UNILATERAL NEGLECT

Unilateral Neglect:
Clinical and Experimental Studies

edited by
Ian H. Robertson
Medical Research Council Applied Psychology Unit, Cambridge, UK

John C. Marshall
Neuropsychology Unit, Radcliffe Infirmary, Oxford, UK

 LAWRENCE ERLBAUM ASSOCIATES, PUBLISHERS
Hove (UK)   Hillsdale (USA)

Lawrence Erlbaum Associates Ltd., Publishers
27 Palmeira Mansions
Church Road
Hove
East Sussex, BN3 2FA
U.K.

British Library Cataloguing in Publication Data
Unilateral Neglect : Clinical and
    Experimental Studies. (Brian Damage,
    Behaviour & Cognition Series,
    ISSN 0967-9944)
    I. Robertson, Ian   II. Marshall, John C.
    II. Series
    616.89

    ISBN 0 86377 208 0 (Hbk)
    ISBN 0 86377 218 8 (Pbk)

Author and subject indices by Sue Ramsey
Typeset by DP Photosetting, Aylesbury, Bucks
Printed and bound by BPCC Wheatons, Exeter

Contents

CODA

List of Contributors

Anna Berti, Istituto di Fisiologia Umana, Università degli Studi di Parma, Via Gramsci 14, 43100 Parma, Italy

Leonard Diller, Rusk Institute of Rehabilitation Medicine, NYU MC, 400 East 34th Street, New York, NY 10016, USA

Mirjam Eglin, Department of Neurology, University Hospital, Zurich, Switzerland

Andrew W. Ellis, Department of Psychology, University of York, York YO1 5DD, UK

Martha J. Farah, Department of Psychology, University of Pennsylvania, 3815 Walnut Street, Philadelphia, PA 19104-6196, USA

Brenda M. Flude, Department of Psychology, University of Lancaster, Lancaster LA1 4YF, UK

Guido Gainotti, Institute of Neurology of the Catholic University of Rome, Policlinico Gemelli, Largo A. Gemelli 8, 00168 Rome, Italy

Peter W. Halligan, Rivermead Rehabilitation Centre, Abingdon Road, Oxford OX1 4XD, UK

Glynn W. Humphreys, Cognitive Science Research Centre, School of Psychology, University of Birmingham, Edgbaston, Birmingham B15 2TT, UK

Marcel Kinsbourne, Center for Cognitive Science, Tufts University, 11 Miner Hall, Medford, MA 02155, USA

Elisabetta Làdavas, Dipartimento di Psicologia, Viale Berti Pichat 5, Bologna, Italy

John C. Marshall, Neuropsychology Unit, Radcliffe Infirmary, Woodstock Road, Oxford OX2 6HE, UK

M. Jane Riddoch, Cognitive Science Research Centre, School of Psychology, University of Birmingham, Edgbaston, Birmingham B15 2TT, UK

Ellen Riley, Jewish Home & Hospital for the Aged, 100 West Kingsbridge Road, Bronx, NY 10468, USA

Giacomo Rizzolatti, Istituto di Fisiologia Umana, Università degli Studi di Parma, Via Gramsci 14, 43100 Parma, Italy

Ian H. Robertson, Medical Research Council Applied Psychology Unit, 15 Chaucer Road, Cambridge CB2 2EF, UK

Lynn C. Robertson, Neurology Service 127, Veterans Administration Medical Center, 150 Muir Road, Martinez, CA 94553, or Center for Neuroscience, University of California, Davis, CA 95616-8768, USA

Giuseppe Vallar, Dipartimento di Psicologia, Università "La Sapienza", Via dei Marsi 78, 00185, Roma, Italy

Shaun P. Vecera, Department of Psychology, Carnegie-Mellon University, Pittsburgh, PA 15213, USA

Marcie A. Wallace, Department of Psychology, Carnegie-Mellon University, Pittsburgh, PA 15213, USA

Reinhard Werth, Institut für Soziale Paediatrie und Jugendmedizin, Universität Munchen, Heiglhofstrasse 63, D-8000 München 70, Germany

Andrew W. Young, Department of Psychology, University of Durham, Durham DH1 3LE, UK

Brain Damage, Behaviour and Cognition
Developments in Clinical Neuropsychology

Series Editors
Chris Code, University of Sydney, Australia
Dave Müller, Suffolk College of Higher and Further Education, U.K.

Series Preface

From being an area primarily on the periphery of mainstream behavioural and cognitive science, neuropsychology has developed in recent years into an area of central concern for a range of disciplines. We are witnessing not only a revolution in the way in which brain–behaviour–cognition relationships are viewed, but a widening of interest concerning developments in neuropsychology on the part of a range of workers in a variety of fields. Major advances in brain-imaging techniques and the cognitive modelling of the impairments following brain damage promise a wider understanding of the nature of the representation of cognition and behaviour in the damaged and undamaged brain.

Neuropsychology is now centrally important for those working with brain-damaged people, but the very rate of expansion in the area makes it difficult to keep up with findings from current research. The aim of the *Brain Damage, Behaviour and Cognition* series is to publish a wide range of books which present comprehensive and up-to-date overviews of current developments in specific areas of interest.

These books will be of particular interest to those working with the brain-damaged. It is the editors' intention that undergraduates, postgraduates, clinicians and researchers in psychology, speech pathology and medicine will find this series a useful source of information on important current developments. The authors and editors of the books in this series are experts in their respective fields, working at the forefront of contemporary research. They have produced texts which are accessible and scholarly. We thank them for their contribution and their hard work in fulfilling the aims of the series.

CC and DJM
Sydney, Australia and Ipswich, UK
Series Editors

WHAT IS NEGLECT?

1

The History and Clinical Presentation of Neglect

Peter W. Halligan
Rivermead Rehabilitation Centre, Oxford, UK

John C. Marshall
Neuropsychology Unit, Radcliffe Infirmary, Oxford, UK

Classical visual neglect is one of the simplest of clinical observations and yet one of the most striking. The fact that textbooks are already full of drawings of daisies and clock faces by neglecting patients makes it no less impressive when you first observe it for yourself (Latto, 1984).

WHAT IS NEGLECT?

Of the many neuropsychological consequences that follow right hemisphere brain damage, few are as striking or as puzzling as when a patient without impairment of intellectual functioning appears to ignore, forget or turn away from the left side of space—as if that half of the world had abruptly ceased to exist in any meaningful form (Mesulam, 1985). This "cognitive" inability to respond to objects and people located on the side contralateral to a cerebral lesion is usually known as unilateral neglect.

The condition can be distinguished from the behaviour associated with primary sensory and motor deficits (hemianopia and hemiplegia), although differential diagnosis may be difficult in the acute phase (Heilman, Watson, & Valenstein 1985b). Most of the classical behaviours associated with the diagnosis of neglect cannot be readily explained in terms of sensori-motor deficits: neglect is manifest in free vision and under conditions of testing that do not necessarily require the use of the motorically impaired limb. Although many patients do have visual field cuts and hemiplegia, severe neglect can be seen in cases without such deficits (Halligan, Marshall, &

Wade, 1990). The lesions which produce neglect are not limited to the accepted primary sensory or motor areas. In addition, many neglect behaviours often resolve sooner than those which result from lesions of sensory or motor cortex (Friedland & Weinstein, 1977).

Even a cursory examination of the neglect patient's behaviour suggests that the spatial disorder underlying the condition is conceptually different from what might be expected to follow impairment of basic sensory or motor abilities. Such deficits do not of themselves entail the failure to explore or respond to objects and activities on the affected side of space (Bisiach, Capitani, Luzzatti, & Perani, 1981). Patients with florid neglect often demonstrate a specific lack of awareness and behave as if they were selectively ignoring stimuli on the impaired side. The condition is more appropriately conceptualised as a failure of looking and searching rather that of seeing or moving the eyes *per se* (Mesulam, 1985).

Patients often believe that they have an appropriate representation of their environment and consequently additional problems of denial and minimisation of deficit emerge (Gordon & Diller, 1983). In such patients, unawareness of the deficit appears to be a central feature of the condition. This subjective lack of awareness (anosognosia) creates additional difficulties for the patient's recovery and involvement in rehabilitation programmes. Unawareness of hemianopia and of hemiplegia are often found acutely after brain damage. Levine (1990) suggests that the underlying pathology "is not associated with any immediate sensory experience that uniquely specifies the defect". Hence, he argues, the loss "must be discovered by a process of self-observation and inference". It is possible that neglect may similarly need to be discovered by the patient, although the appropriate compensatory reaction is not clear as in the case of hemianopia. Other patients may show unilateral hallucinations restricted to (non-neglected) right hemispace (Chamorro et al., 1990; Mesulam, 1981), phenomena that further confuse the patient's relationship with reality.

A BRIEF HISTORY OF VISUAL NEGLECT

The first clinical descriptions of neglect, in the second half of the last century, attracted intense speculation from those few neurological researchers

> ... who needed a respite from the intricacies of aphasic localization and classification, and wondered how the other half of the brain lived. The manifestations of hemi-inattention have also excited the imagination of those who marvelled that one could exist in a demi-world where laterality determined reality (Weinstein & Friedland, 1977).

Although left neglect is one of the most striking consequences of damage to the right hemisphere, it did not initially receive the attention given to rarer perceptual disorders such as the object agnosias. One reason for this "neglect" of visual-spatial disorders is that, unlike language or figural perception, the structure of *psychological* space is elusive and difficult to characterise in a precise way (Delis, Robertson, & Balliet, 1985). The very fact that the spatial components of perception are an intrinsic aspect of every visual cognition appears to hinder the scientific appreciation of space (De Renzi, 1982). Evidence of this difficulty can be seen from the diversity of terms that have been used to describe neglect: neglect of the left half of visual space (Brain, 1941); unilateral visual inattention (Allen, 1948); unilateral spatial agnosia (Duke-Elder, 1949); imperception for one half of external space (Critchley, 1953); amorphosynthesis (Denny-Brown & Banker, 1954); left-sided fixed hemianopia (Luria, 1972); hemi-inattention (Weinstein & Friedland, 1977); hemi-neglect (Kinsbourne, 1977); unilateral neglect (Hecaen & Albert, 1978); hemi-spatial agnosia (Willanger, Danielsen, & Ankerhus, 1981); contralesional neglect (Ogden, 1985); dyschiria (Bisiach & Berti, 1987) and directional hypokinesia (Coslett et al., 1990).

Studies of visual neglect can be divided into two periods: (1) early case studies and (2) later, more detailed case series and group studies. The former illustrate some of the difficulties encountered by clinicians attempting to formulate a coherent description of the condition. The majority of these studies fall within the framework of clinical neurology and emphasise neuroanatomy and pathology. The latter attempt to describe the range and types of visual neglect, using a wide variety of operational definitions, clinical tests and pathogical groups.

Hughlings Jackson's single case report of 1876 is among the first well-documented accounts of neglect. The collective term "imperception" was used to refer to a patient with topographical disorientation, visual neglect, dressing apraxia and some signs of dementia. Jackson noted that when asked to read the Snellen visual acuity chart, the patient " ... did not know how to set about [and] began at the right lower corner and tried to read backwards". Other phenomena mentioned include what would now be termed neglect dyslexia (Ellis, Flude, & Young, 1987): the omission or substitution of letters at the beginning of words. The location of the lesion in the posterior part of the right temporal lobe appeared to confirm Jackson's earlier intuition (1874) regarding the "leading" role of the right hemisphere in visuo-spatial processes. It should be added, however, that this case is far from representative of the condition: Jackson's patient demonstrated many other symptoms not intrinsically related to neglect.

Visual neglect was also described at about this time by several German neurologists, but typically only as a minor symptom within a more complex neurological condition. Anton (1883) reported four patients, two of whom, after right-sided lesions, could not perceive passive movements of their left limbs, and ignored what was happening in left extrapersonal space.

An early case of neglect dyslexia (with associated anosognosia) was published by Pick (1898) and, in 1909, a patient who made similar reading errors was described by Balint. In this latter case, neglect dyslexia was found in the more general context of "psychic paralysis of gaze, optic ataxia and spatial impairment of attention" (Balint's Syndrome). In 1913, Zingerle published a case study of a 45-year-old man with hemiplegia, hemianaesthesia and hemianopia following right hemisphere stroke, whose neglect involved both personal and extrapersonal space. Zingerle's distinctive contribution (see Bisiach & Berti, 1987, for an appraisal) was his subsequent analysis, which classified the patient's condition as similar to the "dyschiria" which had been described earlier by Jones (1910) in the case of a patient who had a specific impairment in the appreciation of left-sided personal space despite intact sensory abilities.

Holmes and Poppelreuter

The First World War resulted in large numbers of young soldiers with relatively discrete cerebral lesions. Examination of these men and, in particular, the systematic work of Walter Poppelreuter and Gordon Holmes, led to significant insights into the factors that underlie the complex syndrome variously described as "visuo-constructive" or "visuo-orientational" disability. In discussing the condition of "visual disorientation" or "defective spatial orientation", Holmes (1918) made a critical distinction. Whereas before "visual disorientation" was regarded as primarily a manifestation of visual agnosia, it was now possible to show that visual disorientation could occur without "object agnosia". This distinction subsequently provided the basis for a re-examination of the concept of "visual inattention".

Gordon Holmes' concept of "inattention" was similar to that of Poppelreuter (1917), which for the most part described the elicited response of "extinction" rather than the spontaneous manifestations of visual neglect. This emphasis on extinction was not altogether surprising, since florid symptoms of visual neglect are not typically found after focal penetrating lesions (Kinsbourne, 1977; Mesulam, 1985). Extinction refers to the following situation with fixed gaze: when visual fields are assessed by presentation of a single object (e.g. the clinician's finger), detection appears normal, i.e. both left and right fields are "full to confrontation". However, when two objects are presented at the same time, one in each field, only one of the stimuli is reported. This latter finding is known as "extinction to double simultaneous stimulation". Holmes reports, however, that similar effects can be seen in situations other than conventional visual field testing. For example (Holmes & Horrax, 1919):

> When asked to look at a needle placed on the table, he [the patient] often failed to detect a pencil placed on one side of it, or if there were two pencils, he could only see the one or the other. At one time ... while sitting in the ward, it was noticeable that the patient usually saw only what their eyes were directed on and that they took little interest in what was happening around them (Holmes, 1919) ... attention lacked its normal spontaneity and facility in diverting itself to new objects.

Although both Holmes and Poppelreuter alluded to what may be regarded as neglect behaviours, many of their systematic investigations concerned the failure to attend to peripheral stimuli approaching from one side when stimuli from both sides were presented. Poppelreuter (1917) describes how such phenomena may result from an "organic weakness of attention". The "only possibility of differentiating between hemi-inattention and a 'perceptive' hemianopia", he writes, is to attempt to re-orient attention by actively directing the patient's attention to the "neglected" side. Poppelreuter also emphasised that no explanation of heminattention can ignore the apparent "completion" of simple forms when a segment thereof falls within a "blind" or neglected area: "the totalizing apperception of form is thus capable of compensating considerably for hemianopia as well as for unilateral weakness of attention" (Poppelreuter, 1917).

Like Poppelreuter, Holmes' description of "inattention" goes further than the elicited response of "extinction" and may more accurately be described as a "limitation of visual attention to those objects within the central vision" (Weinstein & Friedland, 1977). Some of these cases would now be described under the label "simultanagnosia". Describing one such case, Holmes and Horrax (1919) wrote:

> It is essentially a disturbance of visual attention; retinal impressions no longer attract notice with normal facility, and if two or more images claim attention, this is liable to concern itself exclusively with, and to be absorbed in, that which is at the moment in macular vision ...

For Holmes, "inattention" was only one of several component features that contributed to a major disturbance of visual orientation. On several occasions, Holmes goes so far as to point out that inattention *per se* is not an essential part of the condition, and may often occur independently of problems with visual orientation (Holmes, 1918; 1919; Holmes & Horrax, 1919). Holmes' analysis of inattention originated within a general evaluation of visual disabilities after predominantly bilateral damage. It is not clear that the concept of unilateral (contralesional neglect) was available to him.

The term "neglect" was first used consistently by Pineas (1931). Pineas described a 60-year-old woman whose *vernachlassigung* (neglect) of the left side was both severe and long-lasting, despite the absence of a field deficit or sensori-motor loss. Pineas concluded that the left half of the body schema and extrapersonal hemispace did not exist for the patient in any meaningful way. Although Holmes (1918), Poppelreuter (1917), Pineas (1931) and Scheller and Seidmann (1931) documented some of the behavioural features of visual neglect and suggested an attentional explanation, it was not considered a specific syndrome until the Second World War and the work of Russell Brain. Brain's article in 1941 was the first report that isolated and characterised some of the main features of visual neglect.

Brain (1941): A Seminal Paper

Brain's (1941) article remains an important milestone in the conceptualisation of neglect as a distinct neurological condition. Brain set out to provide a coherent sub-classification of the syndrome commonly referred to as "visual disorientation". As a clinical description, Brain recognised that the term had become a "loose and comprehensive description covering a number of disorders of function differing in their nature". Although the article lists nine different features, the main classification distinguished between "defective localisation of objects" and what Brain described as "agnosia for the left half of space".

Three cases of each disorder were presented. In the second type, the patients ignored the left side of space, and thus among other peculiarities tended to make inappropriate right-sided turns while following familiar routes. All three patients had large right parieto-occipital lesions and left visual field deficits.

Brain's subsequent analysis is one of the first attempts to describe and explain visual neglect in terms of a disturbance of perceptual space. The main conclusions of the article, which served as the basis for many subsequent investigations, included: (a) indicating a strong association with posterior lesions of the right hemisphere; (b) demonstrating the inadequacy of a purely sensory explanation—visual neglect could not be attributed to a visual field deficit; (c) distinguishing between "visual inattention" and visual neglect; and (d) suggesting that the condition should be distinguished from topographical memory loss, visual agnosia and left–right discrimination problems.

On the question of underlying mechanisms, Brain resurrected the old physiological concept of body schema, which had been used by Head and Holmes (1911) and Zingerle (1913) and which was later incorporated into a psychoanalytic framework by Schilder (1935). As pointed out by Friedland and Weinstein (1977), the concept of body schema was important in that it linked personal and extrapersonal space and emphasised yet again that neglect could not be explained in terms of hemianopia. For Brain (1941):

> ... the patient's behaviour towards the left half of external space is similar to the attitude adopted towards the left half of the body. Since each half of the body is a part of the corresponding half of external space, it is not surprising to find that perception of the body and perception of external space are closely related.

Although the notion of a disruption of the body schema has provided the basis for several attempts to explain perceptual disturbances that relate to personal space (Roth, 1949), the extension of the concept to include disorders of extrapersonal space raises several problems (McGlynn & Schacter, 1989). None the less, Bisiach et al. (1981) suggest that the concept of body schema together with that of "representational space" offer one of the few realistic attempts to explain neglect. The chief difficulty with earlier accounts, Bisiach et al. (1981) argue, stemmed from the fact that "they generally misused the concept of schema to describe a set of disorders, rather than arguing its necessity as an explanatory concept".

Since Brain's (1941) report, investigations of visual neglect have proliferated, both within the tradition of clinical neurology and more recently within neuropsychology (Battersby, Bender, Pollack, & Kahn, 1956; Critchley, 1953; De Renzi, Faglioni, & Scotti, 1970; Faglioni, Scotti, & Spinnler, 1971; Gainotti, 1968; Hecaen, 1962; Heilman, Valenstein, & Watson, 1985a; Oxbury, Campbell, & Oxbury, 1974; Piercy, Hecean, & Ajuriaguerra, 1960; Zarit & Kahn, 1974).

Zangwill (1944–60): The Development of Testing Procedures

Between 1944 and 1960, what may be described as "Zangwill's group" (Ettlinger, Warrington, & Zangwill, 1957; Humphrey & Zangwill 1952; McFie & Zangwill, 1960 ; McFie, Piercy, & Zangwill, 1950; Patterson & Zangwill, 1944, 1945) was particularly productive.

In their initial two papers of 1944 and 1945, Patterson and Zangwill employed for the first time a wide variety of verbal and visuo-constructive tasks designed to assess their patients' visuo-spatial disturbances. These included the use of clock drawing, pointing tasks, spontaneous drawing and copying, and were intended to further refine the concept of visuo-spatial disorientation. Patterson and Zangwill (1944) showed a dissociation between personal and extrapersonal neglect, thus questioning Brain's original contention that a strong association existed between visual neglect and a disturbance of the body schema. They pointed out the effects of stimulus complexity, and also confirmed the variable effect of neglect on many everyday activities. In a subsequent paper, McFie et al. (1950) showed how drawing a scene can dissociate from a verbal description thereof. A 55-year-old master printer manifested difficulties representing the ground plan of his home, while at the same time being able to describe verbally the layout accurately and in detail. Critchley (1953) also showed how neglect could be seen on simple copying and drawing tasks. Ettlinger et al. (1957) demonstrated the need to consider environmental rather than retinopic co-ordinates in the explanation of neglect; they showed that visual neglect persisted even under conditions in which the patient is forced by opto-kinetic nystagmus to fixate the object in the left half of extrapersonal space. In their view, the essential deficit lay not at the level of sensory input, but in a failure to make effective use of this input at a more central level. They also argued that there was no necessary relationship between visual neglect and visuo-constructional disorders.

Re-emergence of Interest in Visual Neglect: 1970–93

The last two decades have seen a phenomenal increase in the number of studies of neglect phenomena (Bisiach & Vallar, 1988; De Renzi, 1982; Heilman, Watson, & Valenstein, 1985a; Jeannerod, 1987; Mesulam, 1985; Prigatano & Schacter, 1991; Riddoch, 1991; Weinstein & Friedland, 1977). This growth of interest is partly due to the potential significance of neglect for theories of normal spatial processing (Delis et al., 1985; Jeannerod, 1987), selective attention (Posner & Rafal, 1987), mental representation (Bisiach & Vallar, 1988; Farah, 1989), awareness (Levine, 1990; McGlynn & Schacter, 1989), and pre-motor planning (Rizzollatti & Camarda, 1987; Tegner & Levander, 1991). In addition, the interest of clinicians and therapists has been attracted; neglect can be a major disability in the acute phases of recovery from stroke and can impede later attempts to rehabilitate the patient (Denes, Semenza, Stoppa, & Lis, 1982; Diller & Weinberg, 1977; Kinsella & Ford, 1980).

From a neuropsychological perspective, neglect today provides a fascinating window on the spatial processes and attentional mechanisms that underlie normal cognition (Bisiach & Berti, 1987). It is now generally accepted that neglect is a disorder which can compromise several modalities and may involve personal, peripersonal, extrapersonal and representational space (Bisiach & Luzzatti 1978: Halsband, Gruhn, & Ettlinger, 1985; Meador, Loring, Bowers, & Heilman, 1987; Rizzollatti & Gallese, 1988). None the less, the condition is far from unitary and can fractionate into a number of dissociable components in terms of sensory modality, spatial domain, laterality of response, motor output and stimulus content (Bellas, Novelly, Eskenazi, & Wasserstein, 1988; Bisiach, Geminiani, Berti, & Rusconi, 1990; Bisiach, Perani, Vallar, & Berti, 1986; Caplan, 1985;

Colombo, De Renzi, & Faglioni, 1976; Costello & Warrington, 1987; Cubelli et al., 1991; Daffner, Ahern, Weintraub, & Mesulam, 1990; De Renzi, Gentillini, & Barberi, 1989; Fujii et al., 1991; Gainotti et al., 1986; Halligan, Manning, & Marshall, 1991b; Halligan & Marshall, 1991; Laplane, 1990; Tegner & Levander, 1991; Young, de Haan, Newcombe, & Hay, 1990).

Recent evidence suggests that the "left" in left neglect may involve several different reference systems, including retinal, head, trunk and gravitational co-ordinates (Bisiach, Capitani, & Porta, 1985; Bradshaw, Pierson-Savage, & Nettleton, 1987; Calvanio, Petrone, & Levine, 1987; Karnath, Schenkel, & Fischer, 1991; Ladavas, 1987). Kinsbourne (1977) has argued that the traditional dichotomising term "hemispatial neglect", which only took account of performance relative to the mid-sagittal plain, is misleading. Rather, there is a gradient across space (Marshall & Halligan, 1989), such that attention is biased away from the left, regardless of the absolute location of the stimulus within the visual field (De Renzi et al., 1989; Kinsbourne 1970; See also Chapter 3, this volume). Patients with neglect often direct their attention to the right-most features of a configuration, even when the entire stimulus is located in the right (intact) visual field (De Renzi et al., 1989).

Further complexities become apparent when one considers reports of word- and object-centred neglect (Caramazza & Hillis, 1990; Driver & Halligan, 1991; Gainotti, Messerli, & Tissot, 1972; Ogden, 1985; see also Chapter 11, this volume). The manifestations of neglect can often be modulated by the overall visual configuration of the stimulus array (Halligan & Marshall, 1988, 1991; Kartsounis & Warrington, 1989; Seron, Coyette, & Bruyer, 1989). These findings suggest that the deployment of attention is influenced by the perceptual parsing of configurations in the non-neglected field. Likewise, "top-down" phenomena are seen in the differential effects of neglect on word and nonword reading (Behrmann, Moscovitch, Black, & Mozer, 1990; Kinsbourne & Warrington, 1962). It is also clear that, in some patients, stimuli in the "neglected" field, while unavailable to "consciousness", may none the less influence responses to stimuli in the non-neglected field (Audet, Bub, & Lecours, 1991; Berti & Rizzolatti, 1992; Karnath & Hartje, 1987; Marshall & Halligan, 1988; Sieroff, Pollatsek, & Posner, 1988; Spinelli et al., 1990; Volpe, Le Doux, & Gazzangia, 1979).

CLINICAL PRESENTATION OF VISUAL NEGLECT

Neglect is commonly seen after stroke or neoplasm; it is often transient with the most conspicuous manifestations in many cases lasting no more than a few weeks (Friedland & Weinstein, 1977). The condition is frequently found in association with a constellation of sensori-motor deficits, including visual field cuts and hemiparesis.

Most reported cases of severe and persistent neglect involve right hemisphere lesions (Critchley, 1953; Hecaen & Albert, 1978; Weintraub & Mesulam, 1988). This apparent asymmetry in presentation has been questioned on the grounds of subject selection, e.g. the exclusion of left hemisphere cases where dysphasia seriously impairs comprehension (Ogden, 1987). However the issue has been addressed by studies which employed unselected patients and simple tasks. These studies have shown consistently that left visual neglect is both more frequent and more severe after right hemisphere damage than is right neglect after left hemisphere damage (Bisiach, Cornacchia, Sterzi, & Vallar, 1984; Caltagirone, Miceli, & Gainotti, 1977; Colombo et al., 1976; Fullerton, McSherry, & Stout, 1986; Gainotti et al., 1972; Oxbury et al., 1974).

Studies that find no significant difference in the frequency of neglect between left and right brain-damaged patients (Albert, 1973; Battersby et al., 1956; Ogden 1985) have usually involved patients with tumours as opposed to the majority of neglect studies which involve stroke patients. Unlike stroke patients where the acute manifestations often resolve rapidly, tumour patients generally run a progressive course, complicated by the effects of oedema, compression and the infiltration of neighbouring brain regions (Vallar & Perani, 1987). Recent studies have shown that despite close matching for lesion locations, tumour and stroke patients demonstrate major differences in their respective neuropsychological impairments (Anderson, Damasio, & Tranel, 1990).

Estimates of the frequency of visual neglect differ considerably and depend on the tests and criteria employed (Halligan & Robertson, 1992). Using different cancellation tasks, Diller and Gordon (1981), Vallar and Perani (1986) and Girotti, Casazza, Musicco, and Avanzini (1983) have estimated that the incidence of visual neglect ranges between 40 and 44% after right hemisphere stroke. Using a battery of six different tests in a group of patients who were on average 2 months post-stroke, Halligan, Marshall, and Wade (1989) found a frequency of 48% in the right brain-damaged group and only 15% in the left brain-damaged group.

Time post-onset is seldom taken into account when considering the frequency of neglect. Most of the large group studies of visual neglect have recruited patients at different times post-onset. Recently, Stone et al. (1991) showed that when stroke patients were assessed after 3 days, neglect was equally common in patients with right and left hemisphere damage, but by 3 months the relative frequency was far greater in the right brain-damaged group.

Neuropsychological assessment of neglect may be difficult due to the additional presence of constructional dyspraxia, optic ataxia and topographical disorientation. Many manifestations (visual, auditory and tactile) can be readily detected by simply observing the patient's everyday interactions. However, clinical observations show that neglect may be task-specific (Horner et al., 1989). Patients with visuo-spatial neglect on drawing, for example, may not necessarily demonstrate neglect on reading or writing tasks (Costello & Warrington, 1987).

In the acute phase, neglect is often characterised by a marked deviation of the head, eyes and trunk away from the contralesional field. During neuropsychological assessment, the patient appears to be "magnetically" drawn to those stimuli and activities located on the ipsilesional side. Careful examination of eye movements at this stage often shows that most scanning saccades are restricted to the ipsilesional side of space (Ishiai, Furukawa, & Tsukagoshi, 1979; Rubens, 1985), although the patient may have full extraocular movements to command (Mesulam, 1985). The absence of leftward eye movements during sleep in neglect patients has recently been reported by Doricci, Guariglia, Paolucci, and Pizzamiglio (1991).

In severe cases, patients fail to recognise their contralateral extremities as their own. They may experience difficulties in remembering left-sided details of internally represented familiar scenes (Meador et al., 1987) and in general only attend to events and objects located on the ipsilesional side of space. Consequently, patients can easily become excessively isolated as a result of their neglect. Some patients will shave or groom only the right side of their body. They may fail to eat food placed on the left side of the plate, fill out only the right half of a form, omit to wear the left sleeve or slipper, forget to place the left foot on the wheelchair rest, etc. They may report personal belongings as missing even when the objects are clearly in front of them and often lose their way travelling between hospital departments. When transferring from a wheelchair, such patients may fall because they have failed to stabilise the chair by locking both sides. They often collide with people and objects on the affected side. Many of these patients also manifest difficulties with the spatial aspects of such basic skills as reading, writing, copying and drawing. In general, their spontaneous behaviour is characterised by what appears to be a gross inattention to the left side of space (Adams & Hurvitz, 1963; Critchley, 1953; Halligan & Robertson, 1992; Piggott & Brickett, 1966).

ILLUSTRATIONS OF VISUAL NEGLECT

Copying

Copying and constructional tasks are among the clearest ways of illustrating the curious and often variable nature of neglect, despite the fact that poor pre-morbid drawing ability and other visuo-motor constructional problems consequent upon lesion may conspire to render some productions difficult

(a)   (b)

FIG. 1.1   (a) Stimulus (cat); (b) patient's copy.

to interpret as "pure" illustrations of neglect. The illustrations used in this chapter were selected from a large database that included many poorly organised reproductions.

Figure 1.1 shows an example of the type of deficit found on copying tasks. The patient's copy of the cat clearly shows left-sided omissions, despite the very reasonable reproduction of right-sided features.

Drawing from Memory

When asked to draw from memory, patients are no longer constrained by the sensory features of the stimulus configuration and must depend on previously acquired information.

Patients tend to confine their productions to the right side of the page. As in copying, the drawings often include an adequate representation of the right side of a figure with the left side entirely omitted or grossly distorted, despite the fact that the figure may be a well-known symmetrical configuration (such as a clock face), which of itself should implicitly demand the full figure. When asked to draw a clock face from memory, some patients with neglect produce an example such as that shown in Fig. 1.2a. All the numbers on the right side have been positioned in roughly the correct locus. Furthermore, the patient has set the clock hands correctly at two o'clock (as requested) and confirms this in writing at the bottom of the figure.

Other patients position all or most of the 12 numbers on the right side of the clock face (Fig. 1.2b). In these cases, the patient appears to have

(a)   (b)

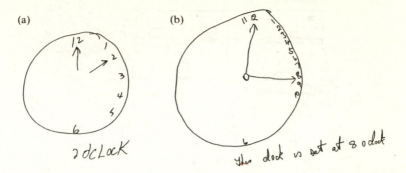

Fig. 1.2   (a) Stimulus (clock face); (b) neglect on a clock face drawing.

transposed details from the left side of the object over into the right. Although examples of this second type of clock face have been described in the literature (Bisiach et al., 1981), they have occasioned little comment. However, the systematic transposition of left-sided details over onto what has been typically regarded as intact *right*-sided space, raises more questions than answers. In order to achieve a successful transposition of the left-sided details in Fig. 1.2b, the patient has to alter the spatial arrangement in right-sided space to accommodate the incoming left-sided numbers while retaining (to some extent) their conventional sequence.

The transposition process itself might be described in terms of either sensory allaesthesia (Joannette & Brouchan, 1984) or neglect-related hypokinesis (Bisiach et al., 1990; Heilman et al., 1985b). However, it is difficult to understand why such patients do not notice or comment on the compression and disruption of right-side features that they have themselves produced. In addition, notice that the time setting that the patient has written at the bottom of the clock face also involves the acceptance of the transposed numbers.

One feature of clock drawing that has rarely been mentioned is that the circumference of the clock face is not usually affected. Perhaps the optimal gestalt of the circle precludes the omission of parts thereof. Another interesting feature of both drawing and copying is that some patients selectively neglect the left side of an object, although the right side of a stimulus further to the left is reproduced. Examples of this object-centred neglect have been reported by Gainotti et al. (1972) and Driver and Halligan (1991). A good illustration of object-centred neglect can be seen in Fig. 1.3. Here the patient was asked to copy a complex scene. Although she attempted to copy all the stimuli except the small figure of the woman on the extreme left, her reproduction shows omissions and/or distortions of features from the left sides of objects at different lateral positions across the stimulus array.

FIG. 1.3   (a) Stimulus; (b) "object-centred" neglect.

Reading (Neglect Dyslexia)

On reading tasks, the right brain-damaged patient with neglect may fail to read the left part of a word or sentence. Text reading often commences in the central portions of the array (Ellis et al., 1987; Kinsbourne & Warrington, 1962; Riddoch, 1991; see also Chapter 11, this volume). Comparable reading errors involving the right side after left brain damage have also been described (Hillis & Caramazza, 1989; Warrington, 1991; Warrington & Zangwill, 1957). In some patients, neglect dyslexia may be the only obvious form of spatial disorder present (Baxter & Warrington, 1983; Costello & Warrington, 1987).

Most of the errors involve the substitution of letters to form alternative words of approximately the same length as the target. Some of the errors are left-sided deletions, particularly where the resultant residue forms a word in its own right. Table 1.1 lists some examples of neglect dyslexia with single words after left and right brain damage.

Prose reading becomes an arduous chore for the patient, especially when the material is unfamiliar and can provide little meaningful context to compensate for the substitutions and omissions. As in the case of drawing and copying, patients (despite in many cases being able to articulate their problem) fail to cue themselves automatically to the affected side.

TABLE 1.1
Examples of Neglect Dyslexia in Right and Left Brain
Damaged Patients

Left Brain Damage[a]		Right Brain Damage[b]	
late	*later*	boat	*coat*
truth	*truck*	cage	*age*
arm	*army*	book	*look*
stop	*steam*	farm	*harm*
south	*soup*	weed	*need*
forest	*forgive*	chair	*hair*
health	*heaven*	belief	*grief*
modern	*modest*	theory	*glory*
unless	*unclean*	treason	*reason*
farmhouse	*farmyard*	climb	*limb*

[a] From Warrington (1991); [b] from Ellis et al. (1987).

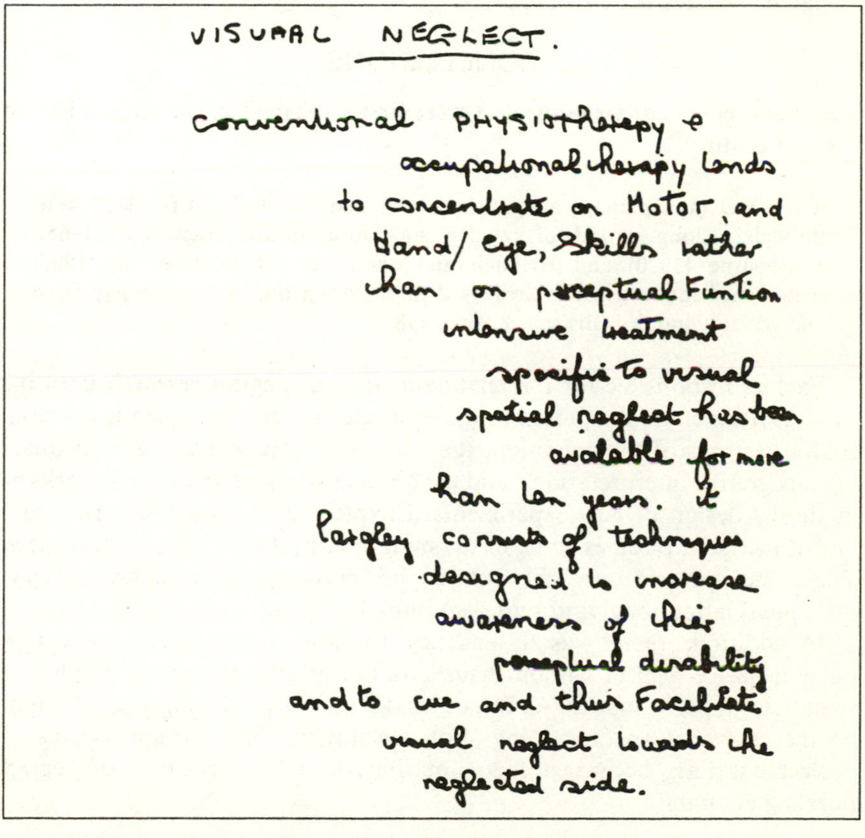

VISUAL NEGLECT.

conventional PHYSIOTherapy &
occupational therapy tends
to concentrate on Motor, and
Hand/eye, Skills rather
than on perceptual Funtion
intensive treatment
specific to visual
spatial neglect has been
available for more
than ten years. it
Largely consists of techniques
designed to increase
awareness of their
perceptual durability
and to cue and their Facilitate
visual neglect towards the
neglected side.

FIG. 1.4   Neglect patient's written performance (dictated passage)

Sometimes they blame their eyesight, maintain that they have lost interest in reading or claim that the target text was meaningless to begin with.

Writing (Neglect Dysgraphia)

Writing may also be affected. The patient may use an uncommonly wide left-sided margin, and hence squeeze most of the text into the right half of the page (Ellis et al., 1987; Hecaen & Marie, 1974; Luria, 1972; Mesulam, 1985). When asked to copy printed or written text, the patient may show selective word or part-word omissions and large spacing errors, in addition to the distinctive crowding of the right side of the page. An example is shown in Fig. 1.4.

There may also be letter and/or stroke additions and omissions (Ellis et al., 1987; Hecaen & Marie, 1974). In Fig. 1.4, it can be seen that the patient has failed to cross many of her t's and dot many of her i's. These omissions have been interpreted by Ellis et al. (1987) in terms of "neglect" of both visual and kinaesthetic feedback.

CONCLUSIONS

Although reports of visual neglect were first published in the second half of the last century,

> it is a fact (and perhaps a significant one) that the study of (neglect) went through a long period of relative stagnation, until Geschwind (1965), Kinsbourne (1970) and Heilman and associates (Heilman et al., 1985) reawakened interest in this area by demonstrating that it could repay fresh and versatile inquiry (Bisiach & Berti, 1987).

Factors responsible for the relative paucity of neglect research until the early 1970s include the failure to differentiate and characterise the essential spatial features of the condition; the widespread acceptance of inadequate infra-cognitive interpretations; and the absence of theoretical frameworks to guide the design of new experiments. Chapter 13, by Marshall, Halligan, and Robertson, outlines some of the main interpretations of visual neglect. These include accounts that place the primary stress upon sensory, perceptual, attentional and representational factors.

In addition, there was a tendency to move away from the actual phenomena of neglect without having fully explored the many perplexing variations in performance. As Bisiach and Rusconi (1990) suggest, "it might be the case that (paraphrasing Wittgenstein) we find certain aspects of neglect puzzling, because we do not find the whole business of neglect puzzling enough".

ACKNOWLEDGEMENTS

This work was supported by the Medical Research Council, Remedi and the Stroke Association.

REFERENCES

Adams, G.F. & Hurvitz, L.J. (1963). Mental barriers to recovery from stroke. *Lancet, 2,* 533–537.

Albert, M. (1973). A simple test of visual neglect. *Neurology, 23,* 658–664.

Allen, I.M. (1948). Unilateral visual inattention. *New Zealand Medical Journal, 47,* 605–617.

Anderson, S., Damasio, H., & Tranel, D. (1990). Neuropsychological impairments associated with lesions caused by tumour or stokes. *Archives of Neurology, 47,* 397–405.

Anton, G. (1883). Beitrage zur klinischen Beurtheilung und zur localisation der Muskelsinnstorungen un Grosshirne. *Stschr. f. Heilk., 14,* 313–348.

Audet, T., Bub, D., & Lecours, A.R. (1991). Visual neglect and left-sided context effects. *Brain and Cognition, 16,* 11–28.

Balint, R. (1909). Seelenlahmung des "Schauens", optische Ataxie, Raumliche Storung der Aufmerksamkeit. *Monatschrift für Psychiatrie and Neurologie, 25,* 51–81.

Battersby, W.S., Bender, M.B., Pollack, M., & Kahn, R.L. (1956). Unilateral spatial agnosia (inattention) in patients with cerebral lesions. *Brain, 79,* 68–93.

Baxter, D. & Warrington, E.K. (1983). Neglect dysgraphia. *Journal of Neurology, Neurosurgery and Psychiatry, 46,* 1073–1078.

Behrmann, M., Moscovitch, M., Black, S., & Mozer, M. (1990). Perceptual and conceptual mechanisms in neglect dyslexia. *Brain, 113,* 1163–1183.

Bellas, D.N., Novelly, R.A., Eskenazi, B., & Wasserstein, J. (1988). The nature of unilateral neglect in the olfactory sensory system. *Neuropsychologia, 26,* 45–52.

Berti, A. & Rizzolatti, G. (1992). Visual processing without awareness: Evidence from unilateral neglect. *Journal of Cognitive Neuroscience, 4,* 345–351.

Bisiach, E. & Berti, A. (1987). Dyschiria: An attempt at its systematic explanation. In M. Jeannerod (Ed.), *Neurophysiological and neuropsychological aspects of spatial neglect.* Amsterdam: North-Holland.

Bisiach, E., Capitani, E., Luzzatti, C., & Perani, D. (1981). Brain and conscious representation of outside reality. *Neuropsychologia, 19,* 543–551.

Bisiach, E., Capitani, E., & Porta, E. (1985). Two basic properties of space representation in the brain. *Journal of Neurology, Neurosurgery and Psychiatry, 48,* 141–144.

Bisiach, E., Cornacchia, L., Sterzi, R., & Vallar, G. (1984). Disorders of perceived auditory lateralisation of the right hemisphere. *Brain, 107,* 37–52.

Bisiach, E., Geminiani, G., Berti, A., & Rusconi, M. (1990). Perceptual and premotor factors of unilateral neglect. *Neurology, 40,* 1278–1281.

Bisiach, E. & Luzzatti, C. (1978). Unilateral neglect of representational space. *Cortex, 14,* 129–133.

Bisiach, E., Perani, D., Vallar, G. & Berti, A. (1986). Unilateral neglect: Personal and extrapersonal. *Neuropsychologia, 24,* 759–767.

Bisiach, E. & Rusconi, M.L. (1990). Breakdown of perceptual awareness in unilateral neglect. *Cortex, 26,* 643–649.

Bisiach, E. & Vallar, G. (1988). Hemineglect in humans. In F. Bollar & J. Graffman (Eds), *Handbook of neuropsychology.* Amsterdam: Elsevier.

Bradshaw, J.L., Nettleton, N.C., Pierson, J.M., Wilson, L.E., & Nathan, G. (1987). Coordinates of extracorporeal space. In M. Jeannerod (Ed.), *Neurophysiological and neuropsychological aspects of spatial neglect.* Amsterdam: North-Holland.

Brain, W.R. (1941). Visual disorientation with special reference to lesions of the right hemisphere. *Brain, 64*, 244–272.

Caltagirone, C., Miceli, G., & Gainotti, G. (1977). Distinctive features of unilateral spatial agnosia in right and left brain damaged patients. *European Neurology, 16*, 121–126.

Calvanio, R., Petrone, P.N., & Levine, D.N. (1987). Left visual spatial neglect is both environment-centred and body-centred. *Neurology, 37*, 1179–1183.

Caplan, B. (1985). Stimulus effects in unilateral neglect? *Cortex, 21.* 69–80.

Caramazza, A. & Hillis, A.E. (1990). Spatial representation of words in the brain implied by studies of unilateral neglect. *Nature, 346*, 267–269.

Chamorro, A., Sacco, R.L., Ciecierski, K., Binder, J.R., Tatemichi, T.K., & Mohr, J.P. (1990). Visual hemineglect and hemihallucinations in a patient with a subcortical infarction. *Neurology, 40*, 1463–1464.

Colombo, A., De Renzi, E., & Faglioni, P. (1976). The occurrence of visual neglect in patients with unilateral cerebral disease. *Cortex, 12*, 221–231.

Coslett, H.B., Bower, D., Fitzpatrick, E., Haws, B., & Heilman, K. (1990). Directional hypokinesia and hemispatial attention in neglect. *Brain, 113*, 475–486.

Costello, A. & Warrington, E.K. (1987). The dissociation of visual neglect and neglect dyslexia. *Journal of Neurology, Neurosurgery and Psychiatry, 50*, 1110–1116.

Critchley, M. (1953). *The parietal lobes.* New York: Hafner.

Cubelli, R., Nichelli, P., Boniot, V., De Tanti, A. & Inzaghi, M.G. (1991). Different patterns of dissociation in unilateral spatial neglect. *Brain and Cognition, 15*, 139–159.

Daffner, K.R., Ahern, G.L., Weintraub, S., & Mesulam, M.M. (1990). Dissociated neglect behaviour following sequential strokes in the right hemisphere. *Annals of Neurology, 28*, 97–101.

Delis, D., Robertson, L.C., & Balliet, R. (1985). The breakdown and rehabilitation of visuo-spatial dysfunction in brain injured patients. *International Rehabilitation Medicine, 5*, 132–138.

Denes, G., Semenza, C., Stoppa, E., & Lis, A. (1982). Unilateral spatial neglect and recovery from hemiplegia: A follow up study. *Brain, 105*, 543–552.

Denny-Brown, D. & Banker, B.Q. (1954). Amorphosynthesis from left parietal lesions. *Archives of Neurology, 71*, 302–313.

De Renzi, E. (1982). *Disorders of space exploration and cognition.* New York: John Wiley.

De Renzi, E., Faglioni, P., & Scotti, G. (1970). Hemispheric contribution to exploration of space through the visual and tactile modality. *Cortex, 6*, 191–203.

De Renzi, E., Gentillini, M., & Barbieri, C. (1989). Auditory neglect. *Journal of Neurology, Neurosurgery and Psychiatry, 52*, 613–617.

Diller, L. & Gordon, W.A. (1981). Interventions for cognitive deficits in brain injured adults. *Journal of Consulting and Clinical Psychiatry, 49*, 822–834.

Diller, L. & Weinberg. J. (1977). Hemi-inattention in rehabilitation: The evolution of a rational remediation programme. In E.A. Weinstein & R.P. Friedland (Eds), *Hemi-inattention and hemispheric specialization.* New York: Raven Press.

Doricci, F., Guariglia, C., Paolucci, S., & Pizzamiglio, L. (1991). Disappearance of left-ward rapid eye movements during sleep in left visual hemi-inattention. *Neuro-Report, 2*, 285–288.

Driver, J. & Halligan, P.W. (1991). Can visual neglect operate in object centred co-ordinates? An affirmative single case study. *Cognitive Neuropsychology, 8*, 475–496.

Duke-Elder, W.S. (1949). *Textbook of opthalmology: Vol.4. The neurology of vision, motor and optical anomalies.* London: C.V. Mosby.

Ellis, A., Flude, B. & Young, A. (1987). "Neglect dyslexia" and the early visual processing of letters, words, and non-words. *Cognitive Neuropsychology, 4*, 439–464.

Ettlinger, G., Warrington, E.K., & Zangwill, O.L. (1957). A further study of visuo-spatial agnosia. *Brain, 80*, 335–361.

Faglioni, P., Scotti, G., & Spinnler, H. (1971). The performance of brain damaged patients in spatial localizations of visual and tactile stimuli. *Brain, 94*, 443–454.

Farah, M.J. (1989). The neuropsychology of mental image. In J.W. Brown (Ed.), *Neuropsychology of visual perception.* Hillsdale, NJ: Lawrence Erlbaum Associates Inc.

Friedland, R. & Weinstein, E. (1971). Hemi-inattention and hemispheric specialization: Introduction and historical review. In E. Weinstein & R. Friedland (Eds), *Hemi-inattention and hemispheric specialization.* New York: Raven Press.

Fujii, T., Fukatsu, R., Kimura, I., Saso, S.I., & Kogure, K. (1991). Unilateral spatial neglect in visual and tactile modalities. *Cortex, 27*, 339–343.

Fullerton, K.J., McSherry, D., & Stout, R.W. (1986). Albert's test: A neglected test of perceptual neglect. *Lancet, 1*, 430–432.

Gainotti, G. (1968). Les manifestations de negligence et d'inattention pour l'hemispace. *Cortex, 4*, 64–91.

Gainotti, G., Messerli, P., & Tissot, R. (1972). Qualitative analysis of unilateral spatial neglect in relation to laterality of cerebral lesions. *Journal of Neurology, Neurosurgery and Psychiatry, 35*, 545–550.

Gainotti, G., Monteleone, D., & Silveri, M.C. (1986). Mechanisms of unilateral spatial neglect in relation to laterality of cerebral lesions. *Brain, 109*, 599–612.

Geschwind, N. (1965). Disconnection syndromes in animals and man. *Brain, 88*, 237–294, 585–644.

Girotti, G., Casazza, M., Musicco, M., & Avanzini, G. (1983). Occulomotor disorders in cortical lesions in man: The role of unilateral neglect. *Neuropsychologia, 21*, 543–55.

Gordon, W.A. & Diller, L. (1983). Stroke: Coping with a cognitive deficit. In T.E. Burish & L.A. Bradley (Eds), *Coping with chronic disease.* San Diego, CA: Academic Press.

Halligan, P.W., Cockburn, J., & Wilson, B. (1991a). The behavioural assessment of visual neglect. *Neuropsychological Rehabilitation, 1*, 5–32.

Halligan, P.W., Manning, L. & Marshall, J.C. (1991b). Hemispheric activation *vs* spatio-motor cuing in visual neglect: A single case study. *Neuropsychologia, 29*, 165–176.

Halligan, P.W. & Marshall, J.C. (1988). How long is a piece of string? A study of line bisection in a case of visual neglect. *Cortex, 24*, 321–328.

Halligan, P.W. & Marshall, J.C. (1991). Left neglect for near but not far space in man. *Nature, 350*, 498–500.

Halligan, P.W., Marshall, J.C., & Wade, D.T. (1989). Visuospatial neglect: Underlying factors and test sensitivity. *Lancet, 2*, 908–911.

Halligan, P.W., Marshall, J.C., & Wade, D.T. (1990). Do visual field deficits exacerbate visuo-spatial neglect. *Journal of Neurology, Neurosurgery and Psychiatry, 53*, 487–491.

Halligan, P.W. & Robertson, I. (1992). The assessment of unilateral neglect. In J. Crawford, W. McKinlay, & D. Parker (Eds), *A handbook of neuropsychological assessment.* Hove: Lawrence Erlbaum Associates Ltd.

Halsband, V., Gruhn, S., & Ettlinger, G. (1985). Unilateral spatial neglect and defective performance in one half of space. *International Journal of Neuroscience, 28*, 173–195.

Head, H. & Holmes, G. (1911). Sensory disturbances from cerebral lesions. *Brain, 34*, 102–254.

Hecaen, H. & Albert, N.L. (1978). *Human neuropsychology.* New York: John Wiley.

Hecaen, H. & Marie, P. (1974). Disorders of written language following right hemispheric lesions: Spatial dysgraphia. In S.J. Dimond & J.G. Beaumont (Eds), *Hemisphere function in the human brain.* London: Elek.

Heilman, K.M., Valenstein, I.E., & Watson, R.I. (1985a). The neglect syndrome. In J.A.M. Fredricks (Ed.), *Handbook of clinical neurology*, (vol. 45:1). Amsterdam: Elsevier.

Heilman, K.M., Watson, R., & Valenstein, E. (1985b). Neglect and related disorders. In K.M. Heilman & E. Valenstein (Eds), *Clinical neuropsychology*, 2nd edn. New York: Oxford University Press.

Hillis, A.E. & Caramazza, A. (1989). The graphemic buffer and attentional mechanisms. *Brain and Language*, *36*, 208–235.

Holmes, G. (1918). Disturbances of visual orientation. *British Journal of Ophthalmology*, *2*, 449–506.

Holmes, G. (1919). Disturbances of visual space perception. *British Medical Journal*, *2*, 230–233.

Holmes, G. & Horrax, G. (1919). Disturbances of spatial orientation and visual attention, with loss of stereoscopic vision. *Archives of Neurology and Psychiatry*, *1*, 385–407.

Horner, J., Massey, E., Woodruff, W., Chase, K., & Dawson, D. (1989). Task-dependent neglect: Computerised tomography size and locus correlations. *Journal of Neuropsychological Rehabilitation*, *3*, 7–13.

Humphrey, M.E. & Zangwill, O.L. (1952). Effects of right-sided occipito-parietal brain injuries in left handed man. *Brain*, *75*, 312–320.

Ishiai, S., Furukawa, T., & Tsukagoshi, H. (1979). Eye fixation patterns in homonymous hemianopia and unilateral spatial neglect. *Neuropsychologia*, *25*, 675–679.

Jackson, J.H. (1874). On the nature of the duality of the brain. *Medical Press and Circular*, *17*, 19 (reprinted in *Brain*, *38*, 80–103, 1915).

Jackson, J.H. (1876) Case of large cerebral tumour without ottic neuritis and with left hemiplegia and imperception. *Royal Opthalmological Hospital Reports*, *8*, 434–444.

Jeannerod, M. (Ed.) (1987). *Neurophysiological and neuropsychological aspects of spatial neglect*. Amsterdam: North-Holland.

Joanette, Y. & Brouchan, M. (1984). Visual allesthesia in manual pointing: Some evidence for a sensorimotor cerebral organization. *Brain and Cognition*, *3*, 152–165.

Jones, E. (1910). Die Pathologie der Dyschirie. *Journal fur Psychologie und Neurologie*, *15*, 145–183.

Karnath, H.O. & Hartje, W. (1987). Residual information processing in the neglected visual half-field. *Journal of Neurology*, *234*, 180–184.

Karnath, H.O., Schenkel, P., & Fischer, B. (1991). Trunk orientation as the determining factor of the "contralateral" deficit in the neglect syndrome and as the physical anchor of the internal representation of body orientation in space. *Brain*, *114*, 1997–2014.

Kartsounis, L.D. & Warrington, E.K. (1989). Unilateral visual neglect overcome by cues implicit in stimulus arrays. *Journal of Neurology, Neurosurgery and Psychiatry*, *52*, 1253–1259.

Kinsbourne, M. (1970). A model for the mechanism of unilateral neglect of space. *Transactions of the American Neurological Association*, *95*, 143–146.

Kinsbourne, M. (1977). Hemi-inattention and hemispheric rivalry. In E.A. Weinstein & R.P. Friedland (Eds), *Hemi-inattention and hemispheric specialization*. New York: Raven Press.

Kinsbourne, M. & Warrington, E.K. (1962). A variety of reading disorders associated with right hemisphere lesions. *Journal of Neurology, Neurosurgery and Psychiatry*, *25*, 339–344.

Kinsella, G. & Ford, B. (1980). Acute recovery patterns in stroke patients. *Medical Journal of Australia*, *2*, 663–666.

Ladavas, E. (1987). Is the hemispatial deficit produced by right parietal lobe damage associated with retinal or gravitational coordinates. *Brain*, *110*, 167–180.

Laplane, D. (1990). La negligence mortice a-t-elle un rapport avec la negligence sensorielle unilaterale? *Revue Neurologie (Paris)*, *146*, 635–638.

Latto, R. (1984). Integration of clinical and experimental investigations of primate visual perception. In F. Reinsoso-Suarez & C. Ajmone-Marsan (Eds), *Cortical integration*. New York: Raven Press.

Levine, D.N. (1990). Unawareness of visual and sensorimotor defects: A hypothesis. *Brain and Cognition, 13*, 233–281.

Luria, A.R. (1972). *The working brain*. New York: Basic Books.

Marshall, J.C. & Halligan, P.W. (1988). Blindsight and insight in visuo-spatial neglect. *Nature, 336*, 766–767.

Marshall, J.C. & Halligan, P.W. (1989). Does the mid-sagittal plane pay any privileged role in "left" neglect? *Cognitive Neuropsychology, 6*, 403–422.

McFie, J., Piercy, M.F., & Zangwill, O.L. (1950). Visual spatial agnosia associated with lesion of the right cerebral hemisphere. *Brain, 73*, 167–190.

McFie, J. & Zangwill, O.L. (1960). Visual-constructive disabilities associated with lesions of the left cerebral hemisphere. *Brain, 82*, 243–259.

McGlynn, S.M. & Schacter, D.L. (1989). Unawareness of deficits in neuropsychological syndromes. *Journal of Clinical and Experimental Neuropsychology, 11*, 143–205.

Meador, K.J., Loring, D.W., Bowers, D., & Heilman, K.M. (1987). Remote memory and neglect syndrome. *Neurology, 37*, 522–526.

Mesulam, M.M. (1981). A cortical network for directed attention and unilateral neglect. *Annals of Neurology, 10*, 309–325.

Mesulam, M.M. (1985). Attention, confusional states and neglect. In M.M. Mesulam (Ed.), *Principles of behavioural neurology*. Philadephia, PA: F.A. Davis.

Ogden, J.A. (1985). Anterior-posterior interhemispheric differences in the loci of lesions producing visual hemi-neglect. *Brain and Cognition, 4*, 59–75.

Ogden, J.A. (1987). The neglected left hemisphere and its contribution to visuo-spatial neglect. In M. Jeannerod (Ed.), *Neurophysiological and neuropsychological aspects of spatial neglect*. Amsterdam: North-Holland.

Oxbury, J.M., Campbell, D.C., & Oxbury, S.M. (1974). Unilateral spatial neglect and impairment of spatial analysis and visual perception. *Brain, 97*, 551–564.

Patterson, A. & Zangwill, O.L. (1944). Disorders of visual space perception associated with lesions of the right cerebral hemisphere. *Brain, 67*, 331–358.

Patterson, A. & Zangwill, O.L. (1945). A case of topographical disorientation associated with a unilateral cerebral lesion. *Brain, 68*, 188–212.

Pick, A. (1898). Uber allegemeine gedachtnisschwache als unmittelbare folge cerebraler herderkrantung. In *Beitrage zur Pathologie und Pathologische Anatomie des Central-ennerven-systems mit bemerkingen zur normalen anatome desselben*, pp. 168–185. Berlin: Karger.

Piercy, M.F., Hecaen, H., & Ajuriaguerra, J. (1960). Constructional apraxia associated with unilateral cerebral lesions. *Brain, 83*, 225–242.

Piggott, R. & Brickett, F. (1966). Visual neglect. *American Journal of Nursing, 66*, 101–105.

Pineas, H. (1931). Ein fall non raumlicher orientierungs-storung mit dsychirie. *Zeitschrift für de ges Neurologie und Psychiatrie, 133*, 180–195.

Poppelreuter, W. (1917). Die strorungan der niederan und hoheren seheistungen durch nerletzung des okzipitalhirns. *Die Psychischen Schadigungen durch Kopfschuss in Kreige (1914/1916)*, Leipzig: Voss.

Posner, M.I. & Rafal, R.D. (1987). Cognitive theories of attention and rehabilitation of attentional deficits. In R.J. Meier, L. Diller, & A.S. Benton (Eds), *Neuropsychological rehabilitation*. London: Churchill Livingstone.

Prigatano, G.P. & Schacter, D.L., (Eds). (1991). *Awareness of deficit after brain injury*. New York: Oxford University Press.

Riddoch, M.J. (Ed.) (1991). *Neglect and the peripheral dyslexias*. Hove: Lawrence Erlbaum Associates Ltd.

Rizzollatti, G. & Camarda, R. (1987). Neural circuits for spatial attention and unilateral neglect. In M. Jeannerod (Ed.), *Neurophysiological and neuropsychological aspects of spatial neglect*. Amsterdam: North-Holland.

Rizzollatti, G. & Gallese, V. (1988). Mechanisms and theories of spatial neglect. In F. Boller & J. Grafman (Eds), *Handbook of neuropsychology*, Vol. 1. Amsterdam: Elsevier.

Robertson, I. (1989). Anomalies in the laterality of omissions in unilateral left visual neglect: Implications for an attentional theory of neglect. *Neuropsychologia, 27,* 157–165.

Roth, M. (1949). Disorders of the body image caused by lesions of the right parietal lobe. *Brain, 72,* 89–111.

Rubens, A. (1985). Caloric stimulation and unilateral visual neglect. *Neurology, 35,* 1019–1024.

Scheller, H. & Seidmann, H. (1931). Zur fage der optischraumlichen agnosie (zugleich ein beitrag der dyslexie). *Monatschrift für Psychiatrie and Neurologie, 81,* 97–188.

Schilder, P. (1935). *The image and appearance of the human body.* London: Kegan, Paul, Trench, and Tubner.

Seron, X., Coyette, F., & Bruyer, R. (1989). Ipsilateral influences on contralateral processing in neglect patients. *Cognitive Neuropsychology, 6,* 475–498.

Sieroff, E., Pollatsek, A., & Posner, M.I. (1988). Recognition of visual letter strings following injury to the posterior visual spatial attention system. *Cognitive Neuropsychology, 5,* 427–449.

Spinelli, D., Guariglia, C., Massironi, M., Pizzamilglio, L., & Zoccolotti, P. (1990). Contrast and low spatial frequency discrimination in hemi-neglect patients. *Neuropsychologia, 28,* 727–732.

Stone, S.P., Wilson, B., Wroot, A., Halligan, P.W., Lange, L.S., Marshall, J.C., & Greenwood, R.J. (1991). The assessment of visuo-spatial neglect after acute stroke. *Journal of Neurology, Neurosurgery and Psychiatry, 54,* 345–350.

Tegner, R. & Levander, M. (1991). Through a looking glass: A new technique to demonstrate directional hypokinesia in unilateral neglect. *Brain, 114,* 1943–1951.

Vallar, G. & Perani, D. (1986). The anatomy of unilateral neglect after right hemisphere stroke lesions: A clinical CT scan correlation study in man. *Neuropsychologia, 24,* 609–622.

Vallar, G. & Perani, D. (1987). The anatomy of spatial neglect in humans. In M. Jeannerod (Ed.), *Neurophysiological and neuropsychological aspects of spatial neglect*. Amsterdam: North-Holland.

Volpe, B.T., Le Doux, J.E., & Gazzangia, M.S. (1979). Information processing in an "extinguished" visual field. *Nature, 282,* 722–724.

Warrington, E.K. (1991). Right neglect dyslexia: A single case study. *Cognitive Neuropsychology, 8,* 193–212.

Warrington, E.K. & Zangwill, O.L. (1957). A study of dyslexia. *Journal of Neurology, Neurosurgery and Psychiatry, 20,* 208–215.

Weinstein, E. & Friedland, R. (1977). *Hemi-inattention and hemispheric specialization.* New York: Raven Press.

Weintraub, S. & Mesulam, M. (1988). Visual hemispatial inattention: Stimulus parameters and exploratory strategies. *Journal of Neurology, Neurosurgery and Psychiatry, 51,* 1481–1488.

Willanger, R., Danielson, V.T., & Ankerhus, J. (1981). Visual neglect in right sided apoplectic lesions. *Acta Neurologica Scandinavica, 64,* 327–336.

Young, A.W., de Haan, E.H., Newcombe, R., & Hay, D.C. (1990). Facial neglect. *Neuropsychologia, 28,* 391–415.

Zarit, S. & Kahn, R. (1974). Impairment and adaption in chronic disabilities: Spatial inattention. *Journal of Nervous and Mental Diseases, 159,* 63–72.

Zingerle, H. (1913). Ueber storrungen der wahrnemung des eigenen koerpers bei organischen gehirnerkrankungen. *Monatschrift für Psychiatrie und Neurologie, 34*, 13–36.

2 The Anatomical Basis of Spatial Hemineglect in Humans

Giuseppe Vallar
Istituto di Clinica Neurologica, Università di Milano, Milano, and Clinica S. Lucia, Roma, Italy

INTRODUCTION

Unilateral spatial neglect may be associated with both left- and right-sided lesions, but is much more frequent and severe after lesion of the right hemisphere. At the clinical level, neglect may be operationally defined as a behavioural disorder whereby a patient fails to explore the half-space contralateral to the cerebral lesion and this deficit cannot be attributed to the impairment of elementary sensori-motor processes. In line with this working definition, neglect is clinically assessed by spatial exploratory tasks, such as pattern crossing (e.g. circles, lines), line bisection, copying, drawing and reading tasks. Most tests involve visual exploration of extrapersonal space, but tactile versions, in which the patient is blindfolded, have been devised. In this type of task, the patient is free to move his or her head and makes use of the non-paretic hand. Under these conditions, the defective exploration of the contralateral half-space cannot be explained in terms of elementary sensori-motor disorders. Consistent with this view, spatial hemineglect is double-dissociated from hemiplegia, hemianopia and hemianaesthesia, even though such disorders are frequently found in patients with neglect (see Bisiach & Vallar, 1988). The precise nature of the processing deficit underlying hemianopia and hemianaesthesia in neglect patients is not clear, however, and recent observations argue cogently for an important role of the impairment of non-peripheral processing components, suggesting that these apparently primary sensory deficits may be themselves

27

a manifestation of neglect (Kooistra & Heilman, 1989; Vallar et al., 1990, 1991a; Vallar, Sandroni, Rusconi, & Barbieri, 1991b). Despite these recent suggestions, the distinction between sensory and neglect components in the genesis of hemianopia and hemianaesthesia cannot be easily drawn by a clinical examination, and the diagnosis of hemineglect is mainly based upon the observation of a defective exploration of the contralateral half-space. Accordingly, in virtually all studies investigating the anatomical correlates of neglect, the presence/absence of the disorder has been assessed by exploratory tasks of the sort mentioned above.

The present chapter comprises four sections and a résumé. First, I review the traditional anatomo-clinical correlation studies, based upon *post-mortem* pathological evidence or upon radiological techniques [brain scan, computerised tomography (CT) and magnetic resonance imaging (MRI)]. All such methods may show structural damage of the brain involving neuronal loss and provide information concerning the site, size and aetiology of the cerebral lesion. I then consider more recent observations, based on imaging methods such as positron emission tomography (PET) and single photon emission computed tomography (SPECT), which may reveal the dysfunction of specific regions of the brain in the absence of structural damage. Next, I discuss the anatomical correlates of a number of discrete components of spatial hemineglect. I follow this up with a discussion of the neural correlates of recovery from hemineglect.

In each section, the discussion will be confined to the neural correlates of hemineglect, operationally defined as a defective exploration of the contralateral half-space, although a number of associated and more or less related disorders (e.g. extinction, allaesthesia, motor neglect, motor impersistence, anosognosia, anosodiaphoria) are frequently listed under the rubric of the "neglect syndrome" (Heilman, Watson, & Valenstein, 1985a). These disorders are frequently associated with neglect, but instances of double dissociations have been reported, such as hemineglect *vs* anosognosia and hemineglect *vs* extinction (see Bisiach & Vallar, 1988). The existence of dissociations such as those mentioned above appears to indicate that the symptom-complex "neglect syndrome" is likely to reflect the anatomical contiguity of cerebral regions involved in the processing of different aspects of personal and extrapersonal space. Seen in this perspective, a symptom-complex such as that of Heilman et al. (1985a) may be regarded as an instance of anatomical, rather than anatomo-functional, syndrome (see discussion in Vallar, 1991a). According to the former view, the neural mechanisms involved in different aspects of spatial processing and awareness may be conceived in terms of complex neural circuits located in adjacent cerebral regions. This would explain both the frequent association of symptoms and the occurrence of dissociated cases. That this is likely to be the case is suggested by the observation in the monkey that small experimental lesions located in adjacent areas may be associated with different patterns of neglect. For instance, the surgical ablation of the postarcuate frontal cortex (area 6) and of the frontal eye fields (area 8) produce neglect for the peripersonal and "far" space, respectively (Rizzolatti, Matelli, & Pavesi, 1983). The two areas are adjacent and even precise experimental lesions performed under microscope control aimed at ablating one area may marginally involve the other (see, for instance, monkey P1 of Rizzolatti et al., 1983). The site and size of naturally occurring lesions, by contrast, are not related to the functional role of the different cerebral areas, but other factors are relevant, such as the vascular territory to which any given cerebral area belongs (see Damasio, 1983). It is then not surprising that in humans, in whom the lesions are produced by natural diseases such as cerebrovascular attacks, tumours and the like, the putative components of the neglect syndrome frequently co-occur, and the observed behavioural dissociations frequently do not have a clear-cut anatomical counterpart (Bisiach, Perani, Vallar, & Berti, 1986a; Bisiach et al., 1986b; Halligan & Marshall, 1991).

ANATOMICAL CORRELATES OF SPATIAL HEMINEGLECT

Since its discovery as a neurological deficit, spatial hemineglect has been regarded as a symptom with a remarkable localising value, which indicates a lesion of the parietal lobe (Adams & Victor, 1985; Brain, 1941; Critchley, 1953; Jewesbury, 1969; McFie, Piercy, & Zangwill, 1950). However, in the last 20 years, the availability of non-invasive radiological techniques has mitigated this conclusion, providing clear evidence that both lesions located outside the parietal lobe and purely subcortical lesions sparing the cortex may produce spatial hemineglect.

Cortico-subcortical Lesions

After the early reports of Zingerle (1913) and Silberpfennig (1941), ample evidence has been accumulated to the effect that right frontal lesions may produce left hemineglect (Castaigne, Laplane, & Degos, 1972; Heilman & Valenstein, 1972a); Van der Linden, Seron, Gillet, & Bredart, 1980). Patients with right neglect associated with left frontal lesions have also been reported (Damasio, Damasio, & Chang Chui, 1980). Systematic anatomo-clinical correlation studies performed on series of patients have, however, shown that the more frequent cortical correlate in humans is a retro-rolandic lesion involving the temporo-parieto-occipital junction. Table 2.1, which draws upon three group studies performed in large series of brain-

TABLE 2.1
Localisation of Lesion in Patients with and without Contralesional Visual
Hemineglect ($N+$, $N-$)

Series	Aetiology	Side of Lesion	Anterior		Posterior		Antero-posterior	
			$N+$	$N-$	$N+$	$N-$	$N+$	$N-$
1. Angiography, pneumoencephalography, surgery[a]	Tumour (mainly)	Right	0	8	10	12	2	9
		Left	0	8	2	6	1	7
2. Computerised tomography[b]	Tumour, cerebrovascular attack, other	Right	2	8	12	6	4	8
		Left	12	4	9	11	4	10
3. Computerised tomography[c]	Cerebrovascular attack	Right	1	11	17	10	16	4

[a] Battersby et al. (1956); [b] Ogden (1985); [c] Vallar and Perani (1986; 1987).

damaged patients collected after the Second World War, summarises the lesion sites in patients with and without visual hemineglect. The three studies differ in a number of important respects, such as aetiology and radiological assessment of the cerebral lesion, time interval between onset of the disease and neuropsychological investigation, behavioural tasks used to detect neglect (see a discussion of the potential biasing effects of these factors in Vallar & Perani, 1987). They concur nevertheless to indicate that left spatial hemineglect is much more frequently associated with right posterior lesions than with right frontal damage. The series of Vallar and Perani (1986) included stroke patients examined within 30 days after stroke onset. In a series of 24 chronic neglect patients assessed 2 or more (median 5) months after stroke onset, Cappa et al. (1991) have confirmed the main role of posterior damage. Thirteen patients (54%) had antero-posterior lesions, 6 (25%) posterior or postero-mesial lesions, while no patient had anterior damage; 5 patients had deep lesions.

The studies of Battersby, Bender, Pollack and Kahn (1956) and Ogden (1985) also included left brain-damaged patients. Battersby et al. (1956) found that right hemineglect, which is less frequent than left hemineglect, also tends to be associated with retro-rolandic lesions. Ogden (1985) reported that right hemineglect produced by left-sided lesions is as frequent, albeit less severe, as left hemineglect produced by right-sided lesions. Secondly, she found an anatomical dissociation, since right hemineglect was associated with anterior lesions. This latter find has not been replicated to date, even though individual cases of right hemineglect produced by left-sided frontal lesions have been reported (e.g. Damasio et al., 1980). One possible explanation for this is that, at variance with Ogden's (1985) findings, in most studies right hemineglect associated with left-sided lesions has been found not to be a frequent phenomenon, preventing therefore meaningful anatomo-clinical correlations. For instance, Hécaen (1972, p. 212), in a large series of patients with unilateral cerebral lesions, assessed surgically or by *post-mortem* examination, found contralateral hemineglect in 56 out of 179 patients with right-sided lesions, and in 1 out of 286 patients with left-sided lesions. Similarly, in the study of Bisiach, Cornacchia, Sterzi and Vallar (1984), who used a visual exploratory task, 15 out of 56 right brain-damaged patients showed left hemineglect, which was absent in the 51 left brain-damaged patients. Vallar et al. (1991c) found visual or tactile contralateral neglect in 23 out of 66 (35%) right brain-damaged patients and in 4 out of 44 (9%) left brain-damaged patients. Over 80% of their patients had suffered a cerebrovascular attack and were investigated within 30 days after stoke onset. The four left brain-damaged patients had a parietal tumour (case 7) and frontal, temporo-insular and subcortical (basal ganglia and white matter) ischaemic lesions (cases 18–20). Two out of four patients, therefore, had anterior lesions (see Ogden, 1985), but the series is too small to warrant definite conclusions.

In a number of studies, the precise site of the right retro-rolandic lesion associated with left spatial hemineglect has been investigated. The available evidence concurs to suggest a pivotal role of lesions involving the infero-posterior regions of the right parietal lobe (Bisiach, Capitani, Luzzatti, & Perani, 1981; Hécaen, Penfield, Bertrand, & Malmo, 1956; Heilman & Valenstein, 1972b; Vallar & Perani, 1986). Figure 2.1 shows the composite contour maps of the posterior right-sided lesions of patients with and without left visual hemineglect. It is apparent that the inferior parietal lobule is damaged in neglect patients, and comparatively spared in unaffected cases. In this latter group, the lesions involve the superior parietal lobule or are located more posteriorly in the occipital regions.

The dissociation between superior and inferior parietal lobe damage is in line with data concerning the anatomical correlates of reaching disorders. In Ratcliff and Davies-Jones' series (1972), non-hemianopic left and right brain-damaged patients with gross impairment of visual localisation in the contralateral half-field had lesions clustering in the superior parietal region. Similarly, the patient of Levine, Kaufman and Mohr (1978), who suffered from a tumour involving the right superior parietal lobule, had misreaching for visual objects without extinction or neglect. A third study relevant here was made by Posner, Walker, Friedrich and Rafal (1984), who suggested a correlation between CT-assessed superior parietal lesions and deficits in the orientation of attention towards targets located in contralateral half-space.

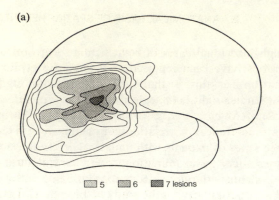

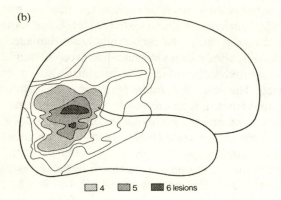

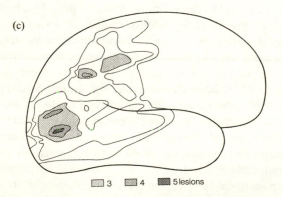

FIG. 2.1. Composite contour maps of the posterior deep-and-superficial right-sided lesions of (a) 8 patients with severe left hemineglect, (b) 6 patients with mild-to-moderate neglect and (c) 10 patients without neglect. The contours drawn on the standard lateral diagram of the brain represent the degree of overlap of the lesions; the outer line indicates the area affected by one lesion only, the next by two and so forth. Reprinted with permission from Vallar and Perani (1986).

The 12 patients of Posner et al. (1984), however, had no or minimal-to-mild signs of contralateral visual hemineglect, as assessed by exploratory tasks, while visual extinction to double simultaneous stimulation was a constant feature. Finally, Kertesz and Dobrowolsky (1981) found an association of left neglect with lesions involving the right fronto-temporo-parietal junction (which includes the inferior parietal lobule), but not with either purely frontal or superior parietal lesions.

These studies indicate that lesions confined to or clustering in the superior parietal regions tend to be associated with disorders such as visual misreaching or extinction, but not with hemineglect. They therefore corroborate the conclusion illustrated in Fig. 2.1 that the crucial cortical correlate of hemineglect is a lesion involving the inferior parietal region. Finally, the data mentioned above provide some indication that the anatomical correlates of visual extinction and hemineglect may be different, suggesting a dissociation between the two disorders (see relevant data in Vallar & Perani, 1986; cf. Heilman et al., 1985a).

The observation that lesions confined to the occipital regions are not associated with hemineglect ties in with the well-known finding that hemianopia and hemineglect are double-dissociated deficits (see, e.g. Bisiach et al., 1986a; Halligan, Marshall & Wade, 1990; Hécaen, 1962; Vallar & Perani, 1986). These anatomical data therefore corroborate the notion that hemineglect cannot be explained in terms of defective sensory processing (see Bisiach & Vallar, 1988). In line with these conclusions, Koehler, Endtz, Te Velde and Hekster (1986) have found that patients anosognosic for homonymous hemianopia have CT-assessed lesions clustering in the inferior-posterior parietal regions, which are spared however in patients aware of their visual field deficit. In these latter patients, by contrast, the lesions superimpose in the occipital lobe. These data suggest a role for the inferior parietal regions in monitoring the function of the visual areas and argue for a close relation between anosognosia for hemianopia and spatial hemineglect.

Vallar et al. (1991b) have shown preserved visual evoked potentials to contralateral stimulation in two right brain-damaged patients with neglect and anosognosia for left hemianopia. The patients were entirely unaware of the left visual half-field stimulation which produced normal evoked potentials. The lesions largely spared the primary sensory occipital areas: one patient had a small ischaemic lesion in the right occipital paraventricular white matter; the second patient an extensive fronto-temporo-parietal infarction. Visual evoked potentials may be used for distinguishing "primarily sensory" hemianopia from visual hemi-inattention. Denial of contralateral hemianopia in neglect patients with CT- or MRI-assessed lesions sparing the primary sensory occipital cortex raises the possibility that the visual field deficit is not sensory in nature.

Subcortical lesions

A consistent association between purely subcortical lesions and hemineglect was discovered only after the introduction of CT scan in clinical practice, even though instances of neglect phenomena in patients with subcortical lesions may be found in the classic literature (Pick, 1898) and in more recent clinico-pathological studies (Oxbury, Campbell, & Oxbury, 1974). A more extensive discussion of the role of subcortical lesions in producing cognitive deficits, such as spatial hemineglect and dysphasia, may be found in Cappa and Vallar (1992).

Thalamus.   Since the late 1970s, a number of individual case reports of CT-assessed right thalamic lesions associated with left hemineglect have been published (Cambier, Elghozi, & Strube, 1980: 3 cases; Schott, Laurent, Mauguière, & Chazot, 1981: 1 case; Watson & Heilman, 1979: 3 cases; Watson, Valenstein, & Heilman, 1981: 1 case). In the patients of Watson and Heilman (1979, case 3) and Cambier et al. (1980, case 1), the thalamic lesion was confirmed by post-mortem examination. The role of thalamic damage in producing hemineglect is also suggested by the observation of spatial and motor neglect after stereotactic lesions performed for the relief of Parkinson's disease (Hassler, 1979; Perani, Nardocci, & Broggi, 1982; Velasco, Velasco, Ogarrio, & Olvera, 1986).

In a number of patients, an *intra-thalamic localisation* of the lesion has been attempted. In case 1 of Cambier et al. (1980), the pathological examination showed a lesion of the pulvinar, and of the ventro-postero-lateral and dorso-medial nuclei. In the patient of Watson et al. (1981), the lesion was reported to involve the postero-ventral and the medial thalamic nuclei, and possibly the antero-inferior pulvinar. The patient of Schott et al. (1981) suffered a haematoma presumably confined to the pulvinar. Graff-Radford et al. (1985) investigated the patterns of neuropsychological deficits associated with ischaemic, well-demarcated lesions of different portions of the thalamus. They found left hemineglect in patients with postero-lateral (one case, with an associated posterior cerebral artery infarction) and medial (one case) right thalamic lesions. The negative cases of Graff-Radford et al. (1985) comprised four postero-lateral, two antero-lateral and two lateral thalamic/posterior limb of internal capsule infarctions. Hirose et al. (1985) reported left hemineglect in four patients with a right posterior thalamic haemorrhage. Case 3 of Cappa, Sterzi, Vallar and Bisiach (1987) had an haemorrhagic lesion involving the right posterior thalamus, and the genu and posterior limb of the right internal capsule. In the clinical study of Bogousslavsky, Regli and Uske (1988b), left hemineglect was associated with ischaemic lesions of the paramedian part of the thalamus (intralaminar and dorsomedial nuclei) and tuberothalamic infarction (ventral-anterior, ventral-lateral, and most of the dorso-medial nuclei).

To summarise, the data from published individual case studies appear to indicate a major role of posterior and medial thalamic damage, as compared with lesions located more anteriorly.

Basal Ganglia. The individual case reports of hemineglect associated with basal ganglia damage are less frequent. Hier, Davis, Richardson and Mohr (1977) briefly mention a "nondominant hemisphere syndrome", including neglect in seven out of nine alert patients with a CT-assessed right putaminal haemorrhage. Damasio and co-workers' (1980) patient had a CT-assessed lesion involving the right putamen, the body of the caudate nucleus and portions of the internal capsule. In the patient of Healton, Navarro, Bressman and Brust (1982), the post-mortem examination revealed an infarction of the head of the right caudate nucleus, putamen, internal and external capsule. Ferro, Kertesz and Black (1987) found evidence of visual hemineglect in 10 out of 15 patients with CT- or MRI-assessed subcortical infarcts, involving the basal ganglia and/or the white matter and the internal capsule. The deficit was severe in only three patients (cases 2, 8 and 9), two of whom (cases 2 and 8) had a substantial involvement of the posterior limb of the internal capsule.

White Matter. Visual hemineglect has been repeatedly found to be associated with CT-assessed lesions involving the posterior limb of the internal capsule, in the vascular territory of the anterior choroidal artery (Bogousslavsky et al., 1988a: 2 cases; Cambier et al., 1983: 3 cases; Ferro & Kertesz, 1984: 1 case; Masson et al., 1983: 3 cases; Vallar et al., 1990: case 2). Case 3 of Stein and Volpe (1983) had a subcortical infarction in the frontal lobe.

These reports of individual patients with subcortical lesions and visual hemineglect suggest a main role of thalamic and basal ganglia damage, followed by white matter lesions. This conclusion has been supported by the group study of Vallar and Perani (1986), who investigated the association of visual hemineglect in a continuous series of 51 patients with CT-assessed vascular subcortical lesions, who were examined within 30 days after stroke onset. In this study, 50% (2/4) of the patients with thalamic lesions, 28% (7/25) of the patients with basal ganglia lesions and 5% (1/19) of the patients with white matter/internal capsule lesions showed neglect. The three patients with extensive lesions involving both the thalamus and the basal ganglia had visual hemineglect. By and large, in line with these findings, Fromm, Holland, Swindell and Reinmuth (1985) found an association between thalamic (1/3 patients) and basal ganglia (3/4 patients) lesions and visual hemineglect. By contrast, two patients with a lacunar stroke in the internal capsule showed no signs of neglect.

These conclusions concerning the different effects of various subcortical lesion sites should consider, however, that the size of the lesion may also play an important role. For instance, in most of Vallar and Perani's (1986) patients with thalamic or basal ganglia lesions, who showed the more consistent association with neglect, the damage also involved the white matter and/or portions of the internal capsule. By contrast, the grey nuclei were spared in patients with lesions confined to the white matter and the internal capsule, who rarely showed signs of hemineglect. The more frequent association of thalamic and basal ganglia damage with neglect might be therefore attributed, at least in part, to the greater lesion volume, since in these patients both the grey and the white matter are involved (see related data, showing a relationship between the size of the subcortical lesion and the occurrence of neuropsychological deficits in Perani et al., 1987).

An indication that the volume of the lesion is not the only factor to be taken into consideration comes from the observation, based on detailed anatomo-clinical correlations in individual patients, that some lesion sites appear to be specifically related to visual hemineglect. This is the case of posterior thalamic and white matter lesions involving the posterior limb of the internal capsule. This pattern of association, together with the well-known finding that the main cortical correlate of human neglect is postero-inferior parietal damage, argues for an important role of a neural circuit comprising as main components the infero-posterior parietal cortex and the thalamic nuclei connected with this cortical area. The pulvinar is likely to be an important part of such a circuit: Located in the posterior part of the thalamus, it receives afferents from structures that in turn receive visual input (among others, the occipital lobe and the superior colliculus). The main output of the pulvinar is conveyed, via the posterior limb of the internal capsule, to the posterior parietal lobe (see more details and references in Hyvarinen, 1982). A similar line of reasoning may be applied to the association between dorso-medial thalamic lesions and neglect, since the nucleus medialis dorsalis provides the major thalamic input to the frontal eye fields (area 8) (see Barbas & Mesulam, 1981; Mesulam, Van Hoesen, Pandya, & Geschwind, 1977; Mesulam, 1985) and lesions of this cortical region produce a severe extrapersonal neglect in the monkey (see data and references in Rizzolatti et al., 1983).

FUNCTIONAL ANATOMY OF HEMINEGLECT

The anatomo-clinical correlation studies reviewed in the previous section are compatible with the view that hemineglect is produced by the disruption of complex neural circuits. This conclusion is also in line with studies in animals, in which neurological deficits broadly comparable to human hemineglect are produced by a range of experimental focal lesions (see reviews in Rizzolatti & Camarda, 1987; Rizzolatti & Gallese, 1988).

Arguments for a network approach to the neural correlates of complex behaviour have also been advanced in different theoretical perspectives in cognitive neuroscience, such as neurobiological research at the cellular and synaptic levels (see Changeux & Dehaene, 1989; Getting 1989) and "distributed processing", "connectionist" or "neural network" modelling of cognitive function (see Morris, 1989; Rumelhart & McClelland; 1986).

The correlation studies discussed in the previous section, in which a given clinical pattern is correlated with a specific lesion site, though compatible with a network approach to cognitive function, do not provide direct and circumstantial support, however. They simply suggest that a number of specific cerebral regions may be more or less important for the operation of a given function. More direct evidence comes from functional imaging techniques, such as positron emission tomography (PET) and single photon emission computed tomography (SPECT), that assess functional activity of the brain in terms of regional cerebral blood flow (rCBF) and metabolism.

In the last 10 years, much evidence has been provided to the effect that a focal structural lesion, such as a stroke or a tumour, may produce a functional derangement in far removed areas, which appear entirely normal on standard CT or MRI assessment (see illustrative examples in Celesia et al., 1984; Kuhl, et al., 1980). This derangement, a revisited and up-to-date version of the classical concept of "diaschisis" (von Monakow, 1914), may be revealed as a pathological reduction of rCBF and metabolism. In these affected areas, the neural cells, though viable, are dysfunctional. The remote effects of diaschisis are produced by the interruption of afferent fibre pathways. So, the lesion of the cerebral region "A", which projects to "B", may produce hypoactivity in "B" (see a review in Feeney & Baron, 1986). These remote effects involve primarily regions ipsilateral to the lesion, which receive major projections from the damaged area (Girault et al., 1985; London et al., 1984). However, a reduction in metabolism in the contra-lateral hemisphere also occurs (see Dobkin et al., 1989; Ginsberg, Reivich, Giandomenico, & Greenberg, 1977; Kiyosawa et al., 1989; for a review, see Andrews, 1991). This mechanism, whereby a lesion affects the function of remote but connected areas, is compatible with the view that cognitive or more basic functions are implemented in neural circuits, comprising a number of interconnected components. This approach has been widely applied to the study of aphasia, showing that language disorders are associated with the dysfunction of a number of interconnected areas, in addition to the structural focal lesion (for a review, see Metter, 1987; 1992).

As for spatial hemineglect, a few studies have attempted to investigate the relationships between diaschisis and the behavioural deficit. In a series of patients suffering from right subcortical stroke, Perani et al. (1987) found that the neglect group had a significantly greater cortical hypoperfusion, as compared with the patients without neglect. In a follow-up study, Vallar et al. (1988) found that behavioural recovery from neglect paralleled reduction

(a)

(b)

(c)

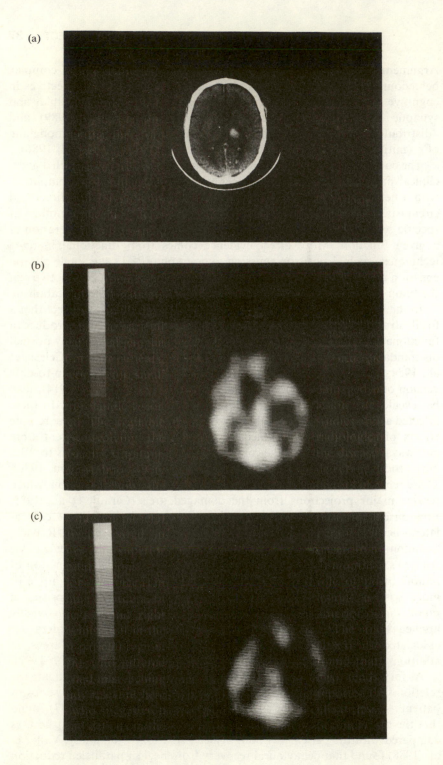

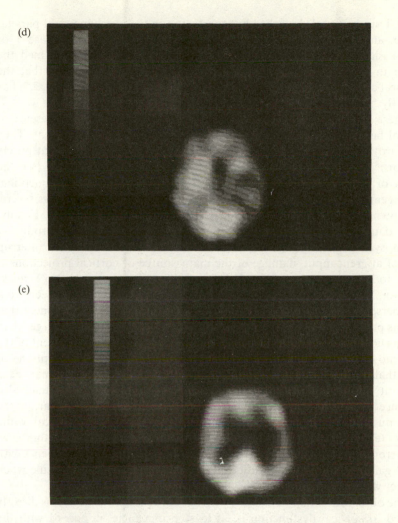

FIG. 2.2. A patient with contralateral hemineglect. (a) CT scan showing a right thalamic haemathoma. (b, c) Initial SPECT (Orbitomeatal line +3.9 and +6.3) showing a large area of hypoperfusion in the fronto-temporo-parietal areas of the right hemisphere. (d, e) Follow-up SPECT (Orbitomeatal line +3.9 and +6.3) showing reduction of cortical hypoperfusion. Reprinted with permission from Vallar et al. (1988).

of cortical hypoperfusion. Figure 2.2 shows one such case, a patient with a right thalamic haematoma and reduction of rCBF in the right fronto-temporo-parietal areas that improved over time.

These results have subsequently been replicated by Bogousslavsky et al. (1988a), who reported two patients with left hemineglect and CT-assessed infarction in the vascular territory of the right anterior choroidal artery. A

SPECT study revealed marked hypoperfusion in the overlying right parietal cortex and, to a lesser extent, in the right frontal cortex. In case 1 of Bogousslavsky et al. (1988a), a post-mortem examination confirmed the lesion in the territory of the anterior choroidal artery, showing that the cerebral cortex was entirely spared. A similar pattern, shown in Fig. 2.3, has recently been reported by Vallar et al. (1990).

These results show that in the case of subcortical damage, the presence of spatial hemineglect is related to the cortical functional derangement. They also provide an explanation of the well-known clinical finding that purely subcortical lesions are not systematically associated with neglect (see the series of Vallar & Perani, 1987): In such negative cases, the functional derangement of the cortico-subcortical circuits is comparatively less severe, as shown by the minor reduction of rCBF (see Perani et al., 1987). Finally, these data may account for the main role of thalamic lesions in producing neuropsychological deficits: As cortical diaschisis is caused by the interruption of afferent input, damage of the main source of cortical projections is likely to be frequently associated with cognitive disorders (see also Franck, Salmon, Sadzot, & Van der Linden, 1986; Pappata et al., 1990). Seen from this perspective, the size effect found by Perani et al. (1987), namely that lesions producing a major cortical hypoperfusion and neglect are larger than lesions not associated with this deficit, reflects the greater involvement of the thalamo-cortical projection, even though the possible disruption of extrathalamic cortical afferents (see Foote & Morrison, 1987) may be a relevant factor. The damage to the thalamocortical projection may also produce cortical diaschisis in the case of structural lesions sparing the thalamus, but involving the internal capsule and the subcortical white matter (e.g. Rousseaux et al., 1986; Vallar et al., 1990). In line with this view, in Ferro and co-workers' (1987) series of right brain-damaged patients with basal ganglia infarction, the lesion also involved the internal capsule when neglect was severe.

The observation that in patients with subcortical lesions neglect is directly related to cortical dysfunction is, at least prima facie, in accord with the traditional view (e.g. Nielsen, 1946) which assigns an exclusive role in cognition to the cerebral cortex (and to the fibre tracts connecting cortical areas). According to this hypothesis, a subcortical lesion produces cognitive deficits only by non-specific effects, such as cortical hypoactivation.

Two arguments, however, militate against this conclusion (see a discussion of this issue in Cappa & Vallar, 1992). The anatomo-clinical observations reviewed in the previous section of this chapter indicate that, while a number of subcortical lesion sites may produce spatial hemineglect, some specific locations appear to show a closer association with the disorder. This is the case of posterior and medial thalamic lesions and of damage to the posterior limb of the internal capsule. The conclusion that

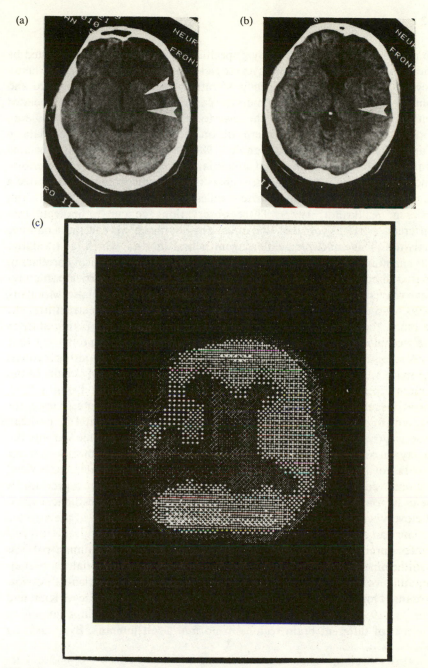

FIG. 2.3. A patient with contralateral hemineglect. (a, b) CT scan showing a right-sided ischaemic lesion in the vascular territory of the anterior choroidal artery. (c) SPECT showing hypoperfusion in the posterior parietal regions of the right hemisphere (the image is inverted, according to neuroradiological conventions). Reprinted with permission from Vallar et al. (1990).

some subcortical areas may play a specific role in cognition is supported by the observations that neuropsychological disorders different from hemineglect are associated with specific intrathalamic lesion sites. Anterior and ventral-lateral left-sided thalamic vascular lesions are frequently associated with aphasia, but this is not the case for posterior thalamic lesions, even though exceptions to this pattern are on record (see a review and data in Cappa, Papagno, Vallar, & Vignolo, 1986). Chronic amnesia is associated with small bilateral medial thalamic infarctions that are located anteriorly and disrupt specific connections, such as the mammillo-thalamic tract (see a review and anatomo-clinical case studies in Graff-Radford, Tranel, Van Hoesen, & Brandt, 1990). These observations concur to indicate that different portions of the thalamus are involved in specific cognitive activities. This conclusion differs from neural models, which, as traditionally maintained (e.g. Nielsen, 1946), argue that the neurological correlate of spatial directed attention is a cortical network, while subcortical structures have only a non-specific activation role (Mesulam, 1981; see also Mesulam, 1990, who assigns more specific roles to some subcortical structures; for instance, the striatum would integrate neural computations taking place in the frontal eye fields with those in the posterior parietal region).

A second line of evidence suggesting that the neural mechanisms involved in spatial representation comprise specific cortico-subcortical circuits comes from studies performed by Deuel in the monkey (Deuel & Collins, 1983, 1984; Deuel, 1987). These experiments represent the counterpart of the human studies mentioned above. Deuel made cortical (frontal or parietal) lesions producing neglect,[1] mapped regional metabolic brain activity (2-deoxyglucose method) by autoradiography, and found hypometabolism in a number of ipsilateral subcortical regions (basal ganglia, thalamus, tectum) far removed from the experimental lesion. Parietal lesions also produced a mild hypometabolism in the ipsilateral visual and somaesthetic cortex. Recovery was associated with reduction of hypometabolism in the affected subcortical regions.

To summarise, the few available functional studies in human patients with hemineglect suggest that the neural mechanisms of spatial representation and awareness may be conceived in terms of neural cortico-subcortical circuits. This conclusion is in line with the study by Metter, Riege, Kuhl and Phelps (1984), who investigated the metabolic relationships among a number of different brain regions in normal adult humans. By measuring

---

[1] Deuel's (1987) operational definition of "neglect" differs from the one adopted in the present chapter. "Neglect" in Deuel's experiments referred to a defective response to stimuli contralateral to the lesion after bilateral simultaneous stimulation and to preference for the ipsilateral hand in all motor activities. In human neuropsychology, these disorders are distinguished from spatial hemineglect and are typically referred to as "extinction" and "motor neglect".

regional cerebral metabolism in a resting state, Metter et al. identified two sets of cerebral regions which show correlated metabolic activities: an inferior system, involving the inferior frontal, Broca's and posterior temporal regions, possibly participating in language-related functions; a superior system comprising the superior and middle frontal gyri, the inferior parietal lobule and the occipital cortex, possibly involved in visuo-spatial processing. The superior frontal region of Metter et al. (1984) includes the frontal eye fields. In the monkey, damage to this region produces a deficit broadly similar to human extrapersonal neglect (Kennard, 1939; Latto & Cowey, 1971a, 1971b; Rizzolatti et al., 1983) and neglect after frontal damage has been repeatedly observed in humans.

A contribution of the frontal regions to the visual exploration of extrapersonal space is also suggested by the intracarotid amobarbital study of Spiers et al. (1990). In a series of 48 patients with epilepsy, they confirmed the hemispheric asymmetry of hemineglect, which was produced only by right-sided injections, and found an association between neglect and EEG slowing in the right frontal areas.

While both human and animal data concur to indicate that the neural mechanisms of spatial representation and awareness should be conceived in terms of cortico-subcortical neural circuits, a difference between man and monkey should be mentioned. In humans, the available CT and functional data suggest that structures such as the inferior parietal lobule may have a particularly relevant role to play. In the monkey, the typical correlate of neglect is a frontal lesion, and parietal neglect is considered somewhat less profound (Hyvarinen, 1982; Lynch, 1980; Lynch & McLaren, 1989), even though neglect deficits after parietal damage have been reported (Denny-Brown & Chambers, 1958; Rizzolatti & Camarda, 1987; Rizzolatti, Genti-lucci, & Matelli, 1985; Rizzolatti et al, 1983; for a discussion of the possible "discontinuity" between the cerebral organisation of spatial representation in man and monkey, see Ettlinger, 1984). This man *vs* monkey difference appears to indicate that in humans the neural network involved in spatial representation is likely to comprise both frontal and parietal systems (such as the frontal eye fields and the inferior parietal lobule), but the parietal component has had a major development. This main role of the parietal regions in spatial representation might possibly be related to the well-known involvement of the human frontal cortex in control and executive functions.

THE FRACTIONATION OF SPATIAL HEMINEGLECT: NEURAL CORRELATES

In the previous sections, spatial hemineglect has been treated as a unitary disorder, basically for the pragmatic reason that the vast majority of the anatomo-clinical correlation studies reviewed have not attempted to distinguish putatively different component deficits. In recent years, however, dissociations between different aspects of neglect have been reported. In this section, the available empirical evidence concerning the neural correlates of such dissociation will be reviewed (see also Chapter 4, this volume).

Premotor vs Perceptual Components of Neglect

A number of anatomo-physiological models of directed attention in extrapersonal space distinguish between "pre-motor" and "perceptual" neural mechanisms. In Mesulam's (1981; 1990) model, the perceptual component provides an internal map of extrapersonal space, while the pre-motor component is involved in the programming and execution of movements (e.g. fixation, reaching) for exploration of such a space. The posterior parietal and the dorso-lateral pre-motor cortices are the major neural correlates of these two systems. Similarly, Heilman et al. (1985a) distinguish between two cortico-subcortical loops: (1) the temporo-parieto-occipital junction, the posterior cingulate gyrus and some thalamic nuclei (ventralis postero-lateralis, medial and lateral geniculate) mediate the perceptual processing of extrapersonal space; (2) the pre-motor cortex, the anterior cingulate gyrus, the basal ganglia and some thalamic nuclei (centromedian parafascicularis, ventral-anterior, ventral-lateral) participate in preparation and execution of motor responses in the extrapersonal space. The mesencephalic reticular formation and the nucleus reticularis thalami are components of both systems.

At the clinical level, distinctions have been drawn between symptoms of the neglect syndrome that may be traced back to the disruption of perceptual and pre-motor systems, respectively.

Perceptual Neglect. The patients' failure to detect contralateral visual or somatosensory[2] stimuli may be a manifestation of perceptual neglect, or

---

[2] Patients with unilateral hemispheric lesions may also fail to respond to auditory free-field stimuli delivered in the contralateral half-space due to perceptual auditory neglect. At variance from hemianopia and hemianaesthesia, the distinction between auditory neglect and a unilateral peripheral hearing loss may easily be drawn, however. A unilateral hearing loss is usually due to a disorder of the peripheral auditory mechanisms or the auditory nerve. Hemispheric lesions typically do not produce a unilateral hearing loss: Both ears are represented in each hemisphere, since the pathways ascending from the brainstem to the cortex are bilateral, even though the contralateral projection is stronger (for a review, see Webster & Garey, 1990). Accordingly, in patients with unilateral hemispheric lesions, a defective response to free-field auditory stimuli delivered in the contralateral half-space is likely to be due to sensory neglect. Furthermore, since the cortical projection is bilateral, patients with a unilateral peripheral deficit may report free-field ipsilateral stimuli, unless they are near-threshold and close to the ear (see also Bisiach et al., 1984). Finally, at variance with patients with a peripheral hearing loss, hemisphere-damaged patients with contralateral auditory neglect are frequently unaware of their deficit.

hemi-inattention (Heilman et al., 1985a). Perceptual visual and somatosensory neglect simulates hemianaesthesia and hemianopia due to primary sensory deficits, however (see Heilman et al., 1985a; Kennard, 1939; Silberpfennig, 1941). A distinction between the sensory and perceptual components of these disorders cannot easily be drawn by clinical examination (but see Kooistra & Heilman, 1989 for the case of perceptual visual neglect vs hemianopia). The demonstration of preserved physiological responses (evoked potentials, skin conductance) to undetected tactile or visual stimuli indicates that hemianopia or hemianaesthesia may be due to perceptual neglect, rather than to a primary sensory disorder (Vallar et al., 1991a; 1991b).

The few published cases of patients with a left visual field deficit due, at least in part, to perceptual visual neglect, have had extensive antero-posterior or posterior lesions. The right sensory occipital cortex was spared in the two patients of Vallar et al. (1991b), who had normal evoked potentials to left visual field stimulation. The patient of Kooistra and Heilman (1989) had a right thalamic and medial temporo-occipital infarct. Similarly, the anatomical correlates of perceptual somatosensory neglect in the four cases of Vallar et al. (1991a; 1991b) were extensive antero-posterior or posterior lesions. As shown by the seminal case reports of Silberpfennig (1941), frontal lesions may also produce perceptual visual neglect, or, using his terminology, "pseudohemianopsia". The association of a CT- or MRI-assessed lesion sparing the visual pathways and occipital cortex with a contralateral visual field deficit does not entirely rule out the possibility of a primary sensory disorder, however. Kuhl et al. (1980) have described a patient with a CT-assessed left frontal infarct and contralateral hemianopia: PET revealed hypometabolism not only in the infarcted area, but also in the left thalamus and primary visual cortex. Evidence of processing without awareness, such as normal evoked potentials to undetected stimuli, is therefore needed to conclude that the visual or somatosensory deficit is due, at least in part, to perceptual neglect.

Pre-motor Neglect. Pre-motor neglect ("unilateral, directional, or hemispatial hypokinesia": Heilman et al., 1985a; Watson, Miller, & Heilman, 1978) refers to the patient's reluctance to perform motor activities in the half-space contralateral to the lesion, with either limb, in the absence of primary motor deficits. The clinical exploratory tasks currently used to detect hemineglect do not dissociate the putative input and output factors of the deficit, requiring both a perceptual (visual, tactile-kinaesthetic) analysis of the environment and motor actions in the extrapersonal space. A number of paradigms have therefore been devised to decouple the perceptual and the pre-motor components of neglect. Such studies also provide some information concerning their anatomical correlates.

Heilman et al. (1985b) found that right brain-damaged patients with left neglect initiate motor responses towards the left hemi-space more slowly than towards the right hemispace. Their patients had extensive antero-posterior (three cases), parietal (two cases) and frontal (one case) lesions. Coslett et al. (1990) required their patients to bisect lines placed to the left or right of their body's sagittal midplane, while monitoring their own performance on a TV screen placed in the left or right half-space (see a discussion of Coslett and co-workers' paradigm in Bisiach, Geminiani, Berti, & Rusconi, 1990). In Coslett and co-workers' series, the two patients (cases 1 and 2) with an hypokinetic deficit had antero-posterior lesions, and the one patient (case 3) with a perceptual deficit had a temporo-parietal lesion. The neglect patient F.S. of Bisiach, Berti and Vallar (1985), who had a right subcortical lesion involving the basal ganglia, the internal capsule and the frontal white matter, frequently failed to react to right-sided visual stimuli when he had to respond by pressing a key in the left half-space using the right unaffected hand. Furthermore, F.S.'s detection of left-sided stimuli, grossly defective when the response took place in the left half-space, improved with a right-sided response.

Bisiach et al. (1990) used a pulley device in order to dissociate the direction of visual attention from that of the arm movement in a line bisection task. They found that in the majority of patients, both the perceptual and the pre-motor deficits were determinants of left hemineglect, with an overall prevalence of the perceptual factor. They suggest a trend whereby pre-motor factors contribute to the bisection error of patients with CT-assessed cortical lesions including the frontal lobe more than to the error of patients with exclusively retro-rolandic lesions. The small number of patients (15 cases) and the absence of purely frontal cases prevent firm anatomo-clinical conclusions, however.

In a series of 18 right brain-damaged patients with neglect, Tegnér and Levander (1991) decoupled the direction of visual exploration and of arm movement in a line cancellation task, by using a 90° angle mirror and preventing a direct view of the test sheet. As with Bisiach et al. (1990), Tegnér and Levander suggest an association between lesions including the frontal lobe and directional hypokinesia, while the perceptual component of neglect would be produced by posterior damage.

In the study of Spiers et al. (1990), who found an association between EEG slowing in the right frontal areas and neglect, a visual exploratory test was used. Spiers et al. required their patients to scan a display and to point to the targets ("A" letters interspersed among other letters) with the hand ipsilateral to the injected hemisphere. This task, which does not dissociate the perceptual and the pre-motor factors of neglect, poses important motor demands (eye and arm movements). These may account for the involvement of the frontal lobe.

In a patient with a right-sided ischaemic lesion of the frontal lobe and the basal ganglia, Bottini, Sterzi and Vallar (1992) have shown a selective impairment in tasks requiring the motor exploration of extrapersonal space. The patient showed left visual hemineglect when pointing to targets by making use of the right hand. By contrast, she was entirely accurate when a naming response was required. The patient was also unimpaired on the Wundt-Jastrow illusion test, which involves a perceptual judgement about the length of two black fans, without any limb movement (Massironi et al., 1988).

The pre-motor component of neglect (directional hypokinesia) must be distinguished from *motor neglect* or *négligence motrice* (Castaigne, Laplane, & Degos, 1970; Critchley, 1953). Motor neglect refers to the patient's unwillingness to move the limbs spontaneously contralateral to the lesion in both halves of space, in the absence of primary motor deficits. Patients are able to move the "neglected" limbs, however, when attention is specifically drawn to them by a verbal command. The absence or reduction of movements by the contralateral hand, which characterises motor neglect, lacks the hemispatial dimension of hemineglect, involving both halves of extrapersonal space. Motor neglect may occur in the absence of spatial hemineglect (Castaigne et al., 1970, 1972; de la Sayette et al., 1989; Laplane et al., 1982; Valenstein & Heilman, 1981; Viader, Cambier, & Pariser, 1982). The anatomical correlates of motor neglect include retro-rolandic and frontal left- and right-sided cortico-subcortical lesions (Castaigne et al., 1970, 1972; Laplane et al., 1977; Laplane & Degos, 1983). Right-sided subcortical lesions, involving the head of the caudate nucleus (Valenstein & Heilman, 1981), the anterior limb of the internal capsule (de la Sayette et al., 1989; Viader et al., 1982) and the thalamus (Laplane et al., 1982; Schott et al., 1981; Watson & Heilman, 1979) may also produce motor neglect. In a group study, Barbieri and De Renzi (1989) have confirmed that motor neglect may occur in the absence of spatial hemineglect, suggesting that the two disorders are not produced by the disruption of a single functional mechanism. They did, however, find an hemispheric asymmetry: left motor neglect was present in 5 out of 28 right brain-damaged patients with mild or no paresis, but not in the group of 50 left brain-damaged patients. All five patients with motor neglect had retro-rolandic lesions involving the right parietal lobe. The series of positive patients of Laplane and Degos (1983) included 12 right-sided and 8 left-sided lesions and in 15 out of 20 patients the frontal lobe was involved.

To summarise, unilateral directional hypokinesia is a discrete component deficit of spatial hemineglect, dissociable from perceptual hemispatial disorders. There is some indication that right frontal lesions may play a major role in producing this pre-motor disorder. Right parietal damage, by contrast, seems more closely associated with the perceptual aspects of neglect. Motor neglect is a space-independent disorder, that may occur in the absence of spatial hemineglect. The available anatomo-clinical correlation studies appear to indicate a more frequent association with right-sided subcortical and cortical (both anterior and posterior) lesions.

Extrapersonal vs Personal Components of Hemineglect

In the last 10 years, animal research has shown that lesions of different cerebral areas may produce neglect for the "far" vs "near" extrapersonal space (Rizzolatti et al., 1983; 1985). A broadly similar dissociation between "extrapersonal" vs "personal" neglect has been observed in humans (Bisiach et al., 1986a). In a patient with an extensive right temporo-parietal cortico-subcortical infarction, Halligan and Marshall (1991) showed neglect for "near" (within hand reach) but not "far" extrapersonal space in line bisection tasks. In man, these behavioural dissociations do not appear to have a clear-cut anatomical counterpart in that in the majority of cases the lesions involve the retro-rolandic areas, while some patients have subcortical lesions. However, firmer conclusions are prevented by the limited number of dissociated cases in whom anatomical data are available. The evaluation of this lack of anatomical dissociation in humans should also consider that, in the monkey, the differentiation of neglect for "far" and "near" space has been produced by small lesions of adjacent areas (see Rizzolatti et al., 1983). In contrast, the naturally occurring human lesions are typically much larger. It is finally worth noting that the differentiation of the anatomical correlates of the "pre-motor" vs "perceptual" components of hemineglect is a comparatively easier enterprise: The putatively involved cortical structures (i.e. the pre-motor frontal and the posterior-inferior parietal regions) are well separated spatially and are often damaged in isolation by naturally occurring lesions.

NEURAL MECHANISMS OF RECOVERY FROM HEMINEGLECT

The notion that the neural correlates of spatial representation and awareness involve cortico-subcortical neural circuits may offer insight into the neural mechanisms of recovery. Recovery from hemineglect may be attributed either to the takeover by undamaged cerebral regions (or neural circuits) not primarily committed to spatial representation,[3] or to the regression of diaschisis in areas far removed from, but connected with, the damaged region. According to this latter view, the neural correlates of

---

[3] An early version of this hypothesis may be found in Gowers (1895), who suggested that recovery from aphasia produced by left-sided lesions is subserved by regions of the right hemisphere homologous to the language area.

cognitive functions are, as suggested in the previous sections, complex circuits: A deficit such as neglect reflects—in an early phase after stroke onset—both the structural damage and the dysfunction of remote areas, while recovery is based on restoration of neural activity in connected regions, not directly damaged by the lesion. The few empirical data concerning recovery from hemineglect are consistent with this hypothesis. In the study of Vallar et al. (1988), behavioural recovery from neglect in patients with subcortical lesions paralleled the reduction in hypoperfusion in the undamaged ipsilateral cortex. Similarly, in the monkey, recovery from neglect produced by cortical experimental lesions is associated with a reduction in hypometabolism in connected subcortical ipsilateral structures (Deuel, 1987). The conclusion that regression of diaschisis in ipsilateral regions connected with the structurally damaged areas is a relevant factor in recovery is not confined to neglect, but applies also to other neuropsychological deficits (aphasia: Perani et al., 1987; Vallar, 1991b), and extends to basic neurological disorders (hemiplegia: Dauth, Gilman, Frey, & Penney, 1985; Gilman, Dauth, Frey, & Penney, 1987; hemianopia: Bosley et al., 1987). In all these disorders, recovery was related to a more or less complete regression of hypoperfusion and hypometabolism in the undamaged cortical or subcortical regions of the affected hemisphere, connected with the area destroyed by the structural (natural or experimental) injury.

Also, the follow-up study of Hier, Mondlock and Caplan (1983) argues for a role of the ipsilateral undamaged regions of the right hemisphere, as lesion size and lobar sparing affected recovery rate, which was faster when the lesion was small and spared the frontal lobe. Levine, Warach, Benowitz and Calvanio (1986) have subsequently confirmed the negative effect of lesion size upon recovery from left spatial hemineglect in right brain-damaged patients who have suffered a stroke. They have also found a negative effect of pre-morbid diffuse cortical atrophy. This latter observation is compatible with the view that the integrity of the left hemisphere is important for recovery from neglect, even though it does not provide direct relevant evidence.

In a series of chronic neglect patients, Cappa et al. (1991) found a significant correlation between severity of neglect and lesion volume in a letter cancellation task, but not between severity of neglect and cerebral atrophy. Cappa and co-workers' data do not confirm the negative effect of cortical atrophy found by Levine et al. (1986). The two results are not directly comparable, however, since Cappa et al. did not undertake a follow-up study.

The lesion size effect found by Hier et al. (1983), Levine et al. (1986) and Cappa et al. (1991) is in line with animal data showing that in the monkey, small frontal lesions (Welch & Stuteville, 1958) produce a neglect deficit of shorter duration, as compared with extensive frontal damage (Deuel &

Collins, 1983). Additional support for the role of the undamaged regions of the right hemisphere comes from a recent clinical observation by Daffner, Ahern, Weintraub & Mesulam (1990). A woman suffered a right frontal stroke producing severe left spatial hemineglect, from which she partially recovered. Twenty days later, she had a second stroke in the right parietal lobe, resulting in a worsening of the left neglect.

Hier and co-workers' (1983) finding that recovery from neglect is more rapid and complete than recovery from more basic neurological deficits (e.g. hemiplegia, hemianopia) may be taken as an indication that the neural networks involved in spatial representation are more extensive and redundant than those devoted to primary somatosensory functions. This conclusion comports with the clinical observation (see p.29–36) that a variety of cortical and subcortical lesion sites may be associated with spatial hemineglect.

The empirical evidence reviewed above does not rule out the possibility that regions of the hemisphere contralateral to the cerebral lesion contribute to recovery. A main source of difficulty for the evaluation of the role of the undamaged hemisphere in recovery from hemineglect in humans is that, at variance with the case of aphasia, successive lesions do not provide clear-cut information. In left brain-damaged aphasic patients, a second lesion in the right hemisphere may yield a worsening of the (more or less recovered) aphasic disorder, suggesting a right hemisphere contribution to recovered or residual language (for a review, see Vallar, 1991b). In the case of spatial exploratory disorders, however, bilateral posterior parieto-occipital lesions are associated with global non-lateralised deficits, often collected under the rubric of Balint's syndrome (for a review, see De Renzi, 1982). Recently, neglect has been reported to occur after bilateral posterior lesions, but the deficit is bilateral, involving the lower half-space (altitudinal neglect: Butters, Evans, Kirsch, & Kewman, 1989; Rapcsak, Cimino, & Heilman, 1988). Data of this sort are compatible with the view that the undamaged hemisphere may contribute to behavioural recovery, but do not provide direct evidence favouring such a conclusion, since the bilateral damage is associated with qualitatively different disorders, rather than with a worsening of the lateralised deficit. The observation that even in patients with extensive antero-posterior cortico-subcortical lesions, vestibular stimulation may produce a temporary amelioration of contralateral hemineglect and hemianaesthesia, suggests an involvement of the unda-maged left hemisphere (Cappa et al., 1987; Vallar et al., 1990), even though this finding cannot be regarded as direct evidence.

Further indirect evidence for a contribution of the undamaged hemisphere to recovery comes from the clinical observation that conjugate eye deviation towards the lesion side, a disorder closely related with right-sided lesions and hemineglect (see De Renzi, Colombo, Faglioni, &

Gibertoni, 1982; Marquardsen, 1969; Tijssen, van Gisbergen, & Schulte, 1991), lasts longer in stroke patients with a pre-existing contralateral lesion involving the frontal lobe, as compared with patients in whom the contralateral hemisphere is unaffected (Steiner & Melamed, 1984; see related data in monkeys with bilateral successive lesions of the frontal eye fields in Latto & Cowey, 1971a; 1971b).

Animal experiments involving commissurotomy argue for a contribution of the undamaged hemisphere. In the monkey, unilateral lesions of the frontal eye fields disrupt reaching of visual targets and the deficit is more severe for contralateral stimuli (Crowne, Yeo, & Steele Russell, 1981). This impairment, which recovers over time, may be temporarily restored by commissurotomy. This indicates a role of the undamaged hemisphere, via the callosal commissures, in the recovery process. Also, the deficit produced by the callosal section lessens over time, suggesting that the availability of the callosal pathways is not essential for recovery. This conclusion is supported by the observation that in monkeys a pre-existing commissurotomy does not affect recovery rate from neglect produced by a unilateral frontal lesion. Monkeys who had suffered a commissurotomy before the frontal lesion show a more severe deficit, however (Watson, Valenstein, Day, & Heilman, 1984).

Finally, as some reduction of metabolism occurs also in the hemisphere contralateral to the lesion (see p. 37), regression of diaschisis may be a relevant factor in determining the contribution of the unaffected hemisphere to recovery. Perani et al. (in press) have recently undertaken a PET-neuropsychological follow-up study in a right brain-damaged patient with a CT-assessed subcortical lesion, who recovered from neglect and sensori-motor neurological deficits. In the acute stage (3 days after stroke onset), PET showed hypometabolism in the structurally undamaged cortex of the right hemisphere and in the left hemisphere. Eight months later, glucose metabolism had improved in both hemispheres, paralleling behavioural recovery. In contrast, in a patient with an extensive infarction in the vascular territories of the middle and posterior cerebral arteries, a severe neglect was still present 4 months post-onset, associated with a persistent reduction of metabolic activity in both hemispheres.

In the last few years, behavioural techniques for the rehabilitation of spatial hemineglect have been devised (see Pizzamiglio et al., 1990). Two recent studies provide some limited information concerning the neural correlates of the behavioural effects of rehabilitation. In the neglect patients of Cappa et al. (1991), the rehabilitation training produced an improvement in scanning performance, which was related neither to lesion volume nor to cerebral atrophy. Pantano et al. (1992) measured rCBF by SPECT in right brain-damaged patients with neglect before and after 2 months rehabilitation treatment. They found a significant correlation between behavioural recovery from hemineglect and increase in rCBF in the anterior regions of the left hemisphere and suggest participation of the left frontal areas in the recovery process induced by the treatment.

SUMMARY

1. Anatomo-clinical studies in brain-damaged patients suffering from spatial hemineglect suggest that the neural correlates of spatial representation and awareness should be conceived of in terms of *complex cortico-subcortical neural circuits*. This conclusion is supported by the observation that, both in humans and in animals, a variety of cortical and subcortical lesions may be associated with neglect, and, more directly, by the finding of correlations between neglect and functional derangement in cerebral regions far removed from, but connected with, the structurally damaged areas. In humans, the right inferior-posterior parietal regions and, possibly, the posterior and medial portions of the thalamus and their connections play a very important role. The network committed to spatial representation is more widespread, however, including, among other structures, the pre-motor frontal cortex.

2. Behavioural studies in patients with spatial hemineglect suggest that these disorders, like other neuropsychological deficits, are not unitary in nature. Distinctions between perceptual and pre-motor, personal and extrapersonal components of neglect have been drawn. Animal and human data studies suggest the possibility of a correspondence between some of these behavioural dissociations and discrete anatomical lesional correlates. Studies in the monkey have shown that different aspects of neglect, such as the peripersonal *vs* extrapersonal space dissociation, may be related to the disruption of different neural circuits. The observation of behavioural dissociations in humans, together with the (admittedly limited) evidence that the anatomical correlates of specific manifestations of the neglect syndrome may be different, is compatible with a multiple circuit approach.

3. The few available studies concerning the neural mechanisms of recovery from hemineglect are also consistent with a network view of the neural correlates of spatial representation and awareness. Regression of diaschisis in undamaged portions of the relevant neural circuits in both the affected and the contralateral hemisphere and size of the structural lesion are important factors underlying behavioural recovery.

ACKNOWLEDGEMENTS

This chapter has benefited from the comments of Edoardo Bisiach, who kindly read an earlier version of the manuscript, and the editors. This work was supported by a CNR grant.

REFERENCES

Adams, R.D. & Victor, M. (1985). *Principles of neurology*, 3rd edn. New York: McGraw-Hill.

Andrews, R.J. (1991). Transhemispheric diaschisis. A review and comment. *Stroke, 22*, 943–949.

Barbas, H. & Mesulam, M.M. (1981). Organization of afferent input to subdivisions of area 8 in the rhesus monkey. *Journal of Comparative Neurology, 200*, 407–431.

Barbieri, C. & De Renzi, E. (1989). Patterns of neglect dissociations. *Behavioral Neurology, 2*, 13–24.

Battersby, W.S., Bender, M.B., Pollack, M., & Kahn, R.L. (1956). Unilateral "spatial agnosia" ("inattention") in patients with cerebral lesions. *Brain, 79*, 68–93.

Bisiach, E., Berti, A., & Vallar, G. (1985). Analogical and logical disorders of space. In M.I. Posner & O.S.M. Marin (Eds), *Attention and performance XI*, pp. 239–249. Hillsdale, NJ: Lawrence Erlbaum Associates Inc.

Bisiach, E., Capitani, E., Luzzatti, C., & Perani, D. (1981). Brain and conscious representation of outside reality. *Neuropsychologia, 19*, 543–551.

Bisiach, E., Cornacchia, L., Sterzi, R., & Vallar, G. (1984). Disorders of perceived auditory lateralization after lesions of the right hemisphere. *Brain, 107*, 37–52.

Bisiach, E., Geminiani, G., Berti, A., & Rusconi, M.L. (1990). Perceptual and premotor factors of unilateral neglect. *Neurology, 40*, 1278–1281.

Bisiach, E., Perani, D., Vallar, G., & Berti, A. (1986a). Unilateral neglect: Personal and extrapersonal. *Neuropsychologia, 24*, 759–767.

Bisiach, E. Vallar, G. (1988). Hemineglect in humans. In F. Boller & J. Grafman (Eds), *Handbook of neuropsychology*, Vol. 1, pp. 195–222. Amsterdam: Elsevier.

Bisiach, E., Vallar, G., Perani, D., Papagno, C., & Berti, A. (1986b). Unawareness of disease following lesions of the right hemisphere: Anosognosia for hemiplegia and anosognosia for hemianopia. *Neuropsychologia, 24*, 471–482.

Bogousslavsky, J., Miklossy, J., Regli, F., Deruaz, J.P., Assal, G., & Delaloye, B. (1988a). Subcortical neglect: Neuropsychological, SPECT, and neuropathological correlations with anterior choroidal artery territory infarction. *Annals of Neurology, 23*, 448–452.

Bogousslavsky, J., Regli, F., & Uske, A. (1988b). Thalamic infarcts: Clinical syndromes, etiology and prognosis. *Neurology, 38*, 837–848.

Bosley, T.M., Dann, R., Silver, F.L., Alavi, A., Kushner, M., Chawluk, J.B., Savino, P.J., Sergott, R.C., Schatz, N.J., & Reivich, M. (1987). Recovery of vision after ischemic lesions: Positron emission tomography. *Annals of Neurology, 21*, 444–450.

Bottini, G., Sterzi, R., & Vallar, G. (1992). Directional hypokinesia in spatial hemineglect: A case study. *Journal of Neurology, Neurosurgery and Psychiatry, 55*, 562–565.

Brain, W.R. (1941). Visual disorientation with special reference to lesions of the right cerebral hemisphere. *Brain, 64*, 244–272.

Butters, C.M., Evans, J., Kirsch, N., & Kewman, D. (1989). Altitudinal neglect following traumatic brain injury: A case report. *Cortex, 25*, 135–146.

Cambier, J., Elghozi, D., & Strube, E. (1980). Lésion du thalamus droit avec syndrome de l'hémisphère mineur: Discussion du concept de négligence thalamique. *Revue Neurologique, 136*, 105–116.

Cambier, J., Graveleau, P., Decroix, J.P., Elghozi, D., & Masson, M. (1983). La syndrome de l'artère choroidienne antérieure: Étude neuropsychologique de 4 cas. *Revue Neurologique, 139*, 553–559.

Cappa, S., Sterzi, R., Vallar, G., & Bisiach, E. (1987). Remission of hemineglect and anosognosia after vestibular stimulation. *Neuropsychologia, 25*, 775–782.

Cappa, S.F., Guariglia, C., Messa, C., Pizzamiglio, L., & Zoccolotti, P.L. (1991). CT-scan correlates of chronic unilateral neglect. *Neuropsychology, 5,* 195–204.

Cappa, S.F., Papagno, C., Vallar, G., & Vignolo, L.A. (1986). Aphasia does not always follow left thalamic hemorrhage: A study of five negative cases. *Cortex, 22,* 639–647.

Cappa, S.F., & Vallar, G. (1992). Neuropsychological disorders after subcortical lesions: Implications for neural models of language and spatial attention. In G. Vallar, S.F. Cappa, & C.W. Wallesch (Eds), *Neuropsychological disorders associated with subcortical lesions,* pp.7–41. Oxford: Oxford University Press.

Castaigne, P., Laplane, D., & Degos, J.D. (1970). Trois cas de négligence motrice par lésion rétro-rolandique. *Revue Neurologique, 122,* 234–242.

Castaigne, P., Laplane, D., & Degos, J.D. (1972). Trois cas de négligence motrice par lésion frontale pré-rolandique. *Revue Neurologique, 126,* 5–15.

Celesia, G.G., Polcyn, R.E., Holden, J.E., Nickles, R.J., Koeppe, R.A., & Gatley, S.J. (1984). Determination of regional cerebral blood flow in patients with cerebral infarction: Use of fluoromethane labeled with fluorine 18 and positron emission tomography. *Archives of Neurology, 41,* 262–267.

Changeux, J.P. & Dehaene, S. (1989). Neuronal models of cognitive functions. *Cognition, 33,* 63–109.

Colombo, A., De Renzi, E., & Gentilini, M. (1982). The time course of visual hemi-inattention. *Archiv für Psychiatrie und Nervenkrankheiten, 231,* 539–546.

Coslett, H.B., Bowers, D., Fitzpatrick, E., Haws, B., & Heilman, K.M. (1990). Directional hypokinesia and hemispatial inattention in neglect. *Brain, 113,* 475–486.

Critchley, M. (1953). *The parietal lobes.* London: Hafner Press.

Crowne, D.P., Yeo, C.H., & Steele Russell, I. (1981). The effects of unilateral frontal eye field lesions in the monkey: Visual-motor guidance and avoidance behaviour. *Behavioral Brain Research, 2,* 165–187.

Daffner, K.R., Ahern, G.L., Weintraub, S., & Mesulam, M.M. (1990). Dissociated neglect behavior following sequential strokes in the right hemisphere. *Annals of Neurology, 28,* 97–101.

Damasio, A.R., Damasio, H., & Chang Chui, H. (1980). Neglect following damage to frontal lobe or basal ganglia. *Neuropsychologia, 18,* 123-132.

Damasio, H. (1983). A computed tomographic guide to the identification of cerebral vascular territories. *Archives of Neurology, 40,* 138–142.

Dauth, G.W., Gilman, S., Frey, K.A., & Penney, J.B. (1985). Basal ganglia glucose utilization after recent precentral ablation in the monkey. *Annals of Neurology, 17,* 431–438.

de la Sayette, V., Bouvard, G., Eustache, F., Chapon, F., Rivaton, F., Viader, F., & Lechevalier, B. (1989). Infarct of the anterior limb of the right internal capsule causing left motor neglect: Case report and cerebral blood flow study. *Cortex, 25,* 147–154.

Denny-Brown, D. & Chambers, R.A. (1958). The parietal lobe and behavior. *Research Publications. Association for Research in Nervous and Mental Disease, 36,* 35–117.

De Renzi, E. (1982). *Disorders of space exploration and cognition.* Chichester: John Wiley.

De Renzi, E., Colombo, A., Faglioni, P., & Gibertoni, M. (1982). Conjugate gaze paresis in stroke patients with unilateral damage: An unexpected instance of hemispheric asymmetry. *Archives of Neurology, 39,* 482–486.

Deuel, R.K. (1987). Neural dysfunction during hemineglect after cortical damage in two monkey models. In M. Jeannerod (Ed.), *Neurophysiological and neuropsychological aspects of spatial neglect,* pp. 315–344. Amsterdam: Elsevier.

Deuel, R.K. & Collins, R.C. (1983). Recovery from unilateral neglect. *Experimental Neurology, 81,* 733–748.

Deuel, R.K. & Collins, R.C. (1984). The functional anatomy of frontal lobe neglect in the monkey: Behavioral and quantitative 2-deoxyglucose studies. *Annals of Neurology, 15,* 521–529.

Dobkin, J.A., Levine, R.L., Lagreze, H.L., Dulli, D.A., Nickles, R.J., & Rowe, B.R. (1989). Evidence for transhemispheric diaschisis in unilateral stroke. *Archives of Neurology*, 46, 1333–1336.

Ettlinger, G. (1984). Humans, apes and monkeys: The changing neuropsychological viewpoint. *Neuropsychologia*, 22, 685–696.

Feeney, D.M. & Baron, J.C. (1986). Diaschisis. *Stroke*, 17, 817–830.

Ferro, J.M. & Kertesz, A. (1984). Posterior internal capsule infarction associated with neglect. *Archives of Neurology*, 41, 422–424.

Ferro, J.M., Kertesz, A., & Black, S.E. (1987). Subcortical neglect: Quantitation, anatomy, and recovery. *Neurology*, 37, 1487–1492.

Foote, S.L. & Morrison, J.H. (1987). Extrathalamic modulation of cortical function. *Annual Review of Neuroscience*, 10, 67–95.

Franck, G., Salmon, E., Sadzot, B., & Van der Linden, M.E. (1986). Etude hémodynamique et métabolique par tomographie a émission de positons d'un cas d'atteinte ischémique thalamocapsulaire droite. *Revue Neurologique*, 142, 475–479.

Fromm, D., Holland, A.J., Swindell, C.S., & Reinmuth, O.M. (1985). Various consequences of subcortical stroke: Prospective study of 16 consecutive cases. *Archives of Neurology*, 42, 943–950.

Getting, P.A. (1989). Emerging principles governing the operation of neural networks. *Annual Review of Neuroscience*, 12, 185–204.

Gilman, S., Dauth, G.W., Frey, K.A., & Penney, J.B. (1987). Experimental hemiplegia in the monkey: Basal ganglia glucose activity during recovery. *Annals of Neurology*, 22, 370–376.

Ginsberg, M.D., Reivich, M., Giandomenico, A., & Greenberg, J.H. (1977). Local glucose utilization in acute focal cerebral ischemia: Local dysmetabolism and diaschisis. *Neurology*, 27, 1042–1048.

Girault, J.A., Savaki, H.E., Desban, M., Glowinsky, J., & Besson, M.J. (1985). Bilateral cerebral metabolic alterations following lesions of the ventromedial thalamic nucleus: Mapping by the ^{14}C-deoxyglucose method in conscious rats. *Journal of Comparative Neurology*, 231, 137–149.

Gowers, W.R. (1895). *Manuale delle malattie del sistema nervoso* (Italian translation). Milano: Vallardi.

Graff-Radford, N.R., Damasio, H., Yamada, T., Eslinger, P.J., & Damasio, A.R. (1985). Nonhaemorrhagic thalamic infarction: Clinical, neuropsychological and electrophysiological findings in four anatomical groups defined by computerized tomography. *Brain*, 108, 485–516.

Graff-Radford, N.R., Tranel, D., Van Hoesen, G.W., & Brandt, J.P. (1990). Diencephalic amnesia. *Brain*, 113, 1–25.

Halligan, P.W. & Marshall, J.C. (1991). Left neglect for near but not far space in man. *Nature*, 350, 498–500.

Halligan, P.W., Marshall, J.C., & Wade, D.T. (1990). Do visual field deficits exacerbate visuo-spatial neglect? *Journal of Neurology, Neurosurgery and Psychiatry*, 53, 487–491.

Hassler, R. (1979). Striatal regulation of adverting and attention directing induced by pallidal stimulation. *Applied Neurophysiology*, 42, 98–102.

Healton, E.B., Navarro, C., Bressman, S., & Brust, J.C.M. (1982). Subcortical neglect. *Neurology*, 32, 776–778.

Hécaen, H. (1962). Clinical symptomatology in right and left hemispheric lesions. In V.B. Mountcastle (Ed.), *Interhemispheric relations and cerebral dominance*, pp. 215–243. Baltimore, MD: Johns Hopkins University Press.

Hécaen, H. (1972). *Introduction à la neuropsychologie*. Paris: Larousse.

Hécaen, H., Penfield, W., Bertrand, C., & Malmo, R. (1956). The syndrome of apractoagnosia due to lesions of the minor cerebral hemisphere. *Archives of Neurology and Psychiatry*, 75, 400–434.

Heilman, K.M., Bowers, D., Coslett, H.B., Whelan, H., & Watson, R.T. (1985b). Directional hypokinesia: Prolonged reaction times for leftward movements in patients with right hemisphere lesions and neglect. *Neurology, 35,* 855–859.

Heilman, K.M. & Valenstein, E. (1972a). Frontal lobe neglect in man., *Neurology, 22,* 660–664.

Heilman, K.M. & Valenstein, E. (1972b). Auditory neglect in man. *Archives of Neurology, 26,* 32–35.

Heilman, K.M., Watson, R.T., & Valenstein, E. (1985a). Neglect and related disorders. In K.M. Heilman & E. Valenstein (Eds), *Clinical neuropsychology,* 2nd edn, pp. 243–293. Oxford: Oxford University Press.

Hier, D.B., Davis, K.R., Richardson, E.P., & Mohr, J.P. (1977). Hypertensive putaminal hemorrhage. *Annals of Neurology, 1,* 152–159.

Hier, D.B., Mondlock, J., & Caplan, L.R. (1983). Recovery of behavioral abnormalities after right hemisphere stoke. *Neurology, 33,* 345–350.

Hirose, G., Kosoegawa, H., Saeki, M., Kitagawa, Y., Oda, R., Kanda, S., & Matsuhira, T. (1985). The syndrome of posterior thalamic hemorrhage. *Neurology,* 35, 998–1002.

Hyvarinen, J. (1982). *The parietal cortex of monkey and man.* Berlin: Springer-Verlag.

Jewesbury, E.C.O. (1969). Parietal lobe syndromes. In P.J. Vinken & G.W. Bruyn (Eds), *Handbook of clinical neurology,* Vol. 2, pp.680–699. Amsterdam: North-Holland.

Kennard, M.A. (1939). Alterations in response to visual stimuli following lesions of frontal lobe in monkeys. *Archives of Neurology and Psychiatry, 41,* 1153–1165.

Kertesz, A. & Dobrowolsky, S. (1981). Right-hemisphere deficits, lesion size and location. *Journal of Clinical Neuropsychology, 3,* 283–299.

Kiyosawa, M., Baron, J.C., Hamel, E., Pappata, S., Duverger, D., Riche, D., Mazoyer, B., Naquet, R., & MacKenzie, E.T. (1989). Time course of effects of lesions of the nucleus basalis of Maynert on glucose utilization by the cerebral cortex: Positron tomography in baboons. *Brain, 112,* 435–455.

Koehler, P.J., Endtz, L.J., Te Velde, J., & Hekster, R.E.M. (1986). Aware or non-aware: On the significance of awareness for the localization of the lesion responsible for homonymous hemianopia. *Journal of the Neurological Sciences, 75,* 255–262.

Kooistra, C.A. & Heilman, K.M. (1989). Hemispatial visual inattention masquerading as hemianopia. *Neurology, 39,* 1125–1127.

Kuhl, D.E., Phelps, M.E., Kowell, A.P., Metter, E.J., Selin, C., & Winter, J. (1980). Effects of stroke on local cerebral metabolism and perfusion: Mapping by emission computed tomography of ^{18}FDG and ^{13}NH3. *Annals of Neurology, 8,* 47–60.

Laplane, D. & Degos, J.D. (1983). Motor neglect. *Journal of Neurology, Neurosurgery and Psychiatry, 46,* 152–158.

Laplane, D., Escourolle, R., Degos, J.D., Sauron, B., & Massiou, H. (1982). La négligence motrice d'origine thalamique. *Revue Neurologique, 138,* 201–211.

Laplane, D., Talairach, J., Meininger, V., Bancaud, J., & Orgogozo, J.M. (1977). Clinical consequences of corticectomies involving the supplementary motor area in man. *Journal of the Neurological Sciences, 34,* 301–314.

Latto, R. & Cowey, A. (1971a). Visual field defects after frontal eye-field lesions in monkeys. *Brain Research, 30.* 1–25.

Latto, R. & Cowey, A. (1971b). Fixation changes after frontal eye-field lesions in monkeys. *Brain Research, 30,* 25–36.

Levine, D.N., Kaufman, K.J., & Mohr, J.P. (1978). Inaccurate reaching associated with a superior parietal lobe tumor. *Neurology, 28,* 556–561.

Levine, D.N., Warach, J.D., Benowitz, L., & Calvanio, R. (1986). Left spatial neglect: Effects of lesion size and premorbid brain atrophy on severity and recovery following right cerebral infarction. *Neurology, 36,* 362–366.

London, E.D., McKinney, M., Dam, M., Ellis, A., & Coyle, J.T. (1984). Decreased cortical glucose utilization after ibotenate lesion of the rat ventromedial globus pallidus. *Journal of Cerebral Blood Flow and Metabolism*, 4, 381–390.

Lynch, J.C. (1980). The functional organization of the posterior parietal association cortex. *Behavioral and Brain Sciences*, 3. 485–534.

Lynch, J.C. & McLaren, J.W. (1989). Deficits of visual attention and saccadic eye movements after lesions of parieto-occipital cortex in monkeys. *Journal of Neurophysiology*, 61, 74–90.

Marquardsen, J. (1969). The natural history of acute cerebrovascular disease. *Acta Neurologica Scandinavica*, 45, (suppl. 38).

Massironi, M., Antonucci, G., Pizzamiglio, L., Vitale, M.V., & Zoccolotti, P. (1988). The Wundt-Jastrow illusion in the study of spatial hemi-inattention. *Neuropsychologia*, 26, 161-166.

Masson, M., Decroix, J.P., Henin, D., Dairou, R., Graveleau, P., & Cambier, J. (1983). Syndrome de l'artère choroidienne antérieure: Etude clinique et tomodensitometrique de 4 cas. *Revue Neurologique*, 139, 547–552.

McFie, J., Piercy, M.F., & Zangwill, O.L. (1950). Visual-spatial agnosia associated with lesions of the right cerebral hemisphere. *Brain*, 73, 167–190.

Mesulam, M.M. (1981). A cortical network for directed attention and unilateral neglect. *Annals of Neurology*, 10, 309–325.

Mesulam, M.M. (1985). Patterns of behavioral neuroanatomy: Association areas, the limbic system, and hemispheric specialization. In M.M. Mesulam (Ed.), *Principles of behavioral neurology*, pp. 1–70. Philadelphia, PA: F.A. Davis.

Mesulam, M.M. (1990). Large-scale neurocognitive networks and distributed processing for attention, language and memory. *Annals of Neurology*, 28, 597–613.

Mesulam, M.M., Van Hoesen, G.W., Pandya, D.N., & Geschwind, N. (1977). Limbic and sensory connections of the inferior parietal lobule (area PG) in the rhesus monkey: A study with a new method for horseradish peroxidase histochemistry. *Brain Research*, 136, 393–414.

Metter, E.J. (1987). Neuroanatomy and physiology of aphasia: Evidence from positron emission tomography. *Aphasiology*, 1, 3–33.

Metter, E.J. (1992) Role of subcortical structures in aphasia: Evidence from studies of resting cerebral glucose metabolism. In G. Vallar, S.F. Cappa, & C.W. Wallesch (Eds), *Neuropsychological disorders associated with subcortical lesions*, pp.479–500. Oxford: Oxford University Press.

Metter, E.J., Riege, W.H., Kuhl, D.E., & Phelps, M.E. (1984). Cerebral metabolic relationships for selected brain regions in healthy adults. *Journal of Cerebral Blood Flow and Metabolism*, 4, 1–7.

Monakow, C. von (1914). *Die Lokalisation im Grosshirn und der Abbau der Function durch Kortikale Herde*. Wiesbaden: Bergmann.

Morris, R.G.M. (Ed.) (1989). *Parallel distributed processing: Implications for psychology and neurobiology*. Oxford: Clarendon Press.

Nielsen, J.M. (1946). *Agnosia, apraxia, aphasia: Their value in cerebral localization*, 2nd edn. New York: P.B. Hoeber.

Ogden, J.A. (1985). Anterior-posterior interhemispheric differences in the loci of lesions producing visual hemineglect. *Brain and Cognition*, 4, 59–75.

Oxbury, J.M., Campbell, D.C., & Oxbury, S.M. (1974). Unilateral spatial neglect and impairments of spatial analysis and visual perception. *Brain*, 97, 551–564.

Pantano, P., Di Piero, V., Fieschi, C., Guariglia, C., Judica, A., & Pizzamiglio, L. (1992). Patterns of CBF in the rehabilitation of visuo-spatial neglect. *International Journal of Neuroscience*, 66, 153–161.

Pappata, S., Mazoyer, B., Tran Dinh, S., Cambon, H., Levasseur, M., & Baron, J.C. (1990). Effects of capsular or thalamic stroke on metabolism in the cortex and cerebellum: A positron tomography study. *Stroke, 21*, 519–524.

Perani, D., Nardocci, N., & Broggi, G. (1982). Neglect after right unilateral thalamotomy: A case report. *Italian Journal of the Neurological Sciences, 3*, 61–64.

Perani, D., Vallar, G., Cappa, S., Messa, C., & Fazio, F. (1987). Aphasia and neglect after subcortical stroke: A clinical/cerebral perfusion correlation study. *Brain, 110*, 1211–1229.

Perani, D., Vallar, G., Paulesu, E., Alberoni, M., & Fazio, F. (in press). Left and right hemisphere contribution to recovery from neglect after right hemisphere damage. A [^{18}F] FDG PET study of two cases. *Neuropsychologia.*

Pick, A. (1898). *Beitrage zur Pathologie und pathologischen Anatomie*, pp. 168–185. Berlin: S. Karger.

Pizzamiglio, L., Antonucci, G., Guariglia, C., Judica, A., Montenero, R., Razzano, C., & Zoccolotti, P.L. (1990). *La rieducazione dell'eminattenzione spaziale.* Milano: Masson.

Posner, M.I., Walker, J.A., Friedrich, F.J., & Rafal, R.D. (1984). Effects of parietal injury on covert orienting of attention. *Journal of Neuroscience, 4.* 1863–1874.

Rapcsak, S.Z., Cimino, C.R., & Heilman, K.M. (1988). Altitudinal neglect. *Neurology, 38*, 277–281.

Ratcliff, G. & Davies-Jones, G.A.B. (1972). Defective visual localization in focal brain wounds. *Brain, 95*, 49–60.

Rizzolatti, G. & Camarda, R. (1987). Neural circuits for spatial attention. In M. Jeannerod (Ed.), *Neurophysiological and neuropsychological aspects of spatial neglect*, pp. 289–313. Amsterdam: Elsevier.

Rizzolatti, G. & Gallese, V. (1988). Mechanisms and theories of spatial neglect. In F. Boller & J. Grafman (Eds), *Handbook of neuropsychology*, Vol. 1, pp. 223–246. Amsterdam: Elsevier.

Rizzolatti, G., Gentilucci, M., & Matelli, M. (1985). Selective spatial attention: One center, one circuit, or many circuits? In M.I. Posner & O.S.M. Marin (Eds), *Attention and performance XI*, pp. 251–265. Hillsdale, NJ: Lawrence Erlbaum Associates Inc.

Rizzolatti, G., Matelli, M., & Pavesi, G. (1983). Deficits in attention and movement following the removal of postarcuate (area 6) and prearcuate (area 8) cortex in macaque monkeys. *Brain, 106*, 655–673.

Rousseaux, M., Steinling, M., Petit, H., Lesoin, F., Dubois, F., Vergnes, R. (1986). Perturbations du debit sanguin hemispherique et hematomes cerebraux profonds. *Revue Neurologique, 142*, 480–488.

Rumelhart, D.E., & McClelland, J.L. (Eds) (1986). *Parallel distributed processing.* Cambridge, MA: MIT Press.

Schott, B., Laurent, B., Mauguiére, F., & Chazot, G. (1981). Négligence motrice par hématome thalamique droit. *Revue Neurologique, 137*, 447–455.

Silberpfennig, J. (1941). Contributions to the problem of eye movements: III. Disturbances of ocular movements with pseudohemianopia in frontal lobe tumors. *Confinia Neurologica, 4*, 1–13.

Spiers, P.A., Schomer, D.L., Blume, H.W., Kleefield, J., O'Reilly, G., Weintraub, S., Osborne-Schaefer, P., & Mesulam, M.M. (1990). Visual neglect during intracarotid amobarbital testing. *Neurology, 40*, 1600–1606.

Stein, S. & Volpe, B.T. (1983). Classical "parietal" neglect syndrome after subcortical right frontal lobe infarction. *Neurology, 33*, 797–799.

Steiner, I. & Melamed, E. (1984). Conjugate eye deviation after acute hemispheric stroke: Delayed recovery after previous contralateral frontal lobe damage. *Annals of Neurology, 16*, 509–511.

Tegnér, R. & Levander, M. (1991). Through a looking glass: A new technique to demonstrate directional hypokinesia in unilateral neglect. *Brain, 114*, 1943–1951.

Tijssen, C.C., van Gisbergen, J.A.M., & Schulte, B.M.P. (1991). Conjugate eye deviation: Side, site and size of the hemispheric lesion. *Neurology, 41,* 846–850.

Valenstein, E. & Heilman, K.M. (1981). Unilateral hypokinesia and motor extinction. *Neurology, 31,* 445–448.

Vallar, G. (1991a). Current methodological issues in human neuropsychology. In F. Boller & J. Grafman (Eds), *Handbook of neuropsychology,* Vol. 5, pp. 343–378. Amsterdam: Elsevier.

Vallar, G. (1991b). Hemispheric control of articulatory speech output in aphasia. In G.R. Hammond (Ed.), *Cerebral control of speech,* pp. 387–416. Amsterdam: North-Holland.

Vallar, G., Bottini, G., Sterzi, R., Passerini, D., & Rusconi, M.L. (1991a). Hemianesthesia, sensory neglect and defective access to conscious experience. *Neurology, 41,* 650–652.

Vallar. G. & Perani, D. (1986). The anatomy of unilateral neglect after right hemisphere stroke lesions: A clinical CT/scan correlation study in man. *Neuropsychologia, 24,* 609–622.

Vallar, G. & Perani, D. (1987). The anatomy of spatial neglect in humans. In M. Jeannerod (Ed.), *Neurophysiological and neuropsychological aspects of spatial neglect,* pp. 235–258. Amsterdam: Elsevier.

Vallar, G., Perani, D., Cappa, S.F., Messa, C., Lenzi, G.L., & Fazio, F. (1988). Recovery from aphasia and neglect after subcortical stroke: Neuropsychological and cerebral perfusion study. *Journal of Neurology, Neurosurgery and Psychiatry, 51,* 1269–1276.

Vallar, G., Rusconi, M.L., Geminiani, G., Berti, A., & Cappa, S.F. (1991c). Visual and nonvisual neglect after unilateral brain lesions: Modulation by visual input. *International Journal of Neuroscience, 61,* 229–239.

Vallar, G., Sandroni, P., Rusconi, M.L., & Barbieri, S. (1991b). Hemianopia, hemianesthesia and spatial neglect. *Neurology, 41,* 1918–1922.

Vallar, G., Sterzi, R., Bottini, G., Cappa, S., & Rusconi, M.L. (1990). Temporary remission of left hemianesthesia after vestibular stimulation: A sensory neglect phenomenon. *Cortex, 26,* 123–131.

Van der Linden, M., Seron, X., Gillet, J., & Bredart, S. (1980). Heminegligence par lesion frontale droite: A propos de trois observations. *Acta Neurologica Belgica, 80,* 298–310.

Velasco, F., Velasco, M., Ogarrio, C., & Olvera, A. (1986). Neglect induced by thalamotomy in humans: A quantitative appraisal of the sensory and motor deficits. *Neurosurgery, 19,* 744–751.

Viader, F., Cambier, J., & Pariser, P. (1982). Phenomene d'extinction motrice gauche: Lesion ischèmique du bras antérieur de la capsule interne. *Revue Neurologique, 138,* 213–217.

Watson, R.T. & Heilman, K.M. (1979). Thalamic neglect. *Neurology, 29,* 690–694.

Watson, R.T., Miller, B.D., & Heilman, K.M. (1978). Nonsensory neglect. *Annals of Neurology, 3,* 505–508.

Watson, R.T., Valenstein, E., Day, A.L., & Heilman, K.M. (1984). The effect of corpus callosum lesions on unilateral neglect in monkeys. *Neurology, 34,* 812–815.

Watson, R.T., Valenstein, E., & Heilman, K.M. (1981). Thalamic neglect: Possible role of the medial thalamus and nucleus reticularis in behavior. *Archives of Neurology, 38,* 501–506.

Webster, W.R. & Garey, L.J. (1990). Auditory system. In G. Paxinos (Ed.), *The human nervous system,* pp. 889–944. San Diego, CA: Academic Press.

Welch, K. & Stuteville, P. (1958). Experimental production of unilateral neglect in monkeys. *Brain, 81,* 341–347.

Zingerle, H. (1913). Ueber Storungen der Wahrnehmung des eigenen Korpers bei organischen Gehirnerkrankungen. *Monatsschrift für Psychiatrie und Neurologie, 34,* 13–36.

NEUROPSYCHOLOGICAL PROCESSES UNDERLYING NEGLECT

3 Orientational Bias Model of Unilateral Neglect: Evidence from Attentional Gradients Within Hemispace

Marcel Kinsbourne
Department of Neurology, Boston University School of Medicine and Boston Veterans Administration Medical Center, Boston, Massachusetts, USA

INTRODUCTION

Bizzarre though its symptomatology might be, the syndrome of unilateral extrapersonal neglect affords unique insights into how the brain is organised. The disorder reflects a breakdown in those interactions between the cerebral hemispheres that control shifts of attention along the horizontal meridian of extrapersonal and personal space. Given the well-known conservatism that characterises the evolution of neural mechanisms, the manner in which the hemispheres interact in controlling attention may reflect how they interact more generally in the control of higher mental functions. This discussion reviews evidence for an opponent processor model, which differs in important ways from some currently popular accounts of the mechanism of neglect. After explaining some of the principles involved, I cite informal observations that favour the model, and then proceed to the major task of summarising the by now plentiful evidence from the experimental literature from which the "orientational bias" model gains powerful support.

Evidence from unilateral neglect supports the broad generalisation that lateral interactions in the brain involve reciprocally interactive opponent processors (Kinsbourne, 1974a), both at the level of direct perception and of internal representation. At both levels, attention is directed along a vector resulting from the interaction of paired opponent processors that are controlled by the right and left hemispheres respectively, each of which directs attention towards the opposite end of a visual display. Unilateral neglect results from imbalance between these opponent processors, such that the undamaged one is disinhibited and largely in control, biasing attention towards the opposite side of arrays that are laterally extended in space. This is the orientational bias model of unilateral neglect (Kinsbourne, 1970; 1977; 1987). The opponent interactions occur at multiple levels (Kinsbourne, 1974a; Rizzolatti & Gallese, 1988). Correspondingly, neglect can result from damage to any one of several unilateral structures.

LATERAL INTERACTIONS BETWEEN OPPONENT PROCESSORS

Bisymmetrical motile animals are continually confronted with the challenge of deciding whether to turn right or left, in the presence of potential targets on either side. It is adaptively advantageous for such a decision to be unequivocal, and in animals that swim or locomote this is made possible by reciprocally inhibitory opponent systems. Mutually inhibitory interactions determine the direction of choice, and difference-minimising feedback enables this direction to be finely graded. Difference-minimising feedback is established when an opponent system is so organised, that as the dominant processor progressively inhibits its counterpart, the latter reciprocally inhibits the dominant processor. In this way, the interaction reaches equilibrium at the desired point. It follows that both hemispheres are involved in shifting the direction of orientation across its full range, in both hemispaces. If one of the opponent processors is inactivated, the individual's direction of orientation coincides with the direction in which it is programmed by the now disinhibited intact processor, and adjusting its direction becomes difficult if not impossible. Reciprocal lateral interactions have been well demonstrated even in the invertebrate octopus (studied by Messenger, 1967) and in many mammalian species. Correspondingly, unilateral lesions at appropriate segmental levels generate neglect syndromes in many species (reviewed by Kinsbourne, 1974a). They have in common the property of manifesting attentional gradients.

WHAT IS AN ATTENTIONAL GRADIENT?

Operationally, an attentional gradient is revealed when an animal system- atically orients to the most right-sided (or left-sided) of horizontally aligned stimuli, regardless of whether they straddle the interface between right and left hemispace or are all located within the same hemispace. Most animal experiments that explore neglect syndromes are not set up in such a way that this can be determined, in that the display usually consists of two stimuli, one to the right and one to the left of the midline. Occasionally, an investigator notes the lesioned animal's "heightened compulsive response to ipsilateral stimuli" (Sprague, 1966). More systematic evidence for the attentional gradient derives from the frequently reported occurrence of "circling" after unilateral lesions that cause neglect in experimental animals. Circling occurs when the animal, rather than explore both sides of its environment, systematically turns in the ipsilesional direction (Glick, Jerussi, & Fleischer, 1976). This is not a simple motor bias. Where the experimental arrangement enables analysis, it becomes clear that circling is determined by the location of neighbouring contours, in that the animal perpetually orients and locomotes towards the end of the contour that is most contralateral to the lesion (Wise & Holmes, 1986).

Neglect patients are seldom observed in the overt state of circling that is so familiar in the experimental animal, presumably on account of associated deficits that limit mobility. But ipsilesional biases in exploring the environment are often described, and I have observed patients with transitory neglect due to paroxysmal unilateral epileptic discharge circle (like the lesioned animal) around the periphery of the room, but contralaterally to the discharging focus. A tendency for acute stroke patients with neglect to over-react to visual stimuli introduced from the side ipsilateral to the lesion (Barany, 1913; Silberpfennig, 1941) and to mislocalise to the ipsilesional side of the target (Corin & Bender, 1970) has long been appreciated.

The attentional gradient refers to the extent to which one stimulus rather than another captures attention, and thereby controls behaviour. It is incompatible with the usual account of neglect, well summarised by Bisiach, Capitani and Porta (1985) as implying that "there are circumscribed brain areas in which lesions would result in a representational loss limited to definite regions of (egocentric) space". The reality of the attentional gradient cannot coherently be parleyed into such concepts as distorted representation of space itself. Rather it is referrable to real or imagined objects (figures) in real or imagined space (ground) (see Farah, 1990, for further discussion). Whereas the relative spatial position of a stimulus is a major determinant of its standing on the attentional hierarchy, its absolute location is not. Indeed, a neglect patient may, while manually outlining one object, look directly at another that intersects it, and not notice it (Bisiach & Rusconi, 1990). Attention may be oriented relative to a gravitational, a viewer-centred or an object-centred frame (Driver & Halligan, 1991: see also Chapter 8, this volume). The implications of these phenomena are beyond the scope of this discussion. I simply note that the gradient of neglect may correspond to any of these frames, depending on the situation. Between them, the hemispheres establish the representation in question. When there is a hemispheric lesion that causes neglect, attention across the task-relevant representation is biased accordingly.

The concept of a gradient is probabilistic. There is no point on the gradient at which the probability of detecting a target is zero, although it may be very low. Also, an unreported target may none the less have some effect on the behaviour of particular patients (Marshall & Halligan, 1988; McGlinchey-Berroth et al., in press; Volpe, Le Doux, & Gazzaniga, 1979) and their psychogalvanic response (Vallar et al., 1991). McGlinchey-Berroth et al. elegantly demonstrated priming of lexical decisions by picture primes in the neglected visual territory. That the neglected stimuli are sufficiently elaborated by the visual system to influence percepts was long ago indicated by the observation of Kinsbourne and Warrington (1962) that in "neglect dyslexia", backward completion of tachistoscopically exposed words reflects the number of neglected letters. Conversely, Bender and Krieger (1951) even found that in total darkness, patients could report and localise individual visual stimuli in visual fields that were perimetrically blind.

MODULAR OR INTERACTIVE PROCESSORS FOR LATERAL ATTENDING?

Unilateral neglect, especially when acute, is far more common on the left, after right-sided lesions, than on the right, after left-sided lesions. When it does occur on the right, it is relatively mild (Ogden, 1987). I have discussed the reason for this elsewhere (Kinsbourne, 1987). For present purposes, all relevant studies have involved patients with left neglect. Henceforth, I substitute "left" for "contralesional" and "right" for "ipsilesional". Further anatomical aspects of neglect are discussed by Vallar (see Chapter 2, this volume).

A crucial prediction of the orientational bias model is that attention is not intact within either hemispace in unilateral neglect. Instead, a lateral gradient of attention sweeps right across both hemispaces, such that attention is biased right-ward regardless of the absolute location of the target (Kinsbourne, 1970). This applies both to visual exploration, by covert shift of attention or overt gaze deviation, and the reporting of items simultaneously displayed by brief (tachistoscopic) exposure. Two other types of mechanism have been suggested for unilateral neglect, neither of which makes this prediction. Both assume that separate and independent mechanisms control attention within left and within right hemispace. These mechanisms are modular rather than interactive.

One type of mechanism is predicated on the longstanding assumption that there is impaired functioning within one hemispace, in contrast to preserved function within the other. The hypothesised malfunction takes a traditionally passive "deficit" form. Its most sophisticated instantiation is Bisiach's suggested impairment of representation in the hemispace subserved by the lesioned hemisphere (a refined version of the representational deficit earlier suggested by Zingerle, 1913). Heilman and Watson (1977) refer to attention rather than representation. They incriminate the loss of the selective orienting response towards stimuli in left hemispace. Their model, too, is dichotomous, implying preserved function with respect to one hemispace and impaired function with respect to another. By inference, one processor, responsible for the left hemispace, is impaired, whereas the other, independently responsible for the right hemispace, is intact. Although, as we shall see, the proposition that neglect is referrable to one half of space, rather than to a lateral gradient of attention across objects, is seriously at variance with the facts, even the most recent characterisations of neglect take a similar form. In fact, neglect is not dichotomously organised; when one of two opponent processors is relatively ineffective, the resulting bias is expressed right across the whole visual field. Also, neglect is not of some part of "space", but of stimuli, or parts of stimuli, depending on relative location along the horizontal meridian of the frame within which they are represented. Neglect is display-centred, not space-centred. Yet, neglect is referred to as "information coming from the side of space opposite the lesion" (Posner, Walker, Friedreich, & Rafal, 1984, p. 1863), "defective performance in one half of space" (Halsband, Gruhn, & Ettlinger, 1985), "stimuli or events in the side of space opposite to the lesion" (Bradshaw et al., 1987, p. 41), "stimuli presented contralateral to a hemispheric lesion" (Heilman, Bowers, Valenstein, & Watson, 1987, p. 116), "input on the side of space contralateral to the site of lesion" (Riddoch & Humphreys, 1987, p. 152), "missing visual stimuli in the contralesional half of space" (Ogden, 1987, p. 215), "the contralateral half-space' (Vallar & Perani, 1987, p. 237), "stimuli presented contralateral to the lesion" (Rizzolatti & Camarda, 1987, p. 289), "failure to orient automatically to the side of space opposite to the lesion" (Egelko et al., 1988, p. 213), "stimuli in left hemispace" (Halligan & Marshall, 1989, p. 517), "stimuli presented in the side of space contralateral to the lesion" (Ishiai, Furukawa, & Tsukagoshi, 1989, p. 1485), "unawareness of and inattention to the side of space contralateral to their lesion" (McGlynn & Schacter, 1989, p. 152), "stimuli on the side contralateral to the lesion" (Farah, et al., 1990, p. 335). In each case, the writers assume either that there is a step-function in attention, such that it is intact in one hemispace and impaired in the other, or that the impairment is with respect to space, rather than things in it. Both assumptions are false.

Even the more dynamically conceived class of model, that holds action leftward to be uniformly impaired and action rightward to remain intact, be it a directional impairment of lateral disengagement of attention (Posner et al., 1984), or of limb displacement (Heilman & Valenstein, 1979), retains the implication that function on one side, or in one direction, is normal. It misses the point that action towards the side of the lesion is not merely preserved, but exaggerated. There is no sector of the lateral spatial meridian within which, or towards which, function can be said to be normal.

HEMISPHERE ACTIVATION AND NEGLECT

The functional impairment of one opponent processor in neglect is a matter of degree. Not only is there a seemingly endless gradation of severity of neglect across cases, but even in an individual case, the degree of neglect is variable. Kinsbourne (1970) proposed that the impaired processor should be considered underactivated. Consistent with this interpretation, manipulations likely to affect hemisphere activation have demonstrable effects on the severity of neglect (Kinsbourne, 1974a; 1974b). A striking instance was reported by Silberpfennig (1941). He demonstrated that neglect could be temporarily relieved by irrigating the contralesional ear with ice water. This familiar "caloric" procedure serves transitorily to equate the activation level on the two sides of the brain, correcting the imbalance that gives rise to the pathological gradient in attention. Recently, this observation has been confirmed (Cappa, Sterzi, Vallar, & Bisiach, 1987; Rubens, 1985; Vallar et al., (1990). Another observation that can be most readily understood in terms of manipulating hemisphere activation is the finding that left neglect can be reduced by having the patient perform left hand finger movements (Robertson & North, 1992). If neglect were due to damage to some encapsulated attentional module, such effects would not be expected.

On the assumption that neglect is indeed due to an activational imbalance, Kinsbourne (1977) predicted that neglect would be more severe while the patient is engaged in a verbal than in a spatial task because the verbal activity would lead to activation of the left hemisphere, further aggravating the imbalance, whereas the spatial activity would activate the right hemisphere, and tend to counteract the imbalance. Heilman and Watson (1978) reported findings that were consistent with that prediction. Caplan (1985) interprets his results as being inconsistent with the differential activation prediction, but inspection of his data shows that the hypothesis is partially confirmed. The lateral gradient in accuracy of cancellation performance tends to be steeper for verbal stimuli and, in particular, performance on the right is more accurate when letters rather than symbols are used, a finding that suggests more extreme bias of attention to the right. In a quite different paradigm, Lecours et al. (1987) found that imposing a difficult verbal task elicits right neglect in left brain-damaged patients. In this study, the possibility of significant intra-hemispheric interference arises, perhaps handicapping the left hemisphere with respect to its inhibitory interaction with the right in the control of the direction of attention.

In an animal model of neglect, Deuel and Collins (1983) directly demonstrated the lateral imbalance in activation that Kinsbourne had hypothesised, with the use of metabolic measurements. Mountcastle (1978), among others, has identified single cells in monkey posterior parietal cortex that increase their firing when the animal attends to locations away from fixation, and in humans who attend to one side, cortical blood flow increases in the opposite posterior parietal area (Petersen, Fox, Miesin, & Raichle, 1988).

CLINICAL OBSERVATIONS

Before discussing the experimental evidence for attentional gradients along the lateral meridian of the visual field of patients with left visual neglect, I cite a few clinical observations. As mentioned above, generic clinical descriptions of unilateral spatial neglect typically imply that neglect effectively bisects perception and performance at the midline vertical meridian. Yet not only everyday clinical experience, but even patients' productions that serve as illustrations in articles and textbooks, contradict this supposition. In the acute stage, the patient does not simply ignore the left side of space, but maintains head and eyes turned to the right (De Renzi, Colombo, Faglioni, & Gibertoni, 1982). When the clinician attempts to test for extinction to double simultaneous stimulation, the very placement of one hand to the patient's right renders him or her unable to maintain central fixation. He or she compulsively orients towards the right hand (De Renzi, 1988; Kinsbourne, 1977). Depending on the severity of the neglect, the patient may attend only to the right-sided extreme of the display, more of it, or all but its left-most extension.

Eye movements are conspicuously affected in neglect (see Chapter 5, this volume). Gainotti and Taicci (1971) reported that patients judge the one to the right of two identical stimuli to be the larger. When the patient's eyes are free to scan and search, there is no invisible barrier at the midline, left of which gaze does not stray. Rather, the probability of fixation is less, the further left the target is relative to other stimuli that might compete for attention. This bears on the interpretation of neglect patients' performance when drawing. When patients draw from memory, they naturally fixate wherever their pencil is pointing. Yet, as the drawing gathers form, detail by detail, right to left, the probability that the patient will stop prematurely, leaving out some relatively left-sided details, or will be content with a more perfunctory rendering, with fainter strokes of the pencil, increases. Yet patients express no dissatisfaction when they draw incompletely, at the point of their fixation, but to the relative left of the complete production. Such behaviour is clearly incompatible with the pervasive assumption that the abnormality is in the representation of space. The patient with left neglect has "a rightward bias which remains latent in absence of stimulation" (De Renzi, Gentillini, Faglioni, & Barbieri, 1989, p. 236). It requires rivalry between stimuli to bring it out. The abnormality is in the representation of things and in orienting to things, and increases in proportion to the extent to which the feature or target in question is *relatively* left.

The patient's performance on commonly used tests for neglect exemplifies the same point. The cancellation test (Albert, 1973) requires the patient to scan a laterally extended display, and to cross out all instances that he or she can find of a predesignated target. The test is motivated by the familiar observation that neglect patients miss items to the left. In this test, dichotomous approaches look for a comparison between performance within the left half of the display (impaired) and the right (preserved) (e.g. Heilman & Watson, 1977). But in fact performance is impaired, though to a lesser extent, on the right also (Gainotti & Taicci, 1971). The patient fixates many times as his or her search progresses from right to left. The search does not arrest abruptly at some point or interface at which right hemispace ends and left hemispace begins. Rather, as it progresses leftward, it gradually diminishes. The further left he or she orients, the more difficult it is to orient still further left. Perhaps the build-up of contour to the right is the limiting factor. The following example further dramatises this crucial point.

Patients with left neglect generally fail to respond to left-sided features of visual input, whether they are hemianopic or not. Additionally, they fail to orient leftward in circumstances under which it is normal to do so automatically. None the less, such patients can be coaxed into voluntary leftward gaze, though with increasing difficulty the more their gaze already deviates in that direction. Conversely, when they look to the right, they are apt to overshoot far into right hemispace, typically to the right extreme of whatever display might extend across their visual field. Thus when they open their eyes to view a newspaper unfolded before them and to read from it, they visibly direct their gaze rightward across the test, until it alights on the right-most margin of the printed text (De Renzi et al, 1989; Kinsbourne, 1977). They then read some letters or a word or two, but soon give up, perplexed, blaming their eyesight. They exhibit no awareness of the expanse of text to the left of their biased focus of attention, although their gaze has just swept across it.

The gradient of attention is not unique to the visual modality. In unilateral neglect of person, the notion of a hemineglect of, in this case, personal space, is as inappropriate as the notion of spatial hemineglect. Zingerle (1913) says of the neglect patient that "in his awareness, the body's representation is apparently confined to the right half". In this statement, he exhibits the static thinking typical of his time. There is no evidence for the existence of a body schema in consciousness, bits of which can be nibbled away by disease. There is no set of localised deficits of regional body awareness, which, when fitted together like jigsaw pieces, cover the total body surface. Observation suggests that the representation of somatic awareness is object-centred, not space-centred—the "objects" in this instance being the body parts. We cannot achieve a simultaneous "overfeel" of all the body. We can, however, shift attention to one or another body part at a time, just like to one or other object in a visual display. For all the claims of neglect of one half of the body, clinical observation reveals a systematic inhomogeneity in the extent to which different left-sided parts are neglected. The most intense neglect (and disavowal) pertains to the left upper extremity, the elbow more than the shoulder, and the hand more than the elbow (Bisiach, Meregalli, & Berti, 1990; Bisiach & Geminiani, 1991). Depending on how one assumes the left–right axis of the body to be arranged, one could regard this as constituting an attentional gradient, analogous to that across the visual field. The gradient must refer to body parts independent of any particular spatial position they happen to assume. Moving a patient's left hand to the right of his or her body does not correct the neglect of the hand.

EXPERIMENTAL OBSERVATIONS

Bisection Performance

A frequently used test for neglect requires the patient to bisect horizontal lines. When patients with neglect also have hemianopia, they must view the target line entirely within the ipsilesional half field. None the less, they transect the line to the right of its veridical centre point. This deviation is in the opposite direction from that found in normal subjects (i.e. in normal visual fields). When normal subjects bisect a horizontal line presented within a half field, they tend to make their mark somewhat more towards fixation than is correct, thus overestimating that part of the length of the line which is most nearly central, in contrast to the patient with neglect, whose performance implies an overestimate of the more peripheral segment (to the right). That this pattern of performance is consistent with increased lateral bias of orienting was elegantly demonstrated by Burnett-Stuart, Halligan and Marshall (1991) in a study of bisection of lines varying systematically in inclination between horizontal and vertical. Whether this class of finding can be construed as evidence for an attentional gradient depends on where patients fixate when they attempt the bisection. This point has been elegantly clarified by Ishiai et al. (1989). They monitored eye movements while patients and controls undertook line bisection. Normal controls fixated roughly in the centre, launched exploratory eye movements to either side (though more to the right, illustrating the general rightward bias of intact attention), and bisected accurately. Patients with left neglect fixated somewhere to the right of centre, made a few rightward and no leftward eye movements, and responded with shorter latency than any of the contrast groups. It follows that those six of their eight patients who had left hemianopias, and fixated at the point of transection, could not have seen the left-sided extent of the line they were supposed to bisect. Assuming, none the less, that the subjects were performing the task as instructed, Ishiai et al. attempted to resolve this puzzle by suggesting that the patients were "completing" the lines into the blind half-field, effectively adding on a length equal to that of the segment they could see, and then correctly bisecting the line as it appeared to them (see also Halligan & Marshall, 1988).

The imaginative completion of incomplete figures (Poppelreuter, 1917) is important to an understanding of neglect phenomenology. But Warrington (1962) has shown that only those shapes are completed that appear to have a part missing. That cannot be said of a line, because there is no prior expectation that a line will be of a particular length (see also Halligan & Marshall, 1989, who dismiss a similar argument on empirical grounds). In any case, the suggestion is illogical. It assumes that a patient with neglect can overview the extent (real or imaginary) of a line in order to make the required judgement. In reality, the task of transection as such must be beyond patients with significant neglect, because it requires them to do something of which they are incapable—maintain within conscious visual attention contour on the left as well as on the right of their point of fixation. More likely, patients fixate as far leftward from the right extreme of the line as the severity of their rightward attentional bias permits, and optimistically make their mark at that point. Such behaviour would in addition explain Halligan and Marshall's (1988; 1989) finding that neglect patients who generally bisect to the right of centre may actually "bisect" very short lines to the left of centre. The patient is not now exhibiting a paradoxical right neglect. He is simply not performing a bisection, because that is something he cannot do, but is doing something else, which is as close to the task set as he can get.

The point of transection in a line bisection task is a somewhat variable function of line length (e.g. Bisiach, Bulgarelli, Sterzi, & Vallar, 1983). It may be that even when it is outside awareness, contour exerts a pull on attention, enabling it to shift leftward to a proportional extent in some instances. Such an effect appears to have been demonstrated by Butter, Kirsh and Reeves (1990), when they were able to influence patients' line bisection by presenting flashing lights to the left of the line out of sight in the hemianopanic field. In any case, Ishiai et al. stress that "hemispace did not affect the visual process represented by the eye fixation pattern in the line bisection task. Even if the subjective midpoint was placed on the true midpoint or to the left of it, the eye fixation pattern characteristic of hemianopics with unilateral spatial neglect was constantly observed" (p. 1500).

Completion

Kinsbourne and Warrington (1962) studied neglect "completion" dyslexia tachistoscopically. They found that patients with right hemisphere lesions tended to "complete" a nonword letter grouping briefly exposed to the right of fixation, so as to respond with a real word that incorporates the exposed letters at its end. These word "completions" were explained as due to left neglect, such that the patient was unaware of the absence from the visual display of the inferred left-sided letter groups. Crucial evidence for attentional gradients within the visual half-field was the additional demonstration that this effect obtained even when the stimuli were exposed in such a way that the completed letters, had they been present, would have appeared well to the right of fixation in the "intact" visual field. Similar findings of completion within a half-field have been reported more recently, for instance by Ellis, Flude and Young (1977).

Warrington (1962) demonstrated left-sided completion of incomplete forms in patients with right hemisphere lesions. Again, the form was completed even if it was exposed well within the visual half-field, rather than apposed to the midline. Completion characterised the responses of those hemianopic patients who were unaware of their visual field defects, and this finding was confirmed by Gassell and Williams (1963).

Gradient in Shape Identification

In tachistoscopic work with 82 patients who had sustained unilateral penetrating cerebral missile wounds some 20 years earlier, Kinsbourne (1966) briefly presented random horizontally adjacent four-letter sequences centred on the fixation point. Although none of the subjects exhibited clinical neglect, the right hemisphere group yielded results that suggested a reverse gradient of attention. The highest percentage of correct identification was for the more peripheral of the two letters to the right of the centre, and the lowest for the more peripheral of the two letters on the left. This gradient was the opposite of that found in a control group, and in patients whose brain wounds were left-sided. Like patients with clinically apparent neglect, these patients oriented to the right end of the display, in this case the one most to the right of four letters, and then moved attention stepwise to the left. So even within each half-field, the direction of the implicit scan was right to left.

Even within single shapes attention is biased to the right. Egelko et al. (1988) presented patients with a matching-to-sample task, and found that for shapes within each half-field, as well as at fixation, they made more mismatches based on failure to observe fine detail on the left than on the right side of the shape that they chose in error.

Gradient Demonstrated by Reaction Time

Làdavas (1987) required patients who had right brain damage with left extinction to respond to a target flashed for 250 msec in one of two boxes, presented both in the left half-field, symmetrically to either side of fixation, or both in the right half-field. In each case, the patients responded more quickly to the stimulus on the right, even though in the latter condition that stimulus is the more peripheral of the two. Làdavas, Del Pesce and Provinciali (1989), again using a reaction time task, showed that both patients with right hemisphere damage and with left hemisphere damage respond more quickly when they shift their attention in a direction towards the side of the lesion, even within the same visual half-field. As predicted by the orientational bias theory, this effect was more marked in the case of the right-damaged patients (see Rizzolatti, Gentilucci, & Matelli, 1985, for similar effects in monkeys with surgically induced neglect). There was even a double dissociation, with a control group performing better than the patients on the more central target, but the patients doing better on the target more peripherally to the right (Làdavas, Petronio, & Umilta, 1990). This demonstrates the pathologically enhanced attention to the extreme right stimulus posited by the orientational bias model. The observation of a condition under which patients actually do better than controls is rare in neuropsychology, and dramatises the difference between the attentional gradient model, with which it is consistent, and deficit models, with which it is not.

De Renzi et al (1989) asked right brain-damaged patients with and without unilateral neglect and controls to search for a target letter among four locations along the lateral plane, the first at fixation and the fourth most peripheral in the right half-field. The patients with neglect yielded their fastest responses when the target was in the right-most position, and progressively slower responses as it moved towards the centre. The contrast groups showed no effect of location on reaction time. This study demonstrates the attentional gradient in neglect with particular clarity.

Eglin, Robertson and Knight (1989) measured neglect patients' search times for predesignated targets, while varying the number of distractors to the right of the target. They found that search would proceed with normal latency even to the left of the midline when there were no right-sided distractors (see also Kaplan, Verfaellie, Meadows, & Caplan, 1991).

Neglect of Represented Displays

Bisiach, Luzzatti and Perani (1979) had neglect patients view shapes through a slit at fixation, behind which the target was moved from one side to the other. They found that the patients, like normals, could identify the shapes, and thus must have displayed in representational space (i.e. as a visual image) what they perceived successively at a single point at fixation. However, their reports revealed that as in direct perception, so in imaged perception, the representation was imperfect towards the left. We took advantage of this methodology to demonstrate a gradient of attention

(Mijovic, Liederman, & Kinsbourne, 1991). Fixating a slot, patients viewed a nesting set of laterally adjacent angles, arranged from more to less acute, in increments of 5°, from 5° to 60°. The patients themselves pulled the display from one side to the other so as to scan it through the slot, but could only view one stimulus at a time. The task was matching-to-sample. A sample angle was mounted just above the slot, and the subjects had to display in the slot the corresponding element in the array. The patients systematically selected an exemplar that was several positions to the right of the normal controls' choice, regardless of the direction in which they had moved the display, and of whether the angle was more or less acute than the correct match. Evidently, the extent of build-up of contour on the right of the successively constructed representation, systematically biased the patients' choices.

Our experiment illustrates how orientational bias theory can clarify the way in which neglect patients establish representations. Bisiach and Luzzatti's (1978) classical demonstration of hemineglect for visualised information about landmarks to either side of the Piazza del Duomo did not address this question, because they did not record the probability of retrieval relative to position along the lateral meridian within a half-representation. I predict that in representation, as in perception, the appropriately designed experiment will uncover a gradient, rather than the right-left dichotomy assumed by Bisiach and Luzzatti. This prediction has recently been confirmed by Dr Bisiach (pers. comm.).

Gravitational and Retinotopic Co-ordinates Deconfounded

The independence of the left-right gradient from retinotopic co-ordinates was elegantly demonstrated by Làdavas (1987). She had subjects with neglect tilt their heads 90° to the right or to the left, and projected stimuli simultaneously to the same visual half-field, but to the right and left respectively in terms of gravitational co-ordinates. The findings conformed to a clear attentional gradient, in that the responses were faster to the stimulus that was relatively to the gravitational right within the rotated visual half-field. A similar demonstration was independently accomplished by Calvanio, Petrone and Levine (1987), and their findings were confirmed by Farah et al. (1990). These findings refute a model proposed by Rizzolatti et al. (1985). They had drawn attention to their earlier finding that in monkey postarcuate frontal cortex, neurons that represent the more medial aspects of the visual field more often respond to stimuli from both sides of the midline than neurons that represent the more peripheral sectors of the field (Rizzolatti, Scandolara, Matelli, & Gentilucci, 1981). Làdavas's and Calvanio and co-workers' findings decisively dissociate the distribution of attention in neglect from the retinotopic distribution of the receptive fields of the neurons in question. A direct test using a reaction time paradigm similarly lends support to a directional orientation bias hypothesis as against Rizzolatti's representational view. Perhaps the most dramatic demonstration has been accomplished very recently. Karnath, Schenkel and Fischer (1991) showed that the deficit in latency of leftward saccadic movement in left neglect could be corrected by having the patients turn their trunk to the left. Yet again, a passive model is shown to be inadequate in explaining neglect symptomatology (see Chapter 9, this volume).

Interestingly, Robertson and Lamb (1988; 1989) have adduced evidence that in at least one variant of normally occurring laterality effects, object-centred rather than retinotopic relations determine the direction of asymmetry in performance, in this case, in response latency. As Efron (1990) has remarked, "It is obvious that these results cannot be explained in terms of Kimura's direct/indirect access theory—indeed, they reflect a fatal flaw in it" (p. 52). However, they are quite compatible with hemisphere activation theory, which deals in terms of how input is represented, rather than by which channel it reaches the cerebral cortex. Curiously, Efron appears to assume that positing a scan automatically invalidates a hemispheric origin for the effect. As examples already reviewed attest, this is by no means the case.

Attention Controlled by the Disconnected Hemisphere

In patients whose corpus callosum is inactivated by surgery or naturally occurring disease, each hemisphere is found to have its independent attentional system (Luck, Hillyard, Mangun, & Gazzaniga, 1989). It responds directly only to stimuli within the contralateral visual half-field. Whether each hemisphere is in addition to be expected to exhibit ipsilateral neglect depends on the model that is applied. The model that proposes that whereas the right hemisphere programmes attention bilaterally, the left is attentive only to the right half-field (Heilman & Valenstein, 1979), predicts uniform and total neglect of left space when the left hemisphere is in action, but no neglect at all of right space when the right hemisphere is active. The experimental findings are grossly at variance with these expectations. Neglect of the left is so subtle in the split-brain state that several studies have failed to find it altogether (Gordon, Bogen, & Sperry, 1971: Joynt, 1977; Sperry, Gazzaniga, & Bogen, 1969). Others have found it only minimally present for a limited period of time after callosal section (Plourde & Sperry, 1984; Wilson, Reeves, Gazzaniga, & Culver, 1977). Moreover, as we shall see, several studies that do report minimal neglect in split-brain patients find it bilaterally.

The orientational bias model, though it refers the locus of opponent interaction to brainstem rather than forebrain commissures, does predict a degree of attentional bias when one hemisphere only is engaged in a task, on account of the loss of the callosum's equilibrating function (Kinsbourne, 1974b). Normally, when one hemisphere is activated by direct stimulation or because the individual has undertaken a task for which it is specialised, activation spreads across the corpus callosum to activate the other hemisphere also. After callosal section, the unused hemisphere remains unactivated, and thus relatively unprepared to process stimuli that come its way without warning. When both hemispheres are independently activated, each generates an uncorrected contralateral attentional bias. Trevarthen and I demonstrated bilateral simultaneous completion on the part of the disconnected hemispheres (Trevarthen, 1974). When different shapes that were incomplete at the vertical meridian were presented simultaneously in the two visual fields, each hemisphere completed the shape presented in its half-field. We also found the one on the left of two letters that were simultaneously exposed in a memory scanning reaction time task was neglected (reviewed by Kinsbourne, 1974b). Whereas in the previous case the task was one that either hemisphere can undertake, the verbal task in the memory scanning study appears to have elicited task-specific left hemisphere activation, and thus the predicted left neglect. Sine, Soufi and Shah's (1984) callosally lesioned patient exhibited left neglect when drawing a clock with his right hand. Goldenberg (1986) found left neglect during right hand use by a patient with anterior callosal disconnection. A well-studied callosally disconnected patient of Kashiwagi et al. (1990) demonstrated left neglect in a number of tasks presented to the left hemisphere, and on one of several tasks presented to the right. All of these findings support the orientational model, because the neglect was within a visual half-field, and therefore demonstrated the gradient effect which this model predicts.

Most recently, Làdavas and Gazzaniga (in prep.) have applied to split-brain subjects the technique of 90° head tilt discussed above. They exposed stimuli within a visual half-field, but to the gravitational right and left, given the head tilt. They found a robust gradient of attention for these two stimuli, although both were presented to the same hemisphere, to half-fields that are retinotopically superior and inferior. It becomes clear that each hemisphere is specialised to represent the opposite side of gravitational space, independent of retinotopic location.

Disengage Impairment

Posner et al. (1984) found a disproportionately increased latency of response to a left-sided stimulus when patients with right parietal lesions were induced to attend to the right of the location of the target—by misleading them (giving them an invalid cue) as to where to expect the target to appear. They inferred that these patients found it hard to disengage from their focus of attention in order to move their attention leftward, and that this was so even if both focus and target were in the right visual half-field. But calling this a disengage deficit when it applies only to an intended attentional shift in one direction does not capture the essence of the phenomenon. Difficulty in disengaging attention should not be affected by the direction in which the subject intends to shift. But imbalance between opponent processors predicts this finding. Impaired representation of left hemispace does not.

Contrary to Morrow and Ratcliff (1987), a directional disengage deficit, if it exists, falls far short of doing justice to neglect symptomatology. Inability to disengage towards the left cannot explain the lack of awareness of left-sided information, even in peripheral vision. Most crucially, it cannot explain why patients with right parietal lesions feel such a "magnetic attraction" (De Renzi et al., 1989, p. 232) to the right side of any display in the first place, and begin their search of displays from that side. Also, neglect patients who are too severe to use Posner's paradigm are impaired in moving their attention leftward, whether they are currently "engaged" in attending somewhere or not. Indeed, as Posner, Walker, Friedreich and Rafal (1987) have remarked, neglect patients are slow to respond to left-sided stimuli, even if they appear to be focusing on them (see also Làdavas, 1987).

The Focus of Attention in Neglect

The statement that patients with neglect attend to the extreme right end of a display is a correct but insufficient characterisation. Even at the right extreme, the patient appears to lack overview. Let us return to the patient attending to the right edge of the text of an unfolded newspaper. It is not found that he easily sweeps his gaze up and down that margin, observing a vertical column of letters or words. He does sluggishly shift focus, usually downwards, one or two lines, but soon abandons his still highly focused search. That is, neglect attention is not only laterally biased; it is also intensely focused. Recent evidence suggests that this focus, or "zoom", varies to some extent with the nature of the target stimulus. It is more marked when the stimulus is a line than when it is a closed two-dimensional figure (Marshall & Halligan, 1991).

At least when neglect is severe, it is characterised by intense attentional focus, not so much at a point as on a thing. Even at fixation, only one of two superimposed objects may be noticed (Bisiach & Rusconi, 1990). This phenomenon characterises visuo-spatial agnosia (or dorsal simultanagnosia, as it is termed by Farah, 1990). I have interpreted this classical syndrome, that involves an inability to see more than one thing at a time, as representing the left hemisphere specialisation for focused attention when its disinhibited attentional control system operates in isolation (Kinsbourne, 1982). If this is correct, it would have to be demonstrable that the difficulty in observing two or more things at a time exists independently of the neglect. For instance, it should be demonstrable along the vertical meridian.

Robertson (Chapter 12, this volume) suggests that left neglect is compounded of an orientational deficit as here discussed and a general impairment of arousal/vigilance reflecting right hemisphere specialisation for this component of behavioural control. This attractive idea can be further integrated into the clinical neuropsychology of the right hemisphere as follows.

The right hemisphere territory that is typically implicated in left neglect is close to that which, when lesioned, releases visuo-spatial agnosia, and neglect patients do indeed perform poorly on many tests of visuo-spatial analysis (Oxbury, Campbell, & Oxbury, 1974). Furthermore, lesions that cause neglect are well known to be extensive. The likelihood that a patient might at the same time suffer from neglect and visuo-spatial agnosia is considerable. The agnosia would be overshadowed by the neglect, and have to be tested for in specific ways. It would follow that the attentional gradient in left neglect is a gradient of *focused* attention. Attention zooms in on a single form, namely the one most to the right.

If the above analysis is correct, left neglect differs from right neglect in yet one more way than those already hypothesised. Right neglect is predicted to lack the tightly constricted focus of attention. That, too, might tend to render it less conspicuous and less of a handicap. The suggestion that neglect patients frequently also visuo-spatial agnosia is new, and experimental tests remain to be done (see Chapter 8, this volume).

In less severe cases, attention can be shifted leftward to another shape, laboriously and under the influence of volition. But it should not be taken for granted that the patient can keep the present and the previously attended shape in simultaneous overview. A lack of overview may also go some way towards accounting for the notorious failure of neglect patients to draw obvious inferences about the integrity of their body parts from considerations of anatomical continuity. For instance, a patient, disowning his or her left hand, might not be swayed by the evident fact that it is on a continuum, through forearm and upper arm, with the rest of his or her body (Bisiach, Meregalli, & Berti, 1990).

The Impairment in Representation in Neglect

As Bisiach et al. (1983) pointed out, the deficit in neglect is not in perception but in representation. However, the deficit appears to relate not to the representation of space, wherein objects may or may not also be represented, but of objects. Space, like time, seems to be a second-order attribute, represented only very grossly in its own right, but, presumably for adaptive reasons, essentially incorporated into the characterisation of objects. Indeed, vision is 100 times as sensitive to change of position when another stationary object is in the field as when a solitary object is in the field (Wallach, 1968). Which part of space is ignored depends on what is in it, and near it. There are no reports of patients who have scotomata in their mental images, as would be expected if analogue representations of space extended across cortex. It appears that analogue properties of figures and their ground are not coded in isomorphic analogue form in the brain. Of course, they are coded. But the fact that coding represents spatial parameters is no reason why the representing need resemble the represented (Dennett & Kinsbourne, 1992). As for what does the ignoring, it is, as Bisiach and Berti (1990) maintain, unnecessary to posit an internal scanner ("eye") that operates in a biased fashion. There is no known further agency downstream from the scanner, in the service of which the scanner can be assumed to scan. Inste ad, I propose that the representing *is* the experiencing, and biased experiencing is the subjective counterpart of biased representing (Kinsbourne, 1988; 1993).

The difficulties associated with a representational theory of neglect are vividly illustrated by the findings of Bisiach, Cornacchia, Sterzi and Vallar (1984). They reported a rightward bias in auditory localisation on the part of a group of patients with right posterior cerebral lesions. This bias was not limited to left hemispace, as predicted by Bisiach's hemirepresentational deficit theory of neglect. It obtains also for the space ipsilateral to the lesion, as predicted by the orientational bias theory. Bisiach et al. (1984, p. 48) remark: "This suggests that not only the contralateral half of the space representation is affected, but that also the ipsilateral half is impaired". If selective attending is implemented by correspondingly biased representing, then Bisiach's theory may not differ from the orientational bias theory.

The "print-out" of object representations into awareness starts on the right, and, progressing leftward, becomes increasingly indefinite and unstable. The representation remains focalised. A panoramic overview, even of what is to the right, is not available to the patient with severe unilateral neglect. This is so even for information perception which does not require an attentional shift, but is normally available in parallel. The impairment applies equally to print-out from perception and from memory. The depleted representations on the left account for the underrating of left-sided items. Similarly, the fragmentary and sketchy manner in which left-sided body parts become represented in consciousness when "local attention" is shifted towards them presumably accounts for the patient's disdainful attitude towards them. Conversely, as Bisiach and Berti (1987) express it, "what appears as a shift of attention might mean a recoil from daunting representations" (p. 196). If, as seems plausible, intending an act is the subjective counterpart of representing its presumed outcome, then the inability to represent intended actions to the left explains the patient's lack of initiative in that direction. Given the absence of representations, the patient would not be expected to complain about his or her failure to generate leftward intention. To be aware of a difficulty or deficit in action, one has to be able to represent the foiled intention.

CONCLUSION

Cumulatively, the evidence for a gradient of attention across the visual field is convincing. Similar evidence in other modalities is available but relatively sparse. Whether the gradient is linear (see Chapter 8, this volume) and how generally it applies to the various frames of reference within which neglect occurs remains to be determined.

REFERENCES

Albert, M.L. (1973). A simple test of visual neglect. *Neurology, 23*, 658–664.

Barany, R. (1913). Latente Deviation der Augen und Vorbeizeigen des Kopfes bei Hemiplegie und Epilepsie. *Wiener klinische Wochenschrift, 26*, 597–599.

Bender, M.B. & Krieger, H.P. (1951). Visual functions in perimetrically blind fields. *Archives of Neurology and Psychiatry, 65*, 72–79.

Bisiach, E. & Berti, A. (1987). Dyschiria: An attempt at its systematic explanation. In M. Jeannerod (Ed.), *Neurophysiological and neuropsychological aspects of unilateral neglect*, pp.187–201. Amsterdam: North-Holland.

Bisiach, E. & Berti, A. (1990). Waking images and neural activity. In R.G. Kunzendorf & A.A. Sheikh (Eds), *The psychophysiology of mental imagery* (pp. 67–88). Amityville, NY: Baywood.

Bisiach, E., Bulgarelli, C., Sterzi, R., & Vallar, G. (1983). Line bisection and cognitive plasticity of unilateral neglect of space. *Brain and Cognition, 2*, 32–38.

Bisiach, E., Capitani, E., & Porta, E. (1985). Two basic properties of space representation in the brain: Evidence from unilateral neglect. *Journal of Neurology, Neurosurgery and Psychiatry, 48*, 141–144.

Bisiach, E., Cornacchia, L., Sterzi, R., & Vallar, G. (1984). Disorders of perceived auditory lateralization after lesions of the right hemisphere. *Brain, 107*, 37–52.

Bisiach, E. & Geminiani, G. (1991). Anosognosia related to hemiplegia and hemianopia. In G. Prigatano & D.L. Schacter (Eds), *Awareness of deficit after brain injury*. New York: Academic Press.

Bisiach, E. & Luzzatti, C. (1978). Unilateral neglect of representational space. *Cortex, 14*, 129–133.

Bisiach, E., Luzzatti, C., & Perani, D. (1979). Unilateral neglect, representational schema and consciousness. *Brain, 102*, 609-618.

Bisiach, E., Meregalli, S., & Berti, A. (1990). Mechanisms of production control and belief fixation in human visuospatial processing: Clinical evidence from unilateral neglect and misrepresentation. In M.L. Commons, R.J. Herrnstein, S.M. Kosslyn, & D.B. Mumford (Eds), *Models of behavior: Computational and clinical approaches to pattern recognition and concept formation*. Hillsdale, NJ: Lawrence Erlbaum Associates Inc.

Bisiach, E. & Rusconi, M.L. (1990). Breakdown of perceptual awareness in unilateral neglect. *Cortex*, *26*, 643–650.

Bradshaw, J.L., Nettleton, L.C., Pierson, J.M., Wilson, L.E., & Nathan, G. (1987). Coordinates of extracorporeal space. In M. Jeannerod (Ed.), *Neurophysiological and neuropsychological aspects of spatial neglect*, pp. 41–67. Amsterdam: North-Holland.

Burnett-Stuart, G., Halligan, P., & Marshall, J. (1991). A Newtonian model of perceptual distortion in visuo-spatial neglect. *NeuroReport*, *2*, 255–257.

Butter, C.M., Kirsh, N.L., & Reeves, G. (1990). The effect of lateralized dynamic stimuli on unilateral spatial neglect following right hemisphere lesions. *Restorative Neurology and Neuroscience*, *2*, 39–46.

Calvanio, R., Petrone, P.N., & Levine, D.N. (1987). Left visual-spatial neglect is both environment-centered and body-centered. *Neurology*, *37*, 1179–1183.

Caplan, B. (1985). Task factors in unilateral neglect. *Cortex*, *21*, 69–80.

Coppa, S., Sterzi, R., Vallar G., & Bisiach, E. (1987). Remission of hemineglect during vestibular stimulation. *Neuropsychologia*, *25*, 775–782.

Corin, M.S. & Bender, M.B. (1970). Mislocation in visual space with reference to midline at the boundary of a homonymous hemianopia. *Archives of Neurology*, *27*, 252–262.

Dennett, D. & Kinsbourne, M. (1992). Time and the observer: The where and when of consciousness in the brain. *Behavioral Brain Sciences*, *15*, 183–247.

De Renzi, E. (1988). Occulomotor disturbances in hemispheric disease. In C.W. Johnston & F.J. Pirozzolo (Eds), *Neuropsychology of eye movements*. Hillsdale, NJ: Lawrence Erlbaum Associates Inc.

De Renzi, E., Colombo, A., Faglioni, P., & Gibertoni, M. (1982). Conjugate gaze paresis in stroke patients with unilateral damage. *Archives of Neurology*, *39*, 482–486.

De Renzi, E., Gentillini, M., Faglioni, P., & Barbieri, C. (1989). Attentional shift towards the rightmost stimuli in patients with left visual neglect. *Cortex*, *25*, 231–237.

Deuel, R.K. & Collins, R.C. (1983). Recovery from unilateral neglect. *Experimental Neurology*, *81*, 773–748.

Driver, J. & Halligan, P.W. (1991). Can visual neglect operate in object-centered coordinates? An affirmative case study. *Cognitive Neuropsychology*, *8*, 475–496..

Efron, R. (1990). *The decline and fall of hemisphere specialization*. Hillsdale, NJ: Lawrence Erlbaum Associates Inc.

Egelko, S., Riley, E., Simon, D., Diller, L., & Esrachi, O. (1988). Unilateral spatial neglect: Biases in contralateral search and fine spatial attention. *Archives of Clinical Neuropsychology*, *3*, 213–226.

Eglin, M., Robertson, L., & Knight, R.T. (1989). Visual search performance in the neglect syndrome. *Journal of Cognitive Neuroscience*, *1*, 372–285.

Ellis, A.W., Flude, B., & Young, A. (1977). "Neglect dyslexia" and the early visual processing of letters in words and nonwords. *Cognitive Neuropsychology*, *4*, 465–486.

Farah, M.J. (1990). *Visual agnosia*. Cambridge, MA: MIT Press.

Farah, M.J., Brunn, J.L., Wong, A.B., Wallace, M.A., & Carpenter, P.A. (1990). Frames of reference for allocating attention to space: Evidence from the neglect syndrome. *Neuropsychologia*, *28*, 335–347.

Gainotti, G. & Taicci, C. (1971). The relationship between disorders of visual perception and unilateral spatial neglect. *Neuropsychologia*, *9*, 451–458.

Gassell, M.M. & Williams, D. (1963). Visual function in patients with homonymous hemianopia. 3. The completion phenomenon: Insight and attitude to the defect and visual functional efficiency. *Brain*, *86*, 229–260.

Glick, S.D., Jerussi, T.P., & Fleischer, L.N. (1976). Turning in circles: The neuropharmacology of rotation. *Life Sciences*, *18*, 889–896.

Goldenberg, G. (1986). Neglect in a patient with partial callosal disconnection. *Neuropsychologia*, *24*, 397–403.

Gordon, H.W., Bogen, J.E., & Sperry, R.W. (1971). Absence of deconnexion syndrome in two patients with partial section of the neocommissures. *Brain*, *94*, 327–336.

Halligan, P.W., & Marshall, J.C. (1988). How long is a piece of string? A study of line bisection in a case of visual neglect. *Cortex*, *24*, 321–328.

Halligan, P.W. & Marshall, J.C. (1989). Perceptual cueing and perceptuo-motor compatability in visuo-spatial neglect: A single case study. *Cognitive Neuropsychology*, *6*, 423–435.

Halsband, U., Gruhn, S., & Ettlinger, G. (1985). Unilateral spatial neglect and defective performance in one half of space. *International Journal of Neuroscience*, *28*, 173–195.

Heilman, K.M., Bowers, D., Valenstein, E., & Watson, R.T. (1987). Hemispace and hemispatial neglect. In M. Jeannerod (Ed.), *Neurophysiological and neuropsychological aspects of spatial neglect*, pp.115–150. Amsterdam: North-Holland.

Heilman, K.M. & Valenstein, E. (1979). Mechanisms underlying hemispatial neglect. *Annals of Neurology*, *5*, 166–170.

Heilman, K.M. & Watson, R.T. (1977). The neglect syndrome—a unilateral defect of the orienting response. In S. Harnad, R.W. Doty, L. Goldstein, J. Jaynes & G. Krauthamer (Eds), *Lateralization in the nervous system*. New York: Academic Press.

Heilman, K.M. & Watson, R.T. (1978). Changes in the symptoms of neglect induced by changing task strategy. *Archives of Neurology*, *35*, 47–49.

Ishiai, S., Furukawa, T., & Tsukagoshi, H. (1989). Visuospatial processes of line bisection and the mechanisms underlying unilateral spatial neglect. *Brain*, *112*, 1485–1502.

Joynt, R.J. (1977). Inattention syndromes in split-brain man. In E.A. Weinstein & R.P. Friedland (Eds), *Hemi-inattention and hemisphere specialization, Advances in Neurology*, Vol. 18. pp. 33–40. New York: Raven Press.

Kaplan, R.F., Verfaellie, M., Meadows, M.E., & Caplan, L.R. (1991). Changing attentional demands in left hemispatial neglect. *Archives of Neurology*, *48*, 1263–1266.

Karnath, H.O., Schenkel, P., & Fischer, B. (1991). Trunk orientation as the determining factor of the "contralateral" deficit in the neglect syndrome and as physical anchor of the internal representation of body orientation in space. *Brain*, *114*, 1997–2014.

Kashiwagi, A., Kashiwagi, T., Nishikawa, T., Tanabe, H., & Okuda, J. (1990). Hemispatial neglect in a patient with callosal infarction. *Brain*, *113*, 1005–1023.

Kinsbourne, M. (1966). Limitations in visual capacity due to cerebral lesions. In *Proceedings of the 18th International Congress of Psychology*, Moscow (July).

Kinsbourne, M. (1970). A model for the mechanism of unilateral neglect of space. *Transactions of the American Neurological Association*, *95*, 143–146.

Kinsbourne, M. (1974a). Lateral interactions in the brain. In M. Kinsbourne & W.L. Smith (Eds), *Hemispheric disconnection and cerebral function*, pp. 239–259 Springfield, ILL: Thomas.

Kinsbourne, M. (1974b). Mechanisms of hemispheric interaction in the brain. In M. Kinsbourne & W.L. Smith (Eds), *Hemispheric disconnection and cerebral function*, pp. 260–285. Springfield, ILL: Thomas.

Kinsbourne, M. (1977). Hemineglect and hemisphere rivalry. *Advances in Neurology*, *18*, 41–49.

Kinsbourne, M. (1982). Hemispheric specialization and the growth of human understanding. *American Psychologist*, *37*, 411–420.

Kinsbourne, M. (1987). Mechanisms of unilateral neglect, In M. Jeannerod (Ed.), *Neurophysiological and neuropsychological aspects of unilateral neglect*, pp. 69–86. Amsterdam: North-Holland.

Kinsbourne, M. (1988). Integrated field theory of consciousness. In A.J. Marcel & E. Bisiach (Eds), *The concept of consciousness in contemporary science*. Oxford: Oxford University Press.

Kinsbourne, M. (1993). Integrated cortical field model of consciousness. In *Ciba Foundation Symposium on Consciousness*, No. 174, London.

Kinsbourne, M. & Warrington, E.K. (1962). A variety of reading disability associated with right hemisphere lesions. *Journal of Neurology, Neurosurgery and Psychiatry, 25*, 339–344.

Làdavas, E. (1987). Is the hemispatial neglect produced by right parietal lobe damage associated with retinal or gravitation coordinates? *Brain, 110*, 167–180.

Làdavas, E., Del Pesce, M., & Provinciali, L. (1989). Unilateral attentional deficits and hemispheric asymmetries in the control of visual attention. *Neuropsychologia, 27*, 353–366.

Làdavas, E. & Gazzaniga, M.S. (in preparation). Variations in attentional bias in the two disconnected cerebral hemispheres.

Làdavas, E., Petronio, A., & Umilta, C. (1990). The deployment of visual attention in the intact field of hemineglect patients. *Cortex, 26*, 307–317.

Lecours, A.R., Mehler, J., Parente, M.A. et al. (1987). Illiteracy and brain damage. 2. Manifestations of unilateral neglect in testing "auditory comprehension" with iconographic materials. *Brain and Cognition, 6*. 243–265.

Luck, S., Hillyard, S.A., Mangun, G.R., & Gazzaniga, M.S. (1989). Independent hemispheric attentional systems mediate visual search in split-brain patients. *Nature, 342*, 543–545.

Marshall, J.C. & Halligan, P.W. (1988) Blindsight and insight in visuospatial neglect. *Nature, 336*, 766–767.

Marshall, J.C. & Halligan, P.W. (1991). A study of plane bisection in four cases of visual neglect. *Cortex, 27*, 277–284.

McGlinchey-Berroth, R., Milberg, W.P., Verfaellie, M., Alexander, M., & Kilduff, P. (in press). Semantic processing in the neglected visual field: Evidence from a lexical decision task. *Brain*.

McGlynn, S.M. & Schacter, D.L. (1989). Unawareness of deficits in neuropsychological syndromes. *Journal of Clinical and Experimental Neuropsychology, 11*, 143–205.

Messenger, T.B. (1967). The effect on locomotion of lesions to the visuomotor system in Octopus. *Proceedings of the Royal Society of London (Biology), 167*, 252–281.

Mijovic, D., Liederman, J., & Kinsbourne, M. (1991, June). *Unilateral neglect: Absence of hypokinesia in an angle-matching task*. Paper presented to the TENNET Conference, Montreal.

Morrow, L.A. & Ratcliff, G. (1987). Attentional mechanisms in clinical neglect. *Journal of Clinical and Experimental Neuropsychology, 9*, 74–75 (abstract).

Mountcastle, V.B. (1978). Brain mechanisms of directed attention. *Journal of the Royal Society of Medicine, 71*, 14–27.

Ogden, J.A. (1987). The "neglected" left hemisphere and its contribution to visuospatial neglect. In M. Jeannerod (Ed.), *Neurophysiological and neuropsychological aspects of spatial neglect*. Amsterdam: North-Holland.

Oxbury, J.M., Campbell, D.C., & Oxbury, S.M. (1974). Unilateral spatial neglect and impairment of spatial analysis and visual perception. *Brain, 97*, 551–564.

Petersen, S.E., Fox, P.T., Miesin, F.M., & Raichle, M.E. (1988). Modulation of cortical visual responses by direction of spatial attention measured by PET. *Association of Research in Vision and Ophthalmology*, p. 22 (abstract).

Plourde, G. & Sperry, R.W. (1984). Left hemisphere involvement in left spatial neglect from right-sided lesions: A commissurotomy study. *Brain, 107*, 95–106.

Poppelreuter, W. (1917). *Die psychischen Schadigungen durch Kopfschuss im Kriege 1914/1916: 1. Die Storungen der Niederen und Hoheren Seeleistungen durch Verletzung des Okzipitalhirns*. Leipzig: Voss.

Posner, M.I., Walker, J.A., Friedreich, F.J., & Rafal, R.D. (1984). Effects of parietal injury on covert orienting of attention. *Journal of Neuroscience, 4*, 1863–1974.

Posner, M.I., Walker, J.A., Friedreich, F.J., & Rafal, R.D. (1987). How do the parietal lobes direct covert attention? *Neuropsychologia, 25*, 135–145.

Reuter-Lorenz, P.A., Kinsbourne, M., & Moscovitch, M. (1990). Hemispheric control of spatial attention. *Brain and Cognition*, *12*, 240–266.

Riddoch, M.J. & Humphreys, G.W. (1987). The effect of cueing on unilateral neglect. *Neuropsychologia*, *21*, 589–599.

Rizzolatti, G. & Camarda, R. (1987). Neural circuits for spatial attention and unilateral neglect. In M. Jeannerod (Ed.), *Neurophysiological and neuropsychological aspects of spatial neglect*, pp. 289–313. Amsterdam: North-Holland.

Rizzolatti, G. & Gallese, V. (1988). Mechanisms and theories of spatial neglect. In F. Boller & J. Grafman (Eds), *Handbook of neuropsychology*, Vol. 1, pp. 223–246. Amsterdam: Elsevier.

Rizzolatti, G., Gentilucci, M. & Matelli, M. (1985). Deficits in attention and movement following the removal of postarcuate (area 6) and prearcuate (area 8) cortex in macaque monkeys. *Brain*, *106*, 655–673.

Rizzolatti, G., Scandolara, C., Matelli, M., & Gentilucci, M. (1981). Afferent properties of periarcuate neurons in macaque monkeys. II. Visual responses. *Behavioral and Brain Research*, *2*, 147–163.

Robertson, I.H. & North, N.N. (1992). Spatio-motor cueing in unilateral left neglect: The role of hemispace, hand and motor activation. *Neuropsychologia*, *30*, 553–563.

Robertson, L.C. & Lamb, M. (1988). The role of perceptual reference frames in visual field asymmetries. *Neuropsychologia*, *26*, 145–152.

Robertson, L.C. & Lamb, M. (1989). Judging the reflection of misoriented patterns in the right and left visual fields. *Neuropsychologia*, *27*, 1081–1089.

Rubens, A.B. (1985). Caloric stimulation and unilateral neglect. *Neurology*, *35*, 1019–1024.

Silberpfennig, J. (1941). Contributions to the problem of eye movements. III. Disturbance of ocular movements with pseudohemianopsia in frontal tumors. *Confinia Neurologica*, *4*, 1–13.

Sine, R.D., Soufi, A., & Shah, M. (1984). Callosal syndrome: Implications for understanding the neuropsychology of stroke. *Archives of Physical Medicine and Rehabilitation*, *65*, 606–610.

Sperry, R.W., Gazzaniga, M.S., & Bogen, J.E. (1969). Interhemispheric relationships: The neocortical commissures; syndromes of hemisphere disconnection. In P.J. Vinken & G.W. Bruyn (Eds), *Handbook of clinical neurology*, Vol. 4, pp. 273–290. Amsterdam: North-Holland.

Sprague, J.M. (1966). Interaction of cortex and superior colliculus in mediation of visually guided behavior in the cat. *Science*, *153*, 1544–1547.

Trevarthen, C. (1974). Functional relations of disconnected hemispheres with the brain stem and with each other: Monkey and man. In M. Kinsbourne & W.L. Smith (Eds), *Hemispheric disconnection and cerebral function*. Springfield, LL: Thomas.

Vallar, G., Bottini, G., Sterzi, R., Passerini, D., & Rusconi, M.L. (1991). Hemianesthesia, sensory neglect, and defective access to conscious experience. *Neurology*, *41*, 650–652.

Vallar, G. & Perani, D. (1987). The anatomy of unilateral neglect after right hemisphere stroke lesions: A clinical CT/scan correlation study in man. *Neuropsychologia*, *24*, 609–622.

Vallar, G., Sterzi, R., Bottini, G., Cappa, S., & Rusconi, M.L. (1990). Temporary remission of left hemianesthesia after vestibular stimulation: A sensory neglect phenomen. *Cortex*, *26*, 123–131.

Volpe, B.T., Le Doux, J.E., & Gazzaniga, M.S. (1979). Information processing of visual stimuli in an "extinguished" field. *Nature*, *282*, 722–724.

Wallach, H.Y. (1968). Informational discrepancy as a basis of perceptual adaption. In S. Friedman (Ed.), *The neuropsychology of spatial behavior*, Homewood, IL: Dorsey Press.

Warrington, E.K. (1962). The completion of visual forms across hemianopic visual field defects. *Journal of Neurology, Neurosurgery and Psychiatry*, *25*, 208–217.

Wilson, D.H., Reeves, A., Gazzaniga, M., & Culver, C. (1977). Cerebral commissurotomy for control of intractable seizures. *Neurology*, *27*, 708–715.

Wise, R.A. & Holmes, L.J. (1986). Circling from unilateral VTA morphine: Direction is controlled by environmental stimuli. *Brain Research Bulletin*, *16*, 267–269.

Zingerle, H. (1913). Uber Storungen der Wahrnehmung des eigenen Korpers bei organischen Gehirnkrankungen. *Monatschrift für Psychiatrie und Neurologie*, *34*, 13–36.

4 Neural Mechanisms of Spatial Neglect

Giacomo Rizzolatti and Anna Berti
Istituto di Fisiologia Umana, Università degli Studi di Parma, Parma, Italy

INTRODUCTION

We have recently advanced a theory of neglect based on the functional properties of the brain areas whose damage produces neglect (Rizzolatti & Berti, 1990). The main points of this theory are as follows:

1. Neglect is primarily a disorder of spatial awareness, that is of the capacity to have a conscious representation of space.
2. Spatial awareness derives from the joint activity of several cortical and subcortical areas, each of which has its own neural space representation.
3. We define as neural space representation the coding of the external world in a system of non-retinal co-ordinates. This coding may be explicit, deriving from egocentric receptive fields, or implicit, deriving from different types of neural computations.
4. Areas in which space representation is constructed are involved in spatial aspects of motor programming; hence the frequent association of motor disturbances with representational deficits.
5. Attentional deficits which may accompany neglect are a secondary consequence of the lesion of space representations. Since spatial representations control specific motor programmes, attentional deficit derives from an imbalance of these programmes.

In this chapter, we will discuss some of the statements presented above and in particular the relation between attention and neglect (outlined in Rizzolatti & Berti, 1990). In addition, we will review some recent clinical observations which show how the representational theory of neglect is heuristically powerful in explaining some intriguing aspects of the syndrome.

ATTENTION AND NEGLECT

An Initial Problem: What Attention Means

Neglect has often been considered a syndrome that is due basically to a disturbance of attention. This idea derives naturally from the observation that patients with neglect ignore ("do not pay attention to") space contralateral to the brain damage; hence the conclusion that these patients have a disorder of attention. It is obvious that, without a precise terminological specification, this interpretation of neglect is more a tautology than a scientific account of the syndrome. Any theory which wants to explain neglect as an attentional disturbance must, first of all, define attention. To rephrase William James (1890): "No one knows what attention is", or, at least, there is no obvious agreement on what different authors mean when they use this term. Secondly, the theory must predict which behavioural and cognitive deficits damage to the attentional mechanism (clearly defined) would produce. If these requests are not fulfilled, a theory of neglect as an "attentional" disturbance is devoid of any scientific value.

Early *vs* Late Selection

William James (1890), pp. 403–404 defined attention as "the taking possession by the mind, in clear and vivid form of one out of what seem several simultaneously possible objects or trains of thought". From this definition, it is clear that, originally, attention was thought of as a mechanism whose function was the selection for perception of external stimuli or internal states. Once attention is defined as selection, the fundamental theoretical problem is to assess how people select information from the environment and how they deal with irrelevant information.

A major controversy on this issue has been the level at which selection occurs. Early selection theorists maintain that elementary features of the visual world, such as contours and lines, which have the attributes of orientation, contrast, length and width, are represented before attentional selection. If the unattended stimuli fall outside the focus of attention, they are filtered out (Broadbent, 1982; Johnston & Dark, 1982; Treisman & Gelade, 1980). In contrast, late selection theorists claim that attention operates after stimulus identification and therefore the irrelevant aspects of the environment are also fully analysed (e.g. Deutsch & Deutsch, 1963). Although the problem is not solved, data on the so-called "interference effect" (e.g. Stroop, 1935) appear to indicate that some processing of the unattended stimuli is carried out beyond the stage of elementary feature analysis. Furthermore, recent data have shown that stimuli that do not interfere with the subject's primary task may also produce a negative priming effect, that is a decrease in performance when such stimuli are followed by others somehow related to them (see Allport, Tipper, & Chmiel, 1985; Driver & Tipper, 1989).

Attention as a Facilitatory Mechanism

Another way to view selective attention is to consider it as a mechanism which facilitates the processing of certain stimuli or certain space positions. This view is based on experiments which show that stimulus cueing increases processing efficiency. The paradigm most commonly used to demonstrate this effect is that described by Posner (1980). In this paradigm, reaction times to stimuli presented at cued and uncued positions in the visual field are measured. The difference between them is taken as an index of the detection efficiency of the cued position. Stimuli at cued positions are presented more frequently than stimuli at uncued positions and the subject has to respond regardless of stimulus location.

Two types of cues have been used: symbolic cues and peripheral cues. *Symbolic cues* are centrally presented symbols (arrows, numbers) which indicate the most likely stimulus position. The subject has to interpret them in order to allocate attention to the correct position. *Peripheral cues* are visual stimuli presented in the correspondence of the location of the imperative stimulus. Peripheral stimuli are thought to attract the subject's attention automatically (e.g. Jonides, 1981). Both symbolic and peripheral cues produce a clear advantage of the cued positions with respect to the uncued ones. These data have been interpreted as evidence that selective attention acts as a mechanism which gives salience to the cued stimuli, rather than as a filter eliminating, partially or totally, irrelevant information. An analogy has been proposed in which the beam of a spotlight illuminates only a part of the space at any one time (Posner, 1980; Remington & Pierce, 1984; see also Umiltà, 1988). In accordance with this metaphor, attention is considered as unitary and it is postulated that in the brain there is a specific, anotomically definable circuit (see Mesulam, 1981; Posner, Walker, Friedrich, & Rafal, 1984) which controls attention. The activity of this circuit can be modulated endogenously (cognitive cues) or externally (peripheral cues). This assumption is not a necessary consequence of empirical data. It is based in part on introspection, but mostly derives from the notion, very popular among cognitive psychologists, that a central processing system, similar to that at the core of digital computers, should exist in the brain (see, e.g. Shallice, 1988). As will be shown later, this aspect of the theory is questionable. Evidence against it will be presented in the next section.

Attention as Selection for Action

A rather different perspective on attentional functions than the traditional ones has been advanced by Allport (1987; 1989). According to his theory, the fundamental purpose of attention is the choice of a specific action directed towards a given object, rather than the selection of a single stimulus among the many that are present in the environment. The senses are considered capable of registering many different stimuli simultaneously. It is the effector system, which is typically limited in its capacity, that carries out one single action at a time. The need for a mechanism for coupling and decoupling perceptual and motor processes is the basis of the attentional mechanism. This mechanism can be triggered externally by particular stimulus conditions or by internally generated states.

An emphasis on the mechanisms responsible for the selection of action is also found in the pre-motor theory of attention (Rizzolatti, 1983; Rizzolatti & Camarda, 1987; Rizzolatti, Riggio, Dascola, & Umiltà, 1987). This theory differs from the filtering or spotlight theories of attention in two ways:

1. In contrast to these theories, it claims that spatial attention is a modular function mediated by several independent neural circuits and not a supramodal mechanism controlling the cognitive activity of the brain as a whole.
2. It maintains that the facilitation of perception due to the attentional mechanism is a consequence of the activation of circuits responsible for motor preparation.

Evidence in favour of the first point comes from a wide range of data, on monkeys as well as humans (see references in Rizzolatti & Gallese, 1988), that indicate a close relationship between motor organisation and attentional behaviour. The strongest evidence is probably the demonstration of dissociations between the capacity of processing stimuli presented in different sectors of space following lesions of different brain centres (Rizzolatti, Gentilucci, & Matelli, 1985). The dissociations are hardly explained by a single attentional centre. Arguments in favour of the second point will be discussed at the end of this chapter.

Can Attentional Theories Explain Neglect?

Even if the precise meaning of "attention" is specified, the question arises as to what is meant when neglect is explained by an attentional deficit. Does it mean that an early or late filtering process has been impaired by the brain lesion? Or that some kind of spotlight mechanism is not working properly? Or that patients are unable to combine the appropriate motor behaviour to the selected stimulus? Or, finally, that some of their pre-motor circuits have been damaged?

As far as the filtering theories are concerned, it appears logical to expect that if some kind of filter is damaged, the patient should have difficulties in selecting the relevant stimuli in the space contralateral to the lesion. The patient will have confused perception due to difficulties in parsing the contralateral field in a clearly defined percept. Contrary to this prediction, patients with neglect ignore the contralesional space, without behaving as if they were perceptually confused due to a non-monitored selection of contralesional stimuli. It would therefore appear to be unrealistic to view neglect as a problem of information filtering.

Allport's (1989) interpretation of attention, although conceptually different from the filtering hypotheses and theoretically very appealing, encounters the same difficulties as the filtering hypotheses in explaining neglect. Indeed, incapacity of coupling and decoupling percepts and motor actions, which are at the core of Allport's theory, should produce incoherent motor behaviour with the performance of apparently meaningless acts.

The spotlight theory proposes that attention "is a limited capacity system that might be identified with conscious awareness" (Posner, 1982). Attention, therefore, is the mechanism that gives salience to different stimuli and allows individuals to become aware of their presence. Thus, if neglect were a disorder of attention in this sense of the term, one should expect patients with neglect to have a complete lack of awareness of any type of stimuli and in any part of space. However, patients' symptomatology does not correspond to these predictions. First, the symptomatology is more severe in the field contralateral to the lesion, whereas it would be bilateral if there was one centre for directing attention. Secondly, both in the monkey and man, several dissociations have been described as far as visual stimuli, space sectors and types of response are concerned. All these dissociations cannot be accounted for by a single attentional centre. Thirdly, as reviewed by Rizzolatti and Gallese (1988), the anatomical connections of the areas whose lesions produce neglect indicate the presence of several independent circuits rather than the presence of only one circuit selectively responsible for attention. Finally, data on the anatomy of the attentional system, gathered from PET studies, provide clear evidence against the idea of a single attentional centre (Corbetta et al., 1990; Posner, Petersen, Fox, &

Raichle, 1988). Areas related to different types of attention have been described in the occipital lobe, the frontal lobe and the cingulate cortex. To date, the parietal areas have been found to be little activated, if at all. While this last observation is most likely due to the materials and tasks employed, there is no doubt that the notion of a single attentional centre or circuit for attention in the cortex has been "falsified" by PET studies.

The demonstration of a multiplicity of areas involved in attention is consistent with the main tenet of the pre-motor theory that attention is not a supramodal function, as claimed by most cognitive psychologists, but a function mediated by several independent circuits (see Rizzolatti & Gallese, 1988). This claim was based essentially on neurophysiological studies in monkeys which indicated that there is no anatomical centre that has a privileged connection with attention. These studies demonstrated that even spatial attention is not a unitary function, but consists of several separate mechanisms mediated by anatomically and functionally independent circuits. There is, however, one neglect finding which appears to be difficult to explain using the pre-motor theory of attention. Lesions which destroy only one sensori-motor circuit often produce neglect for all kinds of stimuli coming from the affected space sector (Rizzolatti, Matelli, & Paresi, 1983). This deficit is observed despite the presence of other circuits able to process the same stimuli in parallel. If attention is a mechanism which facilitates the processing of information, but which is not necessarily required for it, the prediction of the pre-motor theory, in the case of limited lesions, is extinction and not neglect. If, on the other hand, attention is a prerequisite for conscious awareness, the pre-motor theory appears able to accommodate the findings. One wonders, however, whether the term attention is really the most appropriate in this case and whether there is no other term more adequate to describe the phenomenon. Considering the anatomical/physiological organisation of the areas whose lesions produce neglect, the term representation, in our opinion, reflects much better the fundamental mechanism which is destroyed in neglect. We will return to this point in the second part of this chapter.

While the pre-motor theory of neglect does not seem able to explain without further assumptions the fully fledged symptoms of neglect, it can provide an explanation of the fact that patients with neglect may show a gradient of preference for stimuli in the normal field with a better performance for those most ipsilesional (De Renzi, Gentilini, Faglioni, & Barbieri, 1989; Kinsbourne, 1987; Làdavas, Petronio, & Umiltà, 1990; see also Chapters 3 and 9, this volume). It is well established that motor organisation is based on a series of reciprocal inhibitions between competing programmes. This is found at the simple level of motor organisation, as for example in the spinal cord (Sherrington, 1906), but it also observed at higher neural levels. The oculomotor and vestibular systems are classical examples of this type of organisation. If, as the pre-motor theory maintains, there is a close link between motor programming and attention (stimulus processing facilitation), unilateral damage should release the motor programmes in the intact side of the brain from the control usually exerted by the opposite side of the brain, thus favouring the motor and attentional operations in the ipsilateral (normal) visual space. The existence of this kind of interaction between operations in the two visual fields was demonstrated by Sprague (1966). He showed that a stable contralateral hemineglect occurs in cats after large parieto-occipital cortical lesions. A subsequent lesion, either of the ipsilateral superior colliculus or the intertectal commissure, markedly improves the symptomatology, with recovery of the responses in the previously neglected field. The most likely interpretation of this finding is that, after the first lesion, the visuo-motor circuits for ipsilesional orienting responses are liberated from the control of the competing contralateral programmes. The consequence is a prevalence of visuo-motor orienting behaviour towards ipsilesional space and an inhibition of the residual contralateral circuits. The second lesion, by severing the link between competing programmes, restores the residual circuits responsible for head and eye movements towards the previously neglected side and, consequently, restores also the capacity to orient attention towards this side.

In conclusion, this survey of the definitions and theories of attention shows that none of them appears to be sufficient to explain all aspects of the neglect syndrome. In the next section, we will provide evidence that at the core of the disturbance is a deficit of space representation.

REPRESENTATION AND NEGLECT

The definition of neglect as a representational deficit has been revived in the neurological literature by Bisiach and co-workers (Bisiach & Berti, 1987; Bisiach & Luzzatti, 1978; Bisiach, Luzzatti, & Perani, 1979). They showed that neglect can be demonstrated in conditions in which no stimuli are presented to patients who are asked to perform mental operations involving imaging. The most striking result was that their patients were able to reconstruct visually only the ipsilateral half of the requested image. These studies aroused new interest in neglect and offered an alternative to the attentional explanations. However, Bisiach and co-workers' experiment may have an alternative explanation. One can postulate that, although the spatial representation is intact, neglect patients have a lesion of the attentional mechanism which facilitates the ipsilesional representation. We have already discussed the difficulty that attentional interpretations encounter in explaining neglect. However, the possibility that some attentional mechanisms may have a role to play in the phenomenon described by Bisiach and co-workers cannot be ruled out completely (see below).

Neural Representation Theory of Neglect

The neural representation theory of neglect makes two claims about how space is represented in normal subjects: (1) space is represented in several brain centres and, under normal circumstances, the joint activity of these centres is responsible for conscious space awareness; (2) the centres responsible for conscious space awareness code space using viewer-centred co-ordinates. Damage to areas where space is coded in these co-ordinates leads to neglect, while damage to areas where space is coded in retinotopic co-ordinates leads to hemianopia.

Neurophysiological evidence in favour of the first claim is compelling and will not be reviewed here (see Rizzolatti & Gallese, 1988). The second claim is more controversial and requires specification. It can be formulated in two forms. In one form, it says that space is explicitly coded by neurons which have spatial receptive fields. The activity of these neurons signal the location of an object in the space relative to the viewer, independently of eye position. In another form, it postulates that viewer-centred space derives from computation due to neurons whose receptive field is coded in retinotopical co-ordinates.

Empirical evidence in favour of neurons with a spatial viewer-centred receptive field (explicitly spatial, ES) is very strong for the peripersonal space. In monkey area 6, many neurons respond to stimuli presented in particular body-related space sectors, regardless of eye position (Fogassi et al., 1992; Gentilucci, Scandolara, Pigarev, & Rizzolatti, 1983; Gentilucci et al., 1988; Rizzolatti & Gentilucci, 1988). These neurons have bimodal (tactile and visual) fields, with the visual field anchored to the tactile one. A similar organisation is present in area 7b, a parietal area strictly linked to inferior area 6 (Hyvarinen, 1982). Bimodal ES neurons have also been described in area 6 of the cat (Pigarev & Rodionova, 1986).

The existence of spatial neurons is not so obvious in the case of monkey parietal areas involved in the extrapersonal space representation. Studies of area 7a and of an area adjacent to it (LIP) have shown that in these areas several neurons have retinotopically organised receptive fields gated by eye position (Andersen, Essik, & Siegel, 1985, 1987; Sakata, Shibutani, & Kawano, 1980). This finding and the apparent lack of viewer-centred space neurons in the same areas led Andersen et al. (1990) to conclude that viewer-centred space representation derives from the activity of eye-modulated retinotopical neurons. A computational model showing that position in the space could be computed by units with properties similar to those described in area 7a appeared to confirm this point of view (Zipser & Andersen, 1988).

Recent experiments, however, indicate that neurons with a viewer-centred receptive field are not limited to areas related to peripersonal space. Pigarev and Rodionova (1988) demonstrated that in the cat, ES neurons are abundant in the parietal lobe. These neurons are unimodal and respond also to far stimuli. Very recently, ES neurons have also been demonstrated in area V6 of the monkey (Battaglini, Fattori, Galletti, & Zeki, 1990). Thus, although at the present time one cannot rule out completely the hypothesis that the space representation for extrapersonal space might derive from eye modulation of retinotopically organised neurons, this hypothesis appears to be weakened by these new experimental data. It is possible that visual neurons modulated by eye position are an intermediate step between retinotopical maps and explicit spatial representations. Congruent with this point of view are the observations that eye-modulated visual neurons are also present in the retinotopically organised prestriate areas of the occipital lobe (Galletti & Battaglini, 1989) and in the pulvinar (Robinson, McClurkin, & Kertzman, 1990).

Object Analysis and Space

There is general agreement that space and object perception are mediated by the activity of two separate series of cortical areas and that, broadly speaking, the temporal lobe is mostly involved in object perception, whereas the parietal lobe is mostly involved in space perception (Ungerleider & Mishkin, 1982). Object analysis, however, entails two different sets of operations. One concerns object reconstruction from its elementary features and its recognition despite its possible different locations in space and different angles of view. These operations are most likely carried out in the inferotemporal lobe (Gross, 1973). The second set of operations concerns the description of objects in spatial terms. This description requires, in turn, different types of operations. The first is the location of objects with respect to the viewer. The second is the matching of the viewer-centred space with the centre of the object (viewer-centred object representation). An overt example of this matching is represented by head movements which align the head vertical axis with the object even when the object is misplaced with respect to it, even a few degrees. We postulate that a similar object–viewer matching also occurs covertly. Both the location of objects in space and the object–viewer alignment, which are spatial in their essence, are most likely performed in the parietal lobe. The third operation is the extraction of the intrinsic object properties (see Jeannerod, 1988; Arbib, 1981). Neurons coding the intrinsic properties of the object (size, shape, orientation) have been described in inferior parietal lobe (Taira et al., 1991) and in the pre-motor areas connected with it (Rizzolatti et al., 1988). Thus the involvement of the dorsal visual stream of information in object analysis is not a mere supposition but a well-proved fact (see also Goodale & Milner, 1992).

Predictions of the Neural Representation Theory

Once the two claims of neural representation theory are accepted, two main predictions may be advanced as far as the neglect symptoms are concerned: (1) the presence of dissociations between various representational domains (personal, peripersonal and extrapersonal space; space and object representation); and (2) the implicit processing of information within the neglected space. In the next paragraph, we will examine how clinical observations fit with these predictions. Particular emphasis will be given to those data that were not reviewed in our recent article on neglect (Rizzolatti & Berti, 1990).

Dissociations. A dissociation between personal and extrapersonal neglect in man was first described by Bisiach, Perani, Vallar and Berti (1986) in patients with unilateral brain damage. The patients undertook two tasks aimed at assessing unilateral neglect in personal and extrapersonal space. The authors found that personal neglect was much less frequent than extrapersonal neglect. Extrapersonal neglect could, therefore, be seen in the absence of personal neglect. In addition, they also found a patient who showed a severe neglect for personal space without any convincing symptoms of extrapersonal neglect. A similar case has recently been observed by Guariglia and Antonucci (1992). Their patient, whom they studied using a battery of tests specifically devised to assess personal neglect, showed a severe personal neglect while no deficits of any kind were present in extrapersonal space.

Recently, Shelton, Bowers and Heilman (1990) examined the behaviour of normal subjects and of a neglect patient when bisecting lines presented radially (pointing away from the subject) in peripersonal space. The lines were positioned adjacent to the body surface (near peripersonal space), with the line midpoint 30 cm from the body (middle peripersonal space) or 60 cm from it (far peripersonal space). The most striking result was that the patient consistently made a misplacement error towards the near end of the line. Furthermore, the error was small in the near peripersonal space, whereas it was large in the far peripersonal space. The authors interpreted these data as evidence for a subdivision of space representation in sectors (see also Rizzolatti et al., 1983) and as an indication that each of these sectors can be impaired separately.

An opposite dissociation has been observed by Halligan and Marshall (1991). They found a patient who showed a classical extrapersonal neglect when tested on line bisection and other standard tests for the neglect syndrome. However, his deficits were minimal or absent when he had to perform motor action in far space. When requested to bisect a line positioned outside his reaching distance, either with a light pointer or by throwing darts, he performed in the normal range.

Another interesting space dissociation, which was recently reported, is the presence of neglect concerning the vertical dimension—altitudinal neglect (Rapcsak, Cimino, & Heilman, 1988). The deficit is found most frequently in the lower part of the visual space. Halligan and Marshall (1989) found lower field neglect in 18 of 23 patients with neglect, while only 2 presented neglect for the top half of the display, and 3 made the same number of errors in each half.

Deficits along the vertical dimension have previously been described following mesencephalic lesions both in animals and man. Matelli, Olivieri, Saccani & Rizzolatti (1983) found two distinct neglect syndromes in the cat that depended on the mesencephalic commissures that had been cut. The first syndrome occurred after a complete section of the commissure and involved the upper space as well as head and eye movements directed towards this space sector. The second syndrome appeared following the lesion of the posterior commissure and the rostral part of the intertectal commissure. In this case, the disturbances concerned the lower space as well as eye and head movements that were directed downwards. Deficits along the vertical plane were also demonstrated in patients affected by progressive supranuclear palsy (Posner, Cohen, & Rafal, 1982; Rafal & Grimm, 1981). Also in these patients, there was a congruence between the altitudinal deficit and the deficit of eye movements.

A mechanism similar to that described for mesencephalic neglect may be postulated for parietal patients with altitudinal neglect. It is likely that in this case also, circuits are lesioned that are responsible for the representation of a given space sector and for operation on it. The large prevalence of lower space deficits is probably due to the fact that this is the space sector in which manipulations mostly occur (see Previc, 1990). Considering the importance of the parietal lobe for operation in the peripersonal space (see Mountcastle, 1976), it is very likely that lower visual space is particularly richly represented in this part of the brain. Lesions of the parietal lobe, therefore, are more likely to hit the representation of the lower part of the visual space than the upper part.

Recently, another dichotomy has been pointed out regarding neglect. Gainotti, D'Erme, Monteleone & Silveri (1986) noticed that, in copying a complex drawing, a neglect patient ignored the left part of each object depicted in the model, instead of neglecting, as most patients do, the left part of it. Driver & Halligan (1991) observed a patient who behaved in a similar manner to that of Gainotti and co-workers' patient when copying models and during a particular version of the cancellation task. Moreover, they found that the patient had a strong tendency to neglect the left side of stimuli even when they were rotated and the left part of the stimulus was on the right side of the display. These findings were interpreted as the demonstration that some patients have selective difficulties with spatial representations of the objects. Note, however, that the reported deficit implies a distinction between left and right, i.e. the sides of the objects as referred to the viewer. The deficit is therefore a special case of a *viewer-centred* representational deficit rather than an object-centred defect. In a true object-centred representational deficit, a certain part of an object should be constantly neglected, regardless of its position with respect to the viewer. For example, in the case of a rabbit, a patient should always ignore its head or tail independently of where the rabbit is looking. As far as we know, no such cases have been described (see Farah et al., 1990, for a discussion of this point) and, according to our definition of neglect, such cases (if found) would not belong to the domain of neglect.

An explanation in terms of viewer-centred object representation can also be suggested for the findings of Caramazza and Hillis (1990). They described patient N.G. who made reading and spelling errors on the right half of words. The striking feature was that N.G. showed the same pattern of errors irrespective of the spatial arrangement of the stimuli. Since it was the part of the word which was on the right in horizontal normal word presentation which was neglected, even when the word was presented vertically or mirror-reversed, this case suggests that the representation of words is spatially encoded along a horizontal axis referred to the viewer. When the word was presented in a non-canonical way, the subject had to adjust it, so that his subjective midline coincided with the word midline. As mentioned above, this adjustment occurs overtly in the case of object presentation and represents the ideal relation between viewer and object in order to act upon it (for a discussion of neglect dyslexia, see Chapter 11 this volume).

A further case of the viewer-centred object representational deficit has been described by Young, de Haan, Newcombe, and Hay (1990). Their patient showed left neglect only for physiognomic material and no other sign of sensory or representational disorders. Although these authors suggest that the deficit in this case could be due to a disorder of a "face-specific" attentional mechanism, we believe that a representational interpretation explains this finding much better. Indeed, the assumptions of a specific circuit for "face attention" is arbitrary, whereas there is no doubt that there are neural centres specifically related to face representation (Perrett, Mistlin, & Harries, 1989).

Implicit Processing.   The second prediction of our theory is that, given the multiplicity of circuits involved in space representation, neglect patients may show implicit processing of the information coming from the space sector contralateral to the lesion. Volpe, Le Doux and Gazzaniga (1979) showed that patients with right parietal lesion and clinical evidence of extinction were able to name objects when they were presented singly in either field, but denied seeing the left-side stimuli when two visual objects were presented simultaneously to the right and left of the fixation point. Despite the fact that the patients were unable to name the left object in the simultaneous stimuli presentation, they were still able to make a same–different judgement when forced to do so by the examiner. The authors interpret this finding as evidence for the existence of implicit knowledge of the stimuli, even when the patients were unable to name them or were unaware of their presence.

A capacity for processing information in an implicit way has been described by Marshall and Halligan (1988) in a patient with a severe neglect. This patient was repeatedly presented with two drawings of a house, one above the other. The two houses were identical on the right side but were different on the left side. The patient denied any difference between the pairs of houses even when one of them was seen to be burning. None the less, when forced to choose the one in which she would prefer to live, she always chose the one that was not burning.

Recently, Bisiach and Rusconi (1990) replicated Marshall and Halligan's experiment in four patients with neglect, using different kinds of stimuli. They also found that the neglected side of the figure influenced the patients' responses. This influence, however, varied from one patient to another, and was not necessarily related to the meaning of the features which should determine the logically correct choice. For example, two of their patients consistently preferred the burning house. This suggests that it is not necessarily the meaning but sometimes also the mere presence of some low-level sensory factors that may determine choice.

However, a demonstration that in some cases high-level processing can be responsible for the patients' judgement of material presented in the neglected field has been provided by a study on a patient with extinction (Berti et al., 1992). The authors replicated Volpe and co-workers' study using pairs of pictures of identical objects taken from the same or different viewpoints, pairs of different examplars of the same category of objects and pairs of different objects. Patient E.M. could not name left-sided stimuli. However, she was still able to make correct same–different judgements, both in the same and different trials, even when the two objects were physically dissimilar but belonged to the same category. This study showed that patients can make categorical judgements on the objects presented in the extinguishing field even when they are not aware of its identity.

Even more compelling for the issue of implicit processing in neglect patients is a recent study by Berti and Rizzolatti (1992). They demonstrated that in patients with severe neglect, a prime stimulus presented to the neglected visual field can facilitate the responses to target stimuli presented to the normal field. This effect was present when the priming stimulus was physically identical to the target and, most importantly, also when the prime and the target were physically different but belonged to the same category of objects. Note that five out of the seven neglect patients in this study appeared to be hemianopic either on perimetry testing or on confrontation and did not report the presence of any left stimulus in the preliminary part of the experiment. Similar results have been obtained also by McGlinchey-Berroth et al. (in press).

CONCLUSION

It is a classical notion of neurology that after brain damage two types of symptoms can emerge, negative symptoms and positive symptoms (Jackson 1881). Negative symptoms are the direct consequence of the lesion; positive symptoms derive from the release of centres connected with the damaged brain part. Thus, as an example, in the case of spastic paralysis, the negative symptom consists of the inability to perform voluntary movements, whereas the positive manifestation is the increase in muscular tone. We propose a similar interpretation for neglect symptoms. According to this interpretation, the inability to consciously process information coming from the neglected field, represents the neglect negative symptoms. It is due to a lesion of some, or all, of the space representations as defined in the previous paragraphs. The positive symptoms manifest themselves essentially in the shift of processing capacity towards the side ipsilateral to the lesion (for a comprehensive discussion of this symptom, see Chapters 3 and 9, this volume). As a consequence, the right-most stimuli are perceived better and responded to faster. Positive symptoms may aggravate the representational deficit in a similar way. that spasticity aggravates paralysis. They are not, however, the primary cause of neglect.

This interpretation of neglect in terms of positive and negative symptoms fits well with some interesting recent neurological observations. Rubens (1985) showed that a caloric stimulation of the vestibular system, which produces a shift of the eyes towards the neglected side, can improve the neglect symptomatology. This observation was confirmed by Cappa, Sterzi, Vallar and Bisiach (1987), who demonstrated that vestibular stimulation can also improve other representational deficits like anosognosia. The same effect was shown for a productive symptom like somatoparaphrenia (Bisiach & Rusconi, 1991). The stimulation of the vestibular system in the above-cited experiments has, as its primary consequence, an activation of the vestibulo-motor circuits of the damaged side of the brain, which, within limits, compensates for the imbalance between the motor circuits of the two sides of the brain. In turn, according to the pre-motor theory of attention, this compensation improves the attentional mechanisms linked to them. From this, two consequences derive. First, moving attention towards the neglected side decreases the severity of the positive symptoms related to the right shift of processing capacity. Secondly, and most importantly, the activation on the ipsilesional side of the spared centres responsible for space representation determines the restoration of the awareness of the space contralateral to the lesion. It is important to note that an improvement in attention alone cannot explain recovery from anosognosia. It is well known that anosognosic patients often pay a continuous, almost pathological attention to their affected limbs, still continuing to deny the neurological symptoms (see Bisiach, Meregalli, & Berti, 1990). Thus, if vestibular activation only acts through a selective attentional mechanism, one should expect no improvement in the anosognosic symptoms. In contrast, if vestibular activation restores, through activation of the residual circuits, the personal and extrapersonal spatial representations, such improvement can easily be predicted.

Another example of the usefulness of the subdivision of the neglect syndrome into positive and negative symptoms is represented by some data reported by Doricchi, Guariglia, Paolucci and Pizzamiglio (1990). They studied groups of patients with left-sided brain lesions, right-sided brain lesions without neglect and right-sided brain lesions with neglect. All three groups showed a reduction in rapid eye movements towards the contralesional side during paradoxical sleep. However, this reduction was much stronger in the neglect group than in the other two groups. This observation confirms the strict link between the representational deficit of neglect and motor programming. In addition, Doricchi et al. (1990) found that neglect patients who showed significant improvement after a rehabilitation programme continued to present an almost complete lack of contralesional eye movements during paradoxical sleep. The fact that during wakefulness—that is, in a situation in which attentional resources can be called in—there was an improvement, whereas during sleep the basic deficit remained unchanged, suggests that attention is not the primary mechanism responsible for neglect. On the contrary, once it is accepted that the lack of eye movements is an indirect measure of the primary disorder, the findings of Doricchi et al. (1990) fit well with the representational theory. Note that according to this theory, although the representational deficit is primary, its severity can be influenced by attentional pre-motor circuits.

ACKNOWLEDGEMENTS

We would like to thank Edoardo Bisiach for his suggestions and comments. This work was supported by grants from CNR and MPI to G.R.

REFERENCES

Allport, A (1987). Selection for action: Some behavioural and neurophysiological considerations of attention and action. In H. Heuer & A.F. Saunders (Eds), *Perspectives on perception and action*. Hillsdale, NJ: Lawrence Erlbaum Associates Inc.

Allport, A. (1989). Visual attention. In M.I. Posner (Ed.), *Foundation of cognitive science*. Cambridge, MA: MIT Press.

Allport, D.A., Tipper, S.P., & Chmiel, N.R.J. (1985). Perceptual integration and postcategorical filtering. In M.I. Posner & O.M. Marin (Eds), *Attention and performance XI*. Hillsdale, NJ: Lawrence Erlbaum Associates Inc.

Andersen, R.A., Bracewell, R.M., Barash, S., Gnadt, J.W., & Fogassi, L. (1990). Eye position effects on visual, memory, and saccade-related activity in areas LIP and 7a of Macaque. *Journal of Neuroscience, 10*, 1176–1196.

Andersen, R.A., Essik, G.K. & Siegel, R.M. (1985). The encoding of spatial location by posterior parietal neurons. *Science, 230*, 456–458.

Andersen, R.A., Essick, G.K., & Siegal, R.M. (1987). Neurons of area 7 activated by both visual stimuli and oculomotor behaviour. *Experimental Brain Research, 67*, 316–322.

Arbib, M.A. (1981). Perceptual structures and distributed motor control. In V.B. Brooks (Ed.), *Handbook of physiology: The nervous system. II Motor Control*. Washington, DC: American Physiological Society.

Battaglini, P.P., Fattori, P., Galletti, C., & Zeki, S. (1990). The physiology of area V6 in the awake, behaving monkey. *Journal of Physiology, 423*.

Berti, A., Allport, A., Driver, J., Denies, Z., Oxbury, J., & Oxbury, S (1992). Levels of processing for visual stimuli in an "extinguished" field. *Neuropsychologia, 30*, 403–415.

Berti, A. & Rizzolatti, G. (1992). Visual processing without awareness: Evidence from unilateral neglect. *Journal of Cognitive Neuroscience, 4*, 345–351.

Bisiach, E. & Berti, A. (1987). Dyschiria: An attempt at its systemic explanation. In M. Jeannerod (Ed.), *Neurophysiological and neuropsychological aspects of spatial neglect*. Amsterdam: North-Holland.

Bisiach, E. & Luzzatti, C. (1978). Unilateral neglect of representational space. *Cortex, 14*, 129–133.

Bisiach, E., Luzzatti, C., & Perani, D. (1979). Unilateral neglect, representational schema and consciousness. *Brain, 102*, 609–618.

Bisiach, E., Meregalli, S., & Berti, A. (1990). Mechanisms of production control and belief fixation in human visuospatial processing: Clinical evidence from unilateral neglect and misrepresentation. In M.L. Commons, R.J. Herrnstein, S.M. Kosslyn, & D.B. Mumford (Eds), *Quantitative analyses of behavior*, Vol. IX. Hillsdale, NJ: Lawrence Erlbaum Associates Inc.

Bisiach, E., Perani, D., Vallar, G., & Berti, A. (1986). Unilateral neglect: Personal and extrapersonal. *Neuropsychologia, 24*, 759–767.

Bisiach, E. & Rusconi, M.L. (1990). Break-down of perceptual awareness in unilateral neglect. *Cortex, 26*, 643–649.

Broadbent, D.E. (1982). Task combination and selective intake of information. *Acta Psychologica, 50*, 253–290.

Cappa, S., Sterzi, R., Vallar, G., & Bisiach, E. (1987). Remission of hemineglect during vestibular stimulation. *Neuropsychologia, 25*, 775–782.

Caramazza, A. & Hillis, A.E. (1990). Spatial representation of words in the brain implied by studies of a unilateral neglect patient. *Nature, 346*, 267–269.

Corbetta, M., Miezin, F.M., Dobmeyer, S., Shulman, G.L., & Petersen, S.E. (1990). Attentional modulation of neural processing of shape, color, and velocity in humans. *Science, 248*, 1556–1559.

De Renzi, E., Gentilini, M., Faglioni, P., & Barbieri, C. (1989). Attentional shift towards the rightmost stimuli in patients with left visual neglect. *Cortex*, *25*. 231–237.

Deutsh, J.A. & Deutsh, D. (1963). Attention: Some theoretical considerations. *Psychological Review*, *87*, 272–300.

Doricchi, F., Guariglia, C., Paolucci, S., & Pizzamiglio, L. (1990). Severe reduction of leftwards REMs in patients with left unilateral hemiinattention. In J. Horne (Ed.), *Sleep 90*. Bochum: Pontenagel Press.

Driver, J. & Halligan, P. (1991). Can visual neglect operate in object centered coordinates? An affirmative single-case study. *Cognitive Neuropsychology*, *8*, 475–496.

Driver, J. & Tipper, S.T. (1989). On the nonselectivity of "selective" seeing: Contrast between interference and priming in selective attention. *Journal of Experimental Psychology: Human Perception and Performance*, *15*, 304–314.

Farah, M.J., Brunn, L.L., Wong, A.B., Wallace, M.A. & Carpenter, P.A. (1990). Frames of reference for allocating attention to space: Evidence from neglect syndrome. *Neuropsychologia*, *28*, 335–347.

Fogassi, L., Gallese, V., di Pellegrino, G., Fadiga, L., Gentilucci, M., Luppino, G., Matelli, M., Pedotti, A., & Rizzolatti, G. (1992). Space coding by premotor cortex. *Experimental Brain Research*, *89*, 686–690.

Gainotti, G., D'Erme, P., Monteleone, D., & Silveri, M.C. (1986). Mechanisms of unilateral spatial neglect in relation to laterality of cerebral lesions. *Brain*, *109*, 599–612.

Galletti, C. & Battaglini, P.P. (1986). Gaze-dependent visual neurons in area V3A of monkey prestriate cortex. *Journal of Neuroscience*, *9*, 1112–1125.

Gentilucci, M., Fogassi, L., Luppino, G., Matelli, M., Camarda, R., & Rizzolatti, G. (1988). Functional organization of inferior area 6 in the macaque monkey. 1. Somatotopy and control of proximal movements. *Experimental Brain Research*, *71*, 475–490.

Gentilucci, M., Scandolara, C., Pigarev, I.N., & Rizzolatti, G. (1983). Visual responses in the postarcuate cortex (area 6) of the monkey that are independent of eye-position. *Experimental Brain Research*, *50*, 464–468.

Goodale, M.A. & Milner, A.D. (1992). Separate visual pathways for perception and action. *Trends in Neuroscience*, *15*, 20–25.

Gross, C.G. (1973). Visual functions of inferotemporal cortex. In R. Jung (Ed.), *Handbook of sensory physiology, Vol. V11/3*. Berlin: Springer-Verlag.

Guariglia, C. & Antonucci, G. (1992). Personal and extrapersonal space: A case of neglect dissociation. *Neuropsychologia*, *30*, 1001–1009.

Halligan, P.W. & Marshall, J.C. (1989). Is neglect (only) lateral? A quadrant analysis of line cancellation. *Journal of Clinical and Experimental Neuropsychology*, *11*, 793–798.

Halligan, P.W. & Marshall, J.C. (1991). Left neglect for near but not far space in man. *Nature*, *350*, 498–500.

Hyvarinen, J. (1982). Posterior parietal lobe of the primate brain. *Physiological Review*, *62*, 1060–1129.

Jackson, J.H. (1881). Remarks on dissolutions of the nervous system as exemplified by certain post-epileptic conditions. In J. Taylor (Ed.), 1958, *Selected writings of John Hughlings Jackson*, Vol. 2, pp. 12–16. New York: Basic Books.

James, W. (1890). *The principles of psychology*. New York: Holt.

Jeannerod, M. (1988). The neural and behavioural organization of goal-directed movements. Oxford: Oxford University Press.

Johnston, W.A. & Dark, V.J. (1982). In defense of intraperceptual theories of attention. *Journal of Experimental Psychology: Human Perception and Performance*, *10*, 640–654.

Jonides, J. (1981). Voluntary versus automatic control over the mind's eye's movement. In J.B. Long & A.D. Baddeley (Eds), *Attention and performance IX*. Hillsdale, NJ: Lawrence Erlbaum Associates Inc.

Kinsbourne, M. (1987). Mechanisms of unilateral neglect. In M. Jeannerod (Ed.). *Neurophysiological and neuropsychological aspects of spatial neglect.* Amsterdam: North-Holland.

Làdavas, E., Petronio, A. & Umiltà, C. (1990). The deployment of attention in the intact field of hemineglect patients. *Cortex, 26,* 307–317.

Marshall, J.C. & Halligan, P.W. (1988). Blindsight and insight in visuospatial neglect. *Nature, 336,* 766–767.

Matelli, M., Olivieri, M.F., Saccani, A., & Rizzolatti, G. (1983). Upper visual space neglect and motor deficit after section of the midbrain commissures in the cat. *Behavioral Brain Research, 10,* 263–285.

McGlinchey-Berroth, R., Milberg, W.P., Verfaellie, M., Alexander, M., & Kilduff, P.T. (in press). Semantic processing in the neglected field: Evidence from a lexical decision task. *Cognitive Neuropsychology.*

Mesulam, A.A. (1981). A cortical network for directed attention and unilateral neglect. *Annals of Neurology, 10,* 309–325.

Mountcastle, V.B. (1976). The world around us: Neural command functions for selective attention. *Neuroscience Research Program Bulletin, 14,* 147.

Perrett, D.I., Mistlin, A.J., & Harries, M.H. (1989). Seeing faces: The representation of facial information in temporal cortex. In J.J. Kulikowski, C.M. Dickinson, & I.J. Murray (Eds), *Seeing contour and colour.* Oxford: Pergamon Press.

Pigarev, I.N. & Rodionova, E.I. (1986). Neurons with visual receptive fields independent of eye-position in the caudal part of the ventral bank of cat cruciate sulcus. *Neurophysiology (Kiev), 18,* 800–804.

Pigarev, I.N. & Rodionova, E.I. (1988). Neurons with visual receptive fields independent of the position of eyes in cat parietal cortex. *Sensory System, 2,* 245–255 (in Russian).

Posner, M.I. (1980). Orienting of attention. *Quarterly Journal of Experimental Psychology, 32,* 3–25.

Posner, M.I. (1982). Cumulative development of attentional theory. *American Psychologist, 37,* 168–179.

Posner, M.I., Cohen, Y., & Rafal, R.D. (1982). Neural system control of spatial orienting, *Philos. Trans. R. Soc. London ser. B.* 298, 187–198.

Posner, M.I., Petersen, S.E., Fox, P.T., & Raichle, M.E. (1988). Localization of cognitive operations in the human brain. *Science, 240,* 1627–1631.

Posner, M.I., Walker, J.A., Friedrich, F.J., & Rafal, R.D. (1984). Effects of parietal injury on covert orienting of attention. *Journal of Neuroscience, 4,* 1863–1874.

Previc, F.H. (1990). Functional specialization in the lower and upper visual fields in humans: Its ecological origins and neurophysiological implications. *Behavioral and Brain Sciences, 13,* 519–575.

Rafal, R.D. & Grimm, R.J. (1981). Progressive supranuclear palsy: Functional analysis of the response to methysergide and anti-Parkinson agents. *Neurology, 31,* 1507–1518.

Rapcsak, S.Z., Cimino, C., & Heilman, K.M. (1988). Altitudinal neglect. *Neurology, 38,* 277–281.

Remington, R.W. & Pierce, L. (1984). Moving attention: Evidence from time invariant shifts of visual selective attention. *Perception and Psychophysics, 35,* 393–399.

Rizzolatti, G. (1983). Mechanisms of selective attention in mammals. In J.P. Ewert, R.R. Capranica, & D.J. Ingle (Eds), *Advances in vertebrate neuroethology.* London: Plenum Press.

Rizzolatti, G. & Berti, A. (1990). Neglect as a neural representational deficit. *Revue Neurologique, 146,* 626–634.

Rizzolatti, G. & Camarda, R. (1987). Neural circuits for spatial attention and unilateral neglect. In M. Jeannerod (Ed.), *Neurophysiological and neuropsychological aspects of neglect.* Amsterdam: North-Holland.

Rizzolatti, G., Camarda, R., Fogassi, L., Gentilucci, M., Luppino, G., & Matelli, M. (1988). Functional organization of inferior area 6 in the macaque monkey. II. Area F5 and the control of distal movements. *Experimental Brain Research, 71,* 491–507.

Rizzolatti, G. & Gallese, V. (1988). Mechanisms and theories of spatial neglect. In F. Boller & J. Grafman (Eds), *Handbook of neuropsychology,* Vol. 1. Amsterdam: Elsevier.

Rizzolatti, G. & Gentilucci, M. (1988). Motor and visual-motor functions of the promotor cortex. In P. Rakic & W. Singer (Eds), *Neurobiology of neocortex.* Chichester: John Wiley.

Rizzolatti, G., Gentilucci, M., & Matelli, M. (1985). Selective spatial attention: One center, one circuit or many circuits? In M.I. Posner & O.M. Marin (Eds), *Attention and performance, XI.* Hillsdale, NJ: Lawrence Erlbaum Associates Inc.

Rizzolatti, G., Matelli, M. & Pavesi, G. (1983). Deficit in attention and movement following the removal of postarcuate (area 6) and prearcuate (area 8) cortex in monkey. *Brain, 106,* 655–673.

Rizzolatti, G., Riggio, L., Dascola, I., & Umiltà, C. (1987). Reorienting attention across the horizontal and vertical meridians: Evidence in favor of a premotor theory of attention. *Neuropsychologia, 25,* 31–40.

Robinson, D.L., McClurkin, J.W. & Kertzman, C. (1990). Orbital position and eye movement influences on visual responses in the pulvinar nuclei of the behaving macaque. *Experimental Brain Research, 82,* 235–246.

Rubens, A.B. (1985). Caloric stimulation and unilateral visual neglect. *Neurology, 35,* 1019–1024.

Sakata, H., Shibutani, H., & Kawano, K. (1980). Spatial properties of visual fixation neurons in posterior parietal cortex of the monkey. *Journal of Neurophysiology, 43,* 1654–1672.

Shallice, T. (1988). *From neuropsychology to mental structure.* Cambridge: Cambridge University Press.

Shelton, P.A., Bowers, D. & Heilman, K.M. (1990). Peripersonal and personal neglect. *Brain, 113,* 191–205.

Sherrington, C.S. (1906). *The interactive action of the nervous system.* London: Constable. (Second edition 1947, Cambridge, Cambridge University Press.)

Sprague, J.M. (1966). Interaction of cortex and superior colliculus in visually guided behavior in the cat. *Science, 153,* 1544–1547.

Stroop, J.R. (1935). Studies of interference in serial verbal reactions. *Journal of Experimental Psychology, 18,* 643–662.

Taira, M., Mine, S., Georgopoulos, A.P., Murata, A., & Sakata, H. (1991). Parietal cortex neurons of the monkey related to the visual guidance of hand movement. *Experimental Brain Research, 83,* 29–36.

Treisman, A.M. & Gelade, G. (1980). A feature-integration theory of attention. *Cognitive Psychology, 12,* 97–136.

Umiltà, C. (1988). Orienting of attention. In F. Boller & J. Grafman (Eds), *Handbook of neuropsychology,* Vol. 1. Amsterdam: Elsevier.

Ungerleider, L.G. & Mishkin, M. (1982). Two cortical visual systems. In D.J. Ingle, M.A. Goodale, & R.J. Mansfield (Eds), *The analysis of visual behavior.* Cambridge, MA: MIT Press.

Volpe, B.T., Le Doux, J.E., & Gazzaniga, M.S. (1979). Information processing of visual stimuli in an extinguished field. *Nature, 282,* 722–724.

Young, A.W., de Haan, E.H.F., Newcombe, F., & Hay, D.C. (1990). Facial neglect. *Neuropsychologia, 28,* 391–415.

Zipser, D. & Andersen, A. (1988). A back-propagation programmed network that simulates response properties of a subset of posterior parietal neurons. *Nature, 331,* 679–684.

5 The Role of Spontaneous Eye Movements in Orienting Attention and in Unilateral Neglect

Guido Gainotti
*Institute of Neurology of the Catholic University of Rome,
Rome, Italy*

INTRODUCTION

Theories advanced to explain the unilateral neglect syndrome (see Bisiach & Vallar, 1988; De Renzi, 1982; Heilman, Valenstein, & Watson, 1985; Jeannerod, 1987; Weinstein & Friedland, 1977 and Gainotti, D'Erme, & De Bonis, 1989b for reviews) can be broadly classified into two major groups: (1) those that assume that neglect can be explained on the basis of peripheral input/output disturbances; (2) those that consider that disorders at a low level of integration cannot account for several aspects of this syndrome and propose that neglect must be traced back to a central (attentional or representational) disorder. In recent years, clinical and experimental data have convincingly shown, in agreement with the proponents of the second class of interpretations, that neglect phenomena cannot be reduced to disorders of gathering and processing sensory information. This suggests that peripheral factors only play a modulatory and not a causative role in unilateral neglect, and has oriented the interest of researchers almost entirely towards the central attentional and representational theories.

This attitude implies that peripheral and central factors are basically independent rather than strongly reciprocally interconnected. This view, however, is at variance with much data gathered both in normals and in brain-damaged patients, which seem to show that at least one of the peripheral factors (namely, the direction of spontaneous or automatic eye movements) exerts a strong influence upon the central attentional factors. The main scope of the present chapter will, therefore, consist in reviewing evidence supporting this line of thought. In particular, we will focus on a group of investigations prompted by the rather unexpected observation (Rubens, 1985) that severe manifestations of hemineglect can be dramatically improved (at least for short periods) by a caloric vestibular stimulation.

Our main thesis will be that the dramatic reduction of neglect observed after vestibular stimulation is the consequence of a peripheral reflex activity acting both with a direct and with an indirect mechanism. We assume that the facilitation of lateral gaze and head turning towards the neglected half-space (resulting from the elicitation of vestibulo-ocular and vestibulo-spinal reflex activities) can dramatically reduce unilateral neglect, not only because it allows a better visual exploration of the neglected half-space, but also (and perhaps even more) because it automatically orients attention in that direction.

THE SENSORIMOTOR THEORIES OF NEGLECT

The most striking manifestations of neglect usually occur in right brain-damaged patients showing a conjugate gaze deviation towards the right half-space, associated with left homonymous hemianopia and with left-sided somatosensory deficits. Some authors have assumed, therefore, that unilateral neglect may be but a consequence of these elementary sensori-motor disturbances, perhaps superimposed upon a background of wide-spread mental deterioration (Battersby, Bender, Pollack, & Kahn, 1956), which could prevent the patient from adopting adequate compensative strategies.

The best known instance of *sensory defect hypothesis* was presented by Denny-Brown, Meyer and Horenstein (1952), who proposed that the main function of the parietal lobes, usually severely damaged in neglect patients (Gainotti, 1968; Hécaen, 1962; Heilman, Valenstein, & Watson, 1983), may consist in synthesising the spatial aspects of the sensory stimuli. These authors, therefore, ascribed the neglect syndrome (which they called "amorphosynthesis") to a defective spatial summation of multiple sensory data. Although usually considered as a theory viewing neglect as a consequence of a sensory defect, the high-level sensory integration taken into account here makes this hypothesis not too different from modern non-sensory theories. Another version of the sensory defect hypothesis has been proposed by Sprague, Chambers and Steller (1961) in an animal model of neglect provoked in the cat by interrupting the lateral portion of the mesencephalon. Since this part of the brain stem contains ascending sensory pathways, Sprague et al. (1961) concluded that unilateral neglect was due to a loss of patterned afferent input to the forebrain.

Several objections have been raised to these and to similar explanations of the neglect phenomena.

1. The visual fields are often unaffected in cases of unilateral spatial neglect. Although Bisiach et al. (1986) reported that 96% of their neglect patients presented visual field defects on confrontation, it must be stressed that this method is very prone to the influence of attentional factors, which could artificially increase the number of defects not due to "primary" sensory deficits. When the assessment of visual field defects is based on perimetric or campimetric techniques, the incidence of hemianopia in neglect patients is lower, ranging from 50% (Albert, 1973) to 80% (D'Erme, De Bonis, & Gainotti, 1987).

2. Most hemianopic patients (and in particular left brain-damaged patients with right homonymous hemianopia) usually overcome their visual field defects with compensatory movements of the head and eyes (Gainotti, 1968; Meienberg et al., 1981; Meienberg, Harrer, & Wehren, 1986), thus increasing the number of eye fixations directed towards the blind half-field (Ishiai, Furukawa, & Tsukagashi, 1987). No such compensatory activity is generally shown by right brain-damaged patients with unilateral neglect.

3. Unilateral spatial neglect is not limited to the visual modality or to tasks accomplished under visual control. Manifestations of neglect for the left half-space have also been observed during tasks of manual exploration of the right and left parts of space accomplished without visual control (Chedru, 1976; De Renzi, Faglioni, & Scotti, 1970; Gentilini, Barbieri, De Renzi, & Faglioni, 1989; Weintraub & Mesulam, 1987) and during representative tasks, such as the description from memory of familiar surroundings, which do not require the exploration of the external environment or the processing of lateralised sensory stimuli (Bisiach, Capitani, Luzzatti, & Perani, 1981; Halsband, Gruhn, & Ettlinger, 1985; Meador, Loring, Bowers, & Heilman, 1987).

4. Finally, Halligan, Marshall and Wade (1990) have recently shown that the severity of neglect does not significantly differ between neglect patients with and without visual field defects. This observation suggests that visual field defects do not even exacerbate visual spatial neglect.

The *defective exploration hypothesis* stems from the observation that in the most severe forms of unilateral neglect, patients usually show a deviation of the head and eyes towards the lesion side and fail, for example, to orient towards a speaker addressing them from the contralateral half-space.

Schott, Jeannerod and Zahin (1966), therefore, proposed that unilateral neglect might be the consequence of an oculomotor disorder, resulting from a disruption of automatic eye fixation mechanisms, preventing patients from fully exploring the contralateral half-space. More recently, De Renzi (1982) has also proposed that a limitation of eye movements towards the neglected half-space could partly explain unilateral neglect.

A more "central" and more sophisticated version of the defective exploration hypothesis has been proposed by Kinsbourne (1970; 1973; 1974; 1977), who has tried to explain neglect on the basis of an oculomotor imbalance mechanism. According to Kinsbourne, each hemisphere subserves orientation towards the contralateral half-space and tends, when activated, to direct the gaze towards the contralateral spatial field. In the intact brain, the balance between the two sides could be maintained through reciprocal trans-callosal inhibition, but two mechanisms could reduce the orientation tendencies towards the contralateral half-space in unilateral brain-damaged patients: (1) an increased level of trans-callosal inhibition exerted by the normal upon the damaged hemisphere; (2) a defective activation of the damaged hemisphere, diminishing the flow of excitation towards the corresponding orienting apparatus.

The net result of this inter-hemispheric imbalance would be a bias of head and gaze turning towards the half-space ipsilateral to the lesion side (see Chapter 3, this volume, for an overview of Kinsbourne's conceptualisation of neglect and for a summary of the empirical data supporting his model). In more recent years, the hypothesis viewing unilateral neglect as a by-product of disrupted or imbalanced oculomotor mechanisms has been strengthened by the observation that conjugate eye defects, like unilateral spatial neglect, are more frequent and more lasting following right than left hemisphere stroke (De Renzi, Colombo, Faglioni, & Gibertoni, 1982; Mohr et al., 1984) and following right than left intracarotid sodium amytal injection (Meador et al., 1989). On the other hand, the hypothesis which views unilateral neglect as a consequence of a lost capacity to visually explore the contralateral half-space has also raised important objections:

1. Several patients with unilateral neglect do not present obvious oculomotor disorders. According to Hécaen (1962), this disturbance is present in about 85% of patients with hemineglect, but Gainotti (1968) and Albert (1973) have only observed oculomotor disorders in 78 and 64% of their neglect patients, respectively.
2. Hemineglect is more prevalent in right brain-damaged patients on tasks emphasising eye fixation effects (such as drawing simple geometrical figures or recognising small overlapping pictures) than on tasks requiring an exhaustive exploration of the half-space

contralateral to the brain lesion (for a review, see Gainotti, D'Erme, & De Bonis, 1989b).

3. Unilateral neglect is not limited to tasks accomplished under visual control or to tasks requiring the visual exploration of the external environment (see last section for survey). This defect cannot, therefore, be considered as resulting from the inability to explore visually the half-space contralateral to the damaged hemisphere.

REMISSION OF HEMINEGLECT DURING VESTIBULAR STIMULATION

As mentioned in the Introduction, great interest has been shown in recent years in Rubens' (1985) observation that a caloric vestibular stimulation can provoke a transient but dramatic improvement of hemi-inattention in most neglect patients. Rubens, drawing on previous anecdotal observations by Silberpfennig (1941) and Marshall and Maynard (1983), studied the effects of caloric vestibular stimulation on gaze direction and on tests of visual neglect in a group of 18 right brain-damaged patients showing severe manifestations of hemineglect. He reasoned that, if visual neglect is partly due to a gaze and postural turning bias, then caloric vestibular stimulation, producing eye deviation and past-pointing in the direction opposite to this bias, should reduce signs of neglect. His results confirmed the hypothesis, since even in profound neglect patients the caloric-induced vestibular reflex significantly improved both the ability to gaze into the affected field and behaviour on tests of visual neglect.

These results have since been replicated and extended, using the same or similar methodologies, by other authors, who have shown that not only unilateral spatial neglect, but also other (possibly related) signs of right hemisphere damage, can be temporarily reduced by vestibular stimulation. Thus, Cappa, Sterzi, Vallar and Bisiach (1987) have shown that in addition to visual neglect, personal neglect and anosognosia can be temporarily alleviated by caloric vestibular stimulation and, even more recently, Vallar et al. (1990) have demonstrated that this improvement concerns both tasks performed under visual control and tasks performed without visual control. Furthermore, the same authors have shown that, at least in some patients, vestibular stimulation can temporarily reduce defects apparently due to "primary" sensory deficits, such as left hemianaesthesia.

On the other hand, Pizzamiglio et al. (1990) have demonstrated that a temporary reduction in hemineglect can also be obtained by using an optokinetic (instead of a caloric vestibular) stimulation, to provoke a nystagmus with a slow phase opposing the gaze bias shown by neglect patients.

It must be acknowledged, however, that if the remission of hemineglect during caloric vestibular stimulation and comparable manoeuvres is a well-established empirical fact, interpretations of this effect are still controversial. Neither Rubens (1985) nor the authors who have replicated and extended his findings, have entirely attributed the observed remission of hemineglect to an improved capacity to explore visually the half-space contralateral to the damaged hemisphere. Rubens, of course, explicitly assumed that this was the main mechanism, but (owing to the objections to the "defective exploration hypothesis" that we have just mentioned) also took into account the possible role of less elementary and more integrated mechanisms. One of these could be the influence that the vestibular input exerts upon the cortico-limbic-reticular system, implicated by Heilman and co-workers (e.g. Heilman & Valenstein, 1979; Heilman et al., 1985) in the maintenance of hemispheric arousal and readiness to respond to stimuli coming from the contralateral half-space. A second mechanism could consist in the modulation that the vestibular input exerts upon the visual cortical cells (Lahue, Reinis, Landolt, & Money, 1981) and upon the visual tracking neurons of the posterior parietal association cortex, since this modulation could facilitate the visual processing in the defective half-field.

Cappa et al. (1987), Pizzamiglio et al. (1990) and Vallar et al. (1990), on the other hand, were even more reluctant to admit that the effects of vestibular stimulation may be explained simply in terms of a facilitation of ocular movements towards the neglected side, since such a mechanism could not account for the improvement of personal neglect and the regression of anosognosia reported by Cappa et al. (1987), nor the temporary remission of hemianaesthesia and the improvement in extrapersonal neglect in the absence of visual control observed by Vallar et al. (1990). Pizzamiglio et al. (1990) gave a detailed description of the integrated neural mechanism fed by the vestibular system, drawing on a general theoretical model proposed by Jeannerod and Biguer (1987). These authors examined the process of building up the spatial map for directing movements towards the extrapersonal space, reviewing the contribution of eye position signals, head position signals and other signals in the construction of an egocentric body reference system.

They had considered unilateral neglect as an orienting bias produced by a lesion within this central representation of the body reference system, leading to an illusory rotation of the system of reference towards the lesion side. Pizzamiglio et al. (1990) assumed that the body-centred spatial map may be subserved and fed by redundant and independent proprioceptive, visual and vestibular subsystems, which do not need to be simultaneously activated. They proposed that a general imbalance of the spatial reference frame may be observed when a focal brain lesion disconnects this central integrative structure from one or more of the afferent subsystems. In this case, the activation of the remaining subsystems might be sufficient to reduce and partially compensate the spatial bias, which can be observed in a variety of tasks of space exploration.

We do not intend to enter here into a discussion of this explanation or of other similar interpretations. We will limit ourselves to the fact that if an improved visual exploration of the neglected half-space cannot explain phenomena such as the reduction of personal neglect, anosognosia, hemianaesthesia and so on, it is also unlikely that this set of phenomena may be explained by the improved functioning of a higher level integrative structure fed by the vestibular system. We therefore prefer to come back to the simpler and more parsimonious explanation, linking the reduction of hemineglect and of the associated signs of right hemisphere damage to the most obvious consequence of caloric vestibular stimulation, namely the facilitation of ocular movements towards the neglected side. We will propose that this very simple reflex mechanism can perhaps explain the whole set of phenomena observed by Rubens and by the authors who have replicated and extended his findings, provided the following additional assumptions are made:

1. The general mechanism through which vestibular stimulation acts upon personal and extrapersonal neglect, anosognosia and hemi-anaesthesia consists in increasing the level of selective attention paid to the corresponding parts of the body and of extrapersonal space.
2. The facilitation of ocular movements towards the neglected half-space leads to a reduction of neglect and of related phenomena not only because it allows a better visual exploration of the neglected half-space, but also because it automatically orients attention towards this space.

THE INFLUENCE OF ATTENTION UPON SIGNS OF RIGHT HEMISPHERE DAMAGE USUALLY ASSOCIATED WITH NEGLECT

The possibility that not only extrapersonal neglect, but also personal neglect (hemisomatoagnosia) and anosognosia, may be partly due to (or in any case influenced by) central attentional disorders has been repeatedly raised in the history of neuropsychology. Thus, Gentili (1965) maintained that right brain-damaged patients with anosognosia are unaware of their disability because they pay no attention to the left paralysed side of the body and a similar interpretation has been advanced by Critchley (1953) and Frederiks (1963) to explain personal neglect. Therefore, although it may be thought that a rather heterogeneous set of phenomena are described under the headings of anosognosia and of hemisomatoagnosia, it is likely that attentional factors usually interact with other somatosensory, representational and motivational factors in the production of these body-related behavioural disturbances. Even more likely is the link between left-sided anaesthesia and imbalanced distribution of attention, since increasing evidence in recent years has suggested that in right brain-damaged patients the processing of simple somatosensory stimuli may be influenced by high-level attentional factors. Thus, Weiskrantz and Zhang (1987) have shown that detection accuracy of stimuli applied to the left hand of a patient presenting a left-sided anaesthesia was modulated by the level of attention directed towards the stimulated hand. Stimuli were not detected when the patient was passively touched by the examiner on the left hand, but were much more frequently detected when she actively touched the left hand with her unaffected right hand or with a probe held by that hand. Tégner (1989) studied the response to tactile stimuli at the threshold range in two patients with chronic right parietal lesions. On the normal side, response thresholds were low and the number of correct responses increased steeply with increasing stimulus strength, whereas on the left side, the psychometric functions at the threshold range were much less steep and about 10% of the stimuli were not detected independent of the stimulus strength. Both these findings suggest that somatosensory deficits produced by right brain damage are modulated by central attentional factors.

Studies that have used double tactile simultaneous stimulation in various clinical and experimental situations give us further evidence in the same direction. These studies have shown that unilateral spatial neglect and tactile extinction on the body parts contralateral to the damaged hemisphere share important similarities with respect both to hemispheric asymmetries and to rehabilitation strategies. As for the first point, it has been shown that contralateral tactile extinction is more frequent and severe following right than left brain damage both in conditions of spontaneous brain pathology (Gainotti, De Bonis, Daniele, & Caltagirone, 1989a) and after intracarotid amytal injection (Meador & Heilman, 1988). As for the second point, Nocentini, Troisi, Carlesimo and Caltagirone (1990) have recently shown that rehabilitation techniques aiming at ameliorating unilateral spatial neglect by intensively training patients to orient attention towards left half-space also significantly reduce the incidence of contralateral tactile extinctions.

Now, if we accept that anosognosia, personal neglect and somatosensory defects may be due in part to the defective attention paid to the left side of the body, it becomes possible to assume that vestibular stimulation may temporarily ameliorate these symptoms by directing attention towards the left side of personal and extrapersonal space.

DIRECTION OF SPONTANEOUS OR AUTOMATIC EYE MOVEMENTS AND SPATIAL ORIENTING OF ATTENTION

Although several experiments have shown that attention can be allocated to different parts of the spatial field without making overt eye movements (for reviews, see Posner, 1980; Umiltà, 1988), this does not mean that independent processes are involved in the generation of eye movements and in the spatial allocation of attention. Experiments performed in normals by Crovitz and Daves (1962), Remington (1980) and Shepherd, Findlay and Hockey (1986) suggest, for example, a close relationship between eye movements and displacements of attention. In particular, the results obtained by Sheperd et al. (1986) suggest an asymmetric relationship between the two phenomena, since they indicate that it is possible to move attention without making eye movements, but it is not possible to make an eye movement without shifting in the same direction the focus of attention.

It must also be considered that both in experimental and in more ecological situations, effortful and highly controlled operations are necessary to obtain a dissociation between eye movements and spatial allocation of attention, whereas in more spontaneous or automatic conditions, close co-ordination between eye movements and displacements of attention seems essential for a smooth performance. Thus, both experimental data and commonsense considerations suggest that the direction of eye movements usually prompts a corresponding spatial orientation of attention. This suggestion is supported by a consistent body of data obtained in normals and in brain-damaged patients.

Data Gathered in Normals

Gopher (1973) was the first to observe that during dichotic listening tasks, the eyes of subjects tended to orient to and to remain fixated in the direction of the relevant ear and suggested that these eye movements oriented the subjects' attention towards the appropriate part of space. Gopher also noted that the right ear advantage usually observed in verbal dichotic listening tasks increased by directing the gaze towards the right half-space, but disappeared by inverting the direction of gaze (Gopher, 1971, cited in Honoré, Bourdeaud'hui, & Sparrow, 1989). Similar results were obtained by Larmande et al. (1983; 1984) using non-verbal sounds as stimuli, which in a dichotic listening paradigm usually give a left ear advantage. In this case, too, the direction of gaze influenced the spatial allocation of attention, as the left ear advantage was increased by directing the gaze towards the left and reversed by orienting the gaze towards the right. Results obtained by Honoré (1982) when studying the detection of tactile stimuli, are also consistent with the hypothesis of a link between direction of eye movements and spatial allocation of attention. Honoré noted that the detection rate of cutaneous stimuli was higher and the reaction times were shorter when the eyes were turned towards the side stimulated by the examiner.

It must be noted, however, that not all the authors who have performed the above-mentioned experiments have interpreted their data as indicative of a link between direction of gaze and spatial allocation of attention. Larmande et al. (1983; 1984), in particular, have interpreted their data within the theoretical framework proposed by Kinsbourne (1970; 1974; 1977). They assumed that the act of turning the eyes towards one half of space (e.g. the left side) increases the level of activation of the corresponding hemisphere (in this case the right one), thus improving the processing of information coming from the contralateral space (and hence from the left ear) at the expense of stimuli presented at the right ear. This interpretation, which assumes an indirect link (via activation of the contralateral hemisphere) between direction of eye movements and efficiency of performance accomplished in the corresponding spatial field, has recently been tested by Honoré et al. (1989). Among normal subjects examined in a darkened room, Honoré et al. measured reaction times to lateral cutaneous stimulations, when the eyes were directed (a) towards the stimulated area, (b) towards another point within the same hemispace and (c) towards the opposite hemispace. Cutaneous reaction times were shortened only when the stimulation occurred at the centre of the area where the gaze was directed, but not when it occurred at any other point in the same hemispace. These data clearly suggest that eye movements facilitate the processing of stimuli occurring at the centre of the virtual visual field because of a correlative displacement of attention and not because of a resulting activation of the corresponding hemisphere.

Data Gathered in Brain-damaged Patients

Three sets of data obtained in brain-damaged patients are consistent with the hypothesis that the direction of gaze automatically prompts a corresponding displacement of attention.

Among 10 right brain-damaged patients, Larmande and Cambier (1981) studied the incidence of tactile extinction on the left side of the body under various experimental conditions. The lateral orientation of gaze proved to be the most effective variable, as the incidence of extinction decreased when the gaze was oriented towards the left half-space and increased when it was directed to the right. The authors attributed these findings to the hemispheric activation provoked by the act of turning the eyes towards the contralateral half-space; however, the fact that language activities, which certainly induce a left hemisphere activation, were much less effective in increasing the incidence of tactile extinction, weakens this interpretation.

Benin, Perrier, Cambier and Larmande (1988) submitted two patients presenting a pathological gaze deviation towards the right side as a consequence of a brain stem lesion to a non-verbal dichotic listening task. Contrary to what is usually observed in normal conditions, but in agreement with the direction of the pathological gaze deviation, the number of first answers and the overall number of correct responses were greater for the right than for the left ear.

Meador et al. (1987) studied what influence turning the head and eyes of the patient to the right or left side can have upon the severity of neglect observed in a representative task. Their patient, who had lived in the same neighbourhood for over 20 years and who had a thorough knowledge of the families and houses near his home, was asked to imagine (while he was looking straight ahead at the examiner) that he was standing at the end of the street leading to his house.

With this mental set established, he was requested to name the houses on the street. Almost all the houses recalled were in the imagined right half-space, whereas very few were in the left half-space. When, however, he was re-tested with his eyes/head rotated to the left, recall of items lying in the left hemispace improved significantly. Thus, clinical observations and experiments accomplished in normal subjects and in brain-damaged patients consistently show that the direction of eye movements leads to a corresponding spatial orienting of attention. This effect is observed in different types of lateral eye deviation: when this posture is actively assumed by the subject (as in Larmande and co-workers' studies); when it is a consequence of a brainstem lesion producing a pathological gaze deviation (as in Benin and co-workers' study); and when the examiner physically turns the eyes/head of the patient (as in Meador and co-workers' study).

The results of this last investigation are also interesting because they suggest that the direction of gaze is not the only factor which prompts a consensual automatic displacement of attention. Other components of the orienting reaction, such as head turning and trunk turning, are probably part of the same phenomenon, namely an automatic movement of attention towards the part of space pointed at by the body-orienting apparatus. This position, which is in agreement with the recent results of Karnath, Schenkel, and Fischer (1990) that the spatial trunk orientation is an important determining factor of contralateral neglect, is not inconsistent with the results of the caloric vestibular stimulation. The latter, in fact, produces an integrated pattern of reflex activities (comprising the vestibulo-ocular and the vestibulo-spinal reflexes), which synergically orient in the same direction the gaze, head and trunk of the subject.

IMPLICATIONS FOR THEORIES OF UNILATERAL NEGLECT

In previous sections of this chapter, we have tried to demonstrate that lateral eye movements (and the turning movements of the body-orienting apparatus in general) lead to an automatic dislocation of attention towards the corresponding parts of personal and extrapersonal space. We have also suggested that a facilitation of ocular movements and of head turning towards the neglected half-space can explain the transient but dramatic improvement of neglect and of related phenomena observed after vestibular caloric stimulation. These findings, which cannot be simply attributed to an improved visual exploration of the neglected half-space, have been interpreted as the consequence of a less imbalanced distribution of attention, allowing the patient to allocate attention automatically not only to the right, but also to the left half of personal and extrapersonal space.

Our interpretation of the above-mentioned data suggests that the mechanisms disrupted in unilateral neglect are seemingly located within a circuit connecting the central and the peripheral components of a structure subserving the spatial automatic displacements of attention, but does not necessarily point to the more central or to the more peripheral components of this circuit. Various general theories of neglect are, therefore, compatible with our interpretation. Thus, the stress put on the reciprocal interconnections between eye movements and movements of attention could increase the explanatory power of theories suggesting that an elementary oculomotor disorder might play a critical role in unilateral spatial neglect. On the other hand, the automatic nature of the attentional displacements prompted by lateral eye movements could suggest that the attentional bias in unilateral neglect mainly concerns the automatic, rather than the intentional, allocations of attention. This is in line with the view, advanced in previous papers (Gainotti et al., 1989b; Gainotti, D'Erme, & Bartolomeo, 1991), that unilateral neglect may be due to a selective disruption of mechanisms provoking an automatic orienting of attention towards the contralateral half-space, with relative sparing of mechanisms subserving volitional orienting of attention. Similar viewpoints are put forward in this book by Humphreys and Riddoch (Chapter 7) and by Làdavas (Chapter 9).

Finally, our interpretation of the vestibular stimulation experiments is compatible with those theories that assume that more "central" mechanisms of attention are disrupted in unilateral neglect. It is, for example, certainly consistent with Kinsbourne's theory, which views neglect as the consequence of a gaze and postural bias towards the half-space ipsilateral to the lesion side (Kinsbourne, 1977; 1989). It must be added, however, that although it is compatible with all these theories, our interpretation remains neutral as regards the mechanisms proposed to account for one of the most striking aspects of unilateral spatial neglect, namely its prevalence in patients with right hemisphere damage (for reviews, see Bisiach & Vallar, 1988; De Renzi, 1982; Gainotti et al., 1989b; Heilman et al., 1985). Our interpretation of the results obtained with caloric vestibular stimulation can, indeed, be equally well accommodated by: (a) the hypothesis advanced by De Renzi et al. (1982) that the prevalence of neglect in right brain-damaged patients may be due to a right hemisphere superiority for oculomotor functions; (b) our hypothesis which assumes that right hemisphere organisation may be more strongly dependent upon automatic forms of orienting reactions and that therefore a right brain lesion may more easily produce a strongly ipsilaterally imbalanced orienting bias (Gainotti et al., 1991); (c) Kinsbourne's hypothesis, viewing the prevalence of neglect for the left half-space as the exaggeration of a physiological asymmetry, leading normal subjects to orient preferentially towards the right half-space (Kinsbourne, 1987); and (d) Heilman's theory, which considers the prevalence of unilateral neglect in right brain-damaged patients to be due to the different organisation of the receptive fields of right and left parietal attentional neurons (Heilman & Valenstein, 1979; Heilman & Van Den Abell, 1980; Heilman et al., 1985).

The importance of vestibular stimulation experiments for theories of hemineglect must, therefore, be neither underestimated nor overestimated. Although they restrict the strongest candidates to theories which stress central or peripheral aspects of the lateral orienting of attention, they must also be integrated with other data to check for more specific aspects of these different theories, so as to allow for a more precise understanding of the nature of unilateral neglect.

REFERENCES

Albert, M.L. (1973). A simple test of visual neglect. *Neurology*, *23*, 658–664.

Battersby, W.S., Bender, M.B., Pollack, M., & Kahn, R.L. (1956). Unilateral spatial agnosia (inattention) in patients with cerebral lesions. *Brain*, *79*, 68–93.

Benin, C., Perrier, D., Cambier, J., & Larmande, P. (1988). Influence de la déviation pathologique du regard par lésion du tronc cérébral sur l'équilibre inter hémisphérique, étudié par le test d'écoute dichotique non verbal. *Neuropsychologia*, *26*, 753–758.

Bisiach, E., Capitani, E., Luzzatti, C., & Perani, D. (1981). Brain and conscious representation of outside reality. *Neuropsychologia*, *19*, 543–551.

Bisiach, E. & Luzzatti, C. (1978). Unilateral neglect of resprentational space. *Cortex*, *14*, 129–133.

Bisiach, E. & Vallar, G. (1988). Hemineglect in humans. In F. Boller & J. Grafman (Eds), *Handbook of neuropsychology*, Vol. 1. Amsterdam: North-Holland.

Bisiach, E., Vallar, G., Perani, D., Papagno, C., & Berti, A. (1986). Unawareness of disease following lesions of the right hemisphere: Anosognosia for hemiplegia and anosognosia for hemianopia. *Neuropsychologia*, *24*, 471–482.

Cappa, S., Sterzi, R., Vallar, G., & Bisiach, E. (1987). Remission of hemineglect and anosognosia during vestibular stimulation. *Neuropsychologia*, *25*, 775–782.

Chedru, F. (1976). Space representation in unilateral spatial neglect. *Journal of Neurology, Neurosurgery and Psychiatry*, *39*, 1057–1061.

Critchley, M. (1953). *The parietal lobes*. New York: Hafner.

Crovitz, H.F. & Daves, W. (1962). Tendencies to eye movements and perceptual accuracy. *Journal of Experimental Psychology*, *63*, 495–498.

Denny-Brown, D., Meyer, J.S., & Horenstein, S. (1952). The significance of perceptual rivalry resulting from parietal lesions. *Brain*, *75*, 433–471.

De Renzi, E. (1982). *Disorder of space perception and cognition*. New York: John Wiley.

De Renzi, E., Colombo, A., Faglioni, P., & Gibertoni, M. (1982). Conjugate gaze paralysis in stroke patients with unilateral damage. *Archives of Neurology*, *39*, 482–486.

De Renzi, E., Faglioni, P., & Scotti, G. (1970). Hemispheric contribution to the exploration of space through the visual and tactile modalilty. *Cortex*, *6*, 191–203.

D'Erme, P., De Bonis, C., & Gainotti, G. (1987). Influenza dell'emi-inattenzione e dell'emianopsia sui compiti di bisezione di linee nei pazienti cerebrolesi. *Archivio di Psicologia, Neurologia e Psichiatria*, *38*, 193–207.

Frederiks, J.A.M. (1963). Anosognosie et hémiasomatognosie *Revue Neurologique*, *109*, 585–597.

Gainotti, G. (1968). Les manifestations de négligence et d'inattention pour l'hémispace. *Cortex*, *4*, 64–91.

Gainotti, G., De Bonis, C., Daniele, A., & Caltagirone, C. (1989a). Controlateral and ipsilateral tactile exinction in patients with right and left focal brain damage. *International Journal of Neuroscience*, *45*, 81–89.

Gainotti, G., D'Erme, P., & Bartolomeo, P. (1991). Early orientation of attention toward the half space ipsilateral to the lesion in patients with unilateral brain damage. *Journal of Neurology, Neurosurgery and Psychiatry*, *54*, 1082–1089.

Gainotti, G., D'Erme, P., & De Bonis, C. (1989b). Components of visual attention disrupted in unilateral neglect. In J.W. Brown (Ed.), *Neuropsychology of visual perception*, pp. 123–144. Hillsdale, NJ: Lawrence Erlbaum Associates Inc.

Gentili, C. (1965). Corpo come relazione. *Sistema Nervoso*, *17*, 174–187.

Gentilini, M., Barbieri, C., De Renzi, E., & Faglioni, P. (1989). Space exploration with and without the aid of vision in hemisphere-damaged patients. *Cortex*, *25*, 643–651.

Gopher, D. (1973). Eye-movement patterns in selective listening tasks of focused attention. *Perceptual Psychophysics*, *14*, 259–264.

Halligan, P.W., Marshall, J.C., & Wade, D.T. (1990). Do visual field deficits exacerbate visuo-spatial neglect? *Journal of Neurology, Neurosurgery and Psychiatry*, *53*, 487–491.

Halsband, U., Gruhn, S., & Ettlinger, G. (1985). Unilateral spatial neglect and defective performance in one half of space. *International Journal of Neuroscience*, *28*, 173–195.

Hécaen, H. (1962). Clinical symptomatology in right and left hemisphere lesions. In V.B. Mountcastle (Ed.), *Interhemispheric relation and cerebral dominance*. Baltimore, MD: Johns Hopkins University Press.

Heilman, K.M. & Valenstein, E. (1979). Mechanisms underlying hemi-spatial neglect. *Annals of Neurology*, *5*, 166–170.

Heilman, K.M., Valenstein, E., & Watson, R.T. (1983). Localization of neglect. In A. Kertesz (Ed.), *Localization in neuropsychology* (pp. 371–392). New York, NY: Academic Press.

Heilman, K.M., Valenstein, E., & Watson, R.T. (1985). The neglect syndrome. In P.J. Vinken, G.J. Bruyn & H.L. Klawans (Eds), *Handbook of clinical neurology: Vol. 45* (pp. 152–183). Amsterdam: Elsevier Science Publishers.

Heilman, K.M. & Van den Abell, T. (1980). Right hemispheric dominance for attention: The mechanism underlying hemispheric asymmetries of inattention (neglect). *Neurology*, *30*, 327–330.

Honoré, J. (1982). Posture oculaire et attention sélective à des stimuli cutanés. *Neuropsychologia, 20*, 727–730.

Honoré, J., Bourdeaud'hui, M., & Sparrow, L. (1989). Reduction of cutaneous reaction time by directing eyes towards the source of stimulation. *Neuropsychologia, 27*, 3, 367–371.

Ishiai, S., Furukawa, T., & Tsukagashi, H. (1987). Eye-fixation patterns in homonymous hemianopia and unilateral spatial neglect. *Neuropsychologia, 25*, 675–679.

Jeannerod, M. (Ed.) (1987). *Neurophysiological and neuropsychological aspects of spatial neglect.* Amsterdam: North-Holland.

Jeannerod, M. & Biguer, B. (1987). The directional coding of reaching movements. In M. Jeannerod (Ed.), *Neurophysiological and neuropsychological aspects of spatial neglect,* pp. 87–113. Amsterdam: North-Holland.

Karnath, H.O., Schenkel, P., & Fischer, B. (1990). *Trunk orientation as a determining factor of "contralateral" deficit in neglect.* Paper presented at the 8th European Workshop on Cognitive Neuropsychology, Bressanone, January.

Kinsbourne, M. (1970). A model for the mechanism of unilateral neglect of space. *Transactions of the American Neurological Association, 95,* 143.

Kinsbourne, M. (1973). The control of attention by interaction between the cerebral hemispheres. In S. Kornblum (Ed.), *Attention and performance IV.* New York: Academic Press.

Kinsbourne, M. (1974). Direction of gaze and distribution of cerebral thought processes. *Neuropsychologia, 12,* 270–281.

Kinsbourne, M. (1977). Hemineglect and hemispheric rivalry. In E.A. Weinstein & R.P. Friedland (Eds), *Advances in neurology,* Vol. 18. New York: Raven Press.

Kinsbourne, M. (1987). Mechanisms of unilateral neglect. In M. Jeannerod (Ed.), *Neurophysiological and neuropsychological aspects of spatial neglect,* pp. 69–86. Amsterdam: North-Holland.

Lahue, B.H., Reinis, S., Landolt, J.F., & Money, K.E. (1981). Visual–vestibular interactions in visual cortical cells in the cat. *Annals of the New York Academy of Sciences, 374,* 262–273.

Larmande, F., Elghori, D., Sintes, J., Bigot, Th., & Autret, A. (1983). Test d'ecoute dichotique verbal et non verbal chez le sujet normal: influence de létat d'activation hémisphérique. *Revue Neurologique, 139,* 65–69.

Larmande, P., Blanchard, F., Sintes, J., Belin, C., & Autret, A. (1984). Test d'écoute dichotique melodique. Influence de l'état d'activation hémisphérique chez les sujets normaux, musiciens et non musiciens. *Revue Neurologique, 140,* 49–54.

Larmande, P. & Cambier, J. (1981). Influence de l'état d'activation hémisphérique sur le phénoméne d'extinction sensitive chez 10 patients atteints de lésions hemisphériques droites. *Revue Neurologique, 137,* 285–290.

Marshall, C.R. & Maynard, R.M. (1983). Vestibular stimulation for supranuclear gaze palzy: Case Report. *Archives of Physical Medicine and Rehabilitation, 64,* 134–146.

Meador, K.J. & Heilman, K.M. (1988). Right cerebral specialization for tactile attention as evidenced by intracarotid sodium amytal. *Neurology, 38,* 1763–1766.

Meador, K.J., Loring, D.W., Bowers, D., & Heilman, K.M. (1987) Remote memory and neglect syndrome. *Neurology, 37,* 522–536.

Meador, K.J., Loring, D.W., Lee, G.P., Brooks, B.S., Nichols, F.T., Thompson, E.E., Thompson, W.O., & Heilman, K.M. (1989). Hemisphere asymmetry for eye gaze mechanisms. *Brain, 112,* 103–111.

Meienberg, O., Harrer, M., & Wehren, C. (1986) Oculographic diagnosis of hemineglect in patients with homonymous hemianopia. *Journal of Neurology, 233,* 97–101.

Meienberg, O., Zangemeister, W.H., Rosenberg, M., Hoyt, W.F., & Stark, L. (1981). Saccadic eye movement strategies in patients with homonymous hemianopia. *Annals of Neurology, 9,* 537–544.

Mohr, J.P., Rubinstein, L.V., Kase, C.S., Price, T.R., Wolf, P.A., Nichols, F.T., & Tatemichi, T.K. (1984). Gaze palsy in hemispheral stroke: The NINCDS Stroke Data Bank, *Neurology*, *34*, 199 (suppl. 1).

Nocentini, U., Troisi, E., Carlesimo, G.A., & Caltagirone, C. (1990). *Cognitive rehabilitation of hemi-inattentive disorders*. Communication to the 3rd International SISTED Conference, Bologna, April.

Pizzamiglio, L., Frasca, R., Guariglia, C., Incaccia, R., & Antonucci, G. (1990). Effect of optokinetic stimulation in patients with visual neglect. *Cortex*, *26*, 534–540.

Posner, M.I. (1980). Orienting of attention: The VIIth Sir Frederic Bartlett Lecture. *Quarterly Journal of Experimental Psychology*, *32*, 3–25.

Remington, R.W. (1980). Attention and saccadic eye movements. *Journal of Experimental Psychology*, *6*, 726–744.

Rubens, A.B. (1985). Caloric stimulation and unilateral visual neglect. *Neurology*, *35*, 1019–1024.

Schott, B., Jeannerod, M., & Zahin, M.A. (1966). L'agnosie spatiale unilatérale: perturbation en secteur des méchanismes d'exploration et de fixation du regard. *Journal de Medicine de Lyon*, *47*, 169–195.

Shepherd, M., Findlay, J.M., & Hockey, R.J. (1986). The relationship between eye movements and spatial attention. *Quarterly Journal of Experimental Psychology*, *38A*, 475–491.

Silberpfennig, J. (1941). Contributions to the problem of eye movements. III. Disturbances of ocular movements with pseudohemianopia in frontal tumors. *Confinia Neurologica*, *4*, 1–13.

Sprague, J.M., Chambers, W.W., & Steller, E. (1961). Attentive, affective and adaptive behavior in the cat. *Science*, *133*, 165–173.

Tegner, R. (1989). Tactile sensibility in parietal lesions. *Journal of Neurology, Neurosurgery and Psychiatry*, *52*, 669–670.

Umiltà, C. (1988). Orienting of attention. In F. Boller & J. Grafman (Eds), *Handbook of neuropsychology*, Vol. 1. Amsterdam: North-Holland.

Vallar, G., Sterzi, R., Bottini, G., Cappa, S., & Rusconi, L. (1990). Temporary remission of left hemianaesthesia after vestibular stimulation. A sensory neglect phenomenon. *Cortex*, *26*, 123–131.

Weinstein, E.A., & Friedland, R.P. (1977). *Hemi-inattention and hemisphere specialization*. New York: Raven Press.

Weintraub, S. & Mesulam, M.M. (1987). Right cerebral dominance for spatial attention: Further evidence based on ipsilateral neglect. *Archives of Neurology*, *44*, 621–625.

Weiskrantz, L. & Zhang, D. (1987). Residual tactile sensitivity with self-directed stimulation in hemianaesthesia. *Journal of Neurology, Neurosurgery and Psychiatry*, *50*, 632–64.

6

"What" and "Where" in Visual Attention: Evidence from the Neglect Syndrome

Martha J. Farah, Marcie A. Wallace and Shaun P. Vecera
Department of Psychology, Carnegie-Mellon University, Pittsburgh, Pennsylvania, USA

ATTENTION AND REPRESENTATION

Psychologists often speak of "allocating attention to stimuli", but in fact this manner of speaking obscures an important fact about attention. Attention is not allocated to stimuli, but to internal representations of stimuli. Although it may seem pedantic to emphasise such an obvious point, doing so alerts us to the central role of representation in any theory of attention. One cannot explain attention without having specified the nature of the visual representations on which it operates.

The goal of this chapter is to characterise the representations of visual stimuli to which attention is allocated. Two general alternatives will be considered. The first is that attention is allocated to regions of an array-format representation of the visual field. According to this view, when some subset of the contents of the visual field is selected for further, attention-demanding perceptual processing, the attended subset is spatially delimited. In other words, stimuli are selected a *location* at a time. The second alternative is that attention is allocated to a representation that makes explicit the objects in the visual field, but not necessarily their locations, and the attended subset is therefore some integral number of objects. According to this alternative, stimuli are selected an *object* at a time.

In this chapter, we will review what is known about the representation of locations and objects in visual attention from studies of normal subjects and parietal-damaged subjects. The latter include unilaterally damaged subjects who have neglect, and bilaterally damaged subjects, who have a disorder known as "simultanagnosia".

ATTENTION TO LOCATIONS AND OBJECTS: A BRIEF REVIEW OF EVIDENCE FROM NORMAL SUBJECTS

Evidence for Location-based attention

Most research on visual attention in normal subjects has focused on selection of stimuli by spatial location. Visual attention is often compared to a spotlight (e.g. Posner, Snyder, & Davidson, 1980), which is moved across locations in the visual field. One common task used in studying spatial attention is the simple reaction time paradigm developed by Posner and colleagues, in which cues and targets appear to the left and right of fixation as shown in Fig. 6.1. The cue consists of a brightening of the box surrounding the target location and the target itself is a plus sign inside the box. The subject's task is to respond as quickly as possible once the target appears. The cues precede the targets, and occur either at the same location as the target (a "valid" cue) or at the other location (an "invalid" cue). Subjects respond more quickly to validly than invalidly cued targets, and this difference has been interpreted as an attentional effect. Specifically, when a target is invalidly cued, attention must be disengaged from the location of the cue, moved to the location of the target, and re-engaged there before the subject can complete a response. In contrast, when the target is validly cued, attention is already engaged at the target's location, and responses are therefore faster (see Posner & Cohen, 1984).

The hypothesis that attention is shifted across a representation of locations in the visual field also finds striking support from an experiment by Shulman, Remington and McLean (1979). The subjects received cues and targets in far peripheral locations. However, a probe event could occur between the cue and target in an intermediate peripheral location. When the subjects were cued to a far peripheral location and a probe appeared in the intermediate location, they showed facilitation in processing the probe prior to the maximal facilitation of the far peripheral location. These results fit with the idea that if attention is moved from point A to point B through space, then it moves through the intermediate points.

Another representative result supporting spatially allocated visual attention was reported by Hoffman and Nelson (1981). Their subjects were required to perform two tasks: a letter search task, in which the subjects determined which of two target letters appeared in one of four spatial locations, and an orientation discrimination, in which the subjects determined the orientation of a small U-shaped figure. Hoffman and Nelson found that when letters were correctly identified, the orientation of the U-

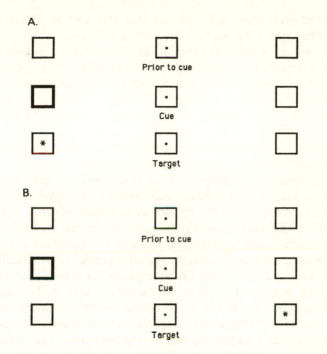

FIG. 6.1. Two sequences of stimulus displays from the simple reaction time paradigm used by Posner and colleagues to demonstrate spatially selective attention. Part A shows a validly cued trial, in which the cue (brightening of one box) occurs on the same side of space as the target (asterisk). Part B shows an invalidly cued trial, in which the cue and target occur in different spatial locations.

shaped figure was better discriminated when it was adjacent to the target letter, compared to when the target letter and U-shape were not adjacent. These results support the hypothesis that attention is allocated to stimuli as a function of their location in visual space.

Evidence for Object-based Attention

In addition to the many results supporting the view that attention is allocated to representations of spatial locations, there are other results suggesting that it is allocated to representations of objects, independent of their spatial location. Perhaps the clearest evidence for object-based attention comes from Duncan (1984). Duncan presented subjects with brief presentations of superimposed boxes and lines, like the ones shown in Fig. 6.2. Each of the two objects could vary on two dimensions: the box could be either short or tall and have a gap on the left or right, and the line could be tilted clockwise or counterclockwise and be either dotted or dashed. The critical finding was that when the subjects were required to make two decisions about the stimuli, they were more accurate when both decisions were about the same object. For example, the subjects were more accurate at reporting the box's size and side of gap, compared to, say, reporting the box's height and the line's texture. This finding fits with the notion that attention is allocated to objects *per se*: It would be more efficient to attend to a single object representation rather than either attending to two object representations simultaneously, or attending to one representation and then the other.

To summarise the findings with normal subjects, there appears to be evidence of both location-based and object-based attention. It is also possible that the findings in support of one type of attention could be explained by the alternative hypothesis. In general, being in the same location is highly correlated with being on the same object and vice versa. This raises the possibility that there is just one type of visual attention, either location-based or object-based. For example, in the type of display shown in Fig. 6.1, the cue–target combination might be seen as forming a single object—a box with a plus inside—when the cue occurs on the same side of space as the target, whereas a box on one side of space and a plus on the other would not be grouped together as a single object. The tendency of the visual system to group stimuli at adjacent spatial locations into objects (the Gestalt principle of grouping by proximity) could be used to explain the effects of spatial location on the allocation of attention in terms of object-based attention. Similarly, evidence for object-based attention could be interpreted in terms of spatial attention. For example, Duncan discusses the possibility that the objects in his experiment may have been perceived as being at different depths, so that shifting attention between objects may in

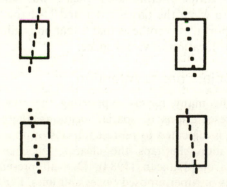

FIG. 6.2.   Examples of stimuli used by Duncan (1984) to demonstrate that attention is object-based.

fact have involved shifting attention to a different depth location. It is, of course, also possible that both types of attention exist. The current state of research with normal subjects does not decisively choose among these alternatives. Let us now turn to the neuropsychological evidence on this issue.

ATTENTION TO LOCATIONS AND OBJECTS AFTER UNILATERAL PARIETAL DAMAGE

Unilateral posterior parietal damage often results in the neglect syndrome, in which patients may fail to attend to the contralesional side of space, particularly when ipsilesional stimuli are present. The neglect syndrome provides clear evidence for a location-based visual attention system, in that what does and does not get attention depends on location, specifically how far to the left or right a stimulus is. Patients with right parietal damage, for example, tend to neglect the left to a greater extent than the right, no matter where the boundaries of perceived objects lay. This fundamentally spatial limitation of attention cannot be explained in terms of object-based attentional processes.

It is, of course, possible that visual attention has both location-based components and object-based components. The following experiments test the possibility that there is an object-based component of attention contributing to neglect patients' performance, as well as the more obvious location-based component.

Object-based Attention in Neglect

We set out to discover whether or not object representations play a role in the distribution of attention in neglect. Eight right parietal-damaged patients with left neglect were given a visual search task, in which they had to name all of the letters they could see in a scattered array. Figure 6.3 shows the two types of stimuli that were used. The patients were simply asked to read as many letters as they could see, and tell us when they were finished. Note that the blob objects are completely irrelevant to the task. Of course, they are perceived by at least some levels of the visual system, and so the question is what, if anything, does that do to the distribution of attention over the stimulus field?

If attention is object-based as well as location-based, then there will be a tendency for entire blobs to be either attended or non-attended, in addition to the tendency for the right to be attended and the left to be non-attended. This leads to different predictions for performance with the horizontal and vertical blobs. Each of the horizontal blobs will be at least partially attended because they extend into the right hemifield. On the hypothesis that attention is allocated to entire objects, then even their left side will receive

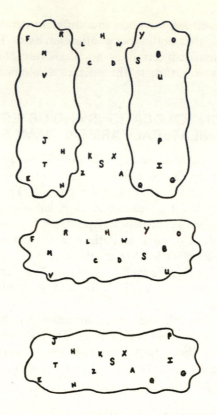

FIG. 6.3. Examples of stimuli used to demonstrate an object-based component to visual attention in neglect patients.

some additional, object-based attention. The hypothesis of object-based attention, therefore, predicts that there will be more attention allocated to the left when the blobs are horizontal and straddle the two sides of space than when they are vertical and each contained within one side. Note that the letters and their locations are perfectly matched for all pairs of horizontal and vertical blobs, so any difference in performance can't be due to differences in the location-based allocation of attention.

We examined two measures of the distribution of attention in the search task. The simplest measure is the number of letters correctly reported from the left-most third of the displays. Consistent with the object-based hypothesis, all but one subject read more letters on the left when the blobs were horizontal and therefore straddled the left and right hemifields. One might wonder whether this measure of performance reflects the effects of the blobs on spatial distribution of attention *per se* over the display, or whether it reflects the effects of the blobs on the subjects' search strategy adopted in the presence of a rightward (i.e. location-based) attentional bias that is not itself affected by the blobs. That is, it is possible that the subjects generally started on the right sides of both kinds of displays, and allowed their search path to be guided by the boundaries of the blobs. This would lead them to read more letters on the left with the horizontal blobs than with the vertical blobs. Our second measure allows us to rule this possibility out. We examined the frequency with which the subjects *started* their searches on the left. Consistent with an effect of the blobs on the distribution of attention at the beginning of each visual search, all of the subjects started reading letters on the left more often with the horizontal blobs than with the vertical blobs.

The results of this experiment suggest that objects do affect the distribution of attention in neglect, and imply that visual attention is object-based as well as location-based. These results do not tell us much about how the visual attention system identifies objects, aside from the low-level figure–ground segregation processes that are required to parse the displays shown in Fig. 6.3 into blob objects. Does knowledge also play a role in determining what the visual attention system takes to be an object?

What Does the Attention System Know about "Objects" in Neglect?

In order to find out whether the damaged attention system in neglect takes knowledge about objects into account when allocating attention, or merely takes objects to be the products of low-level grouping principles, we followed up on a phenomenon first observed by Sieroff, Pollatsek and Posner (1988; Brunn & Farah, 1991). They observed that neglect patients are less likely to neglect the left half of a letter string if the string makes a word than if it makes a nonword. For example, patients are less likely to omit or misread the "t" in "table" than in "tifcl". Sieroff and Posner have assumed that the spatial distribution of attention is the same when reading words and nonwords, and that the difference in reading performance for words and nonwords is attributable to top-down support from word representations "filling in" the missing low-level information. However, there is another possible explanation for the superiority of word over nonword reading in neglect patients, in terms of object-based attentional processes. Just as a blob object straddling the two hemifields causes a reallocation of attention to the leftward extension of the blob, because attention is being allocated to whole blobs, so, perhaps, might a lexical object straddling the two hemifields cause a reallocation of attention to the leftward extension of the word. Of course, this would imply that the "objects" that attention selects can be defined by very abstract properties such as familiarity of pattern, as well as low-level physical features.

In order to test this interpretation of Sieroff and co-workers' observation, and thereby determine whether familiarity can be a determinant of objecthood for the visual attention system, we devised the following two tasks. In one task, we showed word and nonword letter strings printed in different colours, as shown in Fig. 6.4, and asked patients to both read the letters and to name the colours—half read the letters first, half named the colours first. Colour naming is a measure of how well they are perceiving the actual stimulus, independent of whatever top-down support for the orthographic forms there might be. If there is a reallocation of attention to encompass entire objects, in this case lexical objects, then patients should be more accurate at naming the colours on the left sides of words than nonwords. In a second task, we used line bisection to assess the distribution of attention during word and nonword reading. Here, the task was to mark the centre of the line that was presented underneath a letter string. If there is a reallocation of attention to encompass the entire word, then line bisection should be more symmetrical with words than nonwords.

In both tasks, we replicated Seiroff et al., in that more letters from words than nonwords were read in both experiments. Was this despite identical distributions of attention in the two conditions, or was attention allocated more to the leftward sides of word than nonword letter strings? The answer was found by looking at performance in the colour-naming and line-bisection conditions. In both of these tasks, performance was significantly

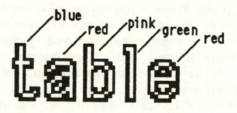

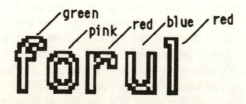

FIG. 6.4. Examples of stimuli used by Brunn and Farah (1991) to demonstrate that the lexicality of letter strings affects the distribution of visual attention in neglect patients.

better with words than nonwords. This implies that lexical "objects", like the blob objects of the previous experiment, tend to draw attention to their entirety. In terms of the issue of what determines objecthood for the allocation of attention, these results suggest that knowledge does indeed play a role.

To summarise the conclusions that can be drawn from these studies of patients with neglect, it appears that attention is both location-based and object-based. Furthermore, the object representations to which attention can be allocated include such abstract objects as words.

ATTENTION TO LOCATIONS AND OBJECTS AFTER BILATERAL PARIETAL DAMAGE

Patients with bilateral posterior parietal damage sometimes display a symptom known as "simultanagnosia", or "dorsal simultanagnosia" (to distinguish this syndrome from a superficially similar but distinct syndrome that follows ventral visual system damage; see Farah, 1990). They may have full visual fields, but are nevertheless able to see only one object at a time. This is manifest in several ways: When shown a complex scene, they will report seeing only one object; when asked to count even a small number of items, they will lose track of each object as soon as they have counted it and therefore tend to recount it again; if their attention is focused on one object, they will fail to see even so salient a stimulus as the examiner's finger being thrust suddenly towards their face. Not surprisingly, given the typical lesions causing this syndrome, these patients have been described as having a kind of bilateral neglect (e.g. Bauer & Rubens, 1985).

Like neglect, dorsal simultanagnosia seems to involve both location- and object-based limitations on attention. Many authors report better performance with small, foveally located stimuli (e.g. Holmes, 1918; Tyler, 1968), demonstrating the role of spatial limitations on the attentional capacities of these patients. In addition, simultanagnosic patients tend to see one object at a time. Luria and colleagues provided some particularly clear demonstrations of the object-limited nature of the impairment. In one experiment (Luria, Pravdina-Vinarskaya, & Yarbuss, 1963), a patient was shown simple shapes and line drawings, such as a circle, cross, carrot or fork, in a tachistoscope. He could name the stimuli when presented one at a time, whether they were small (6–8°) or large (15–20°). However, when shown simultaneously, even at the smaller size, the patient could not name both. Note that the angle subtended by the pair of smaller stimuli would have been no larger than a single large stimulus. This confirms that there is an object limitation *per se*, rather than a spatial limitation, in the subject's ability to attend to visual stimuli.

Given that the limitation of attention seems not to depend upon size *per se*, is it truly a function of number of objects, or is it merely a limitation on some measure of complexity? The foregoing observations by Luria are consistent with both possibilities, as two shapes taken together are more complex than one. Luria provides some insightful demonstrations to answer this question as well. In a study with a different patient, Luria (1959) presented brief tachistoscopic displays of the kind shown in Fig. 6.5a. He found that both objects were more likely to be seen if he simply connected them with a line! Godwin-Austen (1965) and Humphreys and Riddoch (in press) have replicated this finding with similar patients. This suggests that complexity, in the simple sense of amount of information or contour, is not a limiting factor. Because a line connecting two shapes makes them more likely to be grouped as a single object by Gestalt mechanisms, we can infer that low-level geometric properties of a stimulus, such as continuity or connectivity, help define what the visual attention system takes to be an "object". Luria also presented two versions of the Star of David to this patient (Fig. 6.5b). In one version, the two triangles of the star were the same colour, and would thus group together as a single object, and in the other version the triangles were different colours and therefore more likely to be seen as two distinct but superimposed objects. Consistent with a limitation in number of objects, rather than spatial region or complexity, the patient reported seeing a star in the first kind of display and a single triangle in the second.

The reading ability of patients with dorsal simultanagnosia is also informative about the nature of their attentional limitation. Recall that in neglect, words act more like objects than nonwords, from the point of view of attentional allocation. This is generally true in simultanagnosia as well.

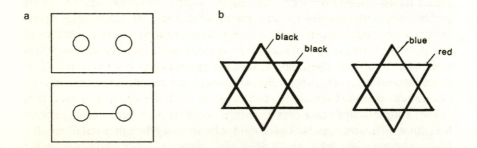

FIG. 6.5.   Examples of stimuli used by Luria (1959) to demonstrate object-based attentional limitations in a dorsal simultanagnosic patient. The patient was more likely to see multiple shapes if they were connected by a line, as shown in (a). When the star shown in (b) was presented in a single colour, the patient saw a star, but when each component triangle was drawn in a different colour, he saw only a single triangle.

Many cases are reported to see a word at a time, regardless of its length or the size of the print.

CONCLUSIONS

Evidence from unilaterally and bilaterally parietal-damaged subjects converges with evidence from normal subjects to suggest that visual attention is allocated to representations of both locations and objects. Let us consider some of the implications of this for our understanding of visual attention and its physiological substrates.

Representation and Visual Attention

The hypotheses of location-based and object-based attention were originally put forth by cognitive psychologists and supported by evidence from normal subjects. However, like any single source of evidence, the research with normal subjects is open to alternative explanations. Neuropsychological evidence is therefore a valuable source of additional constraints on the nature of the representations used by attention. The fundamentally spatial (i.e. left *vs* right) nature of the attentional limitation of neglect patients provides strong evidence that visual attention acts on representations of spatial location. In addition, in experiments with neglect patients in which location was held constant, we found evidence for a distinct object-based component of attention as well. Perhaps the most dramatic evidence for object-based attention comes from the study of patients with bilateral parietal damage. The most salient limitation on what can and cannot be attended to in dorsal simultanagnosia is the limitation on the number of objects, almost entirely independent of the complexity or size of the objects.

In addition to complementing the evidence from normal subjects to object-based attention, the neuropsychological evidence also tells us something new about object-based attention, namely that knowledge-based factors such as familiarity and meaningfulness help to determine what the attention system takes to be an object. In contrast to objects such as boxes and lines, which can be individuated on the basis of relatively low-level visual properties such as continuity, words can be identified as objects, distinct from nonwords, only with the use of knowledge. The fact that neglect patients allocate attention differently to words and nonwords, and that dorsal simultanagnosics tend to see whole words and whole complex objects, suggests that the attention system has access to considerable object knowledge.

One possible confusion concerning the role of objects in the allocation of attention involves the frames of reference used in allocating attention to locations in space (see Chapter 9, this volume). In a previously reported study, we found that right parietal-damaged patients neglect the left side of space relative to their own bodies and relative to the fixed environment, but not relative to the intrinsic left/right of an object (Farah et al., 1990). That is, when they recline sideways, the allocation of their attention is determined by where their personal left is (up or down with respect to the fixed environment) as well as where the left side of the environment is. In contrast, when neglect patients view an object with an intrinsic left and right (such as a telephone) turned sideways, the allocation of their attention is not altered. This is not inconsistent with the hypothesis that neglect patients allocate attention to objects. Rather, it implies that, when neglect patients allocate attention to *locations*, those locations are represented with respect to two different co-ordinate systems—viewer-centred and environment-centred— but not to an object-centred co-ordinate system. In other words, attention is allocated to objects as well as to locations, but objects do not help to determine which locations the attention system takes to be "left" and "right".

Visual Attention and the Two Cortical Visual Systems

An influential organising framework in visual neurophysiology has come to be known as the "two cortical visual systems" hypothesis (Ungerleider & Mishkin, 1982). According to this hypothesis, higher visual perception is carried out by two relatively distinct neural pathways with distinct functions. The dorsal visual system, going from occipital cortex through posterior parietal cortex, is concerned with representing the spatial characteristics of visual stimuli, primarily their location in space. Animals with lesions of the dorsal visual system are impaired on tasks involving location discrimination, but perform normally on tasks involving pattern discrimination. Single-cell recordings show that neurons in this region of the brain respond to stimuli dependent primarily on the location of the stimuli, and not their shape or colour. The ventral visual system, going from occipital cortex through inferotemporal cortex, is concerned with representing the properties of stimuli normally used for identification, such as shape and colour. Animals with lesions disrupting this pathway are impaired at tasks that involve shape and colour discrimination, but perform normally on most tasks involving spatial discriminations. Consistent with these findings, recordings from single neurons in inferotemporal cortex reveal little spatial selectivity for location or orientation, but high degrees of selectivity for shape and colour. Some neurons in this area respond selectively to shapes as complex as a hand or even a particular individual's face.

The findings reviewed earlier seem in conflict with the classical view of the two cortical visual systems, in that patients with bilateral damage to the dorsal system suffer a limitation on object-based attention as well as location-based attention. The results from dorsal simultanagnosics and neglect patients seem to imply that the dorsal visual system represents objects, even words. Actually, these results imply only that the dorsal visual system is part of an interactive network, other parts of which have object and word knowledge. An outline of one possible model that would account for these results was proposed by Farah (1990) and is shown in Fig. 6.6.

According to the ideas sketched out in Fig. 6.6, the effects of objects on the allocation of attention can be explained as a result of interactions between the object representations needed for object recognition and the array-format representation of the visual field that is operated on by attention. One of the basic problems in object recognition is to parse the array into regions that correspond to objects, which can then be recognised. This is a difficult problem because objects in the real world often overlap and occlude each other. One good source of help in segmenting the visual field into objects is our knowledge of what objects look like. Unfortunately, this puts us in a chicken-and-egg situation, in that the configuration of features in the array can be used to determine what objects are being seen, but we need to know what objects are being seen to figure out how to parse the features in order to feed them into the object recognition system. A good solution to this kind of problem is what McClelland and Rumelhart (1981) call an interactive activation system, in which the contents of the array put constraints on the set of candidate objects *at the same time as* the set of candidate objects put constraints on how the contents of the array should be segmented. What this means in terms of activation flow in Fig. 6.6 is that the contents of the array are activating certain object representations in the ventral visual system, and that the activated object representations are simultaneously activating the regions of the array that correspond to an object.

The interactive activation relation between the object representations and the array-format representation of the visual field implies that there are two

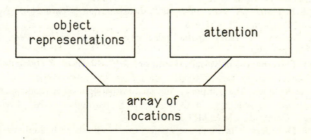

FIG. 6.6. A sketch of the possible relations between location-based representations of the visual world, visual attention, and object representations based on Farah (1990).

sources of activation in the array, both of which will have the potential to engage the dorsal attention system: bottom-up activation from stimulus input, and top-down activation from object representations. Whereas stimulus input can activate any arbitrary configuration of locations, top-down activation from the object system will activate *regions of the array that correspond to objects*. Thus, the dorsal attention system will tend to be engaged by regions of the array that are occupied by objects, including objects defined by the kinds of knowledge stored in the ventral visual system. Whether or not this is the correct interpretation of the object-based attention effects in normal and brain-damaged subjects awaits further experimental tests. At present, it is useful merely as a demonstration that one need not abandon the basic assumptions of the two cortical visual systems hypothesis in order to account for object effects in the attentional limitations of parietal-damaged patients.

ACKNOWLEDGEMENTS

Preparation of this chapter was supported by ONR grant NS0014-89-J3016, NIH career development award K04-NS01405 and NIMH training grant 1-T32-MH19102.

REFERENCES

Bauer, R.M. & Rubens, A.B, (1985). Agnosia. In K.M. Heilman & E. Valenstein (Eds), *Clinical neuropsychology*. New York: Oxford University Press.
Brunn, J.L. & Farah, M.J. (1991). The relation between spatial attention and reading: Evidence from the neglect syndrome. *Cognitive Neuropsychology, 8,* 59–75.
Duncan, J. (1984). Selective attention and the organization of visual information. *Journal of Experimental Psychology: General, 113,* 501–517.
Farah, M.J. (1990). *Visual agnosia: Disorders of object recognition and what they tell us about normal vision.* Cambridge MA: MIT Press.
Farah, M.J., Brunn, J.L., Wong, A.B., Wallace, M., & Carpenter, P.A. (1990). Frames of reference for allocation of spatial attenation: Evidence from the neglect syndrome. *Neuropsychologia, 28,* 335–347.
Godwin-Austen, R.B. (1965). A case of visual disorientation. *Journal of Neurology, Neurosurgery and Psychiatry, 28,* 453–458.
Hoffman, J.E. & Nelson, B. (1981). Spatial selectivity in visual search. *Perception and Psychophysics, 30,* 283–290.
Holmes, G. (1918). Disturbances of visual orientation. *British Journal of Ophthalmology, 2,* 449–468, 506–518.
Humphreys, G.W. & Riddoch, M.J. (in press). Interactions between object and space systems revealed through neuropsychology. In D. Meyer & S. Kornblum (Eds), *Attention and Performance XIV.* Cambridge, MA: MIT Press.
Luria, A.R. (1959). Disorders of "simultaneous perception" in a case of bilateral occipitoparietal brain injury. *Brain, 83,* 437–449.
Luria, A.R., Pravdina-Vinarskaya, E.N., & Yarbuss, A.L. (1963). Disorders of ocular movement in a case of simultanagnosia. *Brain, 86,* 219–228.

McClelland, J.L. & Rumelhart, D.E. (1981). An interactive activation model of context effects in letter perception: Part 1. An account of basic findings. *Psychological Review*, *88*, 375–407.

Posner, M.I. & Cohen, Y. (1984). Components of visual orienting. In H. Bouma & D.G. Bouwhuis (Eds), *Attention and performance X: Control of language processes*, pp. 531–556. Hove: Lawrence Erlbaum Associates Ltd.

Posner, M.I., Snyder, C.R.R., & Davidson, B.J. (1980). Attention and the detection of signals. *Journal of Experimental Psychology: General*, *109*, 160–174.

Shulman, G.L., Remington, R.W., & McLean, J.P. (1979). Moving attention through visual space. *Journal of Experimental Psychology: Human Perception and Performance*, *5*, 522–526.

Sieroff, E., Pollatsek, A., & Posner, M.I. (1988). Recognition of visual letter strings following injury to the posterior visual spatial attention system. *Cognitive Neuropsychology*, *5*, 427–449.

Tyler, H.R. (1968). Abnormalities of perception with defective eye movements (Balint's syndrome). *Cortex*, *3*, 154–171.

Ungerleider, L.G. & Mishkin, M. (1982). Two cortical visual systems. In D.J. Ingle, M.A. Goodale, & R.J.W. Mansfield (Eds), *Analysis of visual behavior*, Cambridge, MA: MIT Press.

7

Interactive Attentional Systems and Unilateral Visual Neglect

Glyn W. Humphreys and M. Jane Riddoch
Cognitive Science Research Centre, School of Psychology,
University of Birmingham, Birmingham, UK

INTRODUCTION

Patients with unilateral visual neglect exhibit a range of behavioural phenomena. Most obviously, the patients may fail to respond to stimuli presented on the side of space contralateral to their lesion—they may fail to eat food on one side of the plate, to cancel lines on one side of a sheet, to draw one half of an object, or to read words on one side of a text. Patients may tend to under-use the limbs on one side of their body, even though movement and sensation are intact (e.g. LaPlane & Degos, 1983). They may also deny the existence of any behavioural difficulties (McGlynn & Schacter, 1989). These different behavioural manifestations likely reflect functionally separate, though frequently co-occurring disorders, and indeed, at least some of these different symptoms dissociate from one another (e.g. Bisiach et al., 1986; LaPlane & Degos, 1983). Our concern in this chapter is not with the neglect syndrome in general, but with unilateral visual neglect in particular. By this term, we refer to specific problems that patients may exhibit in responding to visual stimuli presented contralateral to the side of their lesion. Thus our usage of the generic term "neglect" should be understood in this rather more limited application. The functional account of unilateral visual neglect that we offer is unlikely to apply to all aspects of the neglect syndrome.

Our discussion of unilateral visual neglect is focused on a distinction between two representational and three attentional theories. By a representational theory, we refer to the possibility that, following brain damage, a patient may have impairment to some form of visual representation which makes explicit particular kinds of information about a stimulus. By an attentional theory, we refer to the possibility that there may be an impairment within a system that usually modulates our ability to orient to and select stimuli in the visual world. Our assumption is that an orienting process is involved when we move our attention from one object to another. Movements of attention are required in order that new objects are selected for purposeful actions; unattended objects are not selected for action. We return to justify these assumptions. For now we simply note that neglect may be due to patients failing to attend correctly to visual objects. Both representational and attentional accounts will need to explain why neglect is characteristically spatial (as indicated by the term unilateral visual neglect), and how it can result from damage to a normal visual processing system.

REPRESENTATIONAL ACCOUNTS

Bisiach's Account

In their classic study of neglect, Bisiach and Luzzati (1978) asked patients to imagine and report on the buildings in the Piazza del Duomo in Milan. Patients with neglect following a right hemisphere lesion often either failed to report buildings on the left-hand side of the imagined square or they transposed such buildings from the left to the right side of the square; when asked to image from the other side of the square, the patients then neglected the formerly reported buildings (now on the left) and reported the formerly neglected buildings (now on the right). The above result shows that the patients' long-term knowledge of the buildings present in the square was not impaired. Bisiach and Luzzati argued rather that the temporary visual representation, used when imaging the square, was impaired (in particular, the representation for the left half of space was impaired). Further, the same visual representation may mediate everyday visual interactions with the world. Consequently, patients neglect both on imagery tasks and on tasks requiring more direct interactions with the visual environment, such as copying and line cancellation.

Bisiach and Luzzati's account highlights the role of a common representational format in on-line visual interactions and in visual imagery tasks. The nature of the visual representation, the kind of co-ordinate system on which it may be based and thus the kinds of information it makes explicit, was left unspecified. A more articulated representational account has been proposed by Caramazza and Hillis (1990; Rapp & Caramazza, 1991).

Caramazza and Hillis's Account

The account proposed by Caramazza and Hillis (1990) picks up on the kinds of distinction made by Marr (1982) in his general framework for visual processing. Marr distinguished between at least three separate representations mediating object recognition: the primal sketch, the 2½D sketch and the 3D model representation. These representations were distinguished in various ways, including the nature of the co-ordinate system on which they were based, and the primitives defining each representation. The primal sketch and the 2½D sketch, for example, were specified in terms of retinal co-ordinates, so that they preserved information about the relations between the viewer and a represented object. The 3D model representation, in contrast, was presumed to be based on a co-ordinate system whose axes were defined by major geometric characteristics of the represented object; that is, its co-ordinate system was object- rather than viewer-centred. Thus the 3D model representation codes an object in such a way that the resultant description remains invariant with respect to changes in viewpoint. In addition to these differences, the primitives defining the representations differ: The primitives of the primal sketch are contrast-defined edges, those of the 2½D sketch are surface-based orientation vectors, and those of the 3D model representation are volumetric solids.

Marr's suggestion, then, was that multiple descriptions of objects are elaborated during object processing, and that this is *necessarily* the case as these descriptions serve different computational purposes in making different kinds of information explicit. In addition to this, we can add that these descriptions ultimately also subserve different classes of behaviour: Viewpoint-preserving representations will link closely to reaching and locomotion actions, where the spatial relations between the viewer and the world need to be maintained; viewpoint-invariant representations may serve object recognition, enabling the same stored representations to be accessed even when objects are seen from different points of view.

Caramazza and Hillis extend Marr's argument to the task of reading (see also Monk, 1985, for a similar extension). They propose that separate representations are created en route to word recognition. Like Marr, they outline three representations—termed the feature map, the letter shape map and the graphemic description. The feature map can be thought similar to the primal sketch, in that it is based on a retinal co-ordinate system and its primitives are contrast-defined edges. The letter shape map differs from this in two respects. First, its primitives are letter shapes, as opposed to individually coded features (i.e. the features are combined into units). Secondly, its co-ordinate system is said to be string-centred (Caramazza & Hillis, 1990, p. 394), as opposed to being retinally centred. By the term string-centred, Caramazza and Hillis refer to a representation centred on the centre of a letter string rather than the retina. Nevertheless, the dimensions of this representation appear to be fixed by the current view. For instance, the first letter in an English word will normally be assigned a co-ordinate on the left of centre of the letter string map; however, if the word is written from right-to-left, the same letter will then be assigned a co-ordinate on the right of centre. If the word is written vertically, with the first letter at the top, we may presume that the first letter is assigned a co-ordinate to the top of centre in the letter string map. Thus, the dimensions left, right, top, bottom are viewer-based. The third representation, the grapheme description, differs again, in that its primitives are abstract graphemes (letters or letter pairs corresponding to individual phonemes), and these are represented within a "word-centred" representation. This word-centred representation is similar to the above string-centred representation in that it is centred on the middle of a letter string; it differs in that the dimensions are determined by the positions of letters in the word. Now when written right-to-left, a word will be assigned the same grapheme-based representation as when written left-to-right, since the letters fall in the same positions within the word. Since it, too, remains invariant with respect to view and position-shifts, the grapheme-based representation can be thought equivalent to Marr's 3D model representation mediating object recognition. Figure 7.1 provides an illustration of these different hypothesised representations.

Armed with this theoretical distinction between different types of representation, Caramazza and Hillis propose that different patterns of neglect may be expected due to impairment to the different forms of representation. Degradation of one side of the feature map will be akin to a hemianopia; the patient will neglect stimuli that fall on one side of the retina. Unilateral degradation of a letter-shape map will differ in that neglect will occur for letters which lie retinally to the left or right of the centre of the string, but the precise location of the letters on the retina should not matter. Unilateral neglect of a grapheme description will produce a third pattern of neglect, in which letters to one side of the beginning or end of the string will be impaired, irrespective of whether they fall to the right or left of the centre of the string in retinal space.

Evidence consistent with these distinctions between different types of representation mediating word recognition comes from case studies of neglect dyslexic patients (see also Chapter 11, this volume). Following right hemisphere brain damage, patients can make selective reading errors in which they misidentify letters at the *beginnings* of English words (e.g. Ellis, Flude, & Young, 1987; Riddoch, Humphreys, Cleton, & Fery, 1990). This can occur even when the words are projected into the right visual field, ruling out a problem in representing letters on the left-hand side of a retinal

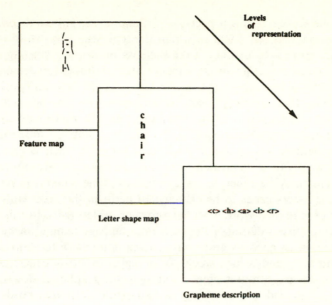

FIG. 7.1.   A framework illustrating Caramazza and Hillis's (1990) account of the different representations mediating visual word recognition.

feature-map (Young, Newcome & Ellis, 1991). In some cases, when the words are inverted, the patients misidentify letters at the *end* of the words (though the ends of words are correctly identified when the words are written normally; Ellis et al., 1987; Riddoch et al., 1990). This is consistent with the patients having problems recovering letters that fall in the same location in the letter-shape map, since the beginnings of normally written words and the ends of inverted words would both fall to the left of centre within such a map. Caramazza and Hillis (1990) reported a neglect dyslexic patient who showed a rather different type of problem. This patient suffered a left hemisphere lesion, producing neglect of items on the right side of space (e.g. letters at the ends of words were misidentified; also the patient bisected lines to the left of centre, neglecting the right). Interestingly, when words were inverted, the patient continued to have problems identifying the end letters, even though they now appeared on the *opposite* side of space, as coded within either a feature- or a letter-shape map. Caramazza and Hillis propose that this patient has an impaired grapheme description, impairing the identification of letters that fall to the right of centre in this description. Since the description is word-centred, the same letters (in this case at the end of the word) will be neglected both when a word is written normally and when it is inverted.

There remain some puzzling aspects to Caramazza and Hillis's theoretical account. One concerns the extent to which the representations within their framework are specific to reading. Take the case of an anagram (e.g. *hte*). When asked to read this as a word, the reader may be thought to construct a grapheme description in which the letters are assigned different positions relative to each other, in comparison to their positions on the page (*the* rather than *hte*). However, this can obviously only be done with known words (in the grapheme description for *the*, the *t* can only be coded to the left of the *h* because *the* is a known lexical item). In such a case, the grapheme description is dependent on the existence of stored lexical knowledge. This may be taken as an extreme example where the relative ordering of the letters needs to be changed to perform the task. However, take the case of reading a word written from right-to-left (*eht*). In this case, aspects of the relative ordering of the letters on the page remain unchanged when the string is assigned its graphemic description (e.g. *h* remains at the centre). A coding system which works from right- to left-of-centre of the letter string on the page, and assigns a coding in the graphemic description from beginning to end of the string, would work both for words and nonwords. Even so, the construction of the graphemic description depends on knowledge specific to reading English (e.g. that letters are read from left-to-right, so that letters at the beginning of the string need to be assigned to the left end of the grapheme description). The rules to construct this representation would thus differ for other languages (e.g. Hebrew, which is written right-to-left), and for more general visual processing (e.g. visual object recognition, where left-to-right or "handedness" assignment seems less important; cf. Hinton & Parsons, 1981). Thus the procedures for generating grapheme descriptions, and the resulting representations, may be specific to reading; in some cases, they may depend on lexical knowledge, in others they may require directionally specific processes which map letters onto lexical knowledge. This overall account may be less satisfying when applied to neglect in tasks other than reading (e.g. line bisection).

Is there evidence for impairment of similar high-level representations in object processing? Driver and Halligan (1991) had patients match shapes in which the differences could occur either to the right or left of the main axis of the shapes. The shapes could also be rotated on the page, so that a difference could occur in the left side of the shape's main axis, but on the right side of the page (when the shape was rotated). They showed that at least some right hemisphere neglect patients missed differences on the left side of the main axis of shapes, even when the differences were on the right side of the page. In such cases, the problem seems linked to a form of representation centred about the shape's main axis (i.e. a problem within an "object-centred representation"). Note that the procedures for generating such an object-centred representation will likely differ from those involved in generating grapheme descriptions in reading. For example, procedures for generating object-centred representations may well depend on encoding salient geometrical characteristics of an object, such as its main axis and its top apex, to serve as a perceptual reference frame (cf. Humphreys, 1983; Marr & Nashihara, 1978), and relating parts of the object to this frame. Procedures for generating grapheme descriptions seem to depend on beginning-to-end orderings of letters. It remains likely that the high-level representations mediating object and word recognition differ. Impairment to one form of representation should not necessarily be related to impairments to the other.

ATTENTIONAL ACCOUNTS

At least three attentional accounts of unilateral neglect can be distinguished, according to whether neglect is thought to be due to: (1) impaired orienting of attention to the neglected side; (2) overly strong orienting of attention to stimuli presented ipsilesionally; and (3) the impaired disengagement of attention once it is oriented to the ipsilesional side. Attentional accounts of neglect have typically been considered because: (1) neglect can be ameliorated by cueing patients to attend to the neglected side (see the section on Impaired Orienting of Attention) and (2) neglect can be exacerbated by presenting stimuli on the non-neglected side simultaneously with stimuli on the neglected side (the phenomenon of extinction). Thus processes sensitive to voluntary (attentional) control, and to competition for selection between simultaneous events (e.g. for identification responses), seem to play a part in the syndrome. We consider each attentional account in turn.

Impaired Orienting of Attention

Riddoch and Humphreys (1983; see also Humphreys & Riddoch, 1992) proposed that neglect occurred because of impaired orienting of attention to stimuli presented contralesionally to the side of current attentional fixation. They had patients carry out a line bisection task and showed that bisection accuracy could be improved by cueing patients to attend voluntarily to the neglected side. Without cueing, patients bisected lines towards the unaffected side. Riddoch and Humphreys suggested that neglect patients bisect lines incorrectly because of an impairment to the processes that normally detect and orient attention in a data-driven way to the end of the line on the neglected side. Nevertheless, processes governing the voluntary control of attention remain intact, so that patients may attend to the neglected side when so instructed. Somewhat similar cueing effects on line bisection have been reported by Halligan, Manning and Marshall (1991), when they placed the patient's hand on the left rather than the right end of the lines to be bisected. Hallilgan et al. suggest that the position of the hand facilitates the patients orienting their attention towards the neglected side of space.

A related proposal was made by Heilman and colleagues (e.g. Heilman & Valenstein, 1979), who tied problems in attentional orienting to right hemisphere lesions. They suggested that the right hemisphere normally controls orienting responses on both sides of space, while the left hemisphere only controls orienting to the contralateral side. Hence problems in orienting attention to left-side signals occur after right hemisphere damage (since the left hemisphere only supports orienting to right-side stimuli); corresponding problems do not occur after left hemisphere damage because the right hemisphere remains capable of supporting orienting responses to stimuli on both sides. The ability of the right hemisphere to support orienting responses to stimuli on both sides of space can be related to the association between neglect and right hemisphere lesions.

Overly Strong Orienting to Ipsilesional Stimuli

A rather different account is that neglect occurs not because of impaired "contralesional orienting" but because of overly strong orienting to the ipsilesional side (see also Chapters 3, 5 and 9, this volume). For example, Làdavas and colleagues (e.g. Làdavas, 1990; Làdavas, Menghini, & Umilta, in press) have argued this based on evidence that right hemisphere patients showing neglect can show faster reaction times (RTs) to targets presented in their right visual field than to targets presented at the centre of the field, when items are presented randomly at different spatial locations. Further, RTs to right-side targets may change little even when the field of presentation is blocked, consistent with these patients chronically orienting attention to the right, under both blocked and random field presentation conditions.

Impaired Disengagement of Attention

The third attentional account, most notably associated with the work of Posner and colleagues (e.g. Posner, Cohen, & Rafal, 1982; Posner, Walker, Friedrich, & Rafal, 1984) holds that neglect is caused by a problem in disengaging attention once it is captured by stimuli presented on the side of space ipsilateral to the lesion. Much of the argument for there being a disengagement problem in neglect is based around the effects of spatial cueing on detection performance in neglect patients. The detection of briefly presented visual stimuli can be facilitated when subjects are cued to their likely location (e.g. Posner, 1980). The facilitatory effects of spatial cueing can be found in patients with right parietal lesions when targets are presented both to their left and to their right visual field. Thus the patients could shift attention to the neglected (left) side when so instructed (see the orienting account, given above). However, when instructed to shift attention into the intact hemifield (i.e. to the right), subjects were then markedly impaired at responding to stimuli presented on the contralesional (left) side. This marked effect of orienting attention incorrectly did not occur when attention was oriented into the impaired field (the left) and targets appeared on the intact (right) side. Posner et al. (1984) argue that the effect of incorrect cueing on the left-side targets arose because the patients had difficulty disengaging attention once it was engaged on right-side cues.

Note that this account differs from the strong ipsilesional-orienting account, in that, according to the disengagement account, patients would not be expected to orient to the non-neglected side in a field absence of stimuli. Consistent with this, d'Erme, Gainotti, Bartolomeo and Robertson (1992) have shown that neglect in detection tasks is increased when stimuli (boxes) are left in the visual field in between trials, with the stimuli to-be-detected being presented within the boxes. Problems in disengaging attention would be expected on occasions when patients engage their attention upon a box in the ipsilateral field.

RELATIONS BETWEEN THE ATTENTIONAL ACCOUNTS: AN INTERACTIVE ATTENTIONAL NETWORK

The three attentional accounts outlined above lay stress on an impairment of one attentional process: either impaired orienting to neglect-side stimuli, overly strong orienting to the non-neglected side, or impaired disengagement of attention from stimuli on the non-neglected side. However, in normality it is likely that attentional operations are determined by a complex network, with several components serving different computational purposes. For instance, normally, the processes that engage and maintain attention upon a given object may interact in an antagonistic way with processes that detect and orient attention to new, salient stimuli at particular locations; also, both of these processes may interact in an inhibitory manner with processes that shift attention voluntarily to a new location (see Humphreys & Riddoch, 1992). Each of these processes, attentional engagement and maintenance, orienting to salient stimuli ("data-driven orienting") and voluntary orienting, can be thought of as a separate component within an attentional network. Activation of the module concerned with data-driven orienting will lead to inhibition of the module concerned with maintaining attention, and also that concerned with voluntarily orienting attention (at least when attention is directed to different locations by the data-driven and voluntary orienting modules). Similarly, maintenance of attention upon an object will lead to inhibition of the orienting modules. A framework outlining this idea of interacting modules within an attentional network is shown in Figure 7.2.

According to this interacting-modules account, an impairment to one component of the network could lead to apparent problems within other components. For instance, consider the possibility that there is a deficit within the orienting module so that either salient differences on one side of space are not registered, or there is a lack of orienting to such differences. This will lead to there being problems in disengaging attention to stimuli presented on the opposite side, since the orienting component will no longer inhibit the maintenance mechanism when salient stimuli are presented on the affected side. Also, although some deficit in orienting to and detecting stimuli on the affected side may be apparent when attention is not engaged on other stimuli, the effects should be exacerbated when attention is maintained elsewhere, since the orienting mechanism should then be subject to inhibition. Posner and co-workers' (1984) work on cueing attention in parietal patients is consistent with this. Remember that Posner et al. found that RTs to stimuli on the contralesional side were particularly impaired when patients were incorrectly cued to the ipsilesional side. In addition, RTs were slower to contralesional than to ipsilesional stimuli even when patients were cued correctly (though this effect was much smaller than the effect when attention was cued incorrectly). This fits with the idea that there is a residual problem in orienting attention to the contralesional side, which is worsened by having patients first disengage attention. A problem in contralesional orienting could also lead to overly strong ipsilesional orienting, since in an environment where visual differences on the

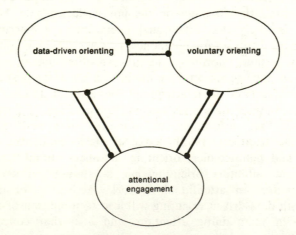

FIG. 7.2.   A framework illustrating three different attentional modules and the way in which these modules might interact in a mutually inhibitory way.

ipsilesional and contralesional sides are equally salient, ipsilesional orienting will dominate.

The interactive-modules account is supported by several findings in the normal literature. For instance, work on so-called "express saccades" (e.g. Fischer, 1986) has shown that the time to initiate saccades to briefly presented peripheral signals is slowed when subjects engage attention elsewhere in the field. If we take saccade initiation time as an indicator of attentional orienting, this work suggests that the orienting response can be inhibited by attentional engagement (see Walker, Findlay, Young, & Welch, 1991, for evidence of a similar but exaggerated effect in neglect patients). Yantis and Jonides (1990) have also shown that the distracting effect of a peripherally presented distractor can be eliminated by having subjects voluntarily engage attention elsewhere, consistent with an automatic orienting mechanism being inhibited by voluntary orienting to another location. Contrasting results come from the work of Müller and Rabbitt (1989), who showed that voluntary orienting to an informative cue could be disrupted by a brief peripheral distractor. The contrast between Müller and Rabbitt's (1989) work and that of Yantis and Jonides (1990) likely reflects the informativeness of the cue for voluntary attention. Inhibition of the data-driven orienting response to the peripheral signal seems only to occur when the cue for voluntary attentional is highly likely to be correct. Here we might think that inhibition of data-driven orienting is directly correlated with the validity of the cue for voluntary attention. However, unless the cue is highly valid, and the voluntary orienting module strongly activated, inhibition from the data-driven module tends to dominate.

SEPARATING THE ACCOUNTS

Can these different accounts of unilateral neglect, both attentional and representational, be separated? In the following sections, we discuss recent research from our laboratory in which we have attempted to tease the different accounts apart.

Controlling for Overly Strong Ipsilesional Orienting

A strong prediction arises from the idea that neglect is due to overly strong orienting to ipsilesional stimuli, namely that neglect should be affected by the nature of the stimulus information in the ipsilesional rather than the contralesional field. The nature of the stimuli in the contralesional field should have little effect, since attention is oriented away from them, to the ipsilesional side.

This prediction can be evaluated in various ways. Consider a visual search task in which a patient is asked to decide whether a given target is present in a visual display. The similarity of the target to the non-targets present can be varied, and search typically becomes more difficult as target–non-target similarity increases (e.g. Duncan & Humphreys, 1989). In the case of neglect patients, the non-targets in the ipsilesional field can be held constant. The question then is, does target–non-target similarity within the contralesional field affect performance? To the extent that only the stimuli in the ipsilesional field are important, the answer to this question should be no.

We have evaluated this in a number of patients showing clear clinical signs of neglect after right parietal lesions (e.g. impaired copying and cancellation; see Riddoch & Humphreys, 1987a). In one search task, patients were asked to decide whether a 45° oriented T target was present among a set of upright (0°) T non-targets; in another, using the same non-targets, the patients were asked to decide whether an inverted T was present. Search for a 45° oriented T is normally considerably easier than search for an inverted T among upright T non-targets (e.g. see Humphreys, Quinlan, & Riddoch, 1989), reflecting the increased similarity of T's and inverted T's (which both contain horizontal and vertical line components) relative to T's and 45° oriented T's (which differ in the orientations of their line components). The main question of interest is: Does detection performance differ for the two types of targets in the contralesional field, when the number of non-targets are kept the same in the ipsilesional field?

Illustrative data are shown in Fig. 7.3, which gives the percentage of correct responses for one right parietal patient, I.J., as a function of the display size (the number of non-targets present within each quadrant of a centrally presented card) in the two search tasks (T *vs* inverted T; T *vs* 45° oriented T). The results indicate that I.J. was worse at detecting targets on the left relative to the right side of a central fixation point, consistent with there being left-side neglect. In addition, the proportion of left-side errors increased in the inverted T relative to the 45° T search task. Note that, in the two search tasks, the non-targets were the same. If I.J.'s neglect was due to chronic ipsilesional orienting, her performance should have been equivalent in the two conditions, since there was no variation in the information present (from non-targets) in the ipsilesional field. Rather, the results show the sensitivity of left-side detections to target–non-target similarity.

The results shown in Fig. 7.3 may of course reflect a general difference between search for a target defined by a single disjunctive feature relative to distractors (T *vs* 45° oriented T), and search for a target defined by a conjunction of features (T *vs* inverted T; which are distinguished only by the conjunction of horizontal and vertical line features). Neglect may be particularly severe for conjunctive stimuli, perhaps because neglect reflects a lack of attention to the contralesional side, so disrupting the coding of conjunctions which are correctly coded only when focally attended (e.g. Treisman, 1988; see Riddoch & Humphreys, 1987a, for discussion of this

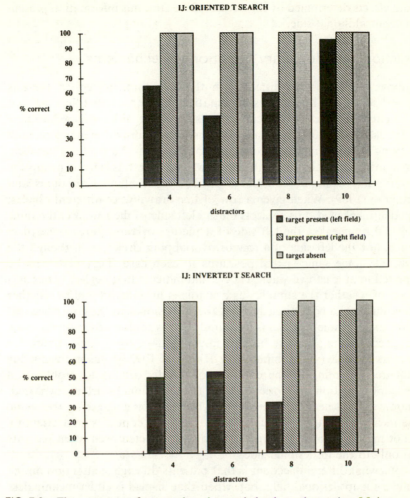

FIG. 7.3. The percentage of correct detection made by the neglect patient I.J. in two visual search tasks: search for a 45° oriented T or for an inverted T against upright T distractors. The data are given for present responses to targets presented to the left and right of a central fixation cross, and for absent responses.

point). Other experiments suggest that this is not the full account. For instance, we have found essentially similar effects in search for disjunctive feature targets as the saliency of the target decreases relative to non-targets (e.g. see Humphreys & Riddoch, 1992). The effect is not confined to search for conjunctive targets.

It is clear that the relative saliency of the contralesional stimulus can determine the amount of neglect. Any explanation of neglect must take into account effects determined by the nature of the stimulus information present on the contralesional side.

Interaction with Voluntary Attentional Mechanisms

The above evidence is consistent with the idea that, in neglect, there is decreased sensitivity to stimulus information in the neglected field, so that only salient differences are detectable. This fits either with the idea that there is a decreased orienting response to salient stimulus differences, or with there being impaired representation and computation of stimulus differences of visual information on the neglected side. However, this is by no means the full story. For example, consider a patient reported by Kartsounis and Warrington (1989). When given a row of line drawings of different objects, this patient neglected those objects on the left side of the row. Yet the same patient did not neglect the left side of a picture of two figures engaged in dialogue, nor the left side of a row of overlapping circles, even though the stimuli fell in the same spatial positions in each case. These data can be interpreted in at least two ways. They could indicate that neglect varies as a function of whether the stimulus as a whole is meaningful and/or whether the stimulus varies continuously from the ipsilesional to the contralesional side. When the whole stimulus is meaningful, or is continuous, patients show less neglect. This might be so because meaningful or continuous stimuli are selected as a whole (see Humphreys & Riddoch, 1992). Thus problems due to impaired orienting to the contralesional side, or due to problems in disengaging attention once orientated to the ipsilesional side, are bypassed. Attention will not need to be disengaged because it is engaged by the whole of the meaningful target stimulus. Also, impaired contralesional orienting may not matter because the whole stimulus is selected even when patients orient only to the ipsilesional side.

A somewhat different account is that patients do engage attention on the display in the ipsilesional field, but, when that display is either meaningless or suggests the presence of contralesional stimuli (because it varies continuously into that field), patients are able to shift attention voluntarily. They then show less neglect. This last account fits with other data showing that voluntary attentional processes can be relatively preserved in neglect (Riddoch & Humphreys, 1983).

That neglect is affected by the meaningfulness of the ipsilesional stimulus is also suggested by data reported by Seron, Coyette and Bruyer (1989). They asked patients showing left-side neglect to identify simple line drawings. The items could be identified from the features present on the right side (e.g. a rhino facing to the right, which might be identified from its horn) or from features on the left (e.g. an axe with its head lying on the left-hand side). Neglect was more severe for the left-feature relative to the right-feature stimuli. More particularly, the information on the right of the left-feature stimuli could either be identified as part of an object (e.g. the handle of the axe) or it was meaningless (e.g. the body of a slug). Neglect was less pronounced if the right-side information could be identified as part of an object. Seron et al. suggest that, for these stimuli, patients were directed by the information present in the right field to voluntarily attend to the identifying features on the left. Neglect was ameliorated by patients using ipsilesional stimuli to direct attention voluntarily to the contralesional side.

Such results indicate that any problems in forming particular types of visual representation, or in orienting to or disengaging attention from stimuli on one side of space, can be modulated by voluntary attentional processes. Thus performance must be understood in terms of interactions between components of the attentional network. Also, whatever is selected for identification seems dependent on the meaningfulness of the stimulus, and not simply on whether the stimulus appears on the ipsilesional or contralesional side of space. Selection seems to be object- rather than space-based. We discuss how this might come about later.

The Lure of Ipsilesional Stimuli: New Data on Copying

In experiments carried out in collaboration with Claire Lowry, we have also examined the effects of features on the left and right sides of objects, using simple copying tasks. These new data further indicate the important interactions that operate between different components of the attentional network, determining neglect.

Patients showing neglect in copying were asked to copy either: (1) drawings of meaningful objects with their identifying features on the left or the right (e.g. an animal facing left or right); (2) drawings of meaningless non-objects formed by substituting features from two real objects (e.g. the arm of a pair of glasses was replaced by a cigarette); and (3) drawings of meaningless patterns. The meaningless objects were taken from a set of non-objects used in an object decision task by Riddoch and Humphreys (1987b). The meaningless patterns were taken from the non-objects used in an object decision task by Kroll and Potter (1984; see Fig. 7.4 for examples). Prior to the experiment, each drawing was divided into quadrants, and a group of independent raters listed the informative features present in each quadrant. This was done in order to separate out parts of the drawing containing informative features from those non-informative parts (the non-informative parts typically being the connecting lines between the informative parts). The informative parts could include what we are terming the identifying features of the object (e.g. the head of an animal), and also features such as a

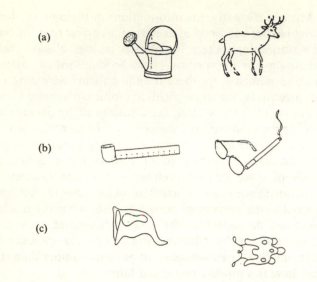

FIG. 7.4.   Examples of (a) real objects, (b) meaningless non-objects and (c) meaningless patterns used in the copying task with the neglect patient A.H.

tail and legs (which may not uniquely specify the identify of a given animal, but which are informative as to the general nature of the object).

The number of omissions made by one neglect patient, A.H., is shown in Fig. 7.5. A.H. had suffered a right parietal lesion, and had a left hemianopia. A.H. made very few omissions on the right-side of the objects, but made considerable left-side omissions. To our surprise, the fewest omissions were made on the meangingless patterns, more were made on the meaningful objects and most were made on the meaningless non-objects. The omissions also varied according to the informativeness of the parts. A.H. tended to miss out non-informative parts relative to the informative features. Perhaps the most striking finding is that, for real objects, there were *no* left-side omissions of informative features when the identifying features of the object were on the left side. However, there were omissions of left-side informative features when the identifying features were on the right (e.g. A.H. might omit the tail of an animal when its head was facing right). This contrasting pattern suggests either that A.H. oriented directly to identifying features when they were present in his neglected field, or that he oriented initially to the right but redirected his attention to the left voluntarily when the right sides of the objects did not contain identifying features. We cannot separate these two possibilities from the present data since A.H. was not under time pressure, and so had time to re-orient attention if required. However, having the identifying feature of the object on the right was very disruptive, leading

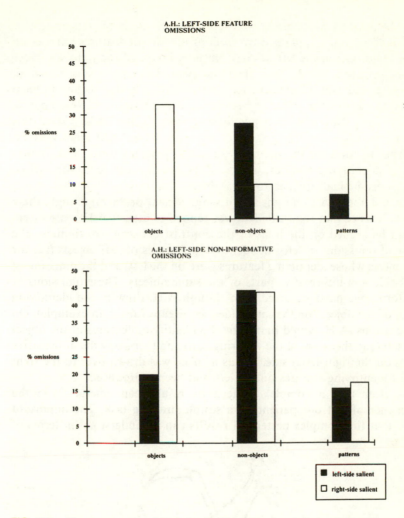

FIG. 7.5. The percentage of omissions of informative and non-informative and non-informative parts of stimuli made in copying by A.H.

to A.H. making left-side omissions of informative and non-informative features alike. This is consistent with A.H. having difficulty disengaging his attention from identifying right-side features (due either to a genuine disengagement problem, or to an orienting problem exacerbated under conditions when attention is engaged).

Given A.H.'s propensity to maintain attention on right-side identifying features, to the neglect of left-side information, we can now explain why meaningless patterns were neglected least and meaningless non-objects most. Meaningless non-objects were concatenations of two separate real objects, and typically contained two sets of identifying features, one set on the right and one on the left. If A.H. initially favoured the right set under these competitive conditions, then he would tend to neglect both informative and non-informative features on the left, due to his problem in disengaging attention from right-side identifying features. Real objects, chosen to have only one set of identifying features, would be spared this problem when the identifying features were on the left and there were no identifying features on the right. Meaningless patterns were by definition devoid of identifying features, and so A.H. was overall less prone to be "stuck" once he had oriented to the right.

Over and above A.H.'s right-side disengagement problem, though, there is other evidence that right-side features tended to attract A.H.'s attention. This can be argued on the basis of the contrast between two findings: the absence of omissions of left-side identifying features of real objects (i.e. for those objects whose identifying features were on the left) and the omission of the left-side non-informative parts of the same objects. These omissions of non-informative parts occurred even though A.H. drew in the identifying features of the objects on the same side (see Figure 7.6 for an example). On such occasions, A.H. would first draw the identifying features of the object on the left (e.g. the spout of the watering can) and then copy the informative features on the right-hand side. It was as if he was drawn over to the right once the identifying features on the left had been reproduced.

It is clear that a complex pattern of results can emerge from the performance of just one patient on a simple drawing task. The important point is that this complex pattern of results can be understood in terms of

FIG. 7.6.   An example of a copy of a watering can by A.H. In this instance, A.H. copied the identifying feature of the spout, from the left side of the depicted object, and then copied the features on the right side of the object.

interactions between components of an attentional network. We have suggested that A.H. is either impaired at orienting to left-side stimuli or that he has problems disengaging attention from right-side features that can be used to identify objects. Subject to the constraints imposed by having identifying features on the right, processes governing the voluntary shifting of attention to the neglected field seem relatively intact. Thus, A.H. will shift attention voluntarily to the left providing the features on the right cannot be used to identify a target object. We suggest this interaction between voluntary attentional control and the presence of identifying features gives rise to his better performance on meaningless patterns than on real objects, and to the better performance on real objects with left-side identifying features than on meaningless objects. In addition, right-side features also seem to "lure" A.H.'s attention, so that once the identifying features on the left of real objects have been drawn, A.H. goes on to reproduce details from the right of the objects, omitting the non-informative details on the left. The lure of right-side features cannot be explained if A.H. simply had a problem in disengaging attention from the right (cf. Posner et al., 1984). However, it would occur either if there was chronic orienting to the right or if there were impaired left-side orienting. A problem in left-side orienting would lead to this behaviour if, following the reproduction of identifying features, A.H.'s next attentional fixation was determined by the relative saliency of orienting cues to the left or right—a competition usually decided in favour of the right.

Attentional Interactions and Neglect Dyslexia

Other evidence indicating the importance of attentional interactions in the behaviour of neglect patients comes from work on neglect dyslexia. The term neglect dyslexia is used to describe patients who make unilateral reading errors, omitting or misidentifying either words from one side of a page or letters from one side of a word (e.g. Kinsbourne & Warrington, 1962). For example, after a right hemisphere lesion, a patient may misidentify letters on the left side of words, showing a left-to-right gradient in the number of letters correctly identified (e.g. Ellis et al., 1987; Warrington, 1991). Riddoch et al. (1990) noted that while this left-to-right gradient was typical for words and orthographically legal (word-like) nonwords, a somewhat different result can occur with unpronounceable (random) letter strings. They reported a left-neglect patient who identified the left-hand (beginning) letter of random letter strings better than the next-to beginning letter, while showing best identification of letters at the right-hand end of the strings. They suggested that, because random letter strings cannot be identified from the letters at the right-hand end of the strings, patients voluntarily shift attention to the left, identifying the left-hand letter.

However, once this is done, the patients then re-orient attention back to the right-hand side, omitting the next-to beginning letter.

Riddoch and co-workers' result can be thought akin to the data we noted in the previous section on the drawing of real objects and meaningless patterns. When there are no identifying features on the right, patients may then attend voluntarily to the left. However, once these left-side features are drawn, attention must be redirected and it is then that "neglect" may be manifest. When not under voluntary control, attention will be directed on the basis of the relative saliency of cues detected via the "orienting module" (see Fig. 7.2). Problems in computing differences on the left, or in responding to the differences computed on the left, will lead to overly strong orienting to the right.

OTHER PHENOMENA IN THE NEGLECT SYNDROME: UNCONSCIOUS PERCEPTION

As we noted at the beginning of this chapter, there are several characteristics of the neglect syndrome. One characteristic apparent in some cases of unilateral visual neglect is that patients may show evidence of having perceived a stimulus even though they deny its presence. Marshall and Halligan (1988) gave their neglect patient two drawings of a house which were identical but for the presence of bright red flames appearing from the window on the left-hand side of one house. The patient denied that there was any difference between the houses but nevertheless tended to choose the one not on fire when asked which house she preferred to live in. Quite similar results have been reported by Bisiach and Rusconi (1990), though they note that their patients sometimes preferred the burning house! Using a somewhat different methodology, Volpe, Le Doux and Gazzaniga (1979) showed that patients could be above chance at making same–different judgements to pairs of pictures briefly presented to the left and right visual fields, while being at chance at reporting the identity of left-side pictures on "different" trials (left- and right-side stimuli being identical on "same" trials). In each of these cases, it has been suggested that there is high-level analysis of the stimulus properties that the patients then deny the presence of or fail to identify. Neglect occurs "in the flow of information between conscious and non-conscious mental systems" (Volpe et al., 1979).

How do such data square with our account of neglect in terms of disruption to components within an interactive attentional system? In broad terms, the account we have offered is agnostic as to the level of representation at which attention is engaged and objects selected. For example, we have suggested that the data-driven orienting module detects the presence of salient stimuli and directs attention to their location. It is tempting also to suggest that the stimulus properties which give rise to data-driven orienting responses are relatively low-level, involving (for instance) low-spatial frequency components of visual stimuli, rapid luminance increments and movement. This would fit with research indicating the potency of such visual properties for capturing attention (e.g. see Jonides & Yantis, 1988; Nakayama & Mackeben, 1989; Yantis & Jonides, 1984, 1990). Nevertheless, it remains possible that the data-driven orienting mechanism responds to high-level descriptions of objects, in which case the potency of low-level properties may reflect a quantitative difference in priority rather than a qualitative difference in the information computed (cf. Duncan, 1981). Salient low-level differences are assigned a higher priority than high-level differences in, for example, the degree of semantic congruence between a stimulus and its surroundings. In the latter case, patients with neglect due to a problem within the data-driven orienting module ought to show high-level processing of stimuli that do not engage attention.

For now, however, it can be argued that the data on unconscious perception in neglect patients are unconvincing. Farah, Monheit, Brunn and Wallace (1991) point out that, in Volpe and co-workers' (1979) study, the advantage for same–different matching over identification may simply be due to less stimulus information being needed for same–different matching for physical identity. They tried to equate the amount of visual information needed in the different tasks by having a forced-choice identification as well as a same–different matching task. Under these conditions, there was no advantage for same–different matching for patients showing contralesional neglect. When the opportunities to use partial visual information are equated, patients are as good at identifying the "neglected" stimuli as they are at judging physical similarity (in the same–different matching task).

Additionally, consider the claim for unconscious perception in forced-choice judgements of stimulus preference (e.g. Marshall & Halligan, 1988). This has typically been made on the basis of relatively few trials, and no attempts have been made to ensure that patients' failure to detect a difference "consciously" between stimuli reflects a response bias (e.g. by requiring patients to use the "same" and "different" response categories equally often). Further, even if a difference between same–different and preference judgements does exist, it is by no means clear that this is due to high-level stimulus properties. Low-level properties such as stimulus complexity, or a lack of good continuation or closure, may well be contributory factors. Indeed, the preference for a burning over a non-burning house shown by two patients reported by Bisiach and Rusconi (1990) could well reflect a different response to low-level stimulus properties relative to the response given by Marshall and Halligan's (1988) patient: Were the preferences due to full high-level interpretation of the drawings, it is unlikely that patients should consistently prefer a burning house!

In sum, we believe the case for full unconscious perception in neglect is unproven. The data remain consistent with an account of unilateral visual neglect as due to impaired orienting to data-driven signals, and with this orienting mechanism specialised for computing low-level stimulus differences.

OBJECT- AND SPACE-SYSTEMS: HIGH-LEVEL REPRESENTATIONS AND NEGLECT

We tentatively suggest, then, that visual attention is oriented on the basis of relatively low-level stimulus differences. However, this does *not* mean that low-level differences alone are selected for action. For instance, even if it is the case that, once engaged, attentional processes enhance low-level processes (e.g. Müller & Humphreys, 1991), the effect of this enhancement may be to facilitate the computation of high-level object descriptions. A framework illustrating how this might come about, proposed by Humphreys and Riddoch (1992), is shown in Fig. 7.7 (see also Chapter 6, this volume, for a strikingly similar account).

Within this framework, low-level stimulus differences generate an attentional orienting response, which leads to attention being engaged on a stimulus at a particular location (cf. the attentional network illustrated in Fig. 7.2). Once attention is engaged, there is feedback to enhance the processing of image features at particular locations.

In parallel with this, object recognition processes are activated, particularly by attentionally enhanced image features. High-level object descriptions feed back to enhance consistent image features further. The object recognition and attentional systems interact by means of their both affecting common image features. Selection takes place when a stable pattern of activation is established across the whole system; for example, by one active object description inhibiting other competing descriptions. Unless

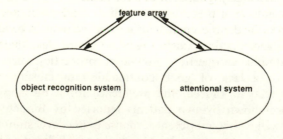

FIG. 7.7   A framework illustrating the interaction between the object recognition and the attentional systems.

such a stable pattern of activation is established, action may not be easily directed to an object, since multiple object descriptions may be available.

According to this framework, the object recognition and attentional systems are not directly connected, but they are yoked together because they affect a common set of image features. In some cases, attention determines selection. For instance, attention to a local part of an object will enhance the features of the part relative to those of the whole object. If the part can be represented as a single object in its own right, object descriptions of the part but not the whole object will be activated and selected.

In other cases, the object recognition system determines selection. For instance, even when attention is directed to a local part of an object, if the whole object and not the part is familiar, there may be stronger activation of the object description for the whole relative to the part. Image features for the whole object will be activated in a top-down manner from the object recognition system. This in turn broadens attentional orienting from the part to the whole object.

How might neglect be conceptualised within this framework? One possibility is that, in neglect, there is enhancement of image features only on the side of space ipsilateral to the lesion (as we have argued earlier, either because of a problem computing stimulus differences on the contralesional side or because of impaired orienting to that side). There can be several consequences of this, depending on the nature of the object and the parts attended. For instance, consider the case of a patient showing left-side neglect when given the glasses–cigarette "non-object" illustrated in Fig. 7.4. Attentional enhancement of the features on the right will lead to the strong activation of a description corresponding to a part of the whole, namely the cigarette. Since this "part", the cigarette, is itself familiar, its image features will be further supported by activation from the object recognition system. Selection will be for the "part" rather than the "whole". Also, since the part is identifiable in its own right, the patient will tend not to orient attention voluntarily to the contralesional side; the net result will be neglect of the left-hand side of the meaningless non-object whole.

Note that it follows that the precise error made will vary considerably with the kind of object presented. If the whole object can be identified from just some attended features, neglect may not be apparent. Neglect may also fail to occur when an attended part cannot be interpreted, prompting a voluntary shift of attention to the non-neglected side. However, if an attended "part" is identifiable as a single object in its own right, neglect is then more likely, because no voluntary shift of attention is prompted, and the whole object will be incorrectly identified as the part.

Neglect patients may therefore respond to whole objects or just to attended parts, and this depends on the interaction between the attentional and the object recognition systems. In essence, top-down activation from the object recognition system forces selection to be object- rather than space-based, since the object selected for action can vary in spatial scale.

The proposal for object-based selection may in fact help explain one puzzling aspect of neglect, namely the tendency of neglect patients to confabulate aspects of stimuli in the neglected field. In their study of "unconscious perception" in neglect, Bisiach and Rusconi (1990) noted that patients sometimes ignored aspects of objects even to the extent that the patients traced over the top of the ignored parts. They presented patients with stimuli such as Marshall and Halligan's (1988) burning house. They remark that sometimes a patient would trace around the house but not the flames, even though parts of the house were occluded by the flames. Within our terms, such effects might occur if patients select a description for a whole object based on the parts within the attended region of field. Top-down filling-in of image features may then lead to completion of the object as imagined rather than as really present, particularly as data-driven image features will not be supported by attentional enhancement.

REPRESENTATIONS, ATTENTION AND BRAIN SITES

We have emphasised that unilateral visual neglect may be conceptualised in terms of a breakdown in an attentional system whose components normally operate (1) to maintain attention at a given location or (2) to orient attention to a new location based either on volition or salient stimulus differences. We believe that, at the very least, any account of neglect is forced to consider the role of attentional processes, given the variance in neglect according to (for instance) whether patients voluntarily shift attention to the neglected side. It is also clear, though, that neglect varies according to the nature of the stimulus information present. It is the interaction between attentional and object recognition processes that determines the behaviour of a given patient on a given occasion. We have outlined two frameworks: one for visual attention and one for the interaction between the attentional system and the object recognition system. Within these frameworks, many of the phenomena of neglect may be captured by the single proposal that patients have difficulty in data-driven orienting to contralesional stimuli. In several places, we have stated that this may either be because of a problem computing the stimulus differences which drive such orienting responses, or because the orienting system fails to respond to computed differences on the contralesional side. Such a problem, in computing stimulus differences, can be related to our initial distinction between representational and attentional theories of visual neglect: A problem in computing stimulus differences could itself be caused by a patient having impaired early visual representations.

It is interesting to speculate that the distinction we have drawn between an attentional system and an object recognition system corresponds to the physiological distinction between a dorsal (occipito-parietal) and a ventral (occipito-temporal) visual system, concerned respectively with spatial processing and object recognition (cf. Desimone & Ungerleider, 1989; Ungerleider & Mishkin, 1982). In the light of this possible correspondence, it is also interesting to note that, classically, unilateral visual neglect is associated with parietal lesions (though this is by no means the only lesion site associated with neglect, it is also possible that other lesion sites are associated with other aspects of the neglect syndrome; see Mesulam, 1981). We can now relate this to the distinction made in the last paragraph, namely between impaired computation of stimulus differences and impaired orienting to computed differences. We suggest that attentional orienting responses arise from activity within the dorsal, spatial processing system, while the computation of stimulus differences arises within the ventral, object recognition system (for physiological evidence on this, see Knierim & van Essen, 1990; Lamme, van Dijk, & Spekreijse, 1992). If this suggestion is correct, and given that neglect is correlated with dorsal rather than ventral lesions, then the pattern of results runs contrary to the idea that there is impaired computation, and therefore representation, of stimulus differences. Rather, the association with dorsal lesions is consistent with neglect being due to impaired orienting to the computed stimulus differences.

VARIETIES OF VISUAL NEGLECT

Although we hold that many aspects of visual neglect can be accounted for by our proposal that patients are impaired at orienting to stimuli presented to the contralesional side of space, we also accept that visual neglect, like the neglect syndrome in general, likely comprises sub-groups of patients with different functional impairments. In particular, it is difficult to understand patients with apparent problems in non-retinally based visual representa- tions (e.g. representations based on object-centred co-ordinates or "grapheme descriptions"), since we envisage that orienting is determined by the computation of stimulus differences at particular retinal locations. We have two suggestions concerning such results. The first is that, in such cases, we witness a different variety of neglect—perhaps even one associated with loss of one side of a high-level visual representation (cf. Caramazza & Hillis, 1990). This proposal is not without difficulty. For instance, it is difficult to reconcile such an apparently high-level representational deficit with the dorsal lesions typically suffered by neglect patients (see above). Also, as we pointed out earlier, impairments of high-level visual representations ought to lead to material-specific problems, rather than an associated pattern of deficits (e.g. both in reading and in line bisection or cancellation; Caramazza & Hillis, 1990). In fact, in patients so far reported with apparent impairments to high-level visual representations, associated deficits have been found across a range of tasks.

An alternative suggestion is that although the data-driven orienting system is activated by retinally based stimulus differences, attentional feedback can be modulated by non-retinal co-ordinate systems. For instance, by means of its yoked relationship to the attentional system, the object recognition system may force attentional feedback to be sensitive to high-level object-centred representations. Thus there may be particularly strong top-down activation from the object recognition system for the main axis of an object, given the important role of the main axis in object representation (e.g. Humphreys, 1983; Marr & Nishihara, 1978). Even if in a given patient there is impaired attentional feedback to image features on one side of space, object-based activation could lead to good perception of the main axis irrespective of its spatial position. Only features which fall on the impaired side of space beyond the main axis may then be poorly perceived (cf. Driver & Halligan, 1991).

These last suggestions are clearly speculative, and a good deal of work is still needed before we develop a full account of the relations between different types of neglect. However, such future developments should remain consistent with the main thrust of our argument, which can be summarised as follows. In normality, visual behaviour is guided by interactions between separate components of an attentional network, and by interactions between this network and an object recognition system. Many aspects of visual neglect can be understood in terms of a breakdown to these normal processes of interaction. Indeed, it is because of the interactive nature of visual processing that neglect is so complex and variable.

ACKNOWLEDGEMENTS

The work reported in this chapter was supported by grants from the Medical Research Council of Great Britain, the Human Science Frontier Programme and the Wolfson Foundation. We thank Ian Robertson, Jon Driver and Martha Farah for comments.

REFERENCES

Bisiach, E. & Luzzati, C. (1978). Unilateral neglect of representational space. *Cortex, 14*, 129–133.

Bisiach, E. & Rusconi, M.L. (1990). Breakdown of perceptual awareness in unilateral neglect. *Cortex, 26*, 1–7.

Bisiach, E., Vallar, G., Perani, D., Papagno, C., & Berti, A. (1986). Unawareness of disease following lesions of the right hemisphere: Anosagnosia for hemiplegia and anosagnosia for hemianopia. *Neuropsychologia, 24*, 471–482.

Caramazza, A. & Hillis, A.E. (1990). Levels of representation, co-ordinate frames, and unilateral neglect. *Cognitive Neuropsychology, 7*, 391–446.

d'Erme, P., Gainotti, G., Bartolomeo, G., & Robertson, I. (1992). The influence of reference boxes on reaction times to lateralized visual stimuli in unilateral spatial neglect. In M.J. Riddoch & G.W. Humphreys (Eds), *Cognitive neuropsychology and cognitive rehabilitation*. Hove: Lawrence Erlbaum Associates Ltd.

Desimone, R. & Ungerleider, L.G. (1989). Neural mechanisms of visual processing in monkeys. In F. Boller & J. Grafman (Eds), *Handbook of neuropsychology*, Vol. 2. Amsterdam: Elsevier.

Driver, J. & Halligan, P. (1991) Can visual neglect operate in object-centred co-ordinates? *Cognitive Neuropsychology, 6*, 475–496.

Duncan, J. (1981). Directing attention in the visual field. *Perception and Psychophysics, 30*, 90–93.

Duncan, J. & Humphreys, G.W. (1989). Visual search and stimulus similarity. *Psychological Review, 96*, 433–458.

Ellis, A.W., Flude, B.M., & Young, A.W. (1987). "Neglect dyslexia" and the early visual processing of letters in words and nonwords. *Cognitive Neuropsychology, 4*, 439–464.

Farah, M.J., Monheit, M.A., Brunn, J.L., & Wallace, M.A. (1991). Unconscious perception of "extinguished" visual stimuli: Reassessing the evidence. *Neuropsychologia, 29*, 949–958.

Fischer, B. (1986). The role of attention in the preparation of visually guided eye movements in monkey and man. *Psychological Research, 48*, 251–257.

Halligan, P.W., Manning, L., & Marshall, J.C. (1991). Hemispheric activation *vs.* spatio-motor cueing in visual neglect: A case study. *Neuropsychologia, 29*, 165–176.

Heilman, K. & Valenstein, E. (1979). Mechanisms underlying hemispatial neglect. *Annals of Neurology, 5*, 166–170.

Hinton, G.E. & Parsons, L. (1981). Frames of references and mental imagery. In J. Long & A.D. Baddeley (Eds), *Attention and performance IX*. Hove: Lawrence Erlbaum Associates Ltd.

Humphreys, G.W. (1983). Reference frames and shape perception. *Cognitive Psychology, 15*, 151–196.

Humphreys, G.W. & Riddoch, M.J. (1992). Interactions between object- and space-vision revealed through neuropsychology. In D.E. Meyer & S. Kornblum (Eds), *Attention and performance XIV*. Hillsdale, NJ: Lawrence Erlbaum Associates Inc.

Humphreys, G.W., Quinlan, P.T., & Riddoch, M.J. (1989). Grouping effects in visual search: Effects with single- and combined-feature targets. *Journal of Experimental Psychology: General, 118*, 258–279.

Jonides, J. & Yantis, S. (1988). Uniqueness of abrupt onset as an attention-capturing property. *Perception and Psychophysics, 43*, 346–354.

Kartsounis, L.D. & Warrington, E.K. (1989). Unilateral neglect overcome by cues implicit in stimulus displays. *Journal of Neurology, Neurosurgery and Psychiatry, 52*, 1253–1259.

Kinsbourne, M. & Warrington, E.K. (1962). A variety of reading disability associated with right-hemisphere lesions. *Journal of Neurology, Neurosurgery and Psychiatry, 25*, 339–344.

Knierim, J.J. & van Essen, D.C. (1990). Spatial organization of suppressive surround effects in neurons of area V1 in alert macaques. *Society for Neuroscience Abstracts, 16*, 523.

Kroll, J.F. & Potter, M.C. (1984). Recognizing words, pictures, and concepts: A comparison of lexical, object, and reality decisions. *Journal of Verbal Learning and Verbal Behavior, 23*, 39–66.

Làdavas, E. (1990). Selective spatial attention in patients with visual extinction. *Brain, 113*, 1527–1538.

Làdavas, E., Menghini, G., & Umilta, C. (in press). On the rehabilitation of hemispatial neglect. In M.J. Riddoch & G.W. Humphreys (Eds), *Cognitive neuropsychology and cognitive rehabilitation*. Hove: Lawrence Erlbaum Associates Ltd.

Lamme, V.A.F., van Dijk, R.W., & Spekreijse, H. (1992). Texture segregation is processed by primary visual cortex in man and monkey. Evidence from VEP experiments. *Vision Research, 32*, 797–807.

LaPlane, D. & Degos, J.D. (1983). Motor neglect. *Journal of Neurology, Neurosurgery and Psychiatry, 46*, 152–158.

Marr, D. (1982). *Vision*. San Francisco, CA: W.H. Freeman.

Marr. D. & Nishihara, H.K. (1978). Representation and recognition of the spatial organization of three-dimensional shapes. *Proceedings of the Royal Society of London, B200*, 269–294.

Marshall, J.C. & Halligan, P.W. (1988). Blindsight and insight in visuo-spatial neglect. *Nature, 336*, 766–767.

McGlynn, S. & Schacter, D.L. (1989). Unawareness of deficits in neuropsychological syndromes. *Journal of Clinical and Experimental Neuropsychology, 11*, 143–205.

Mesulam, M.M. (1981). A cortical network for directed attention and unilateral neglect. *Annals of Neurology, 10*, 309–325.

Monk, A.F. (1985). Co-ordinate systems in visual word recognition. *Quarterly Journal of Experimental Psychology, 37A*, 613–625.

Müller, H.M. & Humphreys, G.W. (1991). Luminance-increment detection: Capacity-limited or not? *Journal of Experimental Psychology: Human Perception and Performance, 17*, 107–124.

Müller, H.M. & Rabbitt, P.M.A. (1989). Reflexive and voluntary orienting of visual attention: Time course of activation and resistance to interruption. *Journal of Experimental Psychology: Human Perception and Performance, 15*, 315–330.

Nakayama, K. & Mackeben, M. (1989). Sustained and transient components of focal visual attention. *Vision Research, 29*, 1631–1647.

Posner, M.I. (1980). Orienting of attention. *Quarterly Journal of Experimental Psychology, 32*, 3–25.

Posner, M.I., Cohen, Y., & Rafal, R.D. (1982). Neural systems control of spatial orienting. *Philosophical Transactions of the Royal Society of London, B298*, 187–198.

Posner, M.I., Walker, J.A., Friedrich, F.J., & Rafal, R.D. (1984). Effects of parietal injury on covert orienting of visual attention. *Journal of Neuroscience, 4*, 1863–1874.

Rapp, B.C. & Caramazza, A. (1991). Spatially determined deficits in letter and word processing. *Cognitive Neuropsychology, 8*, 275–312.

Riddoch, M.J. & Humphreys, G.W. (1983). The effect of cueing on unilateral neglect. *Neuropsychologia, 21*, 589–599.

Riddoch, M.J. & Humphreys, G.W. (1987a). Perceptual and action systems in unilateral visual neglect. In M. Jeannerod (Ed.), *Neurophysiological and neuropsychological aspects of spatial neglect*. Amsterdam: Elsevier.

Riddoch, M.J. & Humphreys, G.W. (1987b). Visual object processing in optic aphasia: A case of semantic access agnosia. *Cognitive Neuropsychology, 4*, 131–185.

Riddoch, M.J., Humphreys, G.W., Cleton, P. & Fery, P. (1990). Interaction of attentional and lexical processes in neglect dyslexia. *Cognitive Neuropsychology, 7*, 479–518.

Seron, X., Coyette, F., & Bruyer, R. (1989). Ipsilateral influences on contralateral processing in neglect patients. *Cognitive Neuropsychology, 6*, 475–498.

Treisman, A. (1988). Features and objects: The Fourteenth Bartless Memorial Lecture. *Quarterly Journal of Experimental Psychology, 40A*, 201–237.

Ungerleider, L.A. & Mishkin, M. (1982). Two cortical visual systems. In D.J. Ingle, M.A. Goodale, & R.J.W. Mansfield (Eds), *Analysis of visual behavior*. Cambridge, MA: MIT Press.

Volpe, B.T., Le Doux, J.E., & Gazzaniga, M.S. (1979). Information processing in an "extinguished" visual field. *Nature, 282,* 722–724.

Walker, R., Findlay, J.M., Young, A.W., & Welch, J. (1991). Disentangling neglect and hemianopia. *Neuropsychologia, 29,* 1019–1027.

Warrington, E.K. (1991). Right neglect dyslexia: A single case study. *Cognitive Neuropsychology, 8,* 193–212.

Yantis, S. & Jonides, J. (1984). Abrupt visual onsets and selective attention: Evidence from visual search. *Journal of Experimental Psychology: Human Perception and Performance, 10,* 601–621.

Yantis, S. & Jonides, J. (1990). Abrupt visual onsets and selective attention: Voluntary versus automatic allocation. *Journal of Experimental Psychology: Human Perception and Performance, 16,* 121–134.

Young, A.W., Newcombe, F., & Ellis, A.W. (1991). Different impairments contribute to neglect dyslexia. *Cognitive Neuropsychology, 8,* 177–192.

8 Attentional Search in Unilateral Visual Neglect

Lynn C. Robertson
Departments of Neurology and Psychiatry, University of California, Davis, and Veterans Administration Medical Center, Martinez, California, USA

Mirjam Eglin
University Hospital, Department of Neurology, Zurich, Switzerland

INTRODUCTION

Patients with severe visual neglect typically come to attention on a neurology ward because of their altered visual scanning behaviour. Eye deviations to the ipsilesional (i.e. intact) side of space and difficulty scanning towards the contralesional (i.e. neglected) side can be seen overtly, especially in the acute stages. Although the frequency of right and left neglect is controversial due to the confounding deficit of aphasia with left hemisphere damage (see Battersby, Bender, Pollock, & Kahn, 1956; De Renzi, 1982; Ogden, 1987; Zarit & Kahn, 1974), the greater severity of neglect with right hemisphere damage at least in the acute stages is well accepted (see De Renzi, 1982; Mesulam, 1981, 1983, 1985; Ogden, 1987; Roy et al., 1987). Acutely, patients with right hemisphere damage are more likely to deviate eyes, head and body towards their intact side than patients with left hemisphere damage. The overt manifestation of visual neglect clearly points to altered search of space. The major question we will address in this chapter is what cognitive mechanisms contribute to the overt scanning deficit?

Before proceeding, it is wise to keep in mind the vast variability inherent in neurological syndromes during the acute stage. Clinical neglect generally requires relatively large lesions to be evident. It usually lasts for only a few weeks or months, and the same patient tested on different days may have quite different profiles (note the dates and performance in Fig. 8.1 of a patient tested in a standard line bisection task). Even patients tested within

169

the same session can show such variability (Marshall & Halligan, 1989). Chronic cases are relatively rare. Neglect typically resolves into double simultaneous extinction where items on the contralateral side to the lesion are ignored only when two items are presented simultaneously side by side. Neglect and extinction probably lie on a continuum with extinction being a less severe form of neglect (see Robertson, 1992). However, there is some controversy over this claim because neglect can be found without extinction. However, the tests for the two have not been equated in any way when defining these conditions clinically, so it is unclear what this dissociation means. It is also important to keep in mind that some explanations of neglect are based on patients with extinction and others on patients with neglect. Some are even based on patients who have no clinical evidence of neglect or extinction at the time of testing, but do have lesions in cortical areas often associated with neglect (most prominently the parietal lobe; but see Heilman, Watson, & Valenstein, 1985; Mesulam, 1985; Rizolatti & Camarda, 1987).

Despite the difficulties in standardising neglect and testing patients with it, a very interesting picture is beginning to emerge from recent studies largely motivated by theories derived from cognitive psychology. Much of the focus has been on the role of attention *vs* spatial representation in visual spatial neglect. Several investigators argue that neglect is due to an attentional deficit (although the argument comes in different forms; Eglin, Robertson, & Knight, 1989; Farah, 1990; Heilman et al., 1985; Kinsbourne, 1987; Làdavas, this volume; Reuter-Lorenz, Kinsbourne, & Moscovitch,

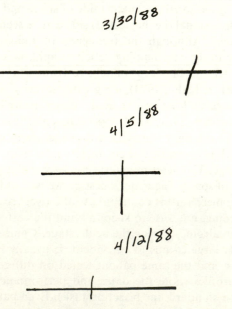

FIG. 8.1.   Changes in line bisection over a two week period as tested at bedside.

1990; Robertson, 1992), while others argue for a deficit in spatial representation (Bisiach & Berti, 1987; De Renzi, 1982; Morrow, 1987). According to the attentional theories, attentional mechanisms are affected directly. According to theories of altered spatial representation, the observed attentional deficits are affected indirectly. In both cases, the overt manifestation of the deficit will be altered visual search.

ATTENTION AND VISUAL NEGLECT

When relying on vision, all animals need some kind of mechanism to tell them where to look next. A system where the eyes would move automatically to whatever is most (or perhaps least) salient in the peripheral visual field would be rather maladaptive. For instance, without control over spatial attention, it would be hopeless to try to keep one's eyes on this sentence until it is finished before moving them to the person who just entered the room. Some mechanism is required that monitors areas of the visual field for potentially important information and other mechanisms to determine when and where the eyes move next or even if they move at all.

The most thorough investigations of the elementary operations of such a system have been reported by Posner and his colleagues (Posner & Petersen, 1990; Posner, Walker, Friedrich, & Rafal, 1984; Posner, Inhoff, Freidrich, & Cohen, 1987a; Posner, Walker, Friedrich, & Rafal, 1987b; Rafal et al., 1988; Rafal & Posner, 1987). In a simple visual task, they were able to break down covert spatial attention into move, engage and disengage operations, each associated with different neural structures in an overall network that guides visual spatial attention (Posner & Cohen, 1984). For the present purpose, the disengage operation is the most important because it is said to be altered in patients with neglect due to middle cerebral artery infarct (Morrow & Ratcliff, 1987), and in patients with extinction and/or more focal parietal lobe damage (Posner et al., 1984, 1987; Rafal, pers. comm.). The basic procedure is as follows. Three boxes appear horizontally across the midline on a computer screen, and the subjects fixate on the central box. A trial begins with one of the two peripheral boxes brightening for a short period of time. This is the cue. After a variable interval (usually 50–1000 msec), an asterisk appears in either peripheral box. The subjects' task is to keep their eyes fixated on the central box and to press a button as soon as the asterisk is detected. Reaction time (RT) to the target in the cued location becomes faster as the interval between cue and target lengthens with an increasing delay in RT when the target appears in the uncued location (invalid location RT minus valid location RT). This difference between valid and invalid RT theoretically reflects the time to disengage covert attention from the cued location, move and engage on the target in the uncued location. Patients with parietal lobe damage detect the asterisk nearly as well in the contralesional and ipsilesional sides of space when it occurs in the cued location (nearly equal ability to move and engage attention to cued locations). However, the delay in responding to the asterisk is increased substantially when it occurs in the uncued location in the neglected field. Patients with parietal lobe damage show an abnormal contralesional delay. When attention must be disengaged from a location on the intact side, there is abnormal delay, and, as with clinical neglect, the delay is worse for right hemisphere groups than for left. Therefore, it is possible that the visual search problems observed in patients with neglect stem from a difficulty in disengaging attention from the ipsilesional side of space once attention has been engaged on an object or location on that side.

These findings are consistent with electrophysiological evidence in monkey, showing that the increased response of many visual cells in parietal lobe (area 7) only occur when the stimulus is relevant to the animal (e.g. predicts food; Bushnell, Goldberg, & Robinson, 1981; Lynch, 1980; Mountcastle, 1978). During free visual search, the cells do not increase firing rate, nor do they do so when the monkey is fixated and the stimulus is not predictive. These data led investigators to conclude that a subset of cells in area 7 are responsible for spatial attention to the object. Posner and co-workers' data suggest a refinement of this conclusion. Rather than the parietal lobe being more involved in spatial attention as a whole, it appears to be involved in the command to disengage attention from its current location. It would make sense that this command would only be sent if a peripheral stimulus were potentially important and would not be sent if attention were not fixated because no disengagement would be required. Although animal studies have not pursued the disengage operation, Posner and co-workers' data suggest that findings from humans could be fruitfully related to investigations into more specific elementary operations in animals.

Recent findings using a very different task (Eglin et al., 1989) are also consistent with the idea that attentional disturbances in patients with neglect reflect a disengage problem in a task that requires visual search. Using feature and conjunction search tasks developed by Treisman and her colleagues (Treisman & Gelade, 1980; Treisman & Gormican, 1988), we varied the side of a predesignated target among a variable number of distractors. Our findings show that patients with neglect have difficulty disengaging from stimulation on the entire half of space ipsilateral to the lesion, but again have no difficulty if target and distractors only appear on the right or left side of the page.

In feature and conjunction search tasks, a target is displayed among a varying number of distractors. The target location varies from trial to trial, and RT to detect its presence or absence is measured. When the target is defined by a unique visual feature (e.g. colour, orientation), the number of distractors make little difference. The target "pops out" from its background. Conversely, when the target is defined by a combination of features (a conjunction), RTs typically increase linearly with the number of distractors in the display. Feature integration theory was developed to accommodate such results (Treisman & Gelade, 1980). It proposes two stages of analysis: an initial stage during which features are detected and a second attentional stage during which conjunctions of features are identified. Feature and conjunction search tasks can be used to determine whether or not a deficit in disengagement of attention from an ipsilateral object is specific to the right or left side of a display and whether it only occurs when attention is involved. Riddoch and Humphreys (1987) addressed these questions in three patients with left neglect due to right hemisphere damage. These subjects were poor at detecting both feature and conjunction targets on the left side. However, error rates were so high in the neglected field that search rates calculated from RT were problematic.

We used a localisation task rather than a presence–absence judgement and timed subjects' ability to point to a target that they knew would be present on every trial (Eglin et al., 1989). Under these conditions, even patients with relatively severe neglect continued to search into the neglected space because they knew that a target must be present. We tested seven patients who were included on a behavioural criterion of neglect: None of them crossed out any lines past the midline of a line cancellation test. RT was measured from stimulus presentation until a pointing response to the target was given. The target and distractor locations varied and were crossed with the right or left side of the display. The number of distractors varied orthogonally with side of display (see Fig. 8.2 for examples).

The most revealing findings were produced by the conjunction search task where serial search was required (see Fig. 8.3). The major findings are as follows:

1. No difference was found in RT to locate the target on the neglected and intact sides *as long as no distractors appeared on the side opposite to the target* (the baseline function with 0 opposite side distractors). In other words, in unilateral displays when there was nothing to attract attention to the intact side, no evidence of unilateral neglect was found.
2. The baseline search rate per item, although slower than in normals, was the same on the intact and neglected side of the displays.
3. In bilateral displays, distractors on the neglected side had no influence on RT when the target was on the intact side. RT increased only as a function of the number of distractors on the intact side as if the contralateral distractors did not exist. Taken together, (1) and (3) demonstrate that neglect was only present when there was stimulation from the intact side (i.e. the presence of objects on that side).

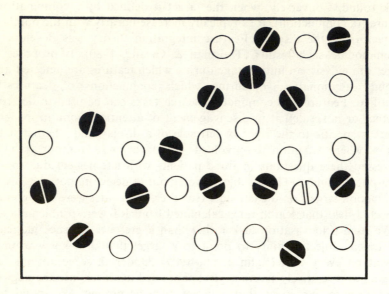

FIG. 8.2.   Example of stimulus used in conjunction search task with target plus 19 distractors on the right side and 10 distractors on the left. Open circles represent red dots and filled circles represent blue dots. Reprinted with permission from Eglin, Robertson, & Knight (1989).

4. All subjects eventually moved into the neglected side if the target was not found on the intact side, and this "contralateral delay" increased as a function of the number of distractors on the intact side. In other words, the degree of contralateral delay increased as the attentional requirements increased on the intact side.
5. The contralateral delay across the midline was disproportional. Each distractor on the intact side added about three times the base search rate to the contralateral delay. Although several explanations are possible, one interpretation is that the patients continued to search the intact side about three times on average before disengaging from the intact half to move to the neglected side.

The contralateral delay is represented in a different way in Fig. 8.4, where RT for each vertical quartile of the displays from the most intact to the most neglected quartile sections is plotted collapsed over all other conditions. There was a gradual increase from the most intact to the most neglected side

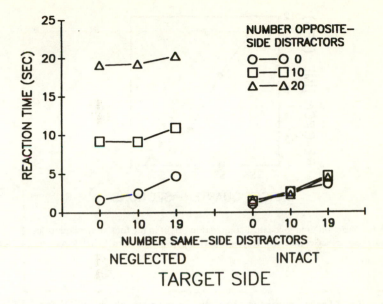

FIG. 8.3.   Reaction time to locate a conjunction target on the intact and neglected side of a display as a function of the number of same-side and opposite-side distractors. Reprinted with permission from Eglin, Robertson, & Knight (1989).

(see also Posner, Inhoff, Freidrich, & Cohen, 1987b), but there was also an abrupt change in the function in the centre. Crossing the midpoint posed a special problem for these patients, but only when stimuli occurred on both sides of the display. In a follow-up study with stable patients with unilateral posterior or anterior lesions without clinical signs of neglect, we did not find this midline problem. However, search still began at the most ipsilateral point to the side of the lesion with RT increasing gradually as the target appeared more towards the neglected side (Eglin, Robertson, & Knight, 1991). For patients with severe neglect, attention was not distributed over space like a single gradient smoothly crossing the midline. The midline of the body defines a spatial frame that demarcates left and right in viewer-centred co-ordinates. The dominance of viewer-centred co-ordinates dissipates over time in patients with neglect, and may be part of the anosognosia that so often co-occurs with syndrome.

It is intriguing that Luck, Hillyard, Mangun and Gazzaniga (1989) have reported evidence in patients with full commissurotomy which suggests that each hemisphere independently guides search on the contralateral side of space. This may account for the fact that distractors on the neglected side have no effect until attention crosses into the contralesional side in patients with neglect.

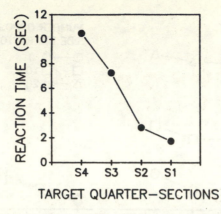

FIG. 8.4.   Reaction time to locate a conjunction target in the four vertical quartiles of the page collapsed over other conditions. Reprinted with permission from Eglin, Robertson, & Knight (1989).

In sum, these findings together suggest at least three different contributions to attentional search deficits in patients with unilateral visual neglect. The first is a directional scanning bias starting at the most ipsilesional stimulus on the intact side. The second is a slowed attentional search rate regardless of field (perhaps a slowed disengage problem from point to point everywhere in the visual field). This could contribute to neglect by increasing the probability of returning to parts of the display that already had been examined. Possibly, inhibitory tagging could be disrupted (Klein, 1988). The third is a difficulty in disengaging from the intact half of the stimulus display to move into the neglected half.

Our findings have been replicated with other displays that do not rely on colour or even on conjoining features (Eglin, Robertson, Knight, & Brugger, submitted). Examples of such stimuli are shown in Fig. 8.5, where the Q pops out from the Os, but to find an O in a field of Qs requires a serial search. The absence of a feature in the target requires a serial search, while the presence of a feature does not (Treisman & Gormican, 1988; Treisman & Souther, 1985). Finally, the contralateral delay can be reduced if the stimuli are grouped by one of the features defining the target (e.g. by colour or by shape) because attention can be allocated to a homogeneous group of items as a whole. Even grouping on the contralateral side can affect the magnitude of neglect (Grabowecky, Robertson, & Treisman, in press) even though a heterogeneous field has no effect on search whatsoever. These findings together show that the number of individual items on the ipsilesional side in a serial search task does not suffice to produce the contralateral delay. Rather, only those items or groups of items that are

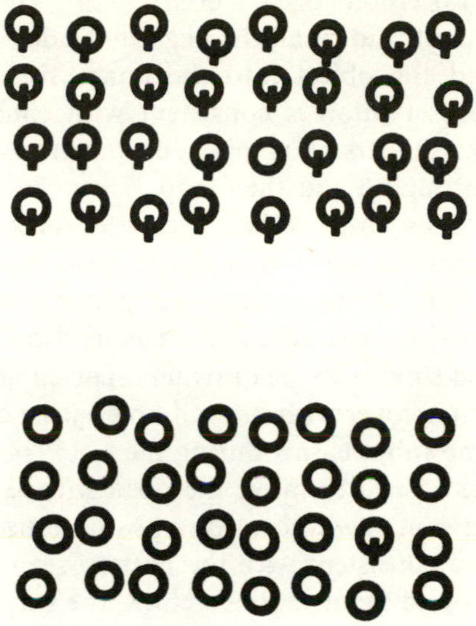

FIG. 8.5.   Example of stimuli. The top display produces functions indicative of serial search and the bottom does not.

serially scanned contribute to the delay in patients with neglect (Eglin et al., submitted). The latter result also suggests intact grouping processes in patients with neglect.

ATTENTION, SPATIAL REPRESENTATION AND NEGLECT

There are clear indications from the foregoing discussion as well as clinical observation that spatial attention is altered in patients with unilateral visual neglect. This does not necessarily mean that attentional mechanisms are affected directly. Attention must be engaged on something (whether an object or a location), and if certain parts of space are weakly represented, then attention will be indirectly affected.

The most prominent competing theory to attentional accounts suggests just this. Bisiach and his colleagues (Bisiach & Berti, 1987; Bisiach, Capitani, Luzzatti, & Perani, 1981; Bisiach & Luzzatti, 1978; Bisiach, Luzzatti, & Perani, 1979) propose that representational space has been altered in unilateral neglect. Patients with left neglect will neglect the left side of a stimulus even when it is visually imagined (Bisiach & Luzzatti, 1978; Bisiach et al., 1981), or when a pattern is presented sequentially by drifting it behind a cut-out slit in central vision (Bisiach et al., 1979). These investigators also found that when patients did recall the neglected side of an imagined scene, they often misplaced the object into the intact side. There was "visual allaesthesia". This observation is consistent with clinical evidence. When drawing in the clock numbers of a clock face, patients with neglect typically do not draw in 1 through 6 and then stop. They are much more likely to place 7 through 11 on or towards the intact side. As shown in Fig. 8.6., the left side seems compressed rather than absent. This does not appear only in drawings. Mijovic (1990) demonstrated that patients with neglect began to move to locations on a covered clock face in a direction that reflected altered spatial representation similar to the drawings. The subjects were first shown a clock face and then a cover with a small hole in the centre was placed on top of it. Thus, all the subjects saw during the test was a cover with a white square cut out. When asked to move the open square to a number on the clock face, initial movement was towards a position that reflected an altered spatial representation consistent with the pattern seen in patient drawings. For instance, when asked to move to 9 o'clock, the subjects might move in a direction towards 2 or 3. As in patient drawings, the left-sided numbers were displaced towards the right within the representation of the clock face. In other studies, Mijovic was able to rule out a directional motor movement bias.

One problem with the representational account is that there are other cases in which patients will draw clock numbers towards the intact side with their eyes open but draw them appropriately when told to close their eyes (Mesulam, 1985). This suggests there may be some cases of neglect that are due to altered spatial representation and others that are not. Also, Mijovic's representational account has difficulty explaining the lack of effect of contralesional distractors on searching for a target on the intact side in the study by Eglin et al. (1989). Visual allaesthesia should increase the number

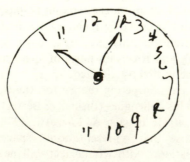

Fig. 8.6.   Example of a patient's drawing of clock numbers.

of distractors perceptually represented on the intact side. If we assume that the number of displaced items increases the more items are present on the neglected side, the slopes on the intact side should increase as the number of distractors on the neglected side increases. This would increase the slopes of the search functions on the intact side relative to the neglected side of space, which did not occur. Neither do the data from Eglin et al. account for the visual allaesthesia observed in clock drawings and the data from Mijovic's study. Visual allaesthesia and contralateral delay likely reflect different components of the neglect syndrome.

NEGLECT AND SPATIAL TRANSFORMATIONS

If the major deficit in neglect is altered spatial representation, it is somewhat surprising that spatial transformations that would seem to require a rather high degree of abstract spatial representation can be made by patients with visual neglect. For instance, Driver and Halligan (1991), Farah et al. (1990) Làdavas (1987; 1990), Calvanio, Petrone and Levine (1987) and Posner et al. (1987) have shown that neglect or extinction are found both on one side of space defined by the body midline, the stimulus display, or by the orthogonal upright environment. When patients with right hemisphere damage and neglect are rotated 90°, viewer-centred and environmentally centred reference frames are orthogonal, yet neglect occurs within both frames. Driver and Halligan (1991) have also shown that neglect can be relative to object-centred frames as well. Same–different judgements for patterns rotated 45° showed neglect for the left side of the objects and did so even when presented entirely within the intact field.

Patients with unilateral left neglect are able to represent differently oriented frames of reference, but then they neglect the left side of each frame. In other words, spatial representations and the deficits within them are stable across orientation and location transformations. This stability does not preclude the possibility that spatial representation is altered consistently on one side across reference frame transformations, but it does make the explanations more complicated and demonstrates that patients with neglect can utilise abstract representations of space in similar ways as normals.

Consistently, there is evidence in normals that directional scanning biases are relative to the orientation of a reference frame. In a series of studies, Robertson and Lamb have shown that a rightward sampling bias to upright patterns continues as a rightward bias in disoriented patterns (Robertson & Lamb, 1988, 1989; Robertson, 1990). When a group of four letters was presented in the left or right visual field and subjects judged whether the letters were normal or reflected (see Fig. 8.7a), a right visual field advantage was observed.[1] When the letters were rotated around the centre fixation point into the upper or lower visual field as in Fig. 8.7b, the advantage was still for the right field *relative* to the orientation of the letters. When the tops of the letters were +90° from upright as in Fig. 8.7b, RT advantage was in the lower visual field, and when they were –90° from upright in the opposite direction as in Fig. 8.7c, RT advantage was in the upper visual field. In both cases, the advantage was for patterns in the relative right field in a reference frame rotated through fixation to correspond to the orientation of the letters

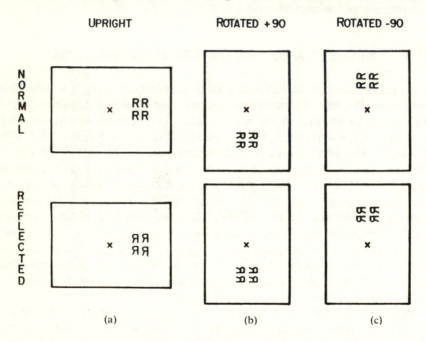

FIG. 8.7.   Example of stimuli used in studies of reference frame effects. All patterns are shown in the right relative field. Reprinted with permission from Robertson & Lamb (1988).

---

[1] The stimulus configuration and task were chosen because a previous study found frame effects with these patterns in a study of frame rotation in mental rotation tasks (Robertson et al., 1987). Obtaining a significant right visual field advantage using letters in a reflection task is by no means guaranteed even in the upright condition. In seven different experiments using such stimuli, a mean right visual field advantage was found on every occasion (8–29 msec), but the advantage only reached significant levels on four of those occasions (with an N between 12 and 16). Obviously, asymmetries and their relation to frames can only be tested if a field advantage is first observed in the upright condition. It should also be noted that the study of frame effects is not limited to right visual field advantage. In order to make a frame interpretation, it is sufficient to have a consistent field advantage (either right or left) over spatial transformations.

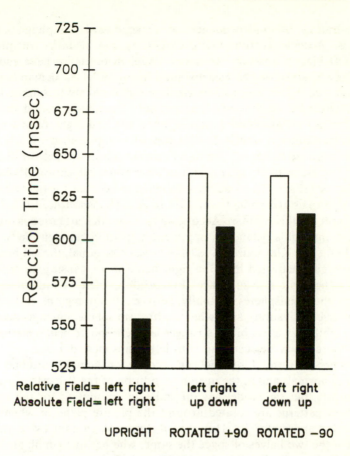

Relative Field= left right   left right   left right
Absolute Field= left right   up down   down up

UPRIGHT   ROTATED +90   ROTATED −90

FIG. 8.8.   Reaction time as a function of display field (both relative and absolute) for the three orientation conditions. Reprinted with permission from Robertson & Lamb (1988).

(see Fig. 8.8). This was the case whether the patterns were normal or reflected ruling out sensory interpretations. As in patients with neglect, scanning biases were consistent across spatial transformation and were rightward in every case.

Other investigators using very different paradigms have also found a rightward advantage in normals (Efron, 1990; Egly & Homa, 1984; Reuter-Lorenz et al., 1990; Werth & Poppel, 1988). Efron and his colleagues (Efron, Yund, & Nichols, 1987, 1990a, 1990b; Yund, Efron, & Nichols, 1990a, 1990b) have repeatedly reported a rightward advantage when subjects must detect a non-linguistic target among a briefly presented display of other non-linguistic targets. Overall target detection was better in the right upper quadrant. This occurred whether the subjects were literate or illiterate, demonstrating the independence of a rightward sampling bias from language processes (Efron, 1990). Obviously, not all tasks will produce a rightward bias in normals. As many visual field studies have shown, the rightward bias can be changed by stimulus and/or task demands (Hellige, 1983), but *all else being equal*, normals are more likely to sample the right side of space before the left. A recent set of studies reported by Reuter-Lorenz et al. (1990) showed that when a left and right bias were pitted against each other, a rightward bias consistently prevailed.

The rightward biases in normals in upright conditions are consistent with a model of hemisphere laterality and attentional allocation developed by Kinsbourne (1975). His model was designed to account for rightward biases in both normals and patients with left neglect (Kinsbourne, 1977; 1987; see also Chapter 3, this volume). According to his model, attention is directed to locations through a balance in opponent activation between the two halves of the brain (see Kinsbourne, 1987). All else being equal, the left hemisphere is more highly activated than the right hemisphere, causing an overall bias towards the right side of space. In addition, there is mutual inhibition between the hemispheres (actually between tectal regions influenced by hemispheric activation) and when right hemisphere damage occurs, the normal inhibitory effect of the stronger left hemisphere bias is disrupted and causes more severe neglect than with left hemisphere damage.

In its present form, this model can account for the rightward bias in many studies in normals and in the upright condition of the Robertson and Lamb experiments, but the model has difficulty in accounting for the rightward bias when patterns are rotated around the picture plane or when subjects with neglect are rotated 90°. However, it is possible that the two hemispheres represent the two halves of space the same, whether the stimuli are spatially defined by sensory channels or transformed via internal mechanisms. This account is consistent with much of the work in imagery and suggests that the subjects may have rotated the letters in the Robertson and Lamb studies around fixation into a viewer-centred frame with the patterns then being channelled through the right or left hemispheres as if they were upright. This issue is critical because Kinsbourne's idea that the vector of attention is determined by opponent processes between the two hemispheres could be extended to imagery tasks if we could show that an image of the pattern was rotated to upright before attentional scanning began. Under such conditions, the image in its imagined space would be analogous to a pattern presented in either the left or right visual field. However, image rotation received little support in studies we conducted to examine this issue (Robertson, 1990).

In one experiment, subjects judged the reflection of rotated letters as in Fig. 8.9. In this case, the patterns were always presented in the left or right visual field. If the subjects rotated letters around fixation to perform the task, then the image of the patterns would be represented in the upper or lower visual field. According to a hemispheric account, no asymmetry should be found. Yet when letters were locally rotated $+90°$, a right visual field advantage was found, and when they were rotated $-90°$, a left visual field advantage was found (Robertson & Lamb, 1989). The fact that rotated letters produced longer RTs than upright letters was also consistent with a mental rotation of some kind. There were four possible rotations that subjects may have used: local rotation of an image, local rotation of a reference frame, global rotation of an image or global rotation of a reference frame. However, in any of these cases, the findings were inconsistent with Kinsbourne's opponent hemisphere activation model.

A local rotation around the centre of the four-lettered pattern would produce an image of the pattern in the field of presentation. In this case, the advantage should not vary as a function of orientation because, whether the letters were oriented plus or minus $90°$, a local rotation would result in image representation in the same visual field as the pattern was presented. Although the magnitude of the field advantage was not the same for $+90°$ and $-90°$, the direction was clearly opposite, as shown in Fig. 8.10. The same logic holds for local rotation of a reference frame. On the other hand, a global rotation of an image around fixation would result in image representation in the upper or lower visual field. Although a field

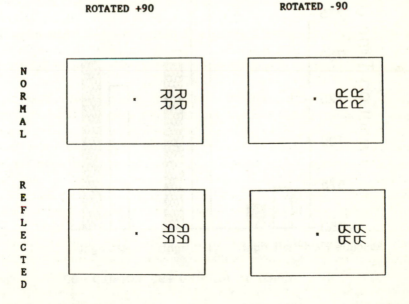

FIG. 8.9. Example of stimuli with a local rotation within the left or right visual field. From Robertson & Lamb (1989).

advantage was found in this experiment commensurate with an upper relative field advantage, a hemispheric explanation is not tenable, since the representation would now be along the up/down axis of the head through the midline. Finally, an upright reference frame may have been rotated into the orientation of the letters. Again, the field advantage in this case would be for the relative upper field within represented space, the difference being that the fields are defined within a rotated space from upright rather than viewer-centred as with image rotation. In its present form, the opponent activation model of differential hemisphere activation cannot account for the consistent field advantage over transformations within this type of rotation either. With a frame rotation, the "image" would not be moved from the right or left visual field, yet the visual field advantage changed to favour the upper relative field.

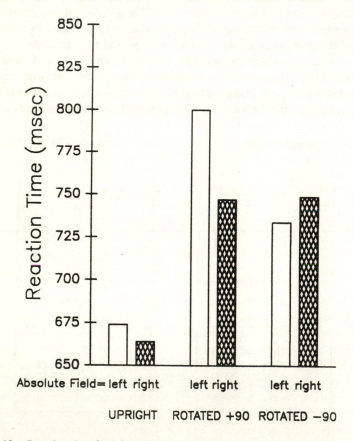

FIG. 8.10.   Reaction time for left and right visual field over the three orientation conditions. From Robertson & Lamb (1991).

These results may be relevant for attentional and/or representational explanations of neglect, even though at first glance they do not seem to fit well with the functional neuroanatomy proposed to underly attentional systems and neglect (e.g. Heilman et al., 1985; Kinsbourne, 1975, 1977, 1987; Mesulam, 1985). There are cases of altitudinal neglect that have been reported consistent with a directional bias along the vertical axis (Butter, Evans, Kirsch, & Kewman, 1989; Rapcsak, Cimino, & Heilman, 1988), and patients with neglect do show directional biases across spatial transformations. Thus, the data we have collected could reflect a right hemisphere dominance in allocating attention along the left/right dimension and up/down dimension. The issue of frame *vs* image rotation then becomes critical in interpreting the effects.

In order to distinguish between the two, we used an orientation priming task similar to the one used by Robertson, Palmer and Gomez (1987) to study frame effects in mental rotation. In this task, a group of letters was oriented plus or minus 90°, and the subject responded whether the letters were normal or reflected as if they were upright. We will call this pattern the prime. A second group of letters then appeared (the target), again either normal or reflected, and the subject made a second reflection judgement. By the pattern of RT to the target, it could be determined whether frame or image rotation occurred when judging the reflection of the prime. To study hemispheric effects, misoriented primes were presented in the lower or upper visual field followed by an upright target in the left or right visual field (see Fig. 8.11a). If the subjects rotated the prime to upright around central fixation to make their first reflection judgement, then the image representation would be as shown in Fig. 8.11b. This should produce faster RTs for a subsequent target presented in a consistent location (Fig. 8.11c) where the image was expected to be compared to an inconsistent location (Fig. 8.11d). If a frame rotation occurred in order to judge the reflection of the prime, then a subsequent upright pattern should not benefit. The data supported frame rotation rather than image rotation. An overall right visual field advantage occurred for the upright target consistent with the previous results, but the prime did not change RT to the target in accordance with image interpretations. A rotation of an image into the right visual field would have facilitated performance for a subsequent pattern presented in the right visual field, and a rotation of an image into the left visual field would have facilitated performance for a subsequent pattern presented in the left visual field. This did not occur. It appears instead that subjects rotated a frame to make their judgements. In other words, together the data suggest that attention is allocated relative to the frame of reference used to analyse the display. We have not yet tested patients with neglect using this procedure, but we do know that neglect can be found within different frames of reference (Calvanio et al., 1987; Driver & Halligan, 1991;

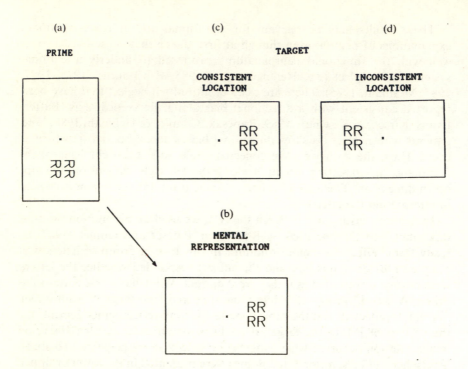

FIG. 8.11.   Example of prime (a) and target (c or d) location and orientation. (b) shows the expected mental representation if a global rotation of an image occurred when responding to the prime.

Farah et al., 1990; Grabowecky et al., in press). The foregoing discussion suggests that the rightward bias found in patients with left neglect may be an exaggerated form of the rightward bias found in normals. It also suggests that mechanisms that select and transform reference frames are intact in these patients with attention being allocated rightward within the frame. It is difficult to know how an opponent process between the two hemispheres could account for an upper or lower visual field bias that is relative to the frame, although Kinsbourne's idea of a vector of attention that is rightward biased has been well supported by the evidence. However, the rightward bias is not relative to the decussation of the visual pathways. Rather, it is relative to the frame of reference that defines the field.

CONCLUSION

It seems fairly clear that the directional scanning biases observed in patients with unilateral visual neglect are due to attentional mechanisms that are either directly or indirectly affected by neural damage. Visual neglect is not limited to the hemisphere of visual input. It has been found relative to viewer-centred, environment-centred and object-centred co-ordinates. It is not information within a visual field but information within the stimulus display in representational space that is neglected. As discussed in the first section, attention can be moved into neglected space as easily as into intact space when the intact field is devoid of task-relevant objects.

As discussed in the second section, the evidence from normals and patient populations together suggests a continuum of attentional bias towards the right of representational space. When all else is equal, information to the right of an adopted reference frame is sampled first. When right hemisphere damage occurs, this tendency is magnified. The case of neglect may be the end-point where everything on one side of the frame is ignored. Because this occurs over spatial transformations, it suggests a link between attentional biases and the reference frame one uses to analyse the scene. It also seems important that various attentional manipulations that can change the basic rightward bias in normals can increase or decrease the amount of neglect observed as well. For instance, normals can be cued to sample the left side of space first as can patients with neglect (Riddoch & Humphreys, 1983; 1987).

Notice that this account of neglect does not solve the issue of whether neglect is due to a direct effect on an attentional mechanism or to altered spatial representation. It is possible that, all else being equal, the right side of space (whether viewer-centred, object-centred or environment-centred) is more strongly represented than the left even in normals, and that it is this inequality that is magnified in patients with unilateral neglect.

Finally, it seems to us that an equally plausible account of an indirect effect on attention as altered spatial representation would be that some lateralised functions attract and/or sustain attention more than others in normals and in patients. With brain injury to a given hemisphere, certain types of information would be missing or weakly represented. For instance, patterns with global forms created from several local forms are responded to in opposite order in patient groups with left or right temporal-parietal (T-P) lesions. Patients with right T-P lesions favour local forms over global, while those with left T-P lesions favour global forms over local (Lamb, Robertson, & Knight, 1990; Robertson & Lamb, 1991; Robertson, Lamb, & Knight, 1988). This occurs whether the pattern is presented in the contralateral or ipsilateral field. Since local elements are typically more frequent than global ones in any visual scene, numerous local elements may be scanned on the ipsilateral side (utilising attention) and produce more severe signs of neglect in patients with right posterior damage, whereas for patients with left posterior damage and a global bias, relatively few global elements will compete for attention. The contralesional deficit would therefore be more severe with right than with left brain damage for hierarchically organised visual scenes. Although this idea is speculative, it does illustrate the fact that there are other possible indirect contributions to attention that could be pursued in addition to a spatial representation one. The current controversy need not be one of attention *vs* spatial representation, but rather the controversy may best be framed as direct effects *vs* indirect effects on attention and indeed even as direct combined with indirect effects that may produce different profiles of neglect. Whatever the case, the role of spatial transformations will have to play a large part in any theory of either normal or defective scanning biases.

ACKNOWLEDGEMENTS

Preparation of this manuscript was partially supported by VA Medical Research funds and by ADAMHA Grant No. AA06637 to L.C.R.

REFERENCES

Battersby, W.S., Bender, M.B., Pollock, M., & Kahn, R.L. (1956). Unilateral "spatial agnosia" (inattention). *Brain, 79*, 68–93.

Bisiach, E. & Berti, A. (1987). Dyschiria: An attempt at its systemic explanation. In M. Jeannerod (Ed.), *Neurophysiological and neuropsychological aspects of spatial neglect.* Amsterdam: Elsevier.

Bisiach, E., Capitani, E., Luzzatti, C., & Perani, D. (1981). Brain and conscious representation of outside reality. *Neuropsychologia, 19*, 543–551.

Bisiach, E. & Luzzatti, C. (1978). Unilateral neglect of representational space. *Cortex, 14*, 129–133.

Bisiach, E., Luzzatti, C., & Perani, D. (1979). Unilateral neglect, representational schema and consciousness. *Brain, 102*, 609–618.

Bushnell, M.C., Goldberg, M.E., & Robinson, D.L. (1981). Behavioral enhancement of visual responses in monkey cerebral cortex I. Modulation in posterior parietal cortex related to selective visual attention. *Journal of Neurophysiology, 46*, 755–772.

Butter, C.M., Evans, J., Kirsch, N., & Kewman, D. (1989). Altitudinal neglect following traumatic brain injury: A case report. *Cortex, 25*, 135–146.

Calvanio, R., Petrone, P.M., & Levine, D.N. (1987). Left visual spatial neglect is both environmental-centered and body-centered. *Neurology, 37*, 1179–1183.

De Renzi, E. (1982). *Disorders of space exploration and cognition.* New York: John Wiley.

Driver, J. & Halligan, P.W. (1991). Can visual neglect operate in object-centered coordinates? An affirmative single-case study. *Cognitive Neuropsychology, 8*, 475–496.

Efron, R. (1990). *Decline and fall of hemispheric specialization.* Hillsdale, NJ: Lawrence Erlbaum Associates Inc.

Efron, R., Yund, E.W., & Nichols, D.R. (1987). Scanning the visual field without eye movements: A sex difference. *Neuropsychologia, 25*, 637–644.

Efron, R., Yund, E.W., & Nichols, D.R. (1990a). Detectability as a function of target location: Effects of spatial configuration. *Brain and Cognition, 12*, 102–116.

Efron, R., Yund, E.W., & Nichols, D.R. (1990b). Visual detectability gradients: The effect of distractors in contralateral field. *Brain and Cognition, 12*, 128–143.

Eglin, M., Robertson, L.C., & Knight, R.T. (1989). Visual search performance in the neglect syndrome. *Journal of Cognitive Neuroscience, 1*, 372–385.

Eglin, M., Robertson, L.C., & Knight, R.T. (1991). Cortical substrates supporting visual search in humans. *Cerebral Cortex, 1*, 262–272.

Eglin, M., Robertson, L.C., Knight, R.T., & Brugger, T. (submitted). Search for simple visual features in patients with visual neglect.

Egly, R. & Homa, D. (1984). Sensitization in the visual field. *Journal of Experimental Psychology, 10*, 778–793.

Farah, M.J. (1990). *Visual agnosia: Disorders of object recognition and what they tell us about normal vision.* New York: Academic Press.

Farah, M.J., Brunn, J.L., Wong, A.B., Wallace, M.A., & Carpenter, P.A. (1990). Frames of reference for allocating attention to space: Evidence from the neglect syndrome. *Neuropsychologia, 28*, 335–347.

Grabowecky, M., Robertson, L.C., & Treisman, A. (in press). Preattentive processes guide visual search: Evidence from patients with unilateral visual neglect. *Journal of Cognitive Neuroscience.*

Heilman, K.M., Watson, R.T., & Valenstein, E. (1985). Neglect and related disorders. In K.M. Heilman & E. Valenstein (Eds), *Clinical neuropsychology.* New York: Oxford University Press.

Hellige, J.B. (1983). Hemisphere × task interaction and the study of laterality. In J.B. Hellige (Ed.), *Cerebral hemisphere asymmetry: Method, theory and application.* New York: Praeger.

Kinsbourne, M. (1975). The mechanisms of hemispheric control of the lateral gradient of attention. In P.M.A. Rabbitt & S. Dornic (Eds), *Attention and performance v.* London: Academic Press.

Kinsbourne, M. (1977). Hemi-neglect and hemispheric rivalry. In E.A. Weinstein & R.P. Friedland (Eds), *Hemi-inattention and hemispheric specialization.* New York: Raven Press.

Kinsbourne, M. (1987). Mechanisms of unilateral neglect. In M. Jeannerod (Ed.), *Neurophysiological and neuropsychological aspects of spatial neglect.* Amsterdam: Elsevier.

Klein, R. (1988). Inhibitory tagging system facilitates visual search. *Nature, 334*, 430–431.

Làdavas, E. (1987). Is the hemispatial deficit produced by right parietal lobe damage associated with retinal or gravitational coordinates? *Brain, 110*, 167–180.

Làdavas, E. (1990). Selective spatial attention in patients with visual extinction. *Brain, 113*, 1527–1530.

Làdavas, E. (1993, this volume). Spatial dimensions of automatic and voluntary orienting components of attention. In I.H. Robertson & J.C. Marshall (Eds), *Unilateral neglect: Clinical and experimental studies.* Hove: Lawrence Erlbaum Associates Ltd.

Lamb, M.R., Robertson, L.C., & Knight, R.T. (1990). Component mechanisms underlying the processing of hierachically organized patterns; Inferences from patients with unilateral cortical lesions. *Journal of Experimental Psychology: Memory, Learning and Cognition, 16*, 471–483.

Luck, S.J., Hillyard, S.A., Mangun, G.R., & Gazzaniga, M.S. (1989). Independent hemispheric attentional systems mediate visual search in split-brain patients. *Nature, 342*, 543–545.

Lynch, J.C. (1980). The functional organization of posterior parietal association cortex. *Behavior and Brain Science, 3*, 485–534.

Marshall, J.C. & Halligan, P.W. (1989). When right goes left: An investigation of line bisection in a case of visual neglect. *Cortex, 25*, 503–515.

Mesulam, M.M. (1981). A cortical network for directed attention and unilateral neglect. *Annals of Neurology, 10*, 309–325.

Mesulam, M.M. (1983). The functional anatomy and hemispheric specialization for directed attention: The role of the parietal lobe and its connectivity. *Trends in Neurosciences, 6*, 384–387.

Mesulam, M.M. (1985). Attention, confusional states and neglect. In M.M. Mesulam (Ed.), *Principles of behavioral neurology.* Philadelphia, PA: F.A. Davis.

Mijovic, D. (1990). *The mechanisms of visual neglect.* Unpublished doctoral dissertation, Boston University.

Morrow, L.A. (1987). Cerebral lesions and internal spatial representation. In P. Ellen & C. Thinus-Blanc (Eds), *Cognitive processes and spatial orientation in animal and man*, Vol. II. Boston, MA: Martinus Nijhoff.

Morrow, L.A. & Ratcliff, G. (1987). Attentional mechanisms in clinical neglect. *Journal of Clinical and Experimental Neuropsychology*, 9, 74–75.

Mountcastle, V.B. (1978). Brain mechanisms for directed attention. *Journal of the Royal Society of Medicine*, 71, 14–28.

Ogden, J.A. (1987). The "neglected" left hemisphere and its contribution to visuospatial neglect. In M. Jeannerod (Ed.), *Neurophysiological and neuropsychological aspects of spatial neglect*. Amsterdam: Elsevier.

Posner, M.I. & Cohen, Y. (1984). Components of visual orienting. In H. Bouma & D. Bowhais (Eds), *Attention and performance X*. Hillsdale, NJ: Lawrence Erlbaum Associates Inc.

Posner, M.I., Inhoff, A.W., Friedrich, F.J., & Cohen, A. (1987a). Isolating attentional systems: A cognitive-anatomical analysis. *Psychobiology*, 15, 107–121.

Posner, M.I. & Petersen, S.E. (1990). The attention system in the human brain. *Annual Review of Neuroscience*, 13, 25–42.

Posner, M.I., Walker, J.A., Friedrich, F.A. & Rafal, R.D. (1984). Effects of parietal injury on covert orienting of attention. *Journal of Neuroscience*, 4, 1863–1874.

Posner, M.I., Walker, J.A., Friedrich, F.A., & Rafal, R.D. (1987b). How do the parietal lobes direct covert attention? *Neuropsychologia*, 25, 235–245.

Rafal, R.D. & Posner, M.I. (1987). Deficits in human visual spatial attention following thalamic lesions. *Proceedings of the National Academy of Sciences*, 84, 7349–7353.

Rafal, R.D., Posner, M.I., Friedman, J.H., Inhoff, A.W., & Bernstein, E. (1988). Orienting of visual attention in progressive supranuclear palsy. *Brain*, 111, 267–280.

Rapcsak, S.Z., Cimino, C.R., & Heilman, K.M. (1988). Altitudinal neglect. *Neurology*, 38, 277–281.

Reuter-Lorenz, P.A., Kinsbourne, M., & Moscovitch, M. (1990). Hemispheric control of spatial attention. *Brain and Cognition*, 12, 240–266.

Riddoch, M.J. & Humphreys, G.W. (1983). The effect of cueing on unilateral neglect. *Neuropsychologia*, 21, 589–599.

Riddoch, M.J. & Humphreys, G.W. (1987). Perceptual and action systems in unilateral visual neglect. In M. Jeannerod (Ed.), *Neurophysiological and neuropsychological aspects of spatial neglect*. Amsterdam: Elsevier.

Rizzolatti, G. & Camarda, R. (1987). Neural circuits for spatial attention and unilateral neglect. In M. Jeannerod (Ed.), *Neurophysiological and neuropsychological aspects of spatial neglect*. Amsterdam: Elsevier.

Robertson, L.C. (1990). *Visual field asymmetries in analyzing rotated letters*. Paper presented at the International Neuropsychological Society Meeting, Innsbruck, Austria (July).

Robertson, L.C. (1992). The role of perceptual organization and search in attentional disorders. In D.I. Margolin (Ed.), *Cognitive neuropsychology in clinical practice*. New York: Oxford University Press.

Robertson, L.C. & Lamb, M.R. (1988). The role of perceptual reference frames in visual field asymmetries. *Neuropsychologia*, 26, 145–152.

Robertson, L.C. & Lamb, M.R. (1989). Judging the reflection of misoriented patterns in the right and left visual fields. *Neuropsychologia*, 27, 1081–1089.

Robertson, L.C. & Lamb, M.R. (1991). Neuropsychological contributions to part–whole organization. *Cognitive Psychology*, 23, 299–330.

Robertson, L.C., Lamb, M.R., & Knight, R.T. (1988). Effects of lesions of temporal-parietal junction on perceptual and attentional processing in humans. *Journal of Neuroscience*, 8, 3757–3769.

Robertson, L.C., Palmer, S.E., & Gomez, L.M. (1987). Reference frames in mental rotation. *Journal of Experimental Psychology: Learning, Memory and Cognition, 13*, 368–379.

Roy, E.A., Reuter-Lorenz, P., Roy, L.G., Copland, S., & Moscovitch, M. (1987). Unilateral attention deficits and hemisphere asymmetries in the control of attention. In M. Jeannerod (Ed.), *Neurophysiological and neuropsychological aspects of neglect*. Amsterdam: Elsevier.

Treisman, A. & Gelade, G. (1980). A feature-integration theory of attention. *Cognitive Psychology, 12*, 97–136.

Treisman, A. & Gormican, S. (1988). Feature analysis in early vision: Evidence from search asymmetries. *Psychological Review, 95*, 15–48.

Treisman, A. & Souther, J. (1985). Search asymmetry: A diagnostic for preattentive processing of separable features. *Journal of Experimental Psychology: General, 114*, 285–310.

Werth, R. & Poppel, E. (1988). Compression and lateral shift of mental coordinate systems in a line bisection task. *Neuropsychologia, 26*, 741–745.

Yund, E.W., Efron, R., & Nichols, D.R. (1990a). Detectability gradients as a function of target location. *Brain and Cognition, 12*, 1–16.

Yund, E.W., Efron, R., & Nichols, D.R. (1990b). Target detection in one visual field in the presence or absence of stimuli in the contralateral field by right and left handed subjects. *Brain and Cognition, 12*, 117–127.

Zarit, S.H. & Kahn, R.L. (1974). Impairment and adaptation in chronic disabilities: Spatial inattention. *Journal of Nervous and Mental Disease, 159*, 63–72.

9 Spatial Dimensions of Automatic and Voluntary Orienting Components of Attention

Elisabetta Làdavas
Dipartimento di Psicologia, Università di Bologna, Bologna, Italy

SELECTIVE ATTENTIONAL DEFICITS FOR DIFFERENT SECTORS OF SPACE

Hemispatial neglect (neglect for the sake of brevity) occurs when patients do not report, respond or orient to stimuli presented contralaterally to the lesioned hemisphere, provided the deficit cannot be attributed to sensory or motor impairments (see, e.g. papers in Jeannerod, 1987). Because neglect is almost always observed after right parietal lesions (Vallar & Perani, 1987), in which follows I will consider only neglect for the left side of space.

Neglect is typically discussed in terms of selective difficulty along the horizontal plane, but there are good reasons to expect neglect for other spatial planes. Objects have a three-dimensional representation and it has been shown that attention can be oriented in depth as well as in the horizontal and vertical dimensions (Gawryszewski, Riggio, Rizzolatti, & Umiltà, 1987). Therefore, if attention can be oriented along each of these dimensions and neglect is defined as a deficit in the orienting component of attention, then it is reasonable to expect attentional deficit related to each of these spatial dimensions. In this section, I will confine myself largely to discuss neglect as a deficit in the automatic orienting component of attention, which can manifest itself in the horizontal dimension as well as in the vertical and depth dimensions. The hypothesis that the attentional deficit is not related to the voluntary orienting component of attention will be also discussed. Moreover, an attempt will be made to explain the deficit by taking into account the pre-motor theory of attention (Rizzolatti, Riggio,

193

Dascola, & Umiltà, 1987; Tassinari, Alioti, Chelazzi, Marzi, & Berlucchi, 1987).

HORIZONTAL DIMENSION

Most of the neuropsychological investigations of human visual neglect have produced an enormous body of data about the perceptual aspect of the deficit and much less attention has been paid to the role of the response coding in determining the deficit. This is surprising because it is well known that normal subjects codify the spatial positions of the stimuli as well as that of the response, and that the employment of one spatial code for the classification of the response determines also the spatial code used for the classification of the stimuli and vice versa. When these spatial codes are applied on the horizontal dimension, the outcome of this mental operation is the specification of the spatial codes "left" and "right" both for stimuli and responses. In the case of space of stimulation, the specification of "left" and "right" codes can be performed for example on the basis of the retinotopic co-ordinates (e.g. left or right visual field) or the environmental co-ordinates (e.g. the relative position of two stimuli). In the case of a manual response, the specification of "left" and "right" codes can be made by taking into account the hand used to respond and its actual position in space (Làdavas & Moscovitch, 1984; Umiltà & Nicoletti, 1990). Since it has been proposed that spatial codes are formed through an attentional process (Umiltà & Liotti, 1987), it is not surprising to find a neglect for the space of stimulation as well as for the space of response. For sake of clarity, I will discuss the two kinds of neglect in two separate sections, although, up to now, there is no empirical evidence for considering them two independent aspects of horizontal neglect.

Neglect for the Space of Stimulation

Definition of Left Space.   Neglect typically affects the left side of space, but the definition of "what is left" depends on the frame of reference adopted by the subject. Objects *per se* do not have intrinsic lefts and rights, and it is the viewer who attributes left and right to objects on the basis of different co-ordinate systems.

In the egocentric frame of reference, the spatial locations of the stimuli are coded according to body co-ordinates (retinal, head and body midline). The relevance of the retinal co-ordinates has been proved, among others, by Làdavas (1987; 1990), who showed that under restricted lateralised presentation of visual stimuli, patients with extinction were less accurate and slower to respond to left than to right visual field stimuli.

In the allocentric frame of reference, the distinction between left and right operates on the basis of stimulus display (display-centred co-ordinates) or object display (object-centred co-ordinates). The relevance of the allocentric co-ordinates is provided by those studies which show that patients with neglect, presented with a visual display, can ignore one side of each individual object in a scene (object-centred co-ordinates) or one side of the scene as a whole (display-centred co-ordinates) (Driver & Halligan, 1991; Gainotti, D'Erme, & De Bonis, 1989). Therefore, it can be said that patients always ignore the left side of a representation, but the co-ordinates according to which left–right spatial codes are formed can vary, probably in accordance with task demands.

The finding that visual neglect manifests itself in object-centred and/or display-centred co-ordinates as well as in body co-ordinates (retinal, head and body midline), is relevant *per se* because it shows that orienting attention in space is a dynamic process which operates according to different systems of co-ordinates and mainly according to task demands. But it must be pointed out that, although this is an important issue, it does not explain in any way why patients with neglect explicitly ignore one side of the display and/or object and/or egocentric space. This issue will be addressed next.

Neglect as a Result of an Hyperattention Deficit.   In order to understand why patients ignore some specific portions of space, it is important to study how the attention of these patients is distributed in the visual field. In a study designed to face this problem (Làdavas, 1990), it was shown that their attention is not equally distributed in the visual field but is focused on the right-most portion of the visual display. Attentional performance of patients with visual extinction was assessed in the experimental condition in which they had to pay attention simultaneously to three spatial positions to the left, right and directly above the fixation stimulus (experiment 1: distributed attention condition) and to only one of the three positions at a time (experiment 2: focused attention condition). The results showed that in experiment 1, the speed (and accuracy) of response to horizontally aligned stimuli increased (decrease in the case of accuracy) gradually from right to left. Reaction times (RTs) to the right stimulus were faster than to the central and left stimuli. Moreover, RTs to the central stimulus were slower than to the right stimulus and faster than to the left stimulus. In contrast, in experiment 2, RTs to the central stimulus were faster than the RTs to the left and right stimuli, and RTs to the right stimulus were faster than the RTs to the left stimulus. More important, speed and accuracy of response to the right stimulus in the distributed attention condition (experiment 1) and in the focused attention condition (experiment 2) were the same. These results showed that, in experiment 1, although the patients were requested to distribute attention simultaneously on the three spatial positions, they focused attention on the right-most stimulus and increased attention to the right was accompanied by decreased attention to the left.

According to several two-stage models of visual attention (for a review, see Umiltà, 1988), attention can be allocated evenly across a large portion of the visual field (i.e. the distributed mode), or can be concentrated on a restricted portion of it (i.e. the focal mode). When attention is in the distributed mode, all possible stimulus positions are processed in parallel at a uniform and relatively slow rate. In the focal mode, processing of the position on which attention is selectively allocated is facilitated, whereas processing of the other positions is inhibited. This is because the area to which attention is allocated can be varied (it can be as small as 1°, or even less), and efficiency of processing decreases as the area covered by attention increases (see, e.g. Castiello & Umiltà, 1990).

On the basis of this model, the results of Làdavas's study seem to suggest that in patients with neglect, spatial attention cannot be allocated to multiple regions of the visual field because it is narrowly focused on the most ipsilesional position. If this interpretation is true, then the deployment of the attentional focus on the right-most position should in turn produce in patients with neglect an enhanced efficiency of processing for the stimuli presented in that position. Therefore, a patient who is presented in the ipsilesional (i.e. intact) visual field with two stimuli horizontally aligned, should process the stimulus on the right relative position faster, not only in comparison with the other stimulus, but also in comparison with control patients. This is because a neglect patient is assumed to have brought focal attention to the right position, whereas the control patients should have distributed attention between the two possible stimulus positions.

This prediction was confirmed by a recent study by Làdavas, Petronio and Umiltà (1990), who showed that neglect patients were faster than controls to respond to the stimuli in the relative right position. Differences in speed and/or accuracy between the two positions could be due to changes in processing efficiency (d') or to changes in response bias (beta). The results of the previous study showed that the effects are attributable to changes in processing efficiency because the differences in response speed were accompanied by congruent differences in sensitivity, whereas no differences in response bias were found.

The findings of Làdavas et al. (1990) and Làdavas (1990) are compatible only with the hypothesis that in patients with neglect, spatial attention cannot be allocated to multiple regions of the visual field because it is narrowly focused on the most ipsilesional area. As a consequence, the benefits in processing efficiency are confined to this area, whereas in adjacent locations only costs are observable. Considering these findings it is possible to define neglect as the result of *hyperattention* for certain sectors of space, as opposed to an attentional deficit for specific locations in space, because the latter effect seems to be a consequence of the former.

Interpretation of the Hyperattentional Deficit. The next point that needs to be addressed is why the affected sector of space is not fixed, but is related to the task, and why patients with neglect show hyperattention for the most ipsilateral stimuli. There are three main hypotheses of neglect.

The *arousal hypothesis* (Heilman, Bowers, Valenstein, & Watson, 1987) maintains that each side of the brain contains its own activating mechanisms and, when one is lesioned, the corresponding hemisphere cannot organise orienting responses towards the contralateral space. This hypothesis cannot explain the first of the points mentioned above. If the deficit is caused by hypoarousal of the right hemisphere, patients should only neglect stimuli shown to the left of fixation, i.e. in the left visual field (LVF). It appears, therefore, that this hypothesis cannot account for the fact that patients may neglect stimuli that are shown in the right visual field (RVF) but are, relatively, on the left (Làdavas, 1987; Rapcsak, Watson, & Heilman, 1987). The authors explained the attentional imbalance within the ipsilesional visual field with reference to the receptive fields of neurons located in cortical structures which appear to be crucially involved in spatial representation (Rapcsak et al., 1987; Rizzolatti, Gentilucci, & Matelli, 1985). They interpreted the right–left attentional asymmetries found in both visual fields in terms of a partial representation of each half of the visual field in attentional areas of both cerebral hemispheres. Rizzolatti et al. (1985), recording from cells in the postarcuate cortex of the monkey, found that of the neurons studied, 29% has exclusively contralateral visual receptive fields, 2% had ipsilateral receptive fields and 69% had bilateral receptive fields. As a consequence, the most lateral part of visual space is represented almost exclusively in one hemisphere, whereas the central part of visual space is represented in both hemispheres. After a lesion in one hemisphere, the capacity to orient to visual stimuli will therefore be affected in the entire visual space, but with a gradient of severity from a maximum in the extreme contralateral hemifield to a minimum in the extreme ipsilateral hemifield.

This hypothesis assumes a fixed relation between the right and left visual fields, as projected through the right and left hemiretinae, and the two hemispheres. It cannot, therefore, account for the attentional bias found in patients with extinction (Làdavas, 1987) and patients with disconnected hemispheres (Làdavas, Del Pesce, Mangun, & Gazzaniga, in press) under the head-tilted condition, because according to the retinal co-ordinates, the two stimuli fall in the upper and lower visual fields. Therefore, we can conclude that this hypothesis (Rapcsak et al., 1987; Rizzolatti et al., 1985) cannot explain the attention imbalance between two separate points on the left–right dimension shown by patients with visual extinction and the two disconnected hemispheres of split-brain patients (see Chapter 3, this volume, for a similar criticism).

According to the *representational hypothesis* (Bisiach & Vallar, 1988), neglect is caused by a deficit in the ability to form a whole representation of space. This hypothesis can explain why the portion of the space affected by the deficit is not fixed, simply by assuming that the space can be represented in different co-ordinate systems. In contrast, this hypothesis cannot explain why neglect patients outperform controls in detecting stimuli which occupy a relative right position in the intact RVF (Làdavas et al., 1990). It is difficult to conceive of a lesion that produces a better representation in some sectors of space.

In contrast, this finding can easily be interpreted within the framework of the orienting hypothesis by assuming that focal attention is "captured" by stimuli that lie in the right-most location. This observation can be consistent with the *directional attentional model* proposed by Kinsbourne, although, as we will see, there are some data which are not in line with his model. Kinsbourne (1977; 1987; see also Chapter 3, this volume) has postulated that each hemisphere is responsible for shifting attention in a contraversive direction, either in the ipsilateral or contralateral half of space, e.g. in the whole space. Damage to one hemisphere would unbalance the attentional system in favour of shifts contraversive to the intact side. This orienting bias would direct attention to the most ipsilesional position and, as a consequence, patients with neglect are faster and more accurate than controls to respond to that spatial position.

Kinsbourne's model implies that the right–left gradient is continuous across the whole field so that costs should increase as a function of the distance of the target from the attended position. This prediction is not supported in Làdavas's (1990) study, because the results obtained in patients with visual extinction showed a discontinuity of this right–left attentional gradient at the junction of the left and right hemisphere. A larger cost was paid when the stimuli were presented at non-attended locations in the hemifield contralateral to the lesion. This phenomenon is observable mainly under restricted lateralised presentation. In free ocular scanning conditions, most patients show an attentional boundary beyond which sustained attention cannot be further directed leftwards. The spatial position of this boundary, however, is not intrinsically linked to the mid-sagittal plane as in the case of restricted laterialised presentation, but to the overall severity of the deficit (Marshall & Halligan, 1989). It must be noted, however, that in this study, the free scanning paradigm renders difficult to determine the exact position of the vertical retinal meridian at any given moment, which of course shifts in accordance with the eyes.

Considering the discontinuity of this right–left attentional gradient at the junction of the left and right hemispace shown by patients with neglect, it must be admitted that the attentional bias towards the right side cannot be the sole explanation of the neglect phenomenon. Therefore, in the case of neglect patients, an additional deficit is likely to play a role. Perhaps not only is attention captured by the right-most location, but, in addition, contralesional stimuli cannot activate the right hemisphere, as suggested by Heilman et al. (1987). The arousal hypothesis maintains that each side of the brain contains its own activation system and, when one system is lesioned, the corresponding hemisphere cannot process sensory information and organise motor responses. As a consequence, there would be a selective loss of the orienting response to the space contralateral to the lesion.

The Pre-motor Theory of Attention.   Another explanation of the discontinuity of this right–left attentional gradient at the junction of the left and right hemispaces is provided by a pre-motor theory of spatial attention (Rizzolatti et al., 1987; Tassinari et al., 1987; see also Chapter 4, this volume). In order to understand how this theory can explain the effect, it is worthwhile introducing an important distinction between overt orienting, which is accompanied by head and eye movements, and purely covert orienting, which can be achieved in the absence of body movements (see, e.g. Posner, 1978; 1980).

As pointed out by Shepherd, Findley and Hockey (1986; also see Umiltà, 1988), the relationship between eye movements and spatial attention can logically manifest itself in three forms. According to the identity hypothesis, the mechanisms involved in the generation of eye movements are identical with those that produce attention shifts. The independence hypothesis maintains that there are two mechanisms, one for eye movements and one for attention shifts, which are not functionally related. A third view, namely the interdependency hypothesis, is that the two mechanisms are neither identical nor completely independent, so that the functioning of one of the two can be facilitated or inhibited by the other.

The identity hypothesis has been disproved by a number of experiments that clearly demonstrated that attention can be directed to different points in space, regardless of eye position (see e.g. Jonides, 1983; Posner, 1978, 1980; Umiltà, 1988). The evidence concerning the independence hypothesis and the interdependence hypothesis is less decisive, even though several attempts have been made to compare them (Klein, 1980; Posner, 1980; Shepherd et al., 1986; Shepherd & Muller, 1989; Remington, 1980; Rizzolatti et al., 1987). All considered, it seems that the evidence available to date favours the interdependence hypothesis. A strong version of this hypothesis was recently proposed by Rizzolatti et al. (1987) and Tassinari et al. (1987), who postulated a strict link between covert orienting of attention and the programming of ocular movements (see also Chapter 5, this volume). The basic idea is that overt orienting and covert orienting are both controlled by the neural mechanisms that are also in charge of saccade programming. Upon the presentation of a stimulus, a motor programme for the saccade is prepared, which specifies the direction and the amplitude of the eye movement. This occurs regardless of whether the saccade is actually executed (i.e. overt orienting) or is not executed (i.e. covert orienting).

It is possible to hypothesise that in patients with a right parietal lobe lesion, the orienting response is under the control of the intact left hemisphere and, therefore, the essential element which characterises the preparation to respond is the specification of the direction "right" as opposed to "left". When the patient has to respond to RVF stimuli, the task does not require any correction of the directional programme, because the system is already prepared to respond to that direction. Conversely, if the subject has to respond to LVF stimuli, the task requires the correction of directional bias, and as a result the emission of response is retarded or, in the case of patients with severe neglect, omitted. This interpretation implies that reorienting of attention is necessary before a manual response can be emitted to a stimulus that appears in a left unattended position. Posner (1980) has suggested that an arbitrary response, that is one not automatically triggered by a stimulus, only occurs through the commitment of conscious attention. In other words, a stimulus must enter the focus of attention and become conscious before an arbitrary response to it can be emitted. If the stimulus does not enter the focus of attention, the response is omitted, even though the stimulus can influence the patient's behaviour without the patient being aware of the stimulus (Bisiach & Rusconi, 1990; Marshall & Halligan, 1988; Volpe, Le Doux, & Gazzaniga, 1979).

Therefore, because the pre-motor theory of attention postulates a strict link between covert orienting of attention and the programming of ocular movements, it can explain the discontinuity of the right–left attentional gradient at the junction of the left and right hemispace found in patients with neglect, as well as the finding that in these patients right attentional shifts are very often associated with a gaze displacement to the right-most position (De Renzi, Gentilini, Faglioni, & Barbieri, 1989). De Renzi, Colombo, Faglioni and Gibertoni (1982) pointed out that gaze displacement to the right-most position, triggered by visual stimulation, can be viewed as a milder manifestation of the phenomenon of eye and head deviation towards the side of lesion. According to these authors, the imbalance between the hemispheric turning apparatuses caused by a unilateral lesion is initially independent of stimulation as far as it is present even in soporose patients having their eyes closed and during sleep. Doricchi, Guariglia, Paolucci and Pizzamiglio (1991) showed that in patients with neglect, the leftward rapid eye movements (REMs) were virtually absent, whereas rightward REMs were present. In contrast, when the deficit is of a milder degree of severity, the patient can control and inhibit the compulsory shift of gaze to the right-most end of the structured space and, as a consequence, the eyes are not any longer deviated towards the right. None the less, it is still possible to observe a rightward attentional bias after an RVF stimulation because the oculomotor system is still programmed to respond in that direction.

On the other hand, this uncontrollable gaze deviation towards the right-most extremity of space is associated with increased time for leftward eye movements and for left shifts of attention. Chedru, Leblanc and Lhermitte (1973) found that marked left unilateral neglect was associated with increased time for leftward eye movements and the degree of asymmetry in eye movement exploration was positively correlated with the degree of unilateral inattention. Moreover, it seems that the deficit can be reduced by asking the patient to turn his or her eyes to the left. Meador et al. (1989) have shown that, when patients with left neglect are requested to imagine a very familiar scene, recall of the items located on the left side of the image is more accurate when they turn their eyes/head to the left.

Within this theoretical framework, other recent data on caloric vestibular stimulation (Cappa, Sterzi, Vallar, & Bisiach, 1987; Vallar et al., 1990) and on the induction of optokinetic nystagmus (Pizzamiglio et al., 1990) fit very well. Either caloric vestibular stimulation or optokinetic nystagmus causes a striking, though temporary, reduction in neglect. Considering that this procedure produces eye deviation towards the neglected side, and that according to the pre-motor theory of attention a motor programme for an eye movement is always accompanied by a corresponding attentional shift, one can well imagine how the eye deviation also renders possible the orienting of attention towards the neglected side.

In conclusion, neglect for the space of stimulation can be regarded as a directional deficit, due to the fact that the component of the motor system which specifies the direction for eye movements or shifts of attention is programmed, by default, to respond only to one direction, e.g. the one ipsilateral to the lesion.

Neglect for Space of Response

In a recent study, Duhamel and Brouchon (1990) stressed the importance of a subtle interplay between afferent (coding of the target) and efferent (coding of the response) processes in the neglect phenomenon. They studied a patient with neglect for the left half of space in a task requiring manual pointing to visual targets located to the left and right visual fields, and found that the difference in speed and accuracy between left and right targets was dependent upon the response condition. They found that the hand contralateral to the lesion was slower than the ipsilateral hand in responding to LVF stimuli and not to RVF stimuli and that the initial spatial position of the responding hand influenced the patient's responses, e.g. the right hand located on the left side of the space was always associated to longer RTs compared to the condition in which it was located on the right side of space. Similar results were found by Halligan, Manning and Marshall (1991), who showed that the position of the responding hand modulates the expression of left neglect in a line bisection task. These findings indicate that hand position in space is taken into account in response preparation and that a lesion on the parietal lobe causes an impairment for the responses emitted in the space contralateral to the lesion.

Considering these results, it seems that in patients with neglect there are at least two components of response coding which can be related and interfere with the stimulus coding: the responding hand (e.g. the left and right hand) and the absolute position of the hand in space (e.g. the left and right space defined according to the body midline). It is known from studies on spatial compatibility effects that there is at least another component of response coding which is taken into account for the emission of response, e.g. the coding of the relative position of the effectors (Nicoletti, Umiltà, & Làdavas, 1984). Considering the relevance of this component, it is not surprising to find neglect also for those responses that require a left–right coding of the relative position of the effectors.

An experimental task in which this third component of response coding is taken into account for the emission of the response requires patients to respond to visual stimuli with the hand ipsilateral to the lesion (the right hand) located on the ipsilesional side (the right side according to the body midline) and left–right finger discrimination. Due to task demands, it is possible to find neglect attributable to left–right finger discriminations and not to the hand used or to the hemispace where the response is emitted. We tested this hypothesis in a study where patients with neglect were presented with two numbers, 1 and 2, shown in the LVF and RVF, and they were required to respond with the index finger to number 1 and the middle finger to number 2, independent of the visual field (Làdavas & Cimatti, in prep.). The results showed that patients with neglect never responded to LVF stimuli, and that responses to RVF stimuli associated with the index finger, which occupied the left position, were slower and less accurate than responses associated with the middle finger, which occupied the right position.

This finding cannot be explained by motor neglect, because the patients respond with the hand ipsilateral to the lesion, or with directional akinesia, because the response does not imply any overt directional response. The results can be explained by taking into account that in these patients there is a motor predisposition to react to the right. When the patient has to respond with the middle finger, which occupies a right position, the task does not require any correction of the directional programme, because the motor system is already prepared to respond towards the right. Conversely, when the patient has to respond with the index finger, which occupies the left position, the task requires the correction of a directional bias, and as a result the emission of the response is retarded or omitted.

If we accept this interpretation, we can conclude that the motor programme responsible for a directional specification of hand movement along the horizontal dimension is biased towards the right and that this bias becomes manifest in any task which requires left–right discriminations. Taking the results of this study into account, as well as those mentioned above, we can conclude that neglect for the space of response manifests itself in tasks which require specification of the hand to be used to respond, for each hand the specification of the hemispace where the hand operates and, finally, in the case of left–right finger discriminations, the specification of the spatial code describing the positions of the fingers.

The observation that the oculomotor system and the motor programme which guides the hand along the horizontal dimension in patients with neglect are biased towards the right can be explained by findings that showed that ocular and manual responses are integrated within a single spatial frame of reference (Fisk & Goodale, 1985; Mather & Fisk, 1985). Additional evidence has been provided by Fries, Swihart and Danek (1989). They reported a patient with a mild left hemianopia and visuo-spatial neglect who could localise LVF stimuli with great difficulty by a series of small ("stair-case") saccades. However, localising eye movements were normal if the visual stimulus had previously been pointed to by the right hand.

VERTICAL DIMENSION

The horizontal dimension is not the only one affected by neglect, because left neglect patients can also show an attentional deficit along the vertical dimension. Other authors have already pointed out the existence of altitudinal neglect (Bender & Teuber, 1948; Rapcsak, Cimino, & Heilman, 1988) and that this deficit can be more pronounced in the lower quadrant of the left hemispace (Halligan & Marshall, 1989). Moreover, Halligan and Marshall (1989) have recently shown that this phenomenon is more evident in the contralateral than in the ipsilateral visual field.

In a recent study, Làdavas and Carletti (in prep.) have tested the hypothesis that neglect for the lower part of the space can appear independently of the neglect field, i.e. also along the vertical meridian. The experimental condition was the same as that used in the experiment designed to test neglect for the space of response, with the exception that the two stimuli (1 or 2) were presented above and below fixation. The results showed that patients were much slower and less accurate to respond to the stimuli presented below than above the fixation mark. The deficit for the lower part of the visual field was much more severe when the bottom stimulus required a left response than when it required a right response, indicating an interaction between neglect for the lower part of the visual field and neglect for the space of response. The observed deficit cannot be sensory in nature, because all of the patients had the lower quadrant of the visual field intact, as assessed by campimetry. Moreover, the magnitude of the deficit was reduced when the patient's attention was cued to the lower visual field. In other words, when Posner's paradigm was used to cue attention to the lower visual field, the difference between up and down was reduced in the same way as the left-side deficit is reduced when the LVF is cued by a central arrow (Làdavas, Menghini, & Umiltà, 1991; Posner, Walker, Friedrich, & Rafal, 1987).

Therefore, the deficit observed along the vertical dimension seems to be attentional in nature, although, at this stage, we cannot say whether the pre-motor theory of attention can accommodate these results. The patients, in fact, did not show, as the theory predicts, any partial or total incapacity to move the eyes or the head vertically. Rizzolatti et al. (1987) proposed the pre-motor theory of attention on the basis of the findings that motor deficits are associated with attentional deficits and the latter are congruent with the former. If the closed relationship between eye movement deficits and attentional shift deficits found for the horizontal dimension in patients with left neglect can be explained by the pre-motor theory of attention, this theory cannot yet account for the neglect found for the lower part of the visual field.

In conclusion, considering the fact that objects have a three-dimensional representation and that attention can be oriented in depth as well as in the horizontal and vertical dimensions (Gawryszewski et al., 1987), it is not surprising to find neglect for each of these spatial dimensions. As far as the depth dimension is concerned, it is worth mentioning some studies (Bisiach, Perani, Vallar, & Berti, 1986; Halligan & Marshall, 1991) that described patients showing personal neglect without having extrapersonal neglect and vice versa, which can be interpreted as a dissociation between the capacity to shift attention in the far and near space (or personal and peripersonal space).

IS THE DEFICIT RELATED TO AUTOMATIC OR VOLUNTARY ORIENTING OF ATTENTION?

An important distinction that emerges from the study of normal subjects is that between voluntary and automatic orienting (Muller & Findley, 1988; Muller & Rabbitt, 1989; Spencer, Lambert, & Hockey, 1988; Yantis & Jonides, 1984). It is known that attention can be directed to the position of an impending target by the use of centrally located cues or peripherally located cues. In the first case, a conventional signal shown at or around fixation indicates the position to which attention must be directed. In the second case, a peripheral marker, in the form of a salient discontinuity in a non-foveal area, is shown near the location to which the stimulus will be presented.

Based on criteria such as capacity demands, resistance to suppression and sensitivity to expectancy, peripheral cues are shown to cause automatic shifts of attention, whereas central cues start voluntary shifts. This has led to the notion that automatic and voluntary orienting can be achieved by two separate mechanisms (Muller & Findley, 1987; Muller & Rabbitt, 1989). In contrast, Posner (1980) and Jonides (1983) assume that there is one mechanism only, which can be triggered automatically by peripheral cues or initiated voluntarily by central cues. In their view, the two modes of orienting are thought to differ only in the ways attention shifts are initiated, rather than in the mechanisms that guide them.

If we consider neglect as an attentional deficit, it can be reasoned that if a single-mechanism subserves automatic and voluntary orienting of attention, neglect patients should be impaired in responding to LVF stimuli both in the peripheral and central cue conditions. In contrast, if the dual-mechanism hypothesis holds true, we should expect the attentional deficit to be associated more with one type of orienting than with the other.

Automatic and voluntary shifts of attention in patients with neglect were tested in two experiments (Làdavas, 1992). In the automatic orienting experiment, an arrow head in the periphery was chosen as the cue that automatically draws attention. In the voluntary orienting experiment, an arrow head at fixation was chosen as the cue that could cause a voluntary shift of attention. In the first experiment, the arrow did not predict the location of the stimulus, whereas in the second experiment the cue was highly predictive of the location of the stimulus. This is because it has been shown that cue validity, i.e. the probability with which the cue predicts the target location, affects the voluntary orienting of attention. There were four possible stimulus locations which were arranged either horizontally or vertically, above, below, to the right or left of a fixation point. The instructions were to respond manually as fast as possible to a visual stimulus, regardless of whether it occurred in a cued or in a non-cued location.

The results showed that when the cue appeared in the same location of the stimulus, patients with neglect never responded to LVF stimuli under the automatic orienting condition, whereas they were much more accurate to respond under the voluntary attention condition. Such results indicate that any deficits in the automatic orienting component of attention can be modulated by voluntary attentional processes (see Chapters 5 and 7, this volume, for a similar view). Therefore, it seems that in patients with neglect, voluntary shifts of attention are preserved and this is probably due to the fact that this function is subserved by the frontal lobe, which in these patients was intact.

If it is true that the frontal lobe mediates voluntary shifts of attention, then opposite results to those obtained in patients with a parietal lesion would be expected in patients with frontal lobe lesions. A recent study by Làdavas, Della Sala, Cimatti and Trivelli (1991) showed that patients with frontal dorsolateral lesions were impaired in the voluntary orienting of attention, whereas their automatic orienting was fairly intact. These patients very rarely responded to stimuli presented in the peripheral field when the stimulus was preceded by a central cue, whereas they always detected the stimulus presented in the peripheral field when it was preceded by a peripheral cue. They also made more false alarms than patients with parietal damage, and this pattern of results appeared only in the peripheral cue condition. The inability shown by patients with a frontal syndrome to voluntary attend a specific spatial position and to suppress the tendency to respond to the peripheral cues, allowed the authors to hypothesise that the frontal lobe mediates the voluntary orienting component of attention. The same anatomical dissociation has been proposed for reflex-like orienting eye movements and volitional eye movements (Guitton, Buchtel, & Douglas, 1985; Doricchi et al., 1991).

These findings seem to support the dual-mechanism hypothesis, which maintains that automatic and voluntary orienting are subserved by separate mechanisms located in different parts of the brain. More specifically, it would seem that the frontal lobe mediates voluntary orienting of attention, whereas the parietal lobe modulates automatic orienting of attention. In particular, it appears that the right parietal lobe mediates automatic orienting towards the left and the left parietal lobe mediates automatic orienting towards the right. Damage to the right hemisphere would unbalance the attentional system in favour of automatic rightward shifts, which can be overcome by a rehabilitation procedure aimed at training the patients to voluntary direct attention to stimuli shown in the neglected contralesional field (Làdavas, Menghini, & Umiltà, in press a & b).

REFERENCES

Bender, M.B. & Teuber, H.L. (1948). Spatial organization of visual perception following injury to the brain. *Archives of Neurology and Psychiatry*, *59*, 39–62.

Bisiach, E., Perani, D., Vallar, G., & Berti, A. (1986). Unilateral neglect: Personal and extra-personal. *Neuropsychologia*, *24*, 759–767.

Bisiach, E. & Rusconi, M.L. (1990). Breakdown of perceptual awareness in unilateral neglect. *Cortex*, *26*, 1–7.

Bisiach, E. & Vallar, G. (1988). Hemineglect in humans. In F. Boller & J. Grafman (Eds), *Handbook of Neuropsychology*, pp. 195–222. Amsterdam: Elsevier.

Cappa, S., Sterzi, R., Vallar, G., & Bisiach, E. (1987). Remission of hemineglect and anosognosia during vestibular stimulation. *Neuropsychologia, 25,* 775–782.

Castiello, U. & Umiltà, C. (1990). Size of the attentional focus and efficiency of processing. *Acta Psychologica, 73,* 195–209.

Chedru, F., Leblanc, M., & Lhermitte, F. (1973). Visual searching in normal and brain-damaged subjects: Contribution to the study of unilateral inattention. *Cortex, 9,* 94–111.

De Renzi, E., Colombo, A., Faglioni, P., & Gibertoni, M. (1982). Conjugate gaze paresis in stroke patients with unilateral damage. *Archives of Neurology, 39,* 482–486.

De Renzi, E., Gentilini, M., Faglioni, P., & Barbieri, C. (1989). Attentional shift towards the rightmost stimuli in patients with left visual neglect. *Cortex, 25,* 231–237.

Doricchi, F., Guariglia, C., Paolucci, S., & Pizzamiglio, L. (1991). Disappearance of leftward rapid eye movements during sleep in the left visual hemi-inattention. *Cognitive Neuroscience and Neuropsychology, 2,* 285–288.

Driver, J. & Halligan, P.W. (1991). Can visual neglect operate in object-centered coordinates? An affirmative single-case study. *Cognitive Neuropsychology, 6,* 475–496.

Duhamel, J.R., & Brouchon, M. (1990). Sensory aspects of unilateral neglect: A single case analysis. *Cognitive Neuropsychology, 7,* 57–74.

Fisk, J.D. & Goodale, M.A. (1985). The organization of eye and limb movements during unrestricted reaching to targets in contralateral and ipsilateral visual space. *Experimental Brain Research, 60,* 159–178.

Fries, W., Swihart, A.A., & Danek, A. (1989). Somatosensory substitution of spatial information improves oculomotor performance in visual neglect. In *Brain damage and rehabilitation: A neuropsychological approach.* Munich: Edition Wissenschaft Kyrill und Method.

Gainotti, G., D'Erme, P., & De Bonis, C. (1989). Aspects cliniques et mecanismes de la négligence visuo-spatiale. *Revue Neurologique, 145,* 626–634.

Gawryszewski, L.D.G., Riggio, L. Rizzolatti, G., & Umiltà, C. (1987). Movements of attention in three spatial dimensions and the meaning of "neutral" cues. *Neuropsychologia, 25,* 19–29.

Guitton, D., Buchtel, H.A., & Douglas, M. (1985). Frontal lobe lesions in man cause difficulties in suppressing reflexive glances and in generating goal-directed saccades. *Experimental Brain Research, 58,* 455–472.

Halligan, P.W., Manning, L. & Marshall, J.C. (1991). Hemispheric activation *vs* spatio-motor cueing in visual neglect: A case study. *Neuropsychologia, 29,* 165–176.

Halligan, P.W. & Marshall, J.C. (1989). Is neglect (only) lateral? A quadrant analysis of line cancellation. *Journal of Clinical and Experimental Neuropsychology, 6,* 793–798.

Halligan, P.W. & Marshall, J.C. (1991). Left neglect for near but not far space in man. *Nature, 350,* 498–500.

Heilman, K.M., Bowers, D., Coslett, H.B., Whelan, H., & Watson, R.T. (1985). Directional hypokinesia. *Neurology, 35,* 855–859.

Heilman, K.M., Bowers, D., Valenstein, E., & Watson, R.T. (1987). Hemispace and hemispatial neglect. In M. Jeannerod (Ed.), *Neurophysiological and neuropsychological aspects of spatial neglect,* pp. 115–150. Amsterdam, North-Holland.

Jeannerod, M. (Ed.) (1987). *Neurophysiological and neuropsychological aspects of spatial neglect.* Amsterdam: North-Holland.

Jonides, J. (1983). Further toward a model of the mind's eye's movement. *Bulletin of the Psychonomic Society, 21,* 247–250.

Kinsbourne, M. (1977). Hemineglect and hemisphere rivalry. In E.A. Weinstein & R.P. Friedland (Eds), *Hemi-inattention and hemisphere specialization,* pp. 41–49. New York: Raven Press.

Kinsbourne, M. (1987). Mechanisms of unilateral neglect. In M. Jeannerod (Ed.), *Neurophysiological and neuropsychological aspects of spatial neglect,* pp. 69–86. Amsterdam: North-Holland.

Klein, R. (1980). Does oculomotor readiness mediate cognitive control of visual attention? In R.S. Nickerson (Ed.), *Attention and performance VIII*, pp. 259–276. Hillsdale, NJ: Lawrence Erlbaum Associates Inc.

Làdavas, E. (1987). Is the hemispatial deficit produced by right parietal lobe damage associated with retinal or gravitational coordinates? *Brain, 110*, 167–180.

Làdavas, E. (1990). Selective spatial attention in patients with visual extinction. *Brain, 113*, 1527–1538.

Làdavas, E. (1992). *Automatic and voluntary orienting of attention: A dissociation between patients with frontal and parietal lesions.* Paper presented at TENNET III, Montreal, 20–22 May.

Làdavas, E. & Carletti, M. (in prep.). Attentional orienting deficit in patients with visual neglect.

Làdavas, E.& Cimatti (in prep.). Directional motor aspects of visual neglect.

Làdavas, E., Della Sala, S., Simatti, D., & Trivelli, C. (1991). *Selective visual attention in patients with frontal lobe lesions.* Paper presented at the Third IBRO World Congress of Neuroscience, Montreal, 4–9 August.

Làdavas, E., Del Pesce, M., Mangun, R., & Gazzaniga, M. (in press). Variations in attentional bias in the two disconnected cerebral hemispheres. *Cognitive Neuropsychology.*

Làdavas, E., Menghini, G., & Umiltà, C. (in press a). On the rehabilitation of hemispatial neglect. In M.J. Riddoch & G.W. Humphreys (Eds), *Cognitive neuropsychology and cognitive rehabilitation.* Hove: Lawrence Erlbaum Associates Ltd.

Làdavas, E., Menghini, G., & Umiltà, C. (in press b). A rehabilitation study of hemispatial neglect. *Cognitive Neuropsychology.*

Làdavas, E. & Moscovitch, M. (1984). Must egocentric and environmental frames of reference be aligned to produce spatial S-R compatibility effects? *Journal of Experimental Psychology: Human Perception and Performance, 10*, 205–215.

Làdavas, E., Petronio, A., & Umiltà, C. (1990). The deployment of visual attention in the intact field of hemineglect patients. *Cortex, 26*, 307–317.

Marshall, J.C. & Halligan, P.W. (1988). Blindsight and insight in visuo-spatial neglect. *Nature, 336*, 766–777.

Marshall, J.C. & Halligan, P.W. (1989). Does the midsagittal plane play any privileged role in "left" neglect? *Cognitive Neuropsychology, 6*, 403–422.

Mather, J.A. & Fisk, J.D. (1985). Orienting to targets by looking and pointing: Parallels and interaction in ocular and manual performance. *Quarterly Journal of Experimental Psychology, 37A*, 315–338.

Meador, K.J., Loring, D.W., Lee, G.P., Brooks, B.S., Nichols, F.T., Thompson, E.E., Thompson, W.O., & Heilman, K.M. (1989). Hemisphere asymmetry for eye gaze mechanisms. *Brain, 112*, 103–111.

Muller, H.J. & Findley, M. (1987). Sensitivity and criterion effects in the spatial cuing of visual attention. *Perception and Psychophysics, 42*, 383–399.

Muller, H.J. & Findley, J.M. (1988). The effect of visual attention on peripheral discrimination threshold in single and multiple element displays. *Acta Psychologica, 69*, 129–155.

Muller, H.J. & Rabbitt, P.M. (1989). Reflexive and voluntary orienting of visual attention: Time course of activation and resistance to interruption. *Journal of Experimental Psychology: Human Perception and Performance, 15*, 315–330.

Nicoletti, R., Umiltà, C., & Làdavas, E. (1984). Compatibility due to the coding of the relative position of the effectors. *Acta Psychologica, 57*, 133–143.

Pizzamiglio, L., Frasca, R., Guariglia, C., Incaccia, R., & Antonucci, G. (1990). Effect of optokinetic stimulation in patients with visual neglect. *Cortex, 26*, 535–540.

Posner, M.I. (1978). *Chronometric exploration of mind.* Hillsdale, NJ: Lawrence Erlbaum Associations Inc.

Posner, M.I. (1980). Orienting of attention. *Quarterly Journal of Experimental Psychology, 32,* 3–25.

Posner, M.I., Walker, J.A., Friedrich, F.A., & Rafal, R.D. (1987). How do the parietal lobes direct covert attention? *Neuropsychologia, 25,* 135–145.

Rapcsak, S.Z., Watson, R.T., & Heilman, K.M. (1987). Hemispace–visual field interactions in visual extinction. *Journal of Neurology, Neurosurgery and Psychiatry, 50,* 1117–1124.

Rapcsak, S.Z., Cimino, C.R., & Heilman, K.M. (1988). Altitudinal neglect. *Neurology, 38,* 277–281.

Remington, R.W. (1980). Attention and saccadic eye movements. *Journal of Experimental Psychology, 6,* 726–744.

Rizzolatti, G. & Camarda, R. (1987). Neural circuits for spatial attention and unilateral neglect. In M. Jeannerod (Ed.), *Neurophysiological and neuropsychological aspects of spatial neglect.* Amsterdam: North-Holland.

Rizzolatti, G., Gentilucci, M., & Matelli, M. (1985). Selective spatial attention: One center, one circuit or many circuits? In M.I. Posner & O.S.M. Marin (Eds), *Attention and performance IX.* Hillsdale, NJ: Lawrence Erlbaum Associates Inc.

Rizzolatti, G., Riggio, L., Dascola, I., & Umiltà, C. (1987). Reorienting attention across the horizontal and vertical meridians: Evidence in favor of a premotor theory of attention. *Neuropsychologia, 25,* 31–40.

Shepherd, M. & Muller, H.J. (1989). Movement versus focusing of attention. *Perception and Psychophysics, 46,* 146–154.

Shepherd, M., Findley, J.M., & Hockey, R.J. (1986). The relationship between eye movements and spatial attention. *Quarterly Journal of Experimental Psychology, 38A,* 475–491.

Spencer, M.B.H., Lambert, A.J., & Hockey, R. (1988). The inhibitory component of orienting, alertness and sustained attention. *Acta Psychologica, 69,* 165–184.

Tassinari, G., Alioti, S., Chelazzi, L., Marzi, C., & Berlucchi, G. (1987). Distribution in the visual field of the costs of voluntary allocated attention and of the inhibitory after-effects of covert orienting. *Neuropsychologia, 25,* 55–71.

Umiltà, C. (1988). Orienting of attention. In F. Boller & J. Grafman (Eds), *Handbook of neuropsychology,* Vol. 1, pp. 175–193. Amsterdam: Elsevier.

Umiltà, C. & Liotti, M. (1987). Egocentric and relative spatial codes in S-R compatibility. *Psychological Research, 49,* 81–90.

Umiltà, C. & Nicoletti, R. (1990). Spatial stimulus–response compatbility. In R.W. Proctor & T.G. Reeve (Eds), *Stimulus–response compatibility: An integrated perspective.* Amsterdam: North-Holland.

Vallar, G. & Perani, D. (1987). The anatomy of spatial neglect in humans. In M. Jeannerod (Ed.), *Neurophysiological and neuropsychological aspects of spatial neglect,* pp. 235–258. Amsterdam: North-Holland.

Vallar, G., Sterzi, R., Bottini, G., Cappa, S., & Rusconi, L. (1990). Temporary remission of left hemianesthesia after vestibular stimulation. A sensory neglect phenomenon. *Cortex, 26,* 123–131.

Volpe, B.T., Le Doux, J.E., & Gazzaniga, M.S. (1979). Information processing of visual stimuli in an "extinguished" field. *Nature, 282,* 722–724.

Yantis, S. & Jonides, J. (1984). Abrupt visual onsets and selective attention: Evidence from visual search. *Journal of Experimental Psychology, 10,* 601–620.

10 Shifts and Omissions in Spatial Reference in Unilateral Neglect

Reinhard Werth
Institut für Soziale Paediatrie und Jugendmedizin, Universität München, München, Germany

INTRODUCTION

Reports about patients who omitted stimuli in one half of the visual field although there was no visual field defect that could explain these omissions, have been published since the end of the last century (Holmes, 1918; Oppenheim, 1885; Pinéas, 1931; Poppelreuter, 1917). Patients who did not "... report, respond, or orient to novel and meaningful stimuli presented in the hemispace contralateral to a brain lesion" were considered as having a hemispatial neglect (Heilman, Bowers, Valenstein, & Watson, 1987, p. 116). The diagnosis of a hemispatial neglect was only regarded as justified if the failure to report, respond or orient to stimuli was not due to a sensory or motor inability (Heilman, 1979).

Patients with a hemispatial neglect may not look to the neglected side on command or in pursuit of a stimulus, or they may only show a decrease in the frequency and amplitude of eye and head movements directed into the affected half of space (Battersby, Bender, Pollack, & Kahn, 1956; Cambier, Elghozi, Graveleau, & Lubetzki, 1984; Chain, Leblanc, Chédru, & Lhérmitte, 1979; Chédru, Leblanc, & Lhérmitte, 1973; Denny-Brown & Banker, 1954; Ogren, Mateer, & Wyler, 1984; Zihl & von Cramon, 1979). Although the patients have no hemianopia, they may not detect stimuli in the visual field contralateral to the lesioned hemisphere if their attention is attracted by an object which is presented in the other half of the visual field (Denny-Brown, Meyer, & Horenstein, 1952; Patterson & Zangwill, 1944). A neglect may also be present in sense modalities other than the visual. A

211

patient may, for example, not orient or respond otherwise to sounds if they are presented in one half of space (Cambier, Elghozi, & Strube, 1980; Gloning, 1965; Koch & von Stockert, 1935; Watson & Heilman, 1979). If patients with neglect are required to explore the peripersonal space tactually without visual control, they may not move their hand into the affected half of space to search tactually for objects (Bisiach, Capitani, & Porta, 1985; Sandifer, 1946). Patients with a severe neglect may never mention the half of space contralateral to the lesioned hemisphere, and they may behave as if this half of space had ceased to exist.

The first section of this chapter deals with omissions of visual stimuli in children where brain damage occurred pre-natally or several days after birth. The following two sections focus on omissions in the half of space ipsilateral to the cerebral lesion in adults and on shifts of visual spatial relations which are observed in the line bisection task.

VISUAL NEGLECT IN CHILDREN

Visual Neglect and Visual Field Defects in Infants

Signs of a neglect of one half of space can already be observed in brain-damaged infants. Whereas healthy infants direct their gaze immediately to light stimuli which are presented in their visual field (Finlay, Quinn, & Ivinskis, 1982; Harris & MacFarlane, 1974; Mohn & van Hoff-van Duin, 1986; Tronick, 1972), brain-damaged infants often do not react to stimuli in one visual hemifield. In the case of these infants, omission of stimuli in one visual hemifield does not allow one to distinguish between a visual field defect and a neglect of one half of space. The diagnosis of a visual neglect rests mainly on the observation that these infants constantly direct their head and eyes into one half of space and on a paucity of eye and head movements directed into the other half of space.

When these infants recover, there is sometimes no gradual widening of the visual field as reported in adult patients (Zihl, 1981; Zihl & von Cramon, 1985), but there is an increase in the frequency of eye and head movements directed to stimuli irrespective of their eccentricity in the visual field. At the same time, the frequency of spontaneous eye and head movements directed to the neglected half of space in the absence of light stimuli increases. The symptoms of a visual neglect may disappear within several weeks or months. A paucity of eye and head movements directed into one half of space and a tendency to omit stimuli in one half of the visual field may, however, persist for many years.

Although visual field defects and a paucity of eye and head movements occur often simultaneously, both disturbances are dissociated. Many children with visual field defects explore the left and right half of space by eye and head movements. On the other hand, children without a visual field defect may not direct their gaze into one half of space. Neither in children nor in adults are visual field defects a necessary or sufficient condition for a paucity of visual exploration of one half of space (Chain, Leblanc, Chédru, Lhérmitte, 1979; Girotti, Casazza, Musicco, & Avanzini, 1983; Meienberg, 1983).

Interaction Between Visual Neglect and a Visual Field Defect

The severity of the omission of visual stimuli is often the consequence of the interaction of a sensory visual impairment and symptoms of a visual neglect. If homonymous hemianopia and a paucity of eye and head movements into the half of space ipsilateral to the blind half of the visual field occur together, the consequences of the visual field defect cannot be compensated by eye and head movements. These patients constantly omit objects in the affected half of space and are severely disabled in everyday life. Neuropsychological therapy should focus on the restitution of compensatory eye and head movements and, if possible, on the restitution of visual functions in the blind area (Zihl, 1981; Zihl & von Cramon, 1985).

Vertical Visual Neglect

In children, objects or light targets may not only be omitted in the left or in the right half of space (Ferro, Pavao Martins, & Tavora, 1984). The following case shows that stimuli may also only be omitted in a region below the horizontal meridian of the visual field. These symptoms of a vertical neglect were present in a 10-year-old boy. When the patient faced a semi-circular screen (luminance: 5 cd/m^2) and fixated a light spot in the centre of the screen, he detected targets (luminance: 240 cd/m^2) on the horizontal meridian up to 90° eccentricity. The patient was asked to shift his gaze as quickly as possible from the central position to the target which was shown at 40° eccentricity on the horizontal meridian. Eye movements were recorded using skin electrodes. The duration of the time intervals between the onset of a target in the left half of the visual field and the beginning of the eye movements (20 trials: $\bar{x} \pm$ s.D. $= 201.8 \pm 37.1$ msec) were not significantly different from the duration of the time intervals between the onset of a target in the right half of the visual field and the beginning of the eye movement (20 trials: $\bar{x} \pm$ s.D. $= 209.6 \pm 38.0$ msec) (t-test: $P > 0.2$).

Targets that were presented with an eccentricity of more than 30° below the horizontal meridian were never detected. However, when the patient was informed that the targets would be presented in an area of more than 30° eccentricity below the horizontal meridian and the location of the targets was shown to him before the test, he could detect all targets. When the targets appeared pseudorandomly in the upper or in the lower half of the visual field, he could not detect targets in the lower visual field.

When asked to shift his gaze as quickly as possible from the central position to a target at 40° eccentricity below or above the fixation point on the vertical meridian, the duration of the interval between the onset of the target and the beginning of the eye movement was longer when the targets were in the lower visual field (20 trials: $\bar{x} \pm$ s.d. = 574.2 ± 100.9 msec) than when the targets were in the upper visual field (20 trials: $\bar{x} \pm$ s.d. = 276.9 ± 54.5 msec.). A computerised tomographic scan showed no cerebral lesion. The EEG exhibited slow-wave activity in the right temporo-occipital region.

The Restitution of Visual Search in Infants

Whereas adult patients and older children can be verbally instructed during therapeutic sessions, young children do not yet understand these instructions or do not easily follow them. These children may, however, start to search visually for objects in the neglected half of space when visual search is reinforced.

The effect of reinforcement on visual exploration of a neglected half of space will be demonstrated with the example of a 2-year-old boy who suffered from a temporo-occipital haemangioma which led to intraventricular bleeding and a dilatation of the lateral ventricles. The right lateral ventricle communicated with a cyst stretching from the white matter in the posterior frontal lobe to the white matter of the occipital lobe. The child suffered from an incomplete left homonymous hemianopia. Between 60° and 70° eccentricity, the left visual field was normal. Following eye and head movements could be elicited when the target moved from a central position into the left or into the right half of space. In everyday life, the child did not orient to objects in the left half of space and continuously bumped into objects on his left.

To test his spontaneous visual search, the child was facing the surface of a semi-circular white screen (luminance: 5 cd/m^2) at a distance of 33 cm fixating a central point. Head movements were recorded using two video-cameras; eye movements were recorded using skin electrodes. When the central light was turned off, a light target (luminance: 240 cd/m^2) appeared either in the right half of the visual field or in the normal visual area in the left visual hemifield. After the onset of the targets, the child turned his eyes and head spontaneously towards the target.

From these testing sessions, the child knew that a target was presented either in the left or in the right half of space after the central point had disappeared. When no target was presented or when the target was in the blind area, he therefore searched for the light stimulus. His visual search was always limited to the right half of space and he never searched for the target on his left. Even on command he did not direct his eyes and his head towards the left half of space.

To elicit eye and head movements directed into the left half of space, an acoustic stimulus was presented together with a light target. Both stimuli were at the same location in the blind area of the visual field. When the child directed his gaze to the sound source and therefore looked at the target which was presented at the same location, he detected a reward (cookie) immediately below the target. The child was allowed to grasp and eat the cookie.

Even after 12 trials in which the child was rewarded for directing his gaze to the left and detecting the light target, the child looked occasionally to the left when the central light disappeared and when no sound was present. Again, detection of the light target without the presence of the acoustic stimulus was rewarded. In the following sessions, the child received a reward if he oriented towards a stimulus which he saw in his right visual hemifield or if, after the offset of the central light, he saw no target in his good visual field and, therefore, searched for the target in the left half of space. After four sessions of about 40 trials each, the child oriented his gaze constantly to the left, if he expected a target, but if the target was not in the normal right half of the visual field. This did not only help to improve visual orientation in everyday life, it was also a prerequisite for the restitution of visual functions in the blind visual field.

VISUAL NEGLECT IN ADULT PATIENTS

Omissions in the Non-Neglected Half of Space

In adult patients in whom symptoms of neglect can be examined in greater detail than in most children, a complicated pattern of omissions and shifts of spatial co-ordinates which may include both halves of space can be observed (Kinsbourne, 1977; 1987).

Two adult patients with right hemisphere lesions who did not suffer from homonymous hemianopia, reported in Werth (1988), neglected the left half of space. Spontaneously, they directed their eyes and head only into the right half of space, they omitted words on the left half of the page when reading, and in the crossing out task (Albert, 1973) they omitted lines on the left-hand side of the paper, irrespective of whether the paper was in front of them, in the left or in the right half of space. The patients omitted petals on the left side of a daffodil they drew from memory, irrespective of whether they drew the flower in the middle or on the right side of a sheet of paper and irrespective of whether the paper was in front of them or in the right hemispace.

Gainotti and co-workers (Gainotti, Messerli, & Tissot, 1972; Gainotti, d'Erme, Monteleone, & Silveri, 1986) reported patients who, when asked to copy a row of figures, omitted the left side of figures, although they copied figures which were to the left of the neglected half of a figure. Similar

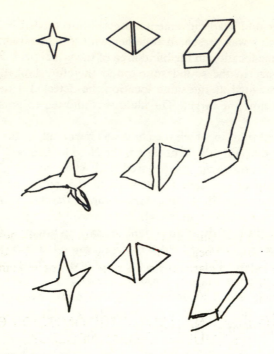

FIG. 10.1. The patients were asked to copy the geometrical figures printed in the top row. Although they copied all of the figures, they omitted the left edge of the figure on the right. From Werth (1988). Reprinted with permission.

performance was found in the above-mentioned patients. They were instructed to copy a row of geometrical figures (star, two triangles, rectangular box). Figure 10.1 shows that all figures were copied, but that both patients omitted the left edge of the box. When the patients were asked to trace with a finger all the lines of the figures which they had copied, they never followed the left edge of the box. Although they were repeatedly asked to examine if the figures were copied completely, they were unable to detect their omission.

Figure 10.2 shows the performance of a female with a left-sided neglect due to a right parietal tumour in a modified crossing-out task. The lines to be crossed out were 7 mm long and were symmetrically distributed among line drawings of geometrical figures on a 23.5 × 8.5 cm sheet of paper. The paper with the lines was about 30° of arc to the right of the mid-sagittal plane of the thorax, i.e. in the right hemispace. The experimenter moved the patient's hand, in which she held a pen, to a line in the middle of the paper, which the patient was supposed to cross out first. The patient was

FIG. 10.2. The patient's task was to cross out all of the short lines between the geometrical figures. The sheet of paper on which the lines were drawn was to the right of the patient's mid-sagittal plane. Arrows indicate the direction in which the patient proceeded. Most of the lines were omitted.

instructed to begin with this line and to cross out all other lines on the paper. Although the patient began the crossing-out task in the middle of the paper, she moved towards the right edge of the paper, omitting most of the stimuli.

THE EXPLANATION OF THE OMISSION OF STIMULI IN VISUAL NEGLECT

Omission of Stimuli due to an Underarousal of One Hemisphere

The omission of stimuli in an area of the visual field cannot be explained by the assumption that one hemisphere contralateral to the neglected half of space is under-aroused due to a defect in a cortico-limbic-reticular loop (Heilman, 1979; Heilman & Valenstein, 1972; Watson, Heilman, Cauthen, & King, 1973). According to this hypothesis, the under-arousal causes a defect in an orienting response which prepares the organism for action. The under-arousal of one hemisphere reduces its ability to prepare for action and the damaged hemisphere becomes akinetic. These patients may have longer reaction times when asked to initiate a response directed towards the half of space contralateral to the under-aroused cerebral hemisphere than when asked to initiate a response directed towards the half of space ipsilateral to the under-aroused hemisphere. Hemispatial akinesia may include eye, head and limb movements (Heilman et al., 1985; 1987).

The short reaction times which were observed in the patient with the vertical neglect when he moved his eyes towards targets on the horizontal meridian contradict the assumption that omission of stimuli in the lower half of the visual field is due to an under-arousal of one or both cerebral hemispheres. On the contrary, both hemispheres detected the targets and induced horizontal eye movements towards the targets in less time than most healthy school children need to complete the same task.

Omissions due to an Inability to Shift Covert Attention

An explanation of these omissions with the assumption that the patient was unable to shift attention into an area more than 30° below the fixation point is also difficult. Poppelreuter (1917) reported that patients with cerebral lesions may have a markedly reduced ability to shift their attention into a given area of the visual field and to expand their field of attention (*Aufmerksamkeitsfeld*) independently of eye movements. Posner (1980) distinguished between "overt orienting", which is observed in eye and head movements, and "covert orienting", which consists of a shift of attention across the visual field. The criterion for a shift of attention into a given area of the visual field is that visual functions in this area improve once the subject is pre-informed of where the stimulus will be presented. In this area, the threshold for the detection will be lower (Bashinski & Bacharach, 1980) and the reaction time will be shorter (Posner, Cohen, & Rafal, 1982) than in an area of the visual field where the subject does not expect the stimulus to appear.

Posner et al. (1982) have shown that adult patients who were unable to move their eyes in a vertical direction due to supranuclear palsy could nevertheless shift covert attention to an area of the visual field below or above the fixation point. The area in which the stimulus was to appear was indicated by a cue (a hexagon which was presented below or above the fixation point), followed by a target to which the patients were asked to respond. When the target was presented in the area indicated by the cue, reaction times were faster than when the target was shown in the area opposite to the area which was indicated by the cue. Under both conditions, the patients were slower to shift their covert attention vertically than when moving their attention horizontally.

In patients with parietal lesions, Posner, Walker, Friedrich and Rafal (1984) found only small differences in reaction times to targets presented in visual hemifields ipsilateral and contralateral to the lesioned hemisphere, respectively, when the location of the target was indicated by a cue beforehand. When the target, however, was presented on the side opposite to the cue, reaction times for the area contralateral to the cerebral lesion were shorter than reaction times to targets on the side ipsilateral to the lesioned hemisphere. Posner et al. (1984) interpreted this finding as a reduced ability to disengage attention from a target while the ability to shift attention towards an area appeared to be almost normal.

Omissions Due to a Loss of Tonic Attention

Normal subjects and even brain-damaged patients can detect targets in an area of their visual field, although they shift their covert attention into another area. The area of the visual field into which the normal subject does not direct his or her attention cannot be compared to the neglected area of the visual field in which a patient is unable to detect stimuli. In the boy with vertical neglect, the neglected visual area was much more impaired in its ability to detect stimuli, when the boy did not expect the targets in this area, than is impaired in normal subjects after attention has been shifted away from this area. When a normal subject directs attention into an area of the visual field, a tonic aspect of attention still appears to be present in the remaining visual field. This tonic attention enables the subject to detect stimuli in unattended areas. At the same time, a phasic aspect of (covert) attention can be shifted from one region to another.

Tonic visual attention is not identical to arousal of one cerebral hemisphere. It is regarded as the activity in neural networks which is necessary for the adequate processing of visual information. The activity in these neural networks is dissociated from the state of arousal in other neural circuits in the same cerebral hemisphere. The activity in the neural systems responsible for maintaining tonic visual attention can be modulated. When the subject expects a visual stimulus in a particular area of the visual field, there may be increased activity of the neurons representing this visual area. This increase in activity may result in a lowering of the threshold for the detection of targets in this area. This corresponds to a shift of phasic (covert) attention. At the same time, the activity of neurons representing other areas of the visual field where no target is expected, may decrease, resulting in an elevation of the threshold for the detection of targets in these areas. Targets can, however, still be detected in these regions of the visual field.

If the activity of neurons representing the unattended areas of the visual field drops below a given level, the subject will no longer be able to detect targets presented in an unattended area. Once activity falls below this level, shifting attention into the formerly unattended area may enhance the activity of the corresponding neurons to an extent that detection of targets again becomes possible. This was, for example, the case in the lower visual field of the boy with vertical neglect. Such a neural network which shifts phasic (covert) attention into areas of the visual field must include a spatial representation of the visual field or it must receive spatial information from other neural networks.

A cerebral lesion may impair the function of these neurons so severely that even the effort needed to shift attention into an area of the visual field may not be enough to increase the activity of the neurons representing this area, to the extent that detection of targets becomes possible. Such a pathological drop in activity may not only result in the functional blindness of an area of the visual field, but awareness for this area may also be extinguished. If this is the case, the patient will not only omit stimuli in this visual area, he or she will also be unaware that he or she is unable to detect stimuli in this area of the visual field.

When patients who suffer from a left visual neglect are asked to draw a daffodil, they may omit the petals on the left. These patients may be unable to detect this omission when the missing half of the flower is in the neglected visual field. Such a patient (Werth, 1988, patient 2) was able, however, to detect the missing petals when he fixated a point in the middle of the flower and when he directed his attention into the neglected half of the visual field. As soon as he stopped to summon his attention to the left half of the visual field, he was completely unaware that in the left half of his visual field one half of the flower was missing.

The site of lesions which cause the omission of visual stimuli shows that there is not one single area of the brain which can be regarded as the neurobiological substrate of tonic and phasic (covert) attention. In humans, the postulated neurons may be localised in the inferior parietal lobe (Heilman, Watson, Valenstein, & Damasio, 1983; Vallar & Perani 1986), in the dorsolateral and medial frontal lobe (Damasio, Damasio, & Chang Chui, 1980; Heilman & Valenstein 1972), the thalamus (Ogren et al., 1984; Watson & Heilman, 1979), the putamen and the nucleus caudatus (Damasio et al., 1980; Hier, Davis, Richardson, & Mohr, 1977; Valenstein & Heilman, 1981).

Defective Co-ordinates in Both Hemispaces

The above examples illustrate that, at least in the case of some patients, a neglect cannot be regarded as a loss of the representation of only one half of space. In the non-neglected half of space, spatial co-ordinates may also be altered; for example, the left half of a sheet of paper which is shown in the non-neglected half of space, may be neglected in a crossing-out task. Also, when a subject is asked to draw a daffodil on the non-neglected right half of the sheet of paper which is in the non-neglected right half of space, the left half of the daffodil may be left out (Fig. 10.3).

These phenomena cannot only be explained by assuming that there is a lack of tonic attention in an area of the visual field. A tentative explanation of these phenomena may derive from the observation that patients with a left-sided neglect have a tendency to direct their gaze to the right. Objects in the right half of space may magnetically attract a patient's gaze (Barany, 1913; De Renzi, Colombo, Faglioni, & Gibertoni, 1982; De Renzi, Gentilini, Faglioni, & Barbieri, 1989; Kinsbourne, 1977, 1987).

FIG. 10.3.   Schematic drawing of the neglected areas of space in different tasks. When the patient is asked to search visually for an object, she may only neglect the left half of space (shaded area in the left half of the figure). If the patient's task is to cross out lines on a sheet of paper which is in the non-neglected right half of space, she may omit the left half of the paper (shaded left half of the square on the right half of the figure). When the patient draws a daffodil on the non-neglected right half of the sheet of paper, the left half of the daffodil may be missing (shaded left half of the schematically drawn flower in the right half of the square).

Figure 10.2 illustrates a patient's tendency to orient her gaze towards the right even if she is forced to start the crossing-out task in the middle of the paper. The tendency to orient gaze to the right is stopped at the right edge of the paper. The right edge of the sheet works as an anchor to prevent the gaze from deviating further to the right. When a patient's gaze and attention are directed to the right edge of the paper, the right edge may become a reference mark for the mental construction of the space in which the patient expects lines to be crossed out and into which eye and head movements are directed. A severe lack of tonic attention in the left half of the visual field may prevent stimuli in the left visual hemifield from being detected and the patient may be unaware that he or she does not detect stimuli in the left visual hemifield. The left half of the sheet of paper—or even more—may not be included in this mentally construed space.

When such patients' task is to draw a daffodil, they start drawing on the right half of the paper. As soon as they start drawing, they must know which part of the figure they are about to draw. The location in which the patients start drawing may become a new reference mark for the development of the space which the drawing will occupy. Within this space, they will plan how to proceed and which part of the figure should be drawn next. This planning of the drawing may be defective in so far as the spatial co-ordinates for the left part of the figure are not developed. They do not direct their gaze into the area where the left part of the figure should be drawn, and a lack of tonic attention in the left hemifield makes it impossible to detect stimuli in this area.

When drawing an object, patients may, therefore, neglect part of an area which they did not neglect when they completed the crossing-out task. Neglect appears, therefore, not only to be a neglect of one hemispace, but also a neglect of the left half of any space into which gaze and attention must be directed with respect to a reference mark to complete a given task.

SHIFTS OF VISUAL CO-ORDINATES

The omissions which were present in the tests described in the last paragraph can also influence patients' performance when asked to solve other visual spatial tasks. A task which is commonly used to test visual spatial competence is the line bisection task (Axenfeld, 1894; Liepmann & Kalmus, 1900). In this test, the patient is asked to indicate the midpoint of a horizontal line by bisecting the line into two equally long sections.

Studies in which normal subjects bisected horizontal lines have yielded unequivocal results. Bisiach, Capitani, Colombo and Spinnler (1976) tested patients with neurological disease but without brain damage. The patients deviated in the mean to the left of the geometrical midpoint when bisecting lines 5–30 cm long. The lines were presented horizontally so that the objective midpoint was in the mid-sagittal plane of the subjects' trunks. Bradshaw, Nettleton, Nathan and Wilson (1985) used lines 8–17 cm long, which were irregularly distributed over a sheet of paper. These subjects also showed a mean left displacement of the subjective midpoint of the lines. A non-significant left displacement of the subjective midpoint of lines from 2.6–20.4 cm long, pseudorandomly distributed over paper, was reported by Scarisbrick, Tweedy, & Kuslawsky (1987).

Schenkenberg, Bradford and Ajax (1980) asked hospitalised subjects without brain disease to bisect horizontal lines 10–20 cm long which were spread over a sheet of paper. The authors found a small deviation to the right when the lines were in the centre of the sheet of paper or in the right half of the paper. The patients deviated slightly to the left when the lines were in the left half of the paper. The subjects tested by Nichelli, Rinaldi and Cubelli (1989) with single lines 8–24 cm long also displayed a small mean right deviation. Liepmann and Kalmus (1900) noted that normal subjects who are asked to bisect horizontal lines do not tend to deviate predominantly to the left or to the right of the true midpoint.

Werth and Pöppel (1988) found no significant deviation to the left or to the right when normal subjects bisected individual lines 4–20 cm long centred on the mid-sagittal plane. Neither did Manning, Halligan and

Marshall's (1990) subjects deviate significantly more to the left than to the right of the geometrical midpoint when they bisected individual lines 1.8–18 cm long. About half of them bisected the lines to the left and half to the right of centre. In this study, the lines were centred on the mid-sagittal plane of the subjects' trunks. It would appear that the unequivocal results of studies with normal subjects when tested with line bisection tasks are due to considerable inter-individual differences in the tendency to bisect horizontal lines to the left or to the right of the geometrical midpoint (Manning et al., 1990).

Liepmann and Kalmus (1900) tested the ability of 10 hemianopic patients without neglect to bisect horizontal lines. The patients with a left homonymous hemianopia but without neglect tended to bisect the lines to the left of the geometrical midpoint. If the patients suffered from a right homonymous hemianopia, they tended to place the subjective midpoint of the line to the right of the true midpoint. This bisection error was greatest when the lines were 4–10 cm long. For very short lines (0.5–2 cm), the bisection error was smaller or disappeared completely.

The deviation which hemianopic patients without neglect show in the line bisection task may, as Liepmann and Kalmus (1900) assumed, be explained by their altered looking strategies. To be able to view the line to be bisected in the good half of their visual field, patients must direct their gaze near the end of the line. Patients with a right homonymous hemianopia, for example, must direct their gaze to the right end of a horizontal line to view the whole line in the unimpaired half of their visual field. They may then bisect the line to the right of the real midpoint.

Normal subjects who are forced by experimental conditions to adopt the same looking strategies make the same error (Werth, 1988). In such experiments, a horizontal line is shown tachistoscopically to the left or to the right of the fixation point. In every presentation, the line is bisected by a vertical bar. The bar bisects the line either at the geometrical midpoint or to the left or to the right of the geometrical midpoint. The nine subjects in Werth's (1988) study were asked to indicate whether the line was bisected at the midpoint or to the left or to the right of the geometrical midpoint. When the horizontal line was presented in the left half of the visual field, the subjects were convinced that the vertical bar bisected the line at the midpoint only if the bar was to the right of the geometrical midpoint. In the experimental trials in which the horizontal line was presented to the right of the fixation point, the subjects assumed that the vertical bar bisected the horizontal line at the midpoint only if the bar was to the left of the geometrical midpoint. In an additional experiment, the horizontal line was presented in the middle of the visual field so that about one-half of the line was in the left half and the other half of the line was in the right half of the visual field. In this case, the subjects made few errors, and they did not tend to deviate more frequently to the left or to the right when estimating the point at which the line was bisected. Thus, the looking strategies which hemianopic patients must adopt to view the entire line to be bisected could, at least in part, explain the performance of hemianopic patients in a line bisection task.

Although there are large between-subject variations in performance in line bisection tasks, the performances of normal subjects and patients with a spatial neglect differ considerably. Patients with a left spatial neglect shift the subjective midpoint much further away from the geometrical midpoint of the line than normal subjects. These patients also shift the subjective midpoint more constantly to the right when bisecting lines of a given length (Bisiach, Bulgarelli, Sterzi, & Vallar, 1983; Heilman & Valenstein, 1972, 1979; Heilman et al., 1983; Patterson & Zangwill 1944; Schenkenberg et al., 1980; Stein & Volpe, 1983; Watson & Heilman, 1979). There are, however, exceptions to this rule. Patients with a left-sided neglect may not deviate more to one side than normal subjects, or they may displace the midpoint of the line to the left of the geometrical midpoint (Denny-Brown et al., 1952; Halligan & Marshall, 1988, 1989; Schenkenberg et al., 1980; Schott, Laurent, Manguière, & Chazot, 1981). Patient 1 reported in Werth (1988), who suffered from a severe left-sided neglect, also did not bisect horizontal lines to the right of the geometrical midpoint. When the patient was asked to bisect horizontally oriented lines 5 and 10 cm long, she bisected both lines considerably to the left of the geometrical midpoint. When asked to point with her finger to each end of the lines before bisection, she bisected both lines correctly.

Halligan and Marshall (1988), Marshall and Halligan (1989) and Tegnér, Levander and Caneman (1990) found that the direction in which patients with a left-sided neglect shift the midpoint of horizontal lines depends on the length of the line to be bisected. The longer the line, the more the line is transected to the right of the geometrical midpoint. Lines shorter than 5 cm were even transected to the left of the true midpoint. The performance of patients with a left-sided neglect when bisecting lines longer than 5 cm may be explained by the assumption that these patients do not register the part of the line which is in the neglected left half of space: The patients only bisect that part of the line of which they are aware.

Patients with a left-sided neglect may, however, also deviate to the right when bisecting horizontal lines of a given length if these lines are presented in the non-neglected right hemispace (see, e.g. Heilman & Valenstein, 1979). As already mentioned, even if an object is in the non-neglected hemispace, one side of the object may not be registered. In some cases, the underestimation of the left extension of a line may be due to the patient's inability to register the whole left extension of the line. The left end of the line may occupy a part of space in which the patient omits the line stimulus when he or she is about to transect the line.

When the task changes, the patient may change the spatial co-ordinates to solve the new task. Now, the previously neglected part of space may no longer be neglected. The new task may be to point with the finger to each end of the lines or to read letters which are printed next to the ends of the lines (Heilman & Valenstein, 1979). Although patients may be able to direct their gaze to both ends of the lines, it does not mean that their assumption about the extensions of the lines is preserved when the requirement changes and they start bisection. Now, they may construe a different space which does not include the whole left half of the line. There is no reason to assume that the spatial co-ordinates remain fixed irrespective of the task which the patients are about to solve. Such task-dependent omissions show that spatial co-ordinates are variable and that the part of space which is neglected may change from task to task.

The results of an experiment with normal subjects support the assumption that the direction of gaze and the distribution of attention in the visual field may influence the visual spatial performance of patients with spatial neglect (Werth, 1988). In this experiment, normal subjects were asked to direct their gaze to a black fixation mark. The mark disappeared and was replaced by a capital letter presented for 13 msec, which the subjects were asked to recognise. When the letter had disappeared, a horizontal line was presented for 50 msec either to the left or to the right of the point where the letter had appeared. This meant that the subjects had to direct their attention to the point where the letter appeared to identify it. Thus the subjects' gaze and attention were directed to a location near the left or near the right end of the horizontal line, depending on whether the line was presented to the left or to the right of the fixation point. Again, a vertical bar which bisected the line either at the midpoint or to the left or to the right of the midpoint was presented together with the line. The subjects were asked to indicate verbally whether the line was bisected at the midpoint or to the left or to the right of the geometrical midpoint.

When the subjects' gaze and attention were directed near the right end of the line, they were convinced that the line was bisected at its midpoint if the vertical bar bisecting the line was to the right of the geometrical midpoint. This meant that the subjects deviated to the right when estimating the midpoint of the horizontal line. Patients with a left-sided neglect also tend to direct their gaze and their attention more to the right side than to the left side of objects like a horizontal line (De Renzi et al., 1989). It may be that this tendency to direct gaze and attention to the right also contributes to the patients' deviation to the right when asked to bisect a horizontal line.

The findings of Bisiach, Geminiani, Berti and Rusconi (1990) support the assumption that the rightward displacement of the subjective midpoint is in part due to unidirectional hypokinesia, i.e. the reluctance of patients to carry out motor activities towards the hemispace contralateral to the lesioned hemisphere. In Bisiach and co-workers' experiments, patients with lesions of the right cerebral hemisphere were asked to move the pointer of a pulley device along a horizontal line either by holding the pointer with two fingers (congruent condition) or by moving it indirectly by means of the pulley device. In the latter case, the pointer could be moved in a given direction by a movement of the hand in the opposite direction (non-congruent condition). The patients were required to indicate the midpoint of the horizontal line by moving the pointer to the geometrical midpoint of the line. The subjective midpoint of the line was displaced to the right of the geometrical midpoint irrespective of whether the patients moved the pointer directly or indirectly by means of the pulley device. In the non-congruent condition, the amount of rightward displacement of the subjective midpoint was, however, smaller than in the congruent condition. The authors concluded from these results that the rightward displacement error is in part due to unilateral hypokinesia, because the patients showed a tendency not to move the arm into the left hemispace.

The results of Halligan, Manning and Marshall (1991) indicate that it is not the use of the left or right hand or the use of the hand being controlled by the damaged hemisphere which determines the degree of displacement of the subjective midpoint in a line bisection task. They asked a patient with a right cerebral lesion to bisect horizontal lines using his left hand. The starting position of the hand was to the right of the right end of the line. The patient's performance was similar to his performance when he used the right hand, commencing the task from the same starting position. The side on which the test started had a more profound effect than which hand was used. This result is still compatible with the theory that the line bisection errors of patients with a left neglect is due to the tendency not to move the hand into the half of space contralateral to the lesioned hemisphere. This hypothesis does not explain, however, why patients with a left-sided neglect bisect short lines to the left of the centre (Halligan & Marshall, 1988; Marshall & Halligan, 1989; Tegnér et al., 1990).

CONCLUSIONS

The symptoms of visual neglect may already be present in infancy when the cerebral lesion occurs pre- or perinatally before brain development is completed. Although visual field defects and a paucity of eye and head movements directed into one half of space are dissociated, the interaction of both impairments leads to a severe omission of stimuli in one half of space. Long-lasting effects of a neglect on the developing brain may be prevented by improving visual search using operant conditioning.

A neglect may not only affect the half of the space or the half of the visual field contralateral to the lesioned hemisphere. The case of a child with a vertical neglect shows that only stimuli in the lower half of the visual field may be omitted, whereas reaction times to targets on the horizontal meridian are not reduced. These symptoms of vertical neglect are neither regarded as an effect of hypokinesia of one cerebral hemisphere (Heilman et al., 1985; 1987) nor as an inability to direct covert attention into the affected region of the visual field (Posner & Rafal, 1987). The omission of stimuli in a region of the visual field is interpreted as the consequence of a loss of tonic attention, which may be compensated for by shifting phasic (covert) attention into this region.

In adult patients in whom the symptoms of neglect can be tested in greater detail than in children, it turns out that besides the left hemispace, stimuli in the non-neglected right half of space may also be omitted. The location and extension of the area in the right half of space which is neglected depends on the task which a patient is asked to complete. The areas in which stimuli are registered in the one task may be neglected in the other task. It appears that, for each task, the patient construes a space within which stimuli are expected to appear. Besides a paucity of eye movements into the neglected area, there may also be a lack of tonic attention and an inability to shift phasic (covert) attention into this area.

The displacement of the subjective midpoint of a horizontal line which is observed in patients with spatial neglect appears to be due to the interaction of many factors. The reduction of motor activities towards the neglected half of space may contribute to the tendency to deviate to the right when the line is bisected. Such hypokinesia cannot, however, explain why a subject is convinced that a line is bisected at the true midpoint when he or she looks at a line which is transected to the right of the geometrical midpoint. Furthermore, the hypokinesia hypothesis cannot explain why patients with a left-sided neglect bisect short lines to the left of centre (Hallilgan & Marshall, 1989). The tendency to direct attention into the left visual hemifield, the starting position of the hand (Halligan et al., 1991), completion of a part of the line (Bisiach et al., 1983; Halligan & Marshall, 1988), the inability to register a section of the line due to a defective mental construction of space, visual field defects, and still unknown mechanisms may interact when patients bisect horizontal lines. All of these possible influences on performance in line bisection tasks may vary considerably between subjects. The influence of each of these factors may also depend on the length of the line to be bisected. Hence, it would not appear that there is only one mechanism to explain the shift of visual spatial co-ordinates observed when patients bisect horizontal lines.

REFERENCES

Albert, M.L. (1973). A simple test of visual neglect. *Neurology*, *23*, 658–664.

Axenfeld, D. (1884). Eine einfache Methode, Hemianopie zu diagnostiziren. *Neurologisches Zentralblatt*, *437*.

Barany, R. (1913). Latente Deviation der Augen und Vorbeizeigen des Kopfes bei Hemiplegie und Epilepsie. *Wiener Klinische Wochenschrift*, *26*, 597–599.

Bashinski, H.S. & Bacharach, V.R. (1980). Enhancement of perceptual sensitivity as the result of selectively attending to spatial locations. *Perception and Psychophysics*, *28*, 241–248.

Battersby, W.S., Bender, M.B., Pollack, M., & Kahn, R.L. (1956). Unilateral "spatial agnosia" ("inattention") in patients with cerebral lesions. *Brain*, *79*, 68–93.

Bisiach, E., Bulgarelli, C., Sterzi, R., & Vallar, G. (1983). Line bisection and cognitive plasticity of unilateral neglect of space. *Brain and Cognition*, *2*, 32–38.

Bisiach, E., Capitani, E., Colombo, A., & Spinnler, H. (1976). Halving horizontal segment: A study on hemisphere damaged patients with cerebral focal lesions. *Archives Suisses de Neurologie, Neurochirurgie et de Psychiatrie*, *118*, 199–206.

Bisiach, E., Capitani, E., & Porta, E. (1985). Two basic properties of space representation in the brain: Evidence from unilateral neglect. *Journal of Neurology, Neurosurgery and Psychiatry*, *48*, 141–144.

Bisiach, E., Geminiani, G., Berti, A., & Rusconi, M.L. (1990). Perceptual and premotor factors of unilateral neglect. *Neurology*, *40*, 1278–1281.

Bradshaw, J.L., Nettleton, N.C., Nathan, G., & Wilson, L. (1985). Bisecting rods and lines. Effects of horizontal and vertical posture on left-side underestimation by normal subjects. *Neuropsychologia*, *23*, 421–425.

Cambier, J., Elghozi, D., Graveleau, P., & Lubetzki, C. (1984). Hémiasomatognosie droite et sentiment d'amputation par lésion gauche sous-corticale. Rôle de la disconnexion calleuse. *Revue Neurologique*, *140*, 256–262.

Cambier, J., Elghozi, D., & Strube, E. (1980). Lésions du thalamus droit avec syndrome de l'hémisphère mineur. *Revue Neurologique*, *136*, 105–116.

Chain, F., Leblanc, M., Chédru, R., & Lhérmitte, F. (1979). Negligence visuelle dans les lésions postérieurs de l'hémisphère gauche. *Revue Neurologique*, *135*, 105–126.

Chédru, F., Leblanc, M., & Lhérmitte, F. (1973). Visual searching in normal and brain damaged subjects (contribution to the study of unilateral inattention). *Cortex*, *9*, 94–111.

Damasio, A.R., Damasio, H., & Chang Chui H. (1980). Neglect following damage to frontal lobe or basal ganglia. *Neuropsychologia*, *18*, 123–132.

Denny-Brown, D. & Banker, B. (1954). Amorphosynthesis from left parietal lesion. *Archives of Neurology and Psychiatry*, *71*, 302–313.

Denny-Brown, D., Meyer, J.S., & Horenstein, S. (1952). The significance of perceptual rivalry resulting from parietal lesion. *Brain*, *75*, 433–471.

De Renzi, E., Colombo, A., Faglioni, P., & Gibertoni, M. (1982). Conjugate gaze paresis in stroke patients with unilateral damage. *Archives of Neurology*, *39*, 482–486.

De Renzi, E., Gentilini, M., Faglioni, P., & Barbieri, C. (1989). Attentional shifts towards the rightmost stimuli in patients with left visual neglect. *Cortex*, *25*, 231–237.

Ferro, J.M., Pavao Martins, I., & Tavora, L. (1984). Neglect in children. *Annals of Neurology*, *15*, 281–284.

Finlay, D., Quinn, K., & Ivinskis, A. (1982). Detection of moving stimuli in the binocular and nasal visual fields by infants three and four months old. *Perception*, *11*, 685–690.

Gainotti, G., D'Erme, P., Monteleone, D., & Silveri, M.C. (1986). Mechanisms of unilateral spatial neglect in relation to laterality of cerebral lesions. *Brain*, *109*, 599–612.

Gainotti, G., Messerli, P., & Tissot, R. (1972). Quantitative analysis of unilateral neglect in relation to laterality of cerebral lesion. *Journal of Neurology, Neurosurgery and Psychiatry*, *35*, 545–550.

Girotti, F., Casazza, M., Musicco, M., & Avanzini, G. (1983). Oculomotor disorders in cortical lesions in man: The role of unilateral neglect. *Neuropsychologia*, *21*, 543–553.

Gloning, K. (1965). *Die cerebral bedingten Störungen des räumlichen Sehens und des Raumerlebens*. Wien: Maudrich.

Halligan, P.W., Manning, L, & Marshall, J.C. (1991). Hemispheric activation vs. spatio-motor cueing in visual neglect: A case study. *Neuropsychologia*, *29*, 165–176.

Halligan, P.W. & Marshall, J.C. (1988). How long is a piece of string? A study of line bisection in a case of visual neglect. *Cortex*, *24*, 321–328.

Halligan, P.W. & Marshall, J.C. (1989). Laterality of motor response in visuo-spatial neglect: A case study. *Neuropsychologia*, *27*, 1301–1307.

Harris, C.M. & MacFarlane, A. (1974). The growth of the effective visual field from birth to seven weeks. *Journal of Experimental Child Psychology*, *18*, 340–348.

Heilman, K.M. (1979). Neglect and related disorders. In K.M. Heilman & E. Valenstein (Eds), *Clinical neuropsychology*, pp. 268–307. Oxford: Oxford University Press.

Heilman, K.M., Bowers, D., Coslett, H.B., Whelan, H., & Watson, R.T. (1985). Directional hypokinesia: Prolonged reaction times for leftward movements in patients with right hemisphere lesions and neglect. *Neurology*, *35*, 855–859.

Heilman, K.M., Bowers, D., Valenstein, E., & Watson, R.T. (1987). Hemispace and hemispatial neglect. In M. Jeannerod (Ed.), *Neurophysiological and neuropsychological aspects of spatial neglect*, pp. 115–150. Amsterdam: Elsevier.

Heilman, K.M. & Valenstein, E. (1972). Frontal lobe neglect in man. *Neurology*, *22*, 660–664.

Heilman, K.M. & Valenstein, E. (1979). Mechanisms underlying hemispatial neglect. *Annals of Neurology*, *5*, 166–170.

Heilman, K.M., Watson, R.T., Valenstein, E., & Damasio, A.R. (1983). Localization of lesion in neglect. In A. Kertesz (Ed.), *Localization in neuropsychology*, pp. 471–492. New York: Academic Press.

Hier, D.B., Davis, K.R., Richardson, E.P., & Mohr, J.P. (1977). Hypertensive putaminal hemorrhage. *Annals of Neurology*, *1*, 152–159.

Holmes, G. (1918). Disturbance of vision by cerebral lesions. *British Journal of Ophthalmology*, *2*, 353–384.

Kinsbourne, M. (1977). Hemi-neglect and hemisphere rivalry. In E.A. Weinstein & R.P. Friedland (Eds), *Hemi-inattention and hemisphere specialization*, pp. 41–47. New York: Raven Press.

Kinsbourne, M. (1987). Mechanisms of unilateral neglect. In M. Jeannerod (Ed.), *Neurophysiological and neuropsychological aspects of spatial neglect*, pp. 69–86. Amsterdam: Elsevier.

Koch, J. & von Stockert, F.G. (1935). Störungen des Körperschemas und ihre Projektion in die Außenwelt. *Klinische Wochenschrift*, *14*, 746–748.

Liepmann, H. & Kalmus, E. (1900). Über eine Augenmaßstörung bei Hemianopikern. *Berliner Klinische Wochenschrift*, *38*, 838–842.

Manning, L., Halligan, P.W., & Marshall, J.C. (1990). Individual variation in line bisection: A study of normal subjects with application to the interpretation of visual neglect. *Neuropsychologia*, *28*, 647–655.

Marshall, J.C. & Halligan, P.W. (1989). When right goes left: An investigation of line bisection in a case of visual neglect. *Cortex*, *25*, 503–515.

Meienberg, O. (1983). Clinical examination of saccadic eye movements in hemianopia. *Neurology*, *33*, 1311–1315.

Mohn, G. & van Hoff-van Duin, J. (1986). Development of the binocular and monocular visual fields of human infants during the first year of life. *Clinical Vision Sciences*, *1*, 51–54.

Nichelli, P., Rinaldi, M., & Cubelli, R. (1989). Selective spacial attention and length representation in normal subjects and in patients with unilateral spatial neglect. *Brain and Cognition*, *9*, 57–70.

Ogren, M.P., Mateer, C.A., & Wyler, A.R. (1984). Alterations in visually related eye movements following left pulvinar damage in man. *Neuropsychologia*, *22*, 187–196.

Oppenheim, H. (1885). Über eine durch eine klinisch bisher nicht verwertete Untersuchungsmethode ermittelte Form der Sensibilitätsstörung bei einseitigen Erkrankungen des Großhirns. *Neurologisches Centralblatt*, *4*, 529–533.

Patterson, A. & Zangwill, O.L. (1944). Disorders of visual space perception associated with lesions of the right cerebral hemisphere. *Brain*, *67*, 331–358.

Pinéas, H. (1931). Ein Fall von räumlicher Orientierungsstörung mit Dyschirie. *Zentralblatt für die gesamte Neurologie und Psychiatrie*, *133*, 180–195.

Poppelreuter, W. (1917). *Die psychischen Schädigungen durch Kopfschuß im Kriege 1914–1916. Bd. I. Die Störungen der niederen und höheren Sehleistungen durch Verletzungen des Okzipithalhirns.* Leipzig: L. Voss.

Posner, M.I. (1980). Orienting of attention. *Quarterly Journal of Experimental Psychology*, *32*, 3–25.

Posner, M.I., Cohen, Y., & Rafal, R.D. (1982). Neural systems control of spatial orienting. *Philosophical Transactions of the Royal Society, London*, *B298*, 17–198.

Posner, M.I. & Rafal R.D. (1987). Cognitive theories of attention and rehabilitation of attentional deficits. In R.J. Meier, A.C. Benton, & L. Diuer (Eds), *Neuropsychological rehabilitation*, pp. 182–201. London: Churchill Livingstone.

Posner, M.I., Walker, J., Friedrich, F.J., & Rafal, R.D. (1984). Effects of parietal injury on covert orienting of attention. *Journal of neuroscience*, *4*, 1863–1874.

Sandifer, P.H. (1946). Anosognosia and disorders of body scheme. *Brain*, *69*, 122–137.

Scarisbrick, D.J., Tweedy, J.R., & Kuslawsky, G. (1987). Hand preference and performance effects on line bisection. *Neuropsychologia*, *25*, 695–699.

Schenkenberg, T., Bradford, D.C., & Ajax, E.T. (1980). Line bisection and unilateral visual neglect in patients with neurologic impairment. *Neurology*, *30*, 509–517.

Schott, B., Laurent, B., Manguière, F., & Chazot, G. (1981). Négligence motrice par hématome thalamique droit. *Revue Neurologique*, *137*, 447–455.

Stein, S. & Volpe, B.T. (1983). Classical "parietal" neglect syndrome after subcortical right frontal lobe infarction. *Neurology*, *33*, 797–799.

Tegnér, R., Levander, M., & Caneman, G. (1990). Apparent right neglect in patients with left visual neglect. *Cortex*, *26*, 455–458.

Tronick, E. (1972). Stimulus control and the growth of the infant's effective visual field. *Perception and Psychophysics*, *11*, 373–376.

Valenstein, E. & Heilman, K.M. (1981). Unilateral hypokinesia and motor extinction. *Neurology*, *31*, 445–448.

Vallar, G. & Perani, D. (1986). The anatomy of unilateral neglect after right hemisphere stroke lesions: A clinical/CT-scan correlation study in man. *Neuropsychologia*, *24*, 609–622.

Watson, R.T. & Heilman, K.M. (1979). Thalamic neglect. *Neurology*, *29*, 290–294.

Watson, R.T., Heilman, K.M., Cauthen, J.C., & King, F.A. (1973). Neglect after cingulectomy. *Neurology*, *23*, 1003–1007.

Werth, R. (1988). *Neglect nach Hirnschädigung. Unilaterale Verminderung der Aufmerksamkeit und Raumrepräsentation.* Berlin: Springer-Verlag.

Werth, R. & Pöppel, E. (1988). Compression and lateral shift of mental coordinate systems in a line bisection task. *Neuropsychologia*, *26*, 741–745.

Zihl, J. (1981). Recovery of visual functions in patients with cerebral blindness. *Neuropsychologia, 18,* 71–77.

Zihl, J. & von Cramon, D. (1979). The contribution of the "second" visual system to directed visual attention in man. *Brain, 102,* 835–856.

Zihl, J. & von Cramon, D. (1985). Visual field recovery from scotomata in patients with postgeniculate damage. *Brain, 108,* 335–365.

11 Neglect and Visual Language

Andrew W. Ellis
Department of Psychology, University of York, York, UK

Andrew W. Young
Department of Psychology, University of Durham, Durham, UK

Brenda M. Flude
Department of Psychology, University of Lancaster, Lancaster, UK

INTRODUCTION

Reading and writing are among the functions commonly affected in unilateral neglect. A patient with left-side neglect following a right parietal lesion will tend to omit the initial words of lines of text, and will make errors on single words which affect the initial letters, for example misreading WINE as "mine" or MESSAGE as "passage". With the exception of Kinsbourne and Warrington (1962), the only treatments of the impact of neglect on reading one can find before the mid-1980s are embedded in more general accounts of the "neglect syndrome" (e.g. Assal & Zander, 1969; Diller & Weinberg, 1977; Friedland & Weinstein, 1977; Gilliat & Pratt, 1952).

The lessons to have been learnt from examining neglect dyslexia through the cognitive neuropsychologist's microscope are, in fact, the lessons that nearly always seem to follow from close inspection of traditional neuropsychological syndromes. The first is that the condition comes in different forms with different properties; the second that at least some of these different forms can dissociate from other symptoms (in this case, other manifestations of unilateral neglect) with which they are commonly associated. Our interpretation and understanding of unilateral neglect, including the effect of neglect on reading and writing, is undergoing major re-assessment and re-evaluation. It follows that any conclusions reached must be regarded as tentative and liable to modification in the light of further investigations.

NEGLECT AND READING I: SPATIAL NEGLECT DYSLEXIA

Spatial Neglect Dyslexia: A Basic Description

Following a series of cerebrovascular accidents, patient V.B. (Ellis, Flude, & Young, 1987a) showed left-side neglect on a wide range of tasks including drawing, line bisection and cancelling letters in arrays. Although her speech production and comprehension were unimpaired, her reading and writing were affected. When reading passages of text, she often failed to attempt words at the beginnings of lines and made errors on a proportion of the words she did attempt.

In their analysis of V.B.'s neglect dyslexia, Ellis et al. (1987a) concentrated on the errors she made in reading single words. From this, it would be easy to convey the impression that V.B. misread most of the words she attempted. She did not. Given unlimited time, she read over 90% of single words correctly. In a number of tests, Ellis et al. were unable to find evidence that V.B.'s accuracy was affected by the frequency of occurrence of stimulus words, their imageability, grammatical class or spelling–sound regularity. Errors showed no significant tendency to be of higher frequency than the target words that elicited them.

The majority of V.B.'s errors involved the initial (left-most) letters of words. Sometimes this involved the simple deletion of initial letters from the target. Examples (in which the target word is shown in capital letters to the left of the arrow and V.B.'s error is to the right) include CLOVE → love, DEARTH → earth, CHAMBER → amber and DRAUGHT → aught. Other errors involved the addition of letters to the beginning of the target word (e.g. ATE → date, LASS → glass). More commonly, however, V.B. substituted letters of the target word with other letters. In the majority of cases, this substitution involved the initial letter only (e.g. EAR → car, SOON → moon, HADDOCK → paddock), but sometimes two or three initial letters were involved (e.g. CABIN → robin, YELLOW → pillow).

Because the prototypical error for V.B. involved substituting letters from the target word with the same number of letters in the error, her misreadings tended to contain the same number of letters as the target words. Examples involving quite different numbers of letters did occur from time to time (e.g. SOCK → hassock, HEIRLOOM → bloom), but overall there was a clear correlation between target length and error length, a phenomenon which had been commented upon previously by Kinsbourne and Warrington (1962).

Ellis et al. (1987a) adopted a fairly strict criterion for what should count as a neglect error for purposes of analysis. This criterion was that the target and error should be identical to the right of an identifiable "neglect point" in each word and should have no letters in common to the left of those two points. Thus in FABLE → table, the neglect point comes after the F in FABLE and after the t in table, whereas in YELLOW → pillow it comes after the E in YELLOW and the i in pillow. Altogether, 66% of V.B.'s errors satisfied this strict criterion, 26% were labelled "visual" (e.g. TSAR → star, MARQUEE → quarrel) and the remaining 8% involved the production of nonwords as responses (e.g. LATCH → flatch, SLAVE → blave).

If V.B. was asked to read a word and also explain what it meant, the definitions she provided were always appropriate to any misreading she made. Thus, she misread RICE as "price" and defined it as "how much for a paper or something in a shop", misread LIQUID as "squid" and defined it as "a kind of sea creature", and misread CLOVER as "lover", producing the definition "partner, or someone you have an affair with; a sweetheart".

V.B.'s identification of words spelled aloud to her was excellent. Her accuracy and error pattern could be changed dramatically by presenting written words in formats other than conventional, horizontal, left-to-right. If a passage of text was rotated clockwise through 90° so that the lines ran from top to bottom rather than from left to right, her performance improved considerably. In particular, she no longer omitted the initial words on each line. If single words were presented upside-down (i.e. rotated through 180°), she managed to read over 65% correctly. Importantly, her neglect errors were now concentrated on the *final* letters, which are on the left when words are upside down, (e.g. PLANT → plane, SCORN → score). Thus, what mattered for V.B.'s neglect dyslexia was the spatial (left-to-right) location of letters in words rather than their first-to-last position. Hence we shall refer to this variety of neglect dyslexia as *spatial neglect dyslexia*.

Length and Lexicality

Behrmann, Moscovitch, Black and Mozer (1990) studied two patients with neglect dyslexia. One of their patients, A.H., would appear to have displayed much the same form of neglect dyslexia as V.B. A.H. made neglect dyslexic errors in the left-most letters of words presented either normally or mirror-reversed. Errors to words displayed vertically were not concentrated on the initial letters. Forty-two per cent of words in conventional format were read correctly, and 61% of errors were neglect errors.

Behrmann et al. (1990) asked A.H. to read words that were either normally spaced or extended by the addition of an extra character space between the letters (cf. HOUSE and H O U S E). Reading accuracy was significantly worse for the extended words than for the normal words. In a study not reported in Ellis et al. (1987a), V.B. was also asked to read words which were either normal or extended. She read 30/40 normal words correctly and 25/40 extended words. While not conclusive, this result is at least compatible with Behrmann and co-workers' finding, and supports the notion that in spatial neglect dyslexia, the initial letters of words are more likely to suffer the effects of neglect (and hence words are more likely to be misread) if the words occupy a greater horizontal extent.

If that is the case, then long words may tend to be read less well than short words. Behrmann et al. (1990) showed that A.H.'s reading accuracy declined from 80% correct to 67% correct across a range of lengths from three to nine letters. Ellis et al. (1987a) failed to obtain a reliable length effect with V.B., but used a narrower range of lengths. Their stimuli were also handwritten, and there may have been a tendency to space out the letters of short words more than long words. There is another factor which may militate against obtaining a length effect. Ellis et al. (1987a) showed that V.B.'s typical neglect error involved the first one or two letters of words, irrespective of their length. Longer words will typically be easier to guess from all except the first one or two letters than will shorter words, and this factor will tend to act against the discovery of an effect of letter length. At present, we do not know whether number of letters or horizontal extent underlies any length effect in spatial neglect dyslexia. This issue will only be resolved by studies which systematically and independently vary the two factors.

Another difference between A.H. and V.B. which may be more apparent than real concerns their performance with real words like SOFA as compared to invented nonwords like BOFA. A.H. showed a dramatic difference in performance between words and nonwords, reading 42% of words accurately in one test as compared with only 3% of nonwords. In contrast, V.B.'s accuracy with nonwords (87.6% correct) was comparable with her performance with words. As with length effects, however, we think that there are good reasons for not jumping straight to the conclusion that A.H.'s and V.B.'s neglect dyslexias were different in some important way. First, V.B.'s reading performance was overall much better than A.H.'s, with V.B. performing at over 85% correct with words as compared with A.H.'s level of around 40–45%. Ellis et al. (1987a) presented data and arguments to suggest that V.B. must have been perceiving many words correctly in their entirety, and that her neglect dyslexia only affected a minority of her attempts at single words. If this is so, then she may also have perceived many nonwords correctly in their entirety.

Comparisons between words and nonwords are also confounded by differences in "guessability". Suppose that a patient is asked to read SOFA, but because of neglect dyslexia only creates a visual representation that is something like -OFA. Provided that the patient knows in advance that the target *is* a word, the item should be read correctly (because there is only one four-letter word ending in -OFA). In contrast, if the target is BOFA, then even if the patient knows that a nonword response is required, it is unlikely to be guessed correctly (because -OFA as a nonword could also be DOFA, NOFA, WOFA, etc.).

A patient like A.H., whose neglect dyslexia is severe, may perceive few or no initial letters correctly, and may be more prone to differences in guessability than a patient with milder neglect dyslexia like V.B. Over and above that is the fact that the potential for differences in guessability to engender apparent lexicality (word–nonword) effects will depend crucially upon the selection of items. Instead of SOFA and BOFA, we could have contrasted PULL with VULL. There are roughly as many four-letter words beginning with a consonant and ending -ULL as there are potential nonwords, so guessability would not favour words here. Overall, though, guessability *would* favour words over nonwords in patients who knew in advance whether the target was a word or a nonword and were clear about the distinction in the first place. A proper comparison taking all these factors into account has yet to be carried out, so a final verdict as to the reality of word–nonword differences in neglect dyslexia cannot be formed.

Word Errors, Letter Errors and Hemianopia

V.B. (Ellis et al., 1987a) omitted words from the beginnings of lines of text. Her misreadings involved a mixture of neglect and visual errors, and her neglect errors involved a mixture of different sorts (e.g. letter deletions *vs* letter substitutions). There are reasons, though, to think that different mechanisms and deficits underlie these different categories of error.

Young, Newcombe and Ellis (1991) reported a patient, S.P., who resembled V.B. in several respects. In text reading, she omitted the initial words of lines, and she made neglect dyslexic errors to single words (e.g. JANGLE → tangle, MARROW → arrow). In fact, S.P. misread more words given unlimited exposure times than did V.B. (29% errors for S.P. compared with around 8% for V.B.), and a higher proportion of her errors met Ellis and co-workers' (1987a) criterion for being counted as neglect errors. Performance improved when words were presented vertically, implying that, as with V.B., S.P.'s neglect dyslexia was determined by the spatial location of letters in words.

In an investigation of whole word omissions *vs* misreadings, S.P. was presented with sheets containing 15 words positioned semi-randomly in an array made from five columns and 15 rows, but with only one word per row and three per column (see Young et al., 1991, figure 3). Across a series of sheets, she was presented with 315 words, with 63 words in each of the five vertical columns. The words were of 4 to 6 letters and shared the common property that the first letter can be either deleted or substituted to produce another words (e.g. FLAP, the F of which can be deleted to lap or substituted to slap). In this task, S.P. made 77 omission errors (complete failures to attempt words) and 48 misreadings, 47 of which were clear neglect errors. Whole-word omissions and neglect dyslexic misreadings showed very different patterns of distribution across the five columns: whole-word omissions were concentrated in the left-most columns, whereas misreadings were distributed much more evenly across the columns. These findings suggest that omissions and misreadings may have somewhat different underlying causes.

Patient J.O.H. of Costello and Warrington (1987) made neglect dyslexic errors on the initial letters of words. He also made errors of substitution, omission and addition to whole words in text, but we are told that these word errors "occurred both to the left and the right and the centre of the page. On no occasion did he fail to 'read' to the end of a line or return to the beginning of the next line. There was no evidence of any unilateral spatial neglect in his reading of prose" (Costello & Warrington, 1987, p. 1114). In contrast, patient V.S.N. of Kartsounis and Warrington (1989) showed severe neglect when attempting paragraphs of text, but minimal neglect dyslexia to single words. When asked to read normal passages of text, he typically failed to attempt more than three words from the extreme right of each line, but he read 94 of a set of 96 single words correctly (only misreading DAYBREAK as "tapebreak" and WAYSIDE as "quayside").

There would seem to be a distinction to be drawn between the form of unilateral neglect that causes patients to omit whole words at the beginnings of lines of text and the form of neglect that causes neglect dyslexic misreadings. Another distinction to be drawn is between those misreadings which affect the initial letters only (neglect errors) and misreadings which affect other portions of words (visual errors). Examples of clear visual errors from V.B. include DIVINE → living, AISLE → praise and MARQUEE → quarrel. We have mentioned already that S.P. misread more words than V.B., but that a higher proportion of her errors were neglect errors. This is because V.B. made a higher proportion of visual errors than S.P. If we consider only real-word errors, and apply Ellis et al. criterion for what is to count as a neglect error, then 94% of S.P.'s errors were neglect errors, whereas the corresponding figure for V.B. was 72%. Ellis et al. (1987a) very strict criterion almost certainly rejects some genuine neglect errors on the grounds of shared letters to the right of the putative neglect point in the target and error words (e.g. INSIDE → fireside, ELBOW → brow). Nevertheless, if visual and neglect misreadings arose from a common underlying deficit, it might be difficult to account for two patients, one of whom (S.P.) makes more errors overall than the other (V.B.) while making a dramatically higher proportion of neglect errors.

All that remains in this section is to compare neglect dyslexic misreadings which involve omissions of initial letters (e.g. LEVER → ever, DEARTH → earth) with misreadings in which initial letters are substituted (e.g. RIVER → liver, SABLE → table). We shall argue that which type of error occurs may depend upon a subtle interaction between neglect dyslexia and another common symptom in patients with neglect dyslexia, namely hemianopia.

Like many patients with neglect, V.B. had a left homonymous hemianopia (blindness to stimuli in the left visual field). Many patients with hemianopia do not show neglect dyslexia, and three of the six neglect dyslexic patients studied by Kinsbourne and Warrington (1962) did not have hemianopias, suggesting that hemianopia cannot be held solely responsible for spatial neglect dyslexia. In addition, Kinsbourne and Warrington (1962), Ellis et al. (1987a) and Young et al. (1991) have all done experiments to show that neglect errors can occur when words are presented entirely within the intact right visual field. Nevertheless, we propose that neglect dyslexia and hemianopia may interact to determine the precise error pattern observed in a particular patient.

Young et al. (1991) contrasted the effect of displaying words entirely within S.P.'s intact right visual field with the effect of presenting words centrally, so that they straddled the boundary between S.P.'s intact right visual field and her hemianopic left visual field. Presentation times were unlimited, so that S.P. was free to move her eyes; what varied was the place at which the word *initially* appeared. With presentation initially in the right visual field, the majority of S.P.'s errors involved substitutions of initial letters (e.g. BAT → eat, BELIEF → relief). With central presentation, a higher proportion of errors involving the simple omission of initial letters was observed (e.g. CAT → at, CHAIR → hair, VALLEY → alley).

We propose that if a word fell entirely within S.P.'s right visual field, then all letters were processed to some degree, and the implicit awareness of the existence of initial letters manifested itself in errors involving substitution rather than simple deletion of initial letters. If a word straddled the boundary between the hemianopic left visual field and the intact right visual field, and if a word was embedded within the right portion of the target word, then the reluctance to scan in the leftwards direction that is known to characterise patients with neglect caused S.P. to stop once she had located a whole word, the result being an omission error. So, for example, if the word CHAIR fell entirely within S.P.'s right visual field, she might read it correctly or make a substitution error (e.g. flair), but if it straddled the boundary between her hemianopic left visual field and her intact right visual field, then she might scan leftwards only until she saw AIR or HAIR and so make an omission.

Thus, it would appear that hemianopia does not *cause* spatial neglect dyslexia, but may interact with it to determine the observed proportions of letter deletions *vs* letter substitutions. Words falling entirely within intact areas of the visual field are likely to be misread by having their initial letters substituted, but letters may be deleted from words falling across the boundary between intact and hemianopic areas of the visual field (especially if the right end forms a familiar word). In sum, we would argue that different underlying deficits are responsible for whole-word omissions, visual errors and neglect errors in spatial neglect dyslexia, and that neglect dyslexia alone (unhindered by interactions with hemianopia) typically results in substitutions rather than deletions of initial letters.

Attention and Spatial Neglect Dyslexia

Riddoch, Humphreys, Cleton and Fery (1991) described a patient, J.B., with a pattern similar to that of both V.B. and S.P. J.B. showed left-sided neglect on a range of tasks including reading following a right temporo-parietal injury. Typical neglect dyslexic errors occurred (e.g. GROSS → cross, BOUGH → slough), with 63% of target–error pairs sharing the same number of letters (indicating a tendency to substitute rather than add or omit initial letters). When words were rotated through 180° so that they were upside-down with their initial letters on the right, J.B. read 91% of words correctly (as good a level of performance as he attained with letters in conventional formats). Fifteen of the 20 errors made to upside-down words involved the left-most (final) letter, with 3 involving central letters and only 2 involving the right-most (initial) letter.

In an earlier study, Riddoch and Humphreys (1983) had sought to test the hypothesis that unilateral neglect is due to a failure to attend to the left sides of objects by showing that neglect is reduced if the patient is required to locate and identify a cue presented to the left of the object. In their experiment, they required neglect patients to bisect horizontal lines with or without a digit to the left of the line. Neglect patients tend to bisect to the right of true centre, presumably because of a failure to respond to the left-most portion of the line. When the digit was present, and had to be reported before the patient bisected the line, this tendency was reduced.

Rather than using digits, Riddoch et al. (1991) placed a hash sign (#) to the left of words that J.B. was to read aloud. Performance improved relative to his reading of the same words on a previous occasion though, as Riddoch et al. admit, their failure to compare reading of words with and without cueing in the same sessions means that the cueing effect might be due to improvement over time in J.B.'s general performance. That said, we can report data on V.B. that seems at least compatible with an attentional account of neglect dyslexia. V.B. was asked to read five-letter words printed in upper-case (capital) letters. The words were printed with either the first two letters in bold and the last three not (e.g. **BROOK**) or the last three bold and the first two not (e.g., **SABLE**. The reasoning was that the letters in bold would be more salient and would attract attention more than those letters not in a bold face. In four different within-session comparisons, V.B.'s scores out of 40 for words with bold initial *vs* non-bold initial letters were 31 *vs* 25, 36 *vs* 33, 31 *vs* 26 and 31 *vs* 26. It would thus seem that increasing the perceptual salience of initial letters improves reading performance in left-sided spatial neglect dyslexia, as an attentional theory would predict.

To summarise, we shall reserve the term "spatial neglect dyslexia" for the tendency to misread the initial letters of words in conventional formats, but the final letters of words presented upside-down or mirror-reversed (i.e. a tendency to misread the left-most letters, however the word is presented). When spatial neglect dyslexia is not complicated by the presence of a hemianopia, the dominant error would appear to be the substitution (rather than the omission) of left-most letters, with the result that target and error words tend to be of similar lengths. Comprehension matches the misreading rather than the target. Words which occupy a greater horizontal extent are more likely to be misread, but it is not yet clear whether an effect of number of letters exists over and above an effect of physical length. Words displayed in vertical format are read much more accurately than words in normal horizontal format. The tendency to omit words at the beginnings of lines of text would appear to be a dissociable symptom with a separate cause, though it is a symptom which often accompanies spatial neglect dyslexia. Visual misreading errors may reflect a third, commonly co-occurring deficit. Finally, the effects of cueing and perceptual salience of initial letters are compatible with the hypothesis that spatial neglect dyslexia results from inattention to left-most letters in strings.

NEGLECT AND READING II: POSITIONAL NEGLECT DYSLEXIA

In contrast to the patients just discussed, whose errors affect the left-most letters of words, patients have been reported whose misreadings affect the final letters of words. As we shall see, their condition cannot be explained as simply the mirror image of left-sided spatial neglect dyslexia. Warrington and Zangwill (1957) reported a patient who made errors on final letters, misreading BEWARE as because, TONGUE as together, and OBTAINED as oblong. A detailed report of another patient, N.G., who made final letter errors has been provided by Hillis and Caramazza (1989; 1991; Caramazza & Hillis, 1991). N.G. was naturally left-handed, though she had been taught to write with her right hand, and had a left hemisphere lesion. N.G. was not aphasic, nor did her short-term memory appear to be seriously impaired (forward span 7; backward span 3). Although she had shown neglect on a variety of tasks in the period immediately following her stroke, by the time that the data discussed here were collected, neglect was only evident in her processing of written language.

When attempting to read sentences, N.G. would occasionally fail to attempt to read the right-most words. Among the words she attempted would be errors focused on the end letters. Thus she read "The quick brown fox jumps over the lazy dog" as "The *quiet* brown fox *jumped* over the lazy *doctor*". She read around 75% of single words correctly, with her errors tending to involve the final letters (e.g. PARK → part, HUMID → human, HOUND → house, SPRINTER → sprinkle). As with V.B., target and error words tended to be of the same length, and comprehension matched the error word rather than the target.

In contrast to patients with spatial neglect dyslexia, N.G. could name all the letters in a word correctly, yet would still misread (and misconstrue) the word. For example, when asked to name the letters in JOURNAL and then read the word, she responded "J, O, U, R, N, A, L , ... journey". This contrasts with V.B. responding to BARRIER as "H, A, R, R, I, E, R ... harrier" and to CANISTER as "B, A, N, I, S, T, E, R ... banister". Asked to name the letters of STATUS *and* define the word, N.G. responded, 'S, T, A, T, U, S ... The Statue of Liberty is very pretty ... The word is statue". To PLANET she responded, "P, L, A, N, E, T ... The plane landed on the other side ... The word is plane".

N.G.'s ability to name the component letters of words she went on to misread shows that her deficit cannot have lain within the earliest stages of visual letter identification. There are other aspects of N.G.'s performance that also suggest a more central locus for her neglect dyslexia. Patients with spatial neglect dyslexia make errors to left-most letters, and so misread the initial letters of ordinary words but the final letters of words presented upside-down or mirror-reversed. With words presented vertically, their errors are no longer concentrated in any particular portion of words. N.G. is different in that she continued to make errors on the final letters of words whatever their orientation. Errors to mirror-reversed words include COMMON → comet, REGULATED → regular and DISCOVERY → disco, while errors to words presented vertically include RANG → ran, BLENDING → blemish and MOTIONLESS → motel. Because N.G.'s errors occur at the ends of words irrespective of their orientation, her neglect dyslexia might be termed *positional neglect dyslexia*. (The term "positional" is taken from Katz and Sevush (1989), whose patient J.M. is claimed to have made errors on initial letters of words irrespective of their orientation, though the evidence upon which that claim is based is less compelling than for N.G.)

Whereas the ability of spatial neglect dyslexics like V.B. to identify words spelled aloud to them can be very good, N.G. made errors on this task that had the same properties as her errors to written words. Examples include "B, A, S, I, S" → brass, "S, P, A, R, R, O, W" → space and "E, A, R, N, S" → earring. These errors suggest that N.G.'s deficit lies at a stage beyond the point at which input from spoken letter names converges with that from written words. N.G.'s reading was also unaffected by extending the horizontal length of words by inserting spaces between letters. This again suggests that N.G.'s deficit is of a less spatial nature than that of V.B. and the other spatial neglect dyslexics.

Ellis et al. (1987a) noted that, for target words of a wide range of different lengths, V.B.'s neglect point fell most frequently after the first letter (from FAT → sat to POPULATION → copulation). Caramazza and Hillis (1991) analysed N.G.'s reading errors and showed that "(1) the vast predominance of errors occurred on the right half of words irrespective of their length; (2) errors occurred at equal rates as a function of absolute distance from the centre of a word; and (3) errors increased 'linearly' as a function of distance from the centre of the word" (p. 406). The evidence for this claim is based on an analysis of N.G.'s errors in which errors were scored at different positions in words ranging in length from four to nine letters. When the results are displayed as in Table 11.1, showing the percentage of errors at each position with the centres of different word lengths aligned, the validity of Caramazza and Hillis's claims can be seen. (Note that this is not the pattern one would expect to see if a short-term memory problem of any sort was preventing N.G. from "holding onto" early letters in words when processing later ones.)

Table 11.2 presents the results of a similar analysis of V.B.'s errors. For this analysis, an error was credited to a given position in a word if the letter in that position was omitted or substituted. Additions to the beginning of words (e.g. TOP → stop) were scored as errors at the initial position. Table 11.1, taken from Caramazza and Hillis (1991), combines N.G.'s neglect and visual errors involving the production of both word and nonword responses to word targets. We discussed earlier the possibility that in spatial neglect dyslexia visual and neglect errors have a different basis. The analysis in Table 11.2 is limited to a corpus of V.B.'s real-word neglect errors (an augmented version of the errors given in the appendix to Ellis et al., 1987a). The restriction to neglect errors, plus the fact that V.B.'s overall error rate was less than N.G.'s, means that the percentages are lower than in Table 11.1 (and are based on smaller numbers). Nevertheless, it can be seen that V.B.'s errors tend to afflict the right halves of words. Thus, although the first position was most error-prone for all lengths, some errors were recorded affecting the first four letters of eight-letter words, whereas only the first two letters of three- and four-letter words were affected (and, in

TABLE 11.1

Percentages of Reading Errors of All Types as Function of Letter Position in Words of Different Lengths for Patient N.G.[a]

Word Length	N					Word Centre ↓				
4	141	0	0	4	15					
5	219	0	0	1	8	18				
6	204	0	0	0	4	8	25			
7	82	0	0	1	4	5	16	31		
8	88	0	0	0	1	3	18	21	34	
	5	0	0	0	0	2	10	23	28	37

[a] From Caramazza and Hillis (1991). Reproduced with permission. n = number of words presented of a given length.

TABLE 11.2

Percentages of Real-word Neglect Dyslexic Reading Errors as a Function of Letter Position in Words of Different Lengths for Patient V.B.[a]

Word Length	N				Word Centre ↓				
3	185			8	1	0			
4	507		9	0	0	0			
5	1035	10	2	0	0	0			
6	501	7	3	1	0	0	0		
7	212	12	5	1	1	1	0	0	
8	153	9	2	2	1	0	0	0	0

[a] Based on a supplemented version of the corpus presented in Ellis et al. (1987a). n = number of words presented of a given length.

fact, only a single error was recorded at the second positions of three- and four-letter targets).

V.B.'s errors to words in normal horizontal format are restricted to the left halves of words, whereas for N.G. the restriction is, of course, to the right halves. It is also true for V.B. as for N.G. that errors increase with distance from the centre. What is not clear is that V.B.'s errors occur at equal rates as a function of absolute distance from the centre of a word, as N.G.'s did. This claim for N.G. is based on the fact that if one scans vertically down the right half of Table 11.1, the error rates look very similar. Thus, the error rates are comparable at the fifth position of five-letter words (18%), the sixth position of seven-letter words (16%) and the seventh position of nine-letter words (23%). That is not true for V.B: for example, the error rates are *not* comparable at the first position of four-letter words

(9%), the second position of six-letter words (3%) and the third position of eight-letter words (2%). We should be cautious in interpreting this observation: Tables 11.1 and 11.2 are based on different error types (all errors for N.G.; real-word neglect errors only for V.B.). Also, N.G. was presented with typewritten words, whereas handwritten words were shown to V.B. and, as noted earlier, there may have been some tendency to space out the letters of short words more than long words. But there is a possible difference here between spatial and positional dyslexia that warrants further investigation.

A possible refutation of the conjecture that all neglect dyslexias are word-centred is provided by patient T.B. of Patterson and Wilson (1991). T.B.'s errors were confined to the initial letter of a word, irrespective of its length. Errors were distributed equally throughout words presented vertically and tended to affect the ends of mirror-reversed words. These observations, plus the fact that his oral spelling and identification of words spelled aloud were both excellent, suggest that T.B.'s neglect dyslexia was spatial rather than positional in nature (though see Caramazza & Hillis, 1991, for discussion).

Patient R.H.R.

Warrington's (1991) patient, R.H.R., was a right-handed man with a small left hemisphere lesion. There was no suggestion of perceptual impairment or unilateral neglect evident in his drawing or cancellation. His speech was fluent without apparent word-finding difficulties, but his reading and spelling were both impaired.

R.H.R. read 55% of a set of common words correctly, and his errors were concentrated towards the ends of words. Fifty-three per cent of his errors to words presented horizontally satisfied Ellis and co-workers' (1987a) criterion for neglect errors except that, being right-sided errors, the target and error words were identical to the *left* of an identifiable neglect point in each word and shared no letters in common to the right of the two neglect points. Examples are CALL → calf, TRUTH → truck and SEASON → seaside. The remaining errors were mostly visual errors (e.g. TOOK → talk, AGREE → argue) or failures to respond.

With vertical presentation of words, R.H.R.'s accuracy fell to 13% correct, and he now made more visual errors than neglect errors. Nevertheless, 25% of his errors continued to satisfy the strict criterion for what should count as a neglect error and, importantly, remained focused on the final letter(s) of the target words. Examples include KING → kite, MARY → march, BLOW → blue and COAT →coach. The fact that R.H.R. continued to make errors on end letters when words were presented vertically, suggests that he should be regarded as a case of positional rather than spatial neglect dyslexia.

Warrington (1991) provides little information on R.H.R.'s spelling, but N.G. showed features which mirrored in a remarkable way her positional neglect dyslexia. But before considering the nature and locus of the impairments in spatial and positional neglect dyslexia, it is helpful to review the impact of unilateral neglect on the production of writing.

SPELLING AND WRITING AND UNILATERAL NEGLECT

We have seen that N.G. made errors on the initial letters of words whether they were presented aurally (by the experimenter spelling the word aloud) or visually, and irrespective of the orientation of written words. N.G.'s spelling and writing showed features which mirrored in a remarkable way her positional neglect dyslexia. In both spelling aloud and writing, N.G. made errors which were again concentrated at the ends of words. These errors typically resulted in the production of nonwords. Examples of her errors in spelling words aloud to dictation include sneeze → S, N, E, E, D, taught → T, A, U, G, H, T, H and events → E, V, E, N, I, S. Examples from writing to dictation include floor → FLOORE, jury → JURD and avoid → AVOILOE. N.G. was more accurate at writing words (33% correct) than nonwords (21% correct), but her spelling or writing of nonwords to dictation showed the same concentration of errors at the ends (e.g. skart → SKARR, remmun → REMNEY, chench → CHEN).

N.G.'s spelling accuracy declined with increasing word length (from 50% correct on four-letter words to 7% correct on eight-letter words). When asked to spell words aloud backwards, she still made errors on the final letters, even though those letters were now the first to be spoken. Thus, asked to spell "absorb" aloud backwards she produced N, W, O, S, B, A (= ABSOWN forwards), and asked to spell "oyster" aloud backwards she produced E, T, S, Y, O (=OYSTE). This demonstrates that her spelling/writing deficit was, like her reading deficit, positional rather than spatial. An analysis similar to that carried out on her reading errors showed that mistakes in spelling and writing also occurred in the right halves of words, whatever their length.

The situation for the patients with spatial neglect dyslexia is different. V.B.'s oral spelling was excellent, as was her identification of words spelled aloud to her, but her attempts at writing contained numerous errors (Ellis, Young, & Flude, 1987b). When writing text, V.B. wrote over towards the right side of the sheet of paper, leaving a wide left margin. In her handwriting, she often failed to go back in order to dot i's and cross t's. Finally, her attempts to write individual words contained frequent errors involving the omission or repetition of letters or letter strokes. J.B. showed the same pattern (Riddoch, 1991), but Ellis et al. (1987b) mention that patient S.P., whose neglect dyslexia is analysed by Young et al. (1991), showed V.B.'s tendencies to write on the right side of the page and to fail to dot i's and cross t's, but did not omit or repeat letters or strokes.

It may be that writing over to the right of the page and failing to dot i's and cross t's reflects the more general visuo-spatial neglect shown by many of the patients with spatial neglect dyslexia. It is obvious why visuo-spatial neglect could cause a patient to ignore the left side of the page in writing. Errors on i's and t's may arise because going back at the end of a word to dot the i's and cross the t's means moving leftwards into the neglected region of space, something which patients with visuo-spatial neglect have difficulty doing. The omissions and repetitions of strokes and letters occurred in V.B. and J.B. but not S.P. Lebrun (1976) used the term "afferent dysgraphia" to refer to this pattern, noting the similarity of these errors to those made by normal subjects writing with their eyes closed, and arguing that letter and stroke omissions and repetitions arise when a patient or a normal writer is unable to use visual and kinaesthetic feedback to monitor and control the complex sequences of movements required in handwriting. Ellis et al. (1987b) asked normal subjects to write with their eyes closed (disrupting visual feedback) and while tapping a finger sequence with the non-writing hand (to interfere with the monitoring of kinaesthetic feedback). They showed that under these conditions normal subjects made letter and stroke repetition errors of the same type and with the same frequency as shown by V.B. writing under normal conditions. It may be that monitoring visual and kinaesthetic feedback is a quasi-attentional function of the normal right parietal lobe which is not directly related to unilateral neglect (because letter and stroke errors do not occur towards one side of words), but which is likely to co-occur with aspects of unilateral neglect as a result of the anatomical proximity of the regions that mediate these functions. Behrmann and co-workers' (1990) report that A.H. showed a spatial neglect dyslexia without afferent dysgraphia supports the proposal that different deficits underlie these two symptom patterns.

Thus, spatial neglect dyslexia appears not to be linked to dysgraphia in any necessary way, but in the one clear case of positional neglect dyslexia reported to date, N.G., there existed a complementarity between the characteristics of reading and writing that looks to be more than coincidental. The question then arises as to whether there exist neglect-related disorders that are specific to spelling and writing and which can occur in the absence of neglect dyslexia.

Caramazza, Miceli, Villa and Romani (1987) reported a patient, L.B., who made letter omission and substitution errors in both writing and spelling aloud, and for both words and nonwords. Reading of familiar words was preserved, though reading of unfamiliar nonwords was impaired (Caramazza, Miceli, Silveri, & Laudanna, 1985). Like normal writers (Wing

& Baddeley, 1980), L.B.'s errors were concentrated in the middles of words. Hillis and Caramazza (1989) report two patients, D.H. and M.L., whose errors resembled L.B.'s, involving letter omissions and substitutions, but M.L.'s errors showed a shift towards the beginnings of words, whereas D.H.'s errors showed a shift towards the ends. In neither case were the beginning or final letters most affected; rather, there was a shift in error focus away from the centre towards the initial (M.L.) or final (D.H.) letters.

One caveat should be entered here. Our knowledge of the distribution of normal errors is derived from a study (Wing & Baddeley, 1980) which combined errors from many different writers. The distribution they obtained, which more or less matches L.B.'s distribution, is a distribution for the population of reasonably skilled writers of English. It may not accurately represent the error distribution of each individual normal writer. It is at least conceivable that there are normal writers whose error distributions are, like those of D.H. and M.L., shifted away from centre. Hence we cannot rule out the possibility that D.H.'s and M.L.'s spelling errors showed similar distributions pre-morbidly, and that the effect of their brain injury has been only to increase their overall tendency to error. Whether or not this is the case, the general point we wish to make is that a discipline like cognitive neuropsychology which pays such close attention to individual differences among patients should also take careful cognisance of individual differences among normal subjects. When comparing patient data against normal data, and especially when differences between patients of similar types are being considered (as with L.B., D.H. and M.L.), it is vital that the normal data should incorporate measures of range and variation, not just central tendency.

That said, the shift in M.L.'s spelling and writing errors towards the beginnings of words was accompanied by a left-side visuo-spatial neglect and very mild neglect dyslexia, while the shift in D.H.'s spelling and writing errors towards the ends of words was accompanied by a mild left-side visuo-spatial neglect and reading errors concentrated on the ends of words. Hence in both cases, the neglect impairment indicated by a shift in spelling and writing errors was not entirely specific, being associated with signs of similarly lateralised neglect in other tasks.

Baxter and Warrington (1983; 1990) describe a left-handed patient, O.R.F., with a right parietal lesion who had a mild fluent aphasia and only a slight left-sided neglect dyslexia. O.R.F. was unable to use his preferred left hand to write because of a left hemiplegia, and his attempts to write using his right hand are described as "extremely slow and hard to decipher". He could, however, attempt to spell aloud. When he did so, his accuracy was affected by the length of words to be spelled, but not by their frequency in the language or by their spelling–sound regularity. The errors he made were concentrated at the beginnings of words. This was true whether he spelled words aloud forwards or backwards.

Baxter and Warrington (1983) suggest that O.R.F. "appeared to be spelling from an 'inner screen'" and that a left-sided neglect reduced the efficiency of this process. Bisiach and co-workers have shown that the report of mental images can be affected by unilateral neglect (Bisiach & Luzzatti, 1978), but as far as we are aware, every patient who has been observed to show neglect of mental images has also shown visuo-spatial neglect when dealing with external visual stimuli (e.g. in drawing or cancellation). O.R.F. is reported as not showing such visuo-spatial neglect for external stimuli or even for non-verbal mental images (D. Baxter, pers. comm.); hence he would not seem to represent a case of imagery neglect without visuo-spatial neglect, but rather a selective neglect dysgraphia caused by a disruption to orthographic representations involved in spelling but not in reading.

NEGLECT AND VISUAL LANGUAGE

Theoretical accounts of the psychological processes underlying reading and spelling/writing differ considerably in their particulars but at the most general level there is broad agreement. A word on a page is a pattern of lines and curves which must undergo processing if it is to be recognised, comprehended and pronounced successfully. First, at least some of the component letters of the word must be identified and the position of letters in the word must be noted. Letter position is important because words may contain the same letters and only differ in their positions (e.g. SLAP/PALS/ALPS/LAPS).

Familiar words come in a wide range of fonts, sizes and formats, and in either UPPER-CASE or lower-case. One way for the reading system to be able to recognise all the different possible versions of a familiar word would be to have each letter string undergo some "normalisation" process resulting in the creation of a positionally encoded sequence of *abstract letter identities* (Coltheart, 1981) or *graphemes* (Caramazza & Hillis, 1991). If, following such normalisation, a string of graphemes is to be recognised as a familiar word, it must be matched against stored representations of all the words known to the reader. The memory structure in which these stored representations are held goes under various names, including the *visual input lexicon* and the *orthographic lexicon*.

Spatial neglect dyslexia affects the left side of both words and nonwords. It is influenced by physical length and salience of letters. Errors to vertical words are randomly dispersed and identification of words presented as oral spellings can be preserved. This pattern is taken by Caramazza and Hillis to indicate that the neglect responsible for spatial neglect dyslexia affects an early stage of visual processing, and an early representation: one which precedes the formation of an abstract graphemic representation. Caramazza and Hillis (1991) suggest that the representation in question is a "stimulus-centred letter shape map" based on left–right not first–last coding.

When word recognition is not affected by hemianopia, the natural error type in spatial neglect dyslexia appears to be the substitution rather than simple deletion of initial letters. Those letters must be processed sufficiently for their presence to be covertly acknowledged in the error. Ellis et al. (1987a) proposed that spatial neglect dyslexia affects the encoding of the identity of letters on the left of strings, but that positional encoding is relatively preserved. Hence, spatial neglect dyslexia might cause a word like FACE to be converted into an abstract graphemic representation that is something like $<->_1$, $<A>_2$, $<C>_3$, $<E>_4$, where the identity of the left-most letter has not been accurately encoded, but its presence has, with the result that the A, C and E are encoded as the second, third and fourth letters, rather than the first, second and third. This representation would activate the entries in the orthographic lexicon of words like LACE and PACE more than it would activate the representation for ACE, so that a misreading is more likely to involve a substitution of the first letter than its deletion.

Positional neglect dyslexia as displayed by N.G. affects final letters irrespective of their spatial positioning, and affects the identification of words from oral spellings as well as in written form. It is not influenced by physical length (nor, we would predict, by manipulations of letter salience). Caramazza and Hillis (1991) note that the characteristics of positional neglect dyslexia are compatible with the suggestion that positional neglect dyslexia affects the abstract graphemic representations themselves (rather than the processes which create the abstract graphemic representations, as in spatial neglect dyslexia).

Cognitive and neuropsychological accounts of the processes underlying spelling and writing propose that the spellings of familiar words are also retrieved from an orthographic lexicon in the form of abstract letter identities or graphemes which are subsequently translated through a series of intermediate stages either into letter names (in spelling aloud), or into arm, hand and finger movements (in handwriting or typing) (see Ellis, 1982; 1988). N.G.'s oral spelling and writing showed word-final errors whose distribution matched that of her reading errors in a remarkably close way, suggesting that the same (disrupted) representation may have been involved in reading, spelling and writing. Caramazza and Hillis (1991) propose that a word-centred, positional, abstract graphemic representation serves both as the input to the orthographic lexicon in reading and as the initial representation of words retrieved from the lexicon in spelling and writing. We have discussed logical reasons why visual word recognition might employ abstract representations (to do with generalising over different formats, fonts and cases). There are also empirical lines of evidence commensurate with this view (see, e.g. Carr, Brown, & Charalambous, 1989; Rayner, McConkie, & Zola, 1980).

Hillis and Caramazza's analysis of N.G. presents the first evidence we are aware of suggesting that a common abstract graphemic representation may be involved in both reading and spelling/writing. A single abstract graphemic representation could, in principle, interface with separate orthographic lexicons for input and output, but the architecture in that case would be somewhat strange. The question of whether reading and spelling/writing are subserved by one lexicon has been much debated but not resolved (see Coltheart & Funnell, 1987; Monsell, 1987), so the idea of a common input–output graphemic representation interfacing with a common input–output orthographic lexicon remains very much within the bounds of possibility.

N.G. could name the letters of words she went on to misread. It could be that spelling aloud involves treating each of the component letters of words as objects, and that her neglect does not affect single objects, showing itself only when object strings are being processed. Finally, N.G. showed the same abstract positional deficit in the reading and writing of unfamiliar nonwords as well as familiar words. There is current debate over whether nonwords are read and written through the intercession of processes distinct from those mediating word reading and spelling, or whether lexical processes can also cope with nonwords (see Patterson & Coltheart, 1987, for a review of the arguments and evidence). Either way, the abstract graphemic representation disrupted in N.G. must be common to both lexical and sublexical processing as well as to both reading and spelling/writing.

Certain architectures for cognition, notably parallel distributed processing systems (Quinlan, 1991), do not (explicitly) honour the distinction between graphemic representations and the lexical units or nodes which recognise or generate them. Within such systems, a familiar word is a pattern engraved across finer grain representations. It could be that N.G.'s positional neglect dyslexia attacks a representation which serves as both input to and output from the orthographic lexicon(s), but we think it at least worth contemplating the possibility that the representation which is disrupted is the orthographic lexicon itself. This would imply that such central representations require their activation levels to be sustained in a manner similar to that by which spatial representations of the external world are sustained.

At this point, arbitrating between rival hypotheses becomes increasingly difficult in the absence of explicit simulations of the processes in question. Mozer and Behrmann (1990) have created a computer model which attempts to show how attentional processes could modulate word recognition, and how "lesioning" such a model could result in phenomena like those seen in spatial neglect dyslexia. Among other things, it provides an account of word omissions and of the superior reading of words than nonwords, though it does not (yet) provide a natural account of other effects, such as the spatial/positional distinction and the dominance of letter substitution over deletion errors. It is early days in the evolution of such models, but the enterprise is clearly a valuable one. We can only learn from attempts to translate sometimes rather vaguely expressed ideas about attention and neglect into working simulations.

Analysis of spatial and positional neglect dyslexias indicates that unilateral neglect can affect at least two separate stages or representations involved in reading and spelling/writing. The studies of patients with neglect-like disorders of writing suggest that still other spatial representations involved in processing visual language may be prone to unilateral neglect.

The letter omissions and substitution errors of Hillis and Caramazza's (1989) patient M.L. tended to occur at the beginnings of words, while the errors of patient D.H. tended to occur at the ends. M.L. also showed a left-side visuo-spatial neglect and (very mild) neglect dyslexia, while D.H.'s spelling and writing errors towards the ends of words were accompanied by a mild left-side visuo-spatial neglect and reading errors concentrated on the ends of words. It is possible that M.L. and D.H. showed positional neglect dyslexias much milder than N.G.'s, resulting in low levels of reading errors and slight shifts in distributions of spelling and writing errors. If so, then M.L. is the first reported case of left-sided positional neglect dyslexia; if not, then as with patient O.R.F. (Baxter & Warrington, 1983; 1990), their disorders will need to be located downstream of the abstract graphemic level affected in N.G. And, if not, future research will need to explore whether, in patients with left hemisphere language dominance, spatial neglect dyslexia is invariably left-sided, resulting from right hemisphere injury, and positional neglect dyslexia invariably right-sided, resulting from left hemisphere injury. Such a state of affairs could arise if the right hemisphere is responsible for maintaining attention across relatively peripheral visual representations of the external world, while the left hemisphere sustains attention (or activation) over more central, but still positionally coded, linguistic representations.

Most patient with neglect dyslexia also show visuo-spatial neglect, including patient N.G. whose positional neglect dyslexia appeared to involve fairly abstract representations (Caramazza & Hillis, 1991; Hillis & Caramazza, 1989; 1991). There are signs, though, that visuo-spatial neglect and neglect dyslexia may dissociate. Patient J.O.H., reported by Costello and Warrington (1987), made errors on the initial letters of words (e.g. MOWER → shower, RAIN → pain), but in visuo-spatial tasks like drawing, cancellation and line bisection he showed signs of *right*-sided neglect. J.O.H. would seem to represent in one individual a double dissociation between a left-sided neglect dyslexia and a right-sided visuo-spatial neglect. Unfortunately, Costello and Warrington's (1987) description of J.O.H. does not provide us with the data that would allow us to confirm that J.O.H.'s neglect dyslexia was spatial in nature. No cases of left-sided positional neglect dyslexia have yet been reported, but it is conceivable (J.O.H. *was* an unusual patient) that J.O.H. may have represented a case of *left*-sided *positional* neglect dyslexia (i.e. the mirror-image of N.G.). If that were the case, conclusions drawn from J.O.H. would not apply automatically to patients with spatial neglect dyslexia. The point is that if, as we now know, neglect dyslexia takes more than one form, then the dissociation of each form with other manifestations of neglect must be established separately. In order to make theoretical progress, we need to know for the left- and right-sided forms of each variety of neglect dyslexia the extent to which that variety can dissociate from neglect in other modalities and for other types of material. If unilateral neglect can affect representations involved in the production of written language, as the study by Hillis and Caramazza (1989) suggests, then we also need to know more about other manifestations of "motor neglect" (Laplane & Degos, 1983) in such patients.

REFERENCES

Assal, G. & Zander, E. (1969). Rappel de la symptomologie neuropsychologique des lésions hémisphériques droites. *Archives Suisses de Neurologie, Neurochirurgie et de Psychiatrie, 105*, 217–239.

Baxter, D.M. & Warrington, E.K. (1983). Neglect dysgraphia. *Journal of Neurology, Neurosurgery and Psychiatry, 46*, 1073–1078.

Baxter, D.M. & Warrington, E.K. (1990). A comment on Hillis and Caramazza's (1989) paper "The graphemic buffer and attentional mechanisms". *Brain and Language, 38*, 615–616.

Behrmann, M., Moscovitch, M., Black, S.E., & Mozer, M.C. (1990). Perceptual and conceptual mechanisms in neglect dyslexia. *Brain, 113*, 1163–1183.

Bisiach, E. & Luzzatti, C. (1978). Unilateral neglect of representational space. *Cortex, 14*, 129–133.

Caramazza, A. & Hillis, A.E. (1991). Levels of representation, co-ordinate frames, and unilateral neglect. *Cognitive Neuropsychology, 7*, 391–445.

Caramazza, A., Miceli, G., Silveri, M.C., & Laudanna, A. (1985). Reading mechanisms and the organisation of the lexicon: Evidence from acquired dyslexia. *Cognitive Neuropsychology, 2*, 81–114.

Caramazza, A., Miceli, G., Villa, G., & Romani, C. (1987). The role of the graphemic buffer in spelling: Evidence from a case of acquired dysgraphia. *Cognition, 26*, 59–85.

Carr, T.H., Brown, J.S., & Charalambous, A. (1989). Repetition and reading: Perceptual encoding mechanisms are very abstractive but not very interactive. *Journal of Experimental Psychology: Learning, Memory and Cognition, 15*, 763–778.

Coltheart, M. (1981). Disorders of reading and their implications for models of normal reading. *Visible Language, 15*, 245–286.

Coltheart, M. & Funnell, E. (1987). Reading and writing: One lexicon or two? In D.A. Allport, D.G. Mackay, W. Prinz, & E. Scheerer (Eds), *Language perception and production: Relationships between listening, speaking, reading and writing*. London: Academic Press.

Costello, A. de L. & Warrington, E.K. (1987). The dissociation of visuospatial neglect and neglect dyslexia. *Journal of Neurology, Neurosurgery and Psychiatry, 50*, 1110–1116.

Diller, L. & Weinberg, J.P. (1977). Hemi-inattention in rehabilitation: The evolution of a rational remediation program. In E.A. Weinstein & R.P. Friedland (Eds), *Hemi-inattention and hemisphere specialisation. Advances in Neurology Vol. 18*. New York: Raven Press.

Ellis, A.W. (1982). Spelling and writing (and reading and speaking). In A.W. Ellis (Ed.), *Normality and pathology in cognitive functions*. London: Academic Press.

Ellis, A.W. (1988). Normal writing processes and peripheral acquired dysgraphias. *Language and Cognitive Processes, 3*, 99–127.

Ellis, A.W., Flude, B.M., & Young, A.W. (1987a). "Neglect dyslexia" and the early visual processing of letters in words and nonwords. *Cognitive Neuropsychology, 4*, 439–464.

Ellis, A.W., Young, A.W., & Flude, B.M. (1987b). "Afferent dysgraphia" in a patient and in normal subjects. *Cognitive Neuropsychology, 4*, 465–486.

Friedland, R.P. & Weinstein, E.A. (1977). Hemi-inattention and hemisphere specialisation: Introduction and historical review. In E.A. Weinstein & R.P. Friedland (Eds), *Hemi-inattention and hemisphere specialisation. Advances in Neurology Vol. 18*. New York: Raven Press.

Gilliat, R.W. & Pratt R.T.C. (1952). Disorders of perception and performance in a case of right-sided cerebral thrombosis. *Journal of Neurology, Neurosurgery and Psychiatry, 15*, 264–271.

Hillis, A.E. & Caramazza, A. (1989). The graphemic buffer and attentional mechanisms. *Brain and Language, 36*, 208–235.

Hillis, A.E. & Caramazza. (1991). The effects of attentional deficits on reading and spelling. In A. Caramazza (Ed.), *Cognitive neuropsychology and neurolinguistics: Advances in models of language processing and impairments*. Hillsdale, NJ: Lawrence Erlbaum Associates Inc.

Kartsounis, L.D. & Warrington, E.K. (1989). Unilateral neglect overcome by cues implicit in stimulus displays. *Journal of Neurology, Neurosurgery and Psychiatry, 52*, 1253–1259.

Katz, R.B. & Sevush, S. (1989). Positional dyslexia. *Brain and Language, 37*, 266–289.

Kinsbourne, M. & Warrington, E.K. (1962). A variety of reading disability associated with right-hemisphere lesions. *Journal of Neurology, Neurosurgery and Psychiatry, 25*, 339–344.

Laplane, D. & Degos, J.D. (1983). Motor neglect. *Journal of Neurology, Neurosurgery and Psychiatry, 46*, 152–158.

Lebrun, Y. (1976). Neurolinguistic models of language and speech. In H. Whitaker & H.A. Whitaker (Eds), *Studies in neurolinguistics*, Vol. 1. New York: Academic Press.

Monsell, S. (1987). On the relation between lexical input and output pathways for speech. In D.A. Allport, D. MacKay, W. Prinz, & E. Scheerer (Eds), *Language perception and production: Relationships between listening, speaking, reading and writing*. London: Academic Press.

Mozer, M.C. & Behrmann, M. (1990). On the interaction of selective attention and lexical knowledge: A connectionist account of neglect dyslexia. *Journal of Cognitive Neuroscience, 2*, 96–123.

Patterson, K. & Coltheart, V. (1987). Phonological processes in reading: A tutorial review. In M. Coltheart (Ed.), *Attention and performance XII: The psychology of reading*. Hove: Lawrence Erlbaum Associates Ltd.

Patterson, K. & Wilson, B. (1991). A ROSE is a ROSE or a NOSE: A deficit in initial letter identification. *Cognitive Neuropsychology, 7*, 447–477.

Quinlan, P.T. (1991). *Connectionism and psychology: A psychological perspective on new connectionist research*. Hemel Hempstead: Harvester Wheatsheaf.

Rayner, K., McConkie, G.W., & Zola, D. (1980). Integrating information across fixations. *Cognitive Psychology, 12,* 206–226.

Riddoch, M.J. (1991). Neglect and the peripheral dyslexias. *Cognitive Neuropsychology, 7,* 369–389.

Riddoch, M.J. & Humphreys, G.W. (1983). The effect of cueing on unilateral neglect. *Neuropsychologia, 21,* 589–599.

Riddoch, M.J., Humphreys, G.W., Cleton, P., & Fery, P. (1991). Interaction of attentional and lexical processes in neglect dyslexia. *Cognitive Neuropsychology, 7,* 479–517.

Warrington, E.K. (1991). Right neglect dyslexia: A single case study. *Cognitive Neuropsychology, 8,* 193–212.

Warrington, E.K. & Zangwill, O.L. (1957). A study of dyslexia. *Journal of Neurology, Neurosurgery and Psychiatry, 20,* 208–215.

Wing, A.M. & Baddeley, A.D. (1980). Spelling errors in handwriting: A corpus and a distributional analysis. In U. Frith (Ed.), *Cognitive processes in spelling.* London: Academic Press.

Young, A.W., Newcombe, F., & Ellis, A.W. (1991). Different impairments contribute to neglect dyslexia. *Cognitive Neuropsychology, 8,* 177–191.

12

The Relationship between Lateralised and Non-lateralised Attentional Deficits in Unilateral Neglect

Ian H. Robertson
Medical Research Council Applied Psychology Unit, Cambridge, UK

INTRODUCTION

Posner and Peterson propose the existence of three broad classes of attentional mechanism—selection, orientation and vigilance/arousal. Posner has suggested that one aspect of orientation (i.e. disengagement) is a central aspect of unilateral neglect.

In the absence of evidence for differing hemispheric specialisation for orientation, it is difficult to explain the preponderance of left over right unilateral neglect once the acute phase is past. The present chapter hypothesises that severe, chronic unilateral neglect may require deficits in at least two attentional systems—disengagement/orientation and arousal/ vigilance. Hence the preponderence of left over right neglect is explained by right hemisphere lesions affecting the vigilance system as well as the orientation system, while left hemisphere lesions only affect the latter. A number of studies are reviewed in the light of this hypothesis and, finally, some mechanisms of recovery from unilateral neglect are discussed, with indirect evidence of compensatory strategies in recovered neglect patients.

Precisely how the lateralised bias of attention and/or representation occurs in unilateral neglect has been the concern of most of the contributors to this volume. The purpose of this chapter is to examine to what extent unilateral neglect tends to be associated with non-lateralised attentional deficits, and to what extent any such deficits might contribute to the nature and natural history of unilateral neglect.

A number of different strands of evidence will be considered in turn: (1) the paradox of neglect (remission rates, laterality and chronicity); (2) evidence for deficits within ipsilesional hemispace; (3) evidence for increased neglect with increased attentional demands on non-visual/spatial aspects of tasks; (4) evidence for greater difficulties in feature *vs* conjunction search among neglect patients; (5) evidence for influence of arousal on neglect. A hypothesis is proposed which suggests that a full account of *chronic* neglect requires one to postulate the co-existence of at least two types of attentional deficit—one lateralised and one non-lateralised. This hypothesis is critically examined in the context of the five strands of evidence described above, and in the context of Posner and Peterson's (1990) model of attention.

THE PARADOX OF NEGLECT: REMISSION RATES, LATERALITY AND CHRONICITY

The neglect paradox can be summarised thus: Recovery in the early stages is rapid and common for left brain-damaged patients, but right brain-damaged patients much less commonly recover completely, though the majority do so. Hier, Mondlock and Caplan (1983b) showed that unilateral spatial neglect (measured by Rey Figure left-side omissions) remitted very rapidly (all patients tested within 7 days of stroke), with the 35/41 patients who showed neglect at first testing taking a median of 8 weeks to recover on this measure. By 12 weeks post-stroke, there was an approximately 75% chance of full recovery. The equivalent figures for "neglect" (defined by "failure to attend to auditory or visual stimuli on one side of space", otherwise unspecified) were 19/41 at intake, with a median 9 weeks to recovery, and an approximately 90% chance of recovery by 12 weeks. Figure 12.1 shows the results. In this study, the "best" remission candidates were: left neglect, prosopagnosia, anosognosia and unilateral spatial neglect on drawing (Rey Figure). Recovery was slower for hemianopia, hemiparesis, motor impersistence and extinction.

Stone et al. (1991) followed up 44 consecutive patients who suffered an acute hemispheric stroke (18 right hemisphere, 26 left hemisphere) at 3 days and then 3 months post-stroke. Figure 12.2 shows the remission rates for the two groups on one of the tests of neglect, a line cancellation test. Altogether, 55% of right hemisphere subjects showed neglect at 3 days, as did 42% of the left brain-damaged subjects. By 3 months, the corresponding figures were 33% and zero, respectively. Hence it would appear from this last study that the incidence of right neglect is only slightly less than that of left neglect in the acute stages, but that recovery from right neglect is both more rapid and more complete. This differential recovery rate will be discussed later in terms of evidence for hemispheric specialisation for certain attentional functions.

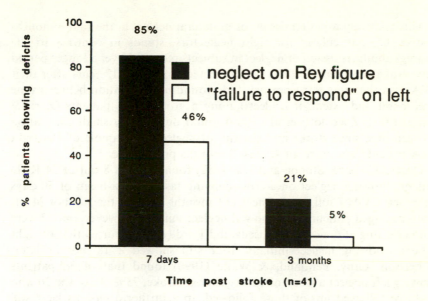

FIG. 12.1.   Recovery from unilateral left neglect (based on data in Hier et al. 1983b).

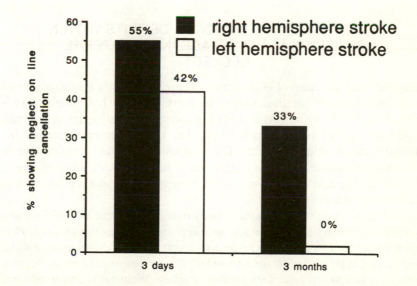

FIG. 12.2.   Recovery from unilateral neglect (based on data in Stone et al. 1991).

This relatively rapid remission of unilateral neglect in the first 3 months post-stroke, particularly for right neglectors, stands in contrast to the findings about remission of neglect in subjects recruited over a longer period post-stroke. Visual neglect has been detected in patients 12 years after their CVA, and the same retrospective study found no correlation between time since onset and extent of neglect among a group of 71 patients (Zarit & Kahn, 1974). Zoccolotti et al. (1989) found only a very small correlation between time since stroke and severity of neglect in a sample of 104 right CVA patients who were all at least 2 months post-stroke.

Denes, Semenza, Stoppa and Lis (1982) found that of 8 out of 24 RBD patients showing neglect on a cross-copying task given a mean of 50 days after their CVA, 7 still showed neglect 6 months later. Of the 5 out of 24 left brain-damaged patients who showed neglect initially, however, only 2 were still neglecting at 6 months. Kinsella and Ford (1985) reported that of eight patients showing neglect initially, four still showed it 18 months later. Robertson, Gray, Pentland, & Waite (1990) found that of 36 patients showing left neglect a mean of 15 weeks post-stroke, 73% (19 of the 26 who could be followed up) of those followed up a further 6 months later still showed clinically significant neglect.

It seems, therefore, that recovery from neglect is poor if subjects are first assessed in the post-acute phase following stroke (more than 2–3 months post-CVA). This contrasts with the relatively rapid remission in the acute phase. This fact will be discussed in the light of data examining non-lateralised attentional deficits in neglect.

EVIDENCE FOR ATTENTIONAL DEFICITS WITHIN IPSILESIONAL HEMISPACE IN UNILATERAL NEGLECT

Weintraub and Mesulam (1987) analysed search times in a cancellation test and found that right brain-damaged patients not only had longer search times on the left than controls and left brain-damaged patients, but also had longer right search times even than the left brain-damaged patients, for whom this was their impaired side. They suggested that this is attributable to the right hemisphere having an attentional role for both sides of space, resulting, in the case of damage to this hemisphere, in both bilateral and unilateral attentional deficits.

Some commentators (Gainotti, Giustolisi, & Nocentini, 1990) have argued that these results are open to an alternative explanation, namely that patients can often neglect with respect to some retintopically based midline which may not be related to the midline of the entire text. For example, in a densely packed visual task such as that used by Weintraub and Mesulam, what may be neglected may relate to a constantly shifting midline within a correspondingly moving narrow attentional field, even when the person is searching to the right side of the stimulus array. By this argument, omissions on the ipsilesional side may reflect simple lateralised neglect of localised areas of the target array. While this argument is an important one, it is not uncommon to observe left neglect patients who neglect at the very right extremity of the stimulus array. Figure 12.3 shows the cancellation performance of such a patient. Such results are difficult to explain by a model of deficit calling on purely lateralised deficits in attention.

Robertson (1989) also proposed a non-lateralised attentional deficit in unilateral left visual neglect, and predicted that one result of this would be a significant increase in right-sided omissions as compared with controls when left neglect patients were cued to the left (in this case by being required to read a simple word under the left stimulus location at the same time as detecting the target stimuli) during the presentation of rapid single or double stimuli. This prediction was substantiated, with left cueing resulting in the equalising of left *vs* right errors among the left neglect patients.

Halligan and Marshall (1990) have shown in a case of unilateral neglect that not only is the displacement of line bisection greater to the right than in normals, but that the standard deviations of displacements of deviations is much greater than in normals. They therefore attribute unilateral neglect to the result of a combination of two distinct impairments: a consistent right-to-left approach to an "indifference zone" or approximate area of perceived middle of the line, and a greater Weber fraction ("a stimulus must be increased by a constant fraction of its value to be just noticeably different"). In other words, there is, apart from the lateralised deficit, a non-lateralised

FIG. 12.3.   Example of cancellation omissions on the extreme right in a case of unilateral left neglect.

deficit in perceptual estimation which leads to a bigger margin of error in the bisection judgements of this neglect subject.

EVIDENCE FOR INCREASED NEGLECT WITH INCREASED DEMANDS UPON ATTENTION

Robertson (1990) found that degree of neglect was highly correlated with the discrepancy between forward and backward digit span. The authors of a previous study which showed this (Weinberg, Diller, Gerstman, & Schulman, 1972) concluded that this reflected a deficit in visuo-spatial representation of the numbers. This conclusion rested, however, on the untested assumption that using a visuo-spatial strategy for the task is advantageous.

The validity of this assumption is cast in doubt by a study by Brooks and Byrd (1988), who showed that giving normals an imagery instruction to visualise the numbers while carrying out digit backward span produced no improvement in performance. This assumption is also challenged by the fact that Robertson (1990) showed that the Paced Auditory Serial Addition test, a test of information processing with no plausible spatial component, was almost as highly correlated with degree of neglect as was the digit discrepancy score. Furthermore, the digit discrepancy score independently predicted a proportion of the variance in neglect even when visuo-spatial capacity (measured by a line orientation test) was partialled out in a multiple-regression. Also, other indices of possible mental deterioration such as verbal memory or perseveration were uncorrelated with degree of neglect, and hence the relationship appears not to be a simple byproduct of severity of brain damage.

All this suggests that the finding of a relationship between severity of neglect on the one hand and digit discrepancy on the other cannot be attributed to lateralised or spatial factors. That digit discrepancy is a valid measure of attentional capacity is supported not only by its correlation with the Paced Auditory Serial Addition test in the present study, but also by the work of Das and Molloy (1975), who showed that backward digit span required a "simultaneous processing" capacity more attentionally demanding than forward digit span.

Rapcsak, Verfaellie, Fleet and Heilman (1989) examined the degree of left hemi-inattention shown by a group of patients in a simple cancellation task under three conditions. The first required the patient to cancel all of a group of simple stimuli. The second required cancellation of only those of a group of similar stimuli which differed from the other stimuli by one simple feature—a "dot" in the top right- or left-hand corner. In the third condition, the stimulus to be cancelled had a dot in the top right- or left-hand corner but, in addition to the foils used in the first condition, there were additional foils which had a dot in the bottom right- or left-hand corner which were also to be ignored. The last condition differed from the other two only in that it required more selective attention from the subjects, i.e. the subjects had to select stimuli from among a greater variety of competing choices. The authors found that the degree of neglect in the latter condition was significantly greater than in the other two, suggesting a deterioration in hemi-inattention under greater non-lateralised attentional load. This finding has subsequently been replicated (Kaplan et al., 1991).

Robertson and Frasca (1992) studied the effect of engaging in an attentionally demanding secondary task (counting backwards in threes from 100) while carrying out a simple visual detection task for briefly presented stimuli. In two out of four patients with left neglect, the latency of response for left stimuli significantly lengthened in comparison to that for right stimuli. An obvious problem with this study, however, is that the "activation" task was primarily verbal and hence by Kinsbourne's theory (see Chapter 3, this volume), the left hemisphere activation should skew attention further to the right, producing the effect attributed in this paper to dual-tasking. In one of these two patients, there was in fact no left–right difference in latency in the non-counting condition, but one emerged when the attentionally demanding secondary task was added.

EVIDENCE FOR RELATIVELY GREATER DIFFICULTY WITH CONJUNCTION VERSUS FEATURE SEARCH AMONG NEGLECT SUBJECTS

Eglin, Robertson and Knight (1989); (see also Chapter 8, this volume) have shown that serial (conjunction) search is more compromised in unilateral neglect than is feature search. Figure 12.4 shows results from this study, indicating that searching for stimuli defined by "conjunctions" of basic perceptual features (requiring serial, focused attention) was much more impaired on the left compared to the right than was search for stimuli defined by basic perceptual features.

Riddoch and Humphreys (1987) had previously demonstrated the same result. It must be noted, however, that feature search is not spared; neither is it parallel, as it is in normals, as evidenced by the slight slope on the feature search curve in Fig. 12.4.

EVIDENCE FOR INFLUENCE OF DEGREE OF AROUSAL UPON NEGLECT

Fleet and Heilman (1986) compared the performance of neglect patients on repeated letter cancellation administrations under two conditions—one with feedback of results, one with no feedback. The feedback consisted simply of them being told the number of errors they had made after each cancellation

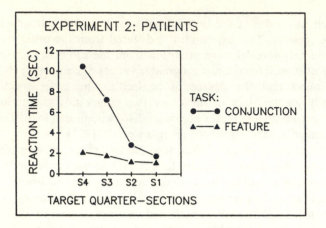

FIG. 12.4.   Feature *vs* conjunction search in unilateral neglect. Reprinted from *Journal of Cognitive Neuroscience, 1,* (4), Eglin et al. (1989), "Visual search performance in the neglect syndrome", by permission of the MIT Press, Cambridge, Massachusetts.

trial. With serial administrations in a short time period, neglect increased in the no-feedback condition, but decreased in the feedback condition. The authors interpret this as being due to improved arousal as a result of feedback of results, causing a reduction in neglect, though of course other interpretations are possible, and the phenomenon cannot unequivocally be attributed to increased arousal.

The apparent association between unilateral neglect and non-lateralised attentional difficulties outlined in the studies just reviewed can now be set in the context of studies of hemispheric lateralisation of attentional function.

EVIDENCE FOR A RIGHT HEMISPHERE SPECIALISATION FOR CERTAIN ASPECTS OF ATTENTION

The following review of a right hemisphere specialisation for certain aspects of attention cannot be exhaustive because of the large number of studies dealing with this issue. The following brief review is therefore highly selective.

Howes and Boller (1975) compared unwarned reaction times to auditory stimuli in left *vs* right CVA subjects, who were matched in terms of size of brain lesion (in fact, the right CVAs had on average slightly smaller lesions). They found that the reaction times of the right CVA group were almost twice those of the left CVA groups (see Fig. 12.5).

Wilkins, Shallice and McCarthy (1987) showed that right frontal lesioned patients showed significantly more errors than left frontal, left temporal or right temporal groups in their capacity to accurately count stimuli appearing

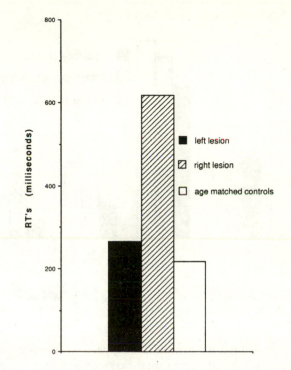

FIG. 12.5.   Simple unwarned auditory reaction times in right CVA, left CVA and aged-matched controls (based on data in Howes & Boller, 1975).

at a rate of one per second. The stimuli consisted of auditory clicks and tactile pulses to the right and left index fingers, respectively (see Fig. 12.6). The results showed that right frontal lesioned patients were particularly poor at sustaining the attention required to count the pulses, whether auditory or tactile, when these pulses occurred at a rate of one per second. In contrast, they were not differentially impaired (in terms of their % deviation from the true value) when the rate of presentation was increased to seven per second. The authors argue that this is evidence for a deficit in sustained attention associated with right frontal lesions, as the one per second task is more demanding of this type of attention than is the seven second per task.

Coslett, Bowers and Heilman (1987) compared auditory unwarned reaction time performance in right and left CVA subjects under two experimental conditions: one in which the reaction time task was performed on its own and one in which it was performed in conjunction with a second

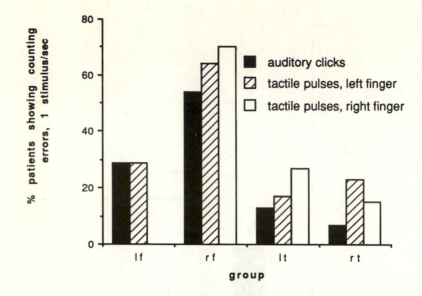

FIG. 12.6.   Errors in counting by lesion group (based on data in Wilkins et al., 1987).

task. The authors argued for a right hemisphere dominance for mediating arousal and hence predicted poorer dual-task performance in right than left brain damage. The results confirmed this. When the second task was added (sorting coins), the mean reaction times (RTs) of the left brain-damaged group rose from 0.3 to 0.5 sec. However, the RTs of the right brain-damaged group rose from 0.5 to 1.3 sec under the dual-task condition. This interaction was statistically significant and could not be attributed to lesion size effects. Half of the right brain-damaged patients showed neglect, whereas all of the left brain-damaged patients were aphasic.

Sandson and Albert (1987) have shown that right brain-damaged patients show significantly more perseveration on tasks such as writing alternative cursive letters (m and n) than do left brain-damaged aphasics or controls. They have also reported a high incidence of perseveration on cancellation shown by neglect patients. Heilman and Van Den Abell (1979) showed that, in normals, lateralised warning stimuli projected to the right hemisphere before a central stimulus reduced RTs significantly more than stimuli projected to the left hemisphere, suggesting a role for phasic activation for the right hemisphere. Heilman, Schwartz and Watson (1978) found that stimulating the ipsilesional arm with an electrode produced lower galvanic skin responses (GSRs) among right brain-damaged patients with neglect than among left brain-damaged aphasics or normals. In contrast, left brain-damaged aphasics showed higher GSRs than normals. This suggested a particular role for the right hemisphere in modulating arousal. Finally, Posner, Inhoff, Friedrich and Cohen (1987) showed that patients with right parietal lesions were greatly affected when a cue was omitted before a target, whereas those with left parietal lesions were not, and deduced from this that patients with right-sided lesions have a particular problem with maintaining alertness.

In conclusion, it appears that the right hemisphere has a particular role in one particular aspect of attention, namely that class of faculties variously described as "alertness", "vigilance", "arousal", and (perhaps) "sustained attention". Given the evidence of Wilkins et al. (1987) that the right frontal lobe is implicated in particular in the maintenance of this function, what is the evidence that the frontal lobes in turn are implicated in neglect?

Vallar (Vallar & Perani, 1986; see also Chapter 2, this volume) reports that a variety of cortical and subcortical lesions may be associated with neglect, including the frontal lobes (e.g. Heilman & Valenstein, 1972), though the inferior parietal lobe is much more commonly associated with the neglect syndrome. He also notes how neglect may be correlated with diaschisis-type hypoperfusion in areas of the brain quite distant from, though connected with, the structurally damaged areas.

Kertesz and Dobrowolski (1981) showed that both neglect and perseveration were significantly worse in patients with frontal and extensive central lesions. Hier at al. (1983b, p. 349) reported that "recovery from constructional apraxia, unilateral spatial neglect on drawing and extinction was more rapid in patients without injury to the right frontal lobe". In contrast, Egelko et al. (1988) found that while neglect seldom occurred in patients with lesions to a single lobe of the brain (based on CT scans), neither frontal nor parietal regions were any more associated with the presence of inattention than were temporal or occipital lesions. They did, however, find an association between lesions in the basal ganglia and unilateral neglect, and there are very strong anatomical connections between the basal ganglia and frontal lobes. They also found that the size of the lesion was correlated with the degree of neglect, a finding also reported by Hier, Mondlock and Caplan (1983a).

There is therefore a small amount of evidence that recovery from neglect may be increased if the right frontal lobe is relatively spared by the lesion, though this can only remain a hypothesis given the present state of the evidence. What is clear, however, is that neglect is associated with large lesions involving several different areas of the brain, and therefore it is at least plausible that more than one attention system may be implicated in chronic neglect. Posner and Peterson's three-factor model of attention will now be considered in the light of this evidence.

POSNER AND PETERSON'S MODEL OF
ATTENTION

According to Posner and Peterson (1990), three interrelated mechanisms, operating semi-autonomously, underlie attention in humans. These are orienting, target detection and alerting. *Orienting* is said to be based in a posterior attentional system, based largely in the posterior parietal lobe, the superior colliculus and the lateral pulvinar nucleus of the posterolateral thalamus, among other areas. Its function is to disengaged from, move to and engage attention to, high-priority stimuli. The right hemisphere is specialised for attention to low spatial frequency stimuli, leading to better detection of large "Gestalt" forms. The left hemisphere is specialised for high spatial frequency "micro" stimuli.

Target detection involves the focal or conscious attention system, which is closely related, functionally and anatomically, to the posterior attention system. It is related to target search and recognition (other than automatic recognition, e.g. of automatically detected word forms), and is to some extent related reciprocally to the third category of attention, *alerting*. Its anatomical basis is possibly the anterior cingulate and supplementary motor areas. Posner and Peterson suggest a possible hierarchy of attentional systems, with the anterior system delegating to the posterior one when it is not occupied with processing other material.

Alerting or vigilance is a system for preparing the brain for processing high-priority signals. It does not improve the processing of the signals, but increases the rate at which attention can respond to stimuli. The right hemisphere—possibly the right prefrontal cortex—appears, according to Posner and Peterson, to be specialised for this, namely for vigilance-type tasks.

Noradrenaline may be the mechanism for alerting, and there is some evidence for a right hemisphere bias in the NA system, and that it is stronger in the frontal cortex, to where it goes first from the locus coeruleus before spreading back into the parietal areas. Hence the alerting system is particularly strong in its effects on the posterior attention system of the right hemisphere. Functionally, the alerting system acts through the posterior system to increase the rate at which high-priority information can be selected for further processing.

OVERVIEW AND HYPOTHESIS

The evidence reviewed above on the role of non-lateralised attentional deficits associated with (mainly left) unilateral neglect can be related to Posner and Peterson's model to explain the apparent paradox of neglect recovery outlined at the beginning of the chapter, namely the differential recovery rates for acute and chronic neglect patients on the one hand, and left *vs* right neglect on the other. The hypothesis suggests that for neglect to be manifest in the acute phase following brain injury, damage to the posterior orientation system may be sufficient. This would explain why the incidence of neglect in right and left brain-damaged patients is more similar in the acute than in the chronic phase, since Posner and Peterson do not suggest any asymmetry in lateralisation of the right and left orientation systems.

It must be noted, however, that Kinsbourne (Chapter 3, this volume) and Robertson and Eglin (Chapter 8, this volume) propose an alternative possible explanation for the right hemisphere preponderance of neglect, drawing on the fact that the left hemisphere is responsible for local *vs* global processing. By this argument, the damaged right hemisphere will lead to a reduction in representation of global forms and to a relative strengthening of representation of local forms. Given that there are by definition more of the latter, the right brain-damaged subject will be confronted with a greater number of stimuli to scan on the ipsilesional side, resulting in a greater degree of neglect of the left side. While this argument accommodates some of the data reviewed above, it does not explain fluctuations in neglect according to attentional factors which are independent of the visual field.

Weintraub and Mesulam (1987), among others, suggest another reason for the right hemisphere preponderance of neglect, i.e. that the right hemisphere has bilateral attentional responsibilities, resulting in bilateral deficits. Such a view implies impairment in quite basic attentional processes and does not rest easily with those findings mentioned above that higher level attentional processes may be implicated in neglect. Furthermore, several studies have failed to establish in normals that the left and right hemispheres differ in their attentional responsibilities in the way that Weintraub and Mesulam describe (e.g. Roy et al., 1987).

The defective vigilance hypothesis is therefore still a strong contender for explaining the low incidence of right neglect. Turning to how recovery from neglect takes place, one can argue that most patients learn spontaneously to compensate for the inattention caused by damage to the posterior attentional system in ways which will be discussed below. However, those patients who have large right hemisphere lesions are also more likely to show deficits in a second attentional system, namely the arousal or vigilance system. By this argument, they do not learn to compensate for the skewed attention of the posterior orientation system, because arousal and vigilance deficits impair the learning of compensatory strategies which in other patients result in improvements in neglect.

What is the evidence that neglect patients recover by such hypothetical compensatory mechanisms? A study by Goodale, Milner, Jakobson and Carey (1990) provides some relevant evidence. They studied a group of nine subjects who had suffered unilateral right hemisphere lesions a mean of 21 weeks after the onset of the lesion. Many of these patients had previously shown signs of unilateral neglect, but by the time they were tested by the authors, there was no clinically significant neglect. The experiment consisted of two tasks, one involving reaching out and touching one of a number of lighted targets presented on a vertical screen in front of the subjects, and the other consisted of requiring the subjects to bisect the distance between two specified targets on the screen.

The brain-damaged patients showed no difference from the controls on their accuracy of touching the targets, while they did show a significant tendency to bisect to the right of the true midpoint of the distance between adjacent targets, suggesting the existence of an enduring subclinical manifestation of left unilateral neglect which was not revealed by standard clinical testing. More interesting, however, were the trajectories of the hand as it reached in to the targets. In both the target and bisection conditions, kinematic video analysis of the reaching movements was made. This revealed that the patients made a wide right arc into the final target, a pattern which was not apparent in the controls. Figure 12.7 shows the movements of patient D53 of the Goodale et al. series during detection as

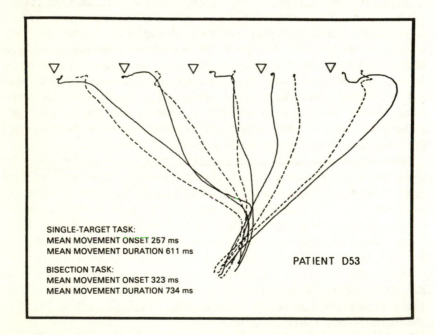

FIG. 12.7.   Limb trajectories of a right brain-damaged subject while reaching out to touch a target. From Goodale et al. (1990). Copyright 1990. Canadian Psychological Association. Reprinted with permission.

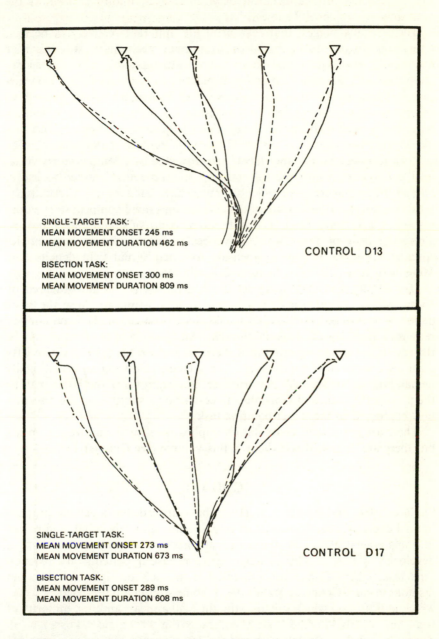

SINGLE-TARGET TASK:
MEAN MOVEMENT ONSET 245 ms
MEAN MOVEMENT DURATION 462 ms

BISECTION TASK:
MEAN MOVEMENT ONSET 300 ms
MEAN MOVEMENT DURATION 809 ms

CONTROL D13

SINGLE-TARGET TASK:
MEAN MOVEMENT ONSET 273 ms
MEAN MOVEMENT DURATION 673 ms

BISECTION TASK:
MEAN MOVEMENT ONSET 289 ms
MEAN MOVEMENT DURATION 608 ms

CONTROL D17

FIG. 12.8. Limb trajectories of two control subjects while reaching out to touch a target. From Goodale et al. (1990). Copyright 1990. Canadian Psychological Association. Reprinted with permission.

well as bisection of the distances between targets. Figure 12.8 shows the pathways of two control subjects.

These results suggest that even after the apparent recovery of neglect, underlying distortions in spatial or attentional mechanisms still exist (for instance, the deficit may have been attributable to a persisting "hypokinesia", namely a difficulty in making movements in the contrale-sional direction). It may be the case that the patients had learned to compensate for their neglect by compensatory visual control. When the patients first sent their arms out on ballistic trajectories, it appears that they did so on the basis of a distorted body-referenced spatial system. The rightward trajectory may then have been corrected by a compensatory visual feedback system, which the subjects had spontaneously learned to use to correct the spatial errors of which they may have been aware. Alternatively, they may not have been aware of the deficits, and these compensatory visual responses may have been elicited by some kind of conditioning process along the lines of those which have been hypothesised in hemianopics spontaneously learning to compensate for their visual field deficits (e.g. Meienberg et al., 1980; Williams & Gassell, 1962).

If it is true that underlying deficits still persist which are obscured by compensatory mechanisms, then it should be possible to cause the basic deficit to re-emerge by presenting a task which is attentionally demanding or requires a high degree of spatial thought. An example of the former may be the results for a case reported in Robertson and Frasca (1992), where left–right differences in response latency only emerged during an attentionally demanding secondary task performance. An example of the latter may be the poor performance of Goodale and co-workers' subjects on the bisection task compared to the target pointing task.

There are important rehabilitation implications for the above arguments but these are discussed elsewhere in this volume (see Chapter 13).

CODA

Shallice (1988) and Posner et al. (1987) have argued that a general-purpose limited-capacity attentional system impairment cannot be what is impaired in unilateral neglect, on the basis of the valid/invalid cue paradigm developed by Posner. This paradigm involves testing patients on a reaction time task, where stimuli are presented to the left or right in a random fashion (Posner, Cohen, & Rafal, 1982). Some stimuli are preceded by a cue, which indicates on which side the stimulus will appear, and in a minority of trials this cue is "invalid", i.e. it indicates the wrong side. Posner et al. demonstrated that subjects with parietal lesions were particularly impaired when they were invalidly cued to the ipsilesional side, with the target appearing on the contralesional side. They argued that a fundamental deficit in neglect is a deficit in a parietal lobe based "disengagement" mechanism, whereby there is difficulty in disengaging in the contralesional direction. Left and right parietal patients did not differ in the extent to which they exhibited this phenomenon.

Posner et al. (1987) studied nine patients with parietal lesions due to CVA, four with left parietal and five with right parietal damage. They compared the performance of these patients on the reaction time paradigm just described under normal conditions *vs* under conditions of a secondary task. If the disengagement attentional system is part of a wider "awareness" or general-purpose limited-capacity attentional system, then addition of the secondary task should cause a more marked disengagement difficulty for invalid cues than normal. Posner et al. did not, however, find this: The secondary task (phoneme monitoring) increased reaction times in both the valid and invalid trials by roughly the same amount.

Shallice and Posner conclude from this that the visual orienting system functions independently of a general-purpose limited-capacity attentional system. How does this square with the hypothesis advanced in the present chapter? First, it should be noted that of the nine subjects in Posner and co-workers' (1987) study, only one showed any signs of visual neglect at the time of testing and two of the subjects were more than 5 years post-stroke. It is possible, therefore, that what the valid/invalid cue paradigm yielded was a subclinical sign of a lasting underlying deficit comparable with Goodale and co-workers' (1990) limb-movement pattern described above. Such a deficit is almost certainly part of a spatial orienting system which is independent of a general purpose limited-capacity attentional system, and so it should not be surprising to find no differential effect of secondary task on valid and invalid trials with the kinds of subjects studied by Posner et al. (1987).

However, such a disengagement deficit is probably not, on its own at least, a sufficient deficit to account for the full florid phenomenon of unilateral neglect, at least in the chronic stage. By the argument of the present chapter, simultaneous damage to the orienting/disengagement and vigilance systems is required for unilateral neglect to persist. Hence in subjects for whom this is the case, then secondary tasks *should* exacerbate neglect, as has been demonstrated in many of the studies described above.

In short, very different conclusions may be derived about the nature of unilateral neglect depending upon the chronicity of the subjects studied. This factor has not sufficiently been taken into account in the neglect literature.

REFERENCES

Brooks, D.A. & Byrd, J. (1988). The effect of internal visualization on digit span performance. *International Journal of Neuroscience*, *43*, 145–147.

Coslett, H.B., Bowers, D., & Heilman, K.M. (1987). Reduction in cerebral activation after right hemisphere stroke. *Neurology*, *37*, 957–962.

Das, J.P. & Malloy, G.N. (1975). Varieties of simultaneous and successive processing in children. *Journal of Educational Psychology*, *67*, 213–220.

Denes, G., Semenza, C., Stoppa, E., & Lis, A. (1982). Unilateral spatial neglect and recovery from hemiplegia: A follow-up study. *Brain*, *105*, 543–552.

Egelko, S., Gordon, W.A., Hibbard, M.R., Diller, L., Lieberman, A., Holliday, R., Ragnarsson, K., Shaver, M.S., & Orazem, J. (1988). Relationship among CT scans, neurological exam and neuropsychological test performance in right brain damaged stroke patients. *Journal of Clinical and Experimental Neuropsychology*, *10*, 539–564.

Eglin, M., Robertson, L.C., & Knight, R.T. (1989). Visual search performance in the neglect syndrome. *Journal of Cognitive Neuroscience*, *1*, 372–385.

Fleet, W.S. & Heilman, K.M. (1986). The fatigue effect in unilateral neglect. *Neurology*, *36*, 258 (suppl. 1).

Gainotti, G., Giustolisi, L., & Nocentini, U. (1990). Contralateral and ipsilateral disorders of visual attention in patients with unilateral brain damage. *Journal of Neurology, Neurosurgery and Psychiatry*, *53*, 422–426.

Goodale, M.A., Milner, A.D., Jakobson, L.S., & Carey, D.P. (1990). Kinematic analysis of limb movements in neuropsychological research; Subtle deficits and recovery of function. *Canadian Journal of Psychology*, *44*, 180–195.

Halligan, P.W., Manning, L., & Marshall, J.C. (1990). Individual variation in line bisection: A study of four patients with right hemisphere damage and normal controls. *Neuropsychologia*, *28*, 1043–1051.

Halligan, P.W. & Marshall, J.C. (1990). Line bisection in a case of visual neglect; Psychophysical studies with implications for theory. *Cognitive Neuropsychology*, *7*, 107–130.

Heilman, K.M., Schwartz, H.D., & Watson, R.T. (1978). Hypoarousal in patients with the neglect syndrome and emotional indifference. *Neurology*, *28*, 229–232.

Heilman, K.M. & Valenstein, E. (1972). Frontal lobe neglect in man. *Neurology*, *22*, 660–664.

Heilman, K.M. & Van Den Abell, T. (1979). Right hemisphere dominance for mediating cerebral activation. *Neuropsychologia*, *17*, 315–321.

Hier, D.B., Mondlock, J., & Caplan, L.R. (1983a). Behavioral abnormalities after right hemisphere stroke. *Neurology*, *33*, 337–334.

Hier, D.B., Mondlock, J., & Caplan, L.R. (1983b). Recovery of behavioural abnormalities after right hemisphere stroke. *Neurology*, *33*, 345–350.

Howes, D. & Boller, F. (1975). Simple reaction time: Evidence for focal impairment from lesions of the right hemisphere. *Brain*, *98*, 317–332.

Kaplan, R.F., Verfaillie, M., Meadows, M.E., Caplan, L.R., Peasin, M.S., & De Witt, D. (1991). Changing attentional demands in left hemispatial neglect. *Archives of Neurology*, *48*, 1263–1266.

Kertesz, A. & Dobrowolski, S. (1981). Right-hemisphere deficits, lesion size and location. *Journal of Clinical Neuropsychology*, *3*, 283–299.

Kinsella, G. & Ford, B. (1985). Hemi-inattention and the recovery patterns of stroke patients. *International Rehabilitation Medicine*, *7*, 102–106.

Meienberg, O., Zangmeister, W., Rosenberg, M., Hoyt, W., & Stark, L. (1980). Saccadic eye movement strategies in patients with homonymous hemianopia. *Annals of Neurology*, *9*, 537–544.

Posner, M.I., Cohen, Y., & Rafal, R.D. (1982). Neural systems control of spatial orienting. *Proceedings of the Royal Society of London*, *B298*, 187–198.

Posner, M.I., Inhoff, A., Friedrich, F.J., & Cohen, A. (1987). Isolating attentional systems: A cognitive-anatomical analysis. *Psychobiology*, *15*, 107–121.

Posner, M.I. & Peterson, S.E. (1990). The attention system of the human brain. *Annual Review of Neuroscience*, *13*, 25–42.

Rapscak, S.Z., Verfaellie, M., Fleet, S., & Heilmann, K.M. (1989). Selective attention in hemispatial neglect. *Archives of Neurology*, *46*, 172–178.

Riddoch, M.J. & Humphreys, G.W. (1987). Perceptual and action systems in unilateral visual neglect. In M. Jeannerod (Ed.), *Neurophysiological and neuropsychological aspects of neglect.* Amsterdam: North-Holland.

Robertson, I. (1989). Anomalies in the lateralisation omissions in unilateral left neglect: Implications for an attentional theory of neglect. *Neuropsychologia*, *27*, 157–165.

Robertson, I. (1990). Digit span and visual neglect: A puzzling relationship. *Neuropsychologia*, *28*, 217–222.

Robertson, I. & Frasca, R. (1992). Attentional load and visual neglect. *International Journal of Neuroscience*, *62*, 45–56.

Robertson, I., Gray, J., Pentland, B., & Waite, L. (1990). Microcomputer-based rehabilitation of unilateral left visual neglect: A randomised controlled trial. *Archives of Physical Medicine and Rehabilitation*, *71*, 663-668.

Roy, E., Reuter-Lorenz, P., Roy, L., Copland, S., & Moscovitch, M. (1987). Unilateral attention deficits and hemispheric asymetries in the control of attention. In M. Jeannerod (Ed.), *Neurophysiological and neuropsychological aspects of neglect.* Amsterdam: North-Holland.

Sandson, J. & Albert, M.L. (1987). Perseveration in behavioural neurology. *Neurology*, *37*, 1736–1741.

Shallice, T. (1988). *From neuropsychology to mental structure.* Cambridge: Cambridge University Press.

Stone, S.P., Wilson, B., Wroot, A., Halligan, P.W., Lange, L.S., Marshall, J.C., & Greenwood, R.J. (1991). The assessment of visuo-spatial neglect after acute stroke. *Journal of Neurology, Neurosurgery and Psychiatry*, *54*, 345–350.

Vallar, G. & Perani, D. (1986). The anatomy of unilateral neglect after right hemisphere stroke lesions: A clinical CT/scan correlation study in man. *Neuropsychologia*, *24*, 609–622.

Weinberg, J., Diller, L., Gerstman, L., & Schulman, P. (1972). Digit span in right and left hemiplegics. *Journal of Clinical Psychology*, *28*, 361.

Weintraub, S. & Mesulam, M. (1987). Right cerebral dominance in spatial attention: Further evidence based on ipsilateral neglect. *Archives of Neurology*, *44*, 621–625.

Wilkins, A.J., Shallice, T., & McCarthy, R. (1987). Frontal lesions and sustained attention. *Neuropsychologia*, *25*, 359–365.

Williams, D. & Gassell, M. (1962). Visual function in patients with homonymous hemianopia. Part 1. The visual fields. *Brain*, *85*, 175–250.

Zarit, S. & Kahn, R. (1974). Impairment and adaptation in chronic disabilities: Spatial inattention. *Journal of Nervous and Mental Diseases*, *159*, 63–72.

Zoccolotti, P., Antonucci, G., Judica, A., Montenero, P., Pizzamiglio, L., & Razzano, C. (1989). Incidence and evolution of the hemineglect disorder in chronic patients with unilateral right brain damage. *International Journal of Neuroscience*, *47*, 209–216.

III

REHABILITATION OF UNILATERAL NEGLECT

13 Prospects for the Rehabilitation of Unilateral Neglect

Ian H. Robertson
Medical Research Council Applied Psychology Unit, Cambridge, UK

Peter W. Halligan
Rivermead Rehabilitation Centre, Oxford, UK

John C. Marshall
Neuropsychology Unit, Radcliffe Infirmary, Oxford, UK

WHY CONSIDER REHABILITATION?

For two main reasons, few previous books on neglect have tackled the issue of rehabilitation. The first is that many experimentalists have not regarded rehabilitation questions as theoretically interesting or informative about the fundamental phenomenon; the second is that clinicians often tend to assume that the phenomenon is transient and of little therapeutic relevance. We argue that both of these views are wrong and that the issue of rehabilitation should have a central place in both theoretical and clinical thinking in this area.

That the rehabilitation of neglect can yield theoretically interesting results is shown by Robertson, North and Geggie (1992), who found that limb activation procedures designed to cue visual scanning to the neglected side appear to have therapeutic effects even when the instruction to scan to the neglected side was omitted. This led on to experimental studies (Robertson & North, 1992) demonstrating that visual scanning was irrelevant to the improvements in performance observed during rehabilitation; the crucial element of rehabilitation appeared to be the presence of voluntary movements by one of the affected limbs in the neglected hemispace (these studies will be described in greater detail below).

That unilateral neglect is of practical clinical importance is demonstrated by a number of studies. At least five have found the presence of neglect to predict poor recovery in everyday life functioning (Denes, Semenza, Stoppa,

& Lis, 1982; Fullerton, McSherry, & Stout, 1986; Henley, Pettit, Todd-Pokropek, & Tupper, 1985; Kinsella & Ford, 1980; Wade, Skilbeck, & Langton Hewer, 1983). Indeed, Denes et al. found that the presence of neglect a mean of 53 days post-stroke was the *only* significant predictor of activities of daily living (ADL) functioning: Severity of lesion, dysphasia and intellectual capacity all failed to show a significant relationship with ADL.

THE ROLE OF THEORIES OF NEGLECT IN DETERMINING THE NATURE OF REHABILITATION

Most attempts at rehabilitation of neglect have hitherto relied on relatively atheoretical attempts to induce patients to scan the neglected hemifield. These studies are based largely on explicit or implicit principles of behaviour therapy. One or two examples of theoretically driven attempts at rehabilitation will be considered later, but the question remains as to whether theory has anything to offer the rehabilitationist.

The most obvious potential contribution relates to fractionation of neglect phenomena, and the chapters in this volume amply demonstrate the complexities and subtypes of neglect which exist. If ways can be developed to reliably assess these subtypes, then it is possible that advances may be made in rehabilitation through tailoring specific treatments to specific subtypes of the disorder (Halligan & Marshall, 1991). Furthermore, it may be the case that some types of neglect are less fundamentally remediable than others, depending, for instance, on the level of representation in the visual system which is hypothesised to be impaired (see, for instance, Caramazza & Hillis, 1990).

The question of non-lateralised attentional loss (see Chapter 8, this volume) is also relevant to clinical issues. If it is the case that neglect patients are particularly limited in their dual-tasking capacity, then requiring them to scan left at the same time as they try to learn new motor and other skills may result in a situation of continual information overload; this in turn may help explain the fact that neglect predicts poor recovery in everyday life functions.

EFFECTIVENESS OF REHABILITATION 1

One of the earliest studies of attempts to remediate visual neglect was by Lawson (1962). He treated two cases of neglect by frequently reminding the patients to "look to the left", and also to use their fingers to guide their vision while reading. They were also encouraged to find the centre of a book or food-tray by using touch and then to use their finger position as a reference point from which to explore systematically the page or tray. It is important to note that Lawson reported that generalisation to untrained tasks was poor.

The New York Studies

Weinberg et al. (1977) carried out a controlled study which involved 20 h of training with 25 right CVA patients suffering from left hemi-inattention, defined by a range of cancellation, reading and other tests. The performance of these patients was compared with that of a randomly selected group of 32 patients satisfying similar criteria. The mean time post-stroke was 10 weeks, though the range was considerable. The control subjects received the same normal occupational therapy programme as the experimental subjects, and no attempt was made to control for the non-specific effects of being in a novel treatment programme.

The experimental treatment consisted of a number of tasks designed to "compensate for faulty scanning habits" (ibid., p. 481). These included, among others, the use of a "scanning machine", reading and cancellation tasks in which the subjects were provided with a thick red vertical line down the left side of the page, and which they were taught to use as an "anchor" by always bringing it into vision before beginning the task in hand. Performance on a wide range of reading, cancellation and other tests showed significant benefit to the treated group relative to the controls, particularly for the group showing severe neglect.

In a partial replication of this study using identical selection criteria, Weinberg et al. (1979) carried out a further randomised trial, in this case with the control group being given an extra hour of occupational therapy each day to match the extra treatment time given to the treatment group. The procedures were similar to the previous study, with the addition of two extra training tasks relating to tactile-location training and length estimation training. The treated group did better than the controls on a number of neuropsychological tests, and again this was particularly prominent among the severe group.

A further partial replication of this type of training procedure was carried out by Young, Collins and Hren (1983), whose results suggested a significant treatment effect. Gordon et al. (1985) attempted a further replication of the training procedures developed by Weinberg et al., though this time not using a randomised design. Instead, one institution supplied the control group for one period, and another institution supplied the experimental group. The two institutions then alternated between control and treatment conditions on an unspecified number of occasions. The experimental ($n = 48$) and control ($n = 29$) subjects were well matched on all neurological and neuropsychological measures. A total of 35 h of training showed the experimental group performing significantly better than the control group on cancellation, arithmetic, reading comprehension, line bisection and on a search task. By four months, however, there were only two significant differences between the two groups, namely the control group showed significantly less lateral bias on Raven's Coloured Progressive Matrices, and the treatment group reported significantly less anxiety and hostility.

Poor Generalisation in Attempted Replications of the New York Studies

In yet another attempt at a replication of Weinberg and co-workers' methods, Webster et al. (1984) used a multiple-baseline by subject single case design with three males showing left neglect. That is, treatment onset was staggered for the three subjects, in order to determine whether improvements in neglect corresponded with the onset of treatment. The outcome measure was performance in navigating an "obstacle course" in wheelchairs, based upon the number of collisions with markers on the course. The training relied on the scanning machine used by Weinberg et al., and lateral scanning was trained while moving in the wheelchair. Significant improvements in wheelchair navigation appeared in each case, though only for frontal collisions with the obstacles, and not with collisions with the rear of the wheelchair.

In replicating this study, Gouvier et al. (1984) reported similar results, though improvement on wheelchair and scanning board performance did not generalise to letter cancellation performance. Another study by this group (Gouvier, Bua, Blanton, & Urey, 1987) supported the view that the effects of training were much more consistently observed in tasks similar to the training procedure. For instance, training using a "light board" (detecting lights on a 2-m wide board) produced improvements on this measure, but not on cancellation, while training in cancellation resulted in improvements in cancellation tests but not on light board performance.

Failure of Computerised Versions of the New York Methods

Robertson Gray, Pentland and Waite (1990) carried out a randomised controlled trial of computerised training with 36 patients suffering from unilateral neglect. One group of 20 subjects received a mean of 15.5 ± 1.8 h of computerised scanning and attentional training, which drew on many of the methods of the New York group (e.g. perceptual anchoring); a second group of 16 subjects received a mean of 11.4 ± 5.2 h of recreational computing selected in order to minimise scanning and timed attentional tasks.

The training consisted of computerised procedures such as matching to sample tasks, where the computer would not accept a response before the subject pressed an "anchor bar" on the left of the touch-sensitive screen. Blind follow-up at the end of training and 6 months follow-up revealed no statistically or clinically significant results between the groups (which were extremely well matched prior to training) on a wide range of relevant tests. This was not because of large improvements on the part of the control group, as neither group showed dramatic improvements in neglect over 6 months.

Conclusions from Early Studies of Neglect Rehabilitation

The rehabilitation of hemi-inattentional disorders is probably the most researched area of neuropsychological rehabilitation outside the domain of the language disorders. The results have tended to be positive, but closer inspection of the data suggests the following:

1. Training effects tend to be restricted to measures which share stimulus characteristics with the training materials. For instance, the Weinberg procedures lean heavily on reading and cancellation training. Testing tends to rely on measures with similar stimulus characteristics, and hence generalisation to different tasks has not been adequately demonstrated.
2. Training effects have not been shown to generalise over time.

EFFECTIVENESS OF REHABILITATION 2: BEHAVIOURAL TRAINING OF STIMULUS-SPECIFIC RESPONSES

The limitations of the New York-based studies have been turned into a virtue in a few other studies of neglect rehabilitation. In other words, the New York studies are viewed as being successful in producing specific responses (compensatory saccades) to specific situations (largely reading/ writing tasks). Such improvements are of fundamental importance to the rehabilitation of individuals, given the importance of reading and writing in everyday life.

A few subsequent studies have eschewed the ambitious aims of Diller and his colleagues and contented themselves with inducing specific response changes to specific stimuli without aiming to produce generalised and spontaneously initiated changes in scanning behaviour. One example of this is the case of Seron, Deloche and Coyette (1989), who attempted to use the New York methods with a severely neglecting patient, and failed to produce improvement. They also attempted self-instructional training and failed with this also. Their final attempt at therapy was, however, successful in reducing the handicapping effects of neglect on the patient's everyday life functioning. The treatment involved a "mental prosthesis", namely a device the size of a cigarette packet which gave a high-pitched buzz at random intervals between 5 and 20 secs. This was placed in the patient's left shirt pocket, and he was encouraged to explore space to find the machine and switch it off. The result was a significant improvement in everyday functioning, where none had been obtained by the previous methods.

Robertson and Cashman (1991) reported a 29-year-old woman with left sensory and visual neglect in the context of frontal lobe difficulties who presented problems in physiotherapy because she walked with her left foot heel-up in a highly unstable planarflex position. She completely failed to learn to lower her heel on walking, which as a result could have led to an eversion injury, despite the fact that she could lower her heel to the floor on command. This was partially attributable to a unilateral left neglect (as well as frontal problems). A pressure-sensitive switch attached to a buzzer on her belt was inserted under her left heel, and a walking programme instituted, with time of heel contact during a 4-m walking test being gradually increased through a process of charting progress and setting goals. Improvements in her walking were charted, which appeared to generalise to everyday life.

Lennon (in press) trained a patient with severe left visual neglect to avoid collisions in the physiotherapy gymnasium by placing large coloured paper markers on the edges of tables, corners, etc., with which he habitually collided. This method is analogous to Weinberg and co-workers' anchoring procedure for reading. The patient was trained to look for these markers, which he learned to do, and also to skirt around the obstacles with which he habitually collided. This he also learned. Once the markers were removed, the improved behaviour was maintained, though it did not generalise beyond the precise topography of the gymnasium and its furniture.

When this patient went home, he made as many collisions as before in the new environment. The procedure was therefore repeated in the home, with markers being placed on the edges with which he habitually collided. The treatment worked as before, and the effects persisted after removal of the paper markers. However, the behaviour change was again limited to the precise topography of his home and there was no further generalisation.

In another study, Lennon (1991) showed how teaching a neglecting person to verbally regulate the steps involved in transferring from a wheelchair produced significant improvement in this functionally important activity.

In summary, the above series of cases illustrates the potential remediability of *specific* responses to specific stimuli. But the conclusions of the previous section still hold, namely that generalised scanning improvements in unilateral neglect as a result of training remain elusive.

EFFECTIVENESS OF REHABILITATION 3: SPATIO-MOTOR CUEING

Theoretical Background: Limb Activation in Visual Neglect

Joanette and Brouchon (1984) described a 64-year-old woman who suffered a right brain CVA and who tended to point to stimuli on her left as if she had seen them on her right. Interestingly, an interaction appeared between the side of space upon which the stimulus appeared and the arm which was used. Only when the right arm was used in response to a left-sided stimulus did the allaesthesia appear. When the other arm was used in response to the same stimulus on the same side, there was no allaesthetic response; performance was reasonably accurate. A subsequent series of cases (Joanette, Brouchon, Gauthier, & Samson, 1986) found that it was not only allaesthetic problems which revealed such an interaction. In a standard stimulus identification procedure, neglect was less severe when the limb contralateral to the lesion was used to point to the target stimuli than when the limb ipsilateral to the lesion was used. In a single case study, Halligan and Marshall (1989) also found that use of the left arm for a cancellation and line bisection task resulted in less neglect.

These findings are in line with the theoretical position of Rizzolatti and Camarda (1987), who propose that spatial attention is based upon a series of circuits largely independent from one another which programme motor plans in a spatial framework. Spatial attention is not seen as a supraordinate function controlling whole-brain activity, but as a property intrinsically linked to pre-motor activity and distributed among a range of centres.

Subsequently, however, Halligan, Manning and Marshall (1991) showed in a series of experiments that the advantage of arm use in reducing neglect was better explained by a spatio-motor cueing process than by an hemispheric activation hypothesis. More specifically, they found that the advantage of left arm use in line bisection was eliminated by having the subject begin the task on the right side of the line, i.e. with the arm crossed over the body midline. This finding does not exclude the possibility that any hypothesised activation effect may be dependent upon limb activation *within left hemispace*, as opposed to limb activation *per se*.

Such results lead to a clear clinical question in the rehabilitation of unilateral left neglect; Is there a stimulus which is reliably present in all the different situations in which the sufferer must operate? One answer to this is the person's *left arm*. In short, the question posed in these studies is whether left arm activation and perceptual anchoring can produce *enduring* and therapeutic improvements in neglect.

A caveat to the approach in question is necessitated by the high incidence of hemiplegia often associated with unilateral neglect. However, Robertson

(1991) has reported one case of severe left hemiplegia where use of the hemiplegic left arm aided by the right arm (and including some minimal left shoulder movement) resulted in a significant reduction in inattention to the left compared to standard right arm performance. Furthermore, in two of the three cases reported below, patients *did* have severe hemiplegias: The movements required were the kind of residual minimal responses which are often possible in hemiplegic patients. Finally, even where there is no movement whatsoever in the left arm, the possibility of using the left arm as a passive perceptual anchor remains.

The first study (reported in Robertson et al., 1992) used a combination of perceptual anchoring training with left arm activation procedures in a case of severe left neglect. Specifically, the patient was trained always to place his partially hemiparetic left arm to the left margin of any activity, and to locate it visually during every stage of concurrent activity (e.g. shaving, eating, reading). The training was associated with improvements in reading, telephone dialling and letter cancellation, without improvement on an untrained task, namely digit backward span.

In the second case reported by Robertson et al., the same basic procedure was used, with one additional element—a device which, like Seron's buzzer, emitted a loud noise at variable intervals. In this case, however, the subject had to prevent the noise being triggered by pressing a large switch with the hemiplegic hand, something which she managed despite her partial hemiplegia. The results of this training were positive. In addition, the woman's husband made daily ratings (baseline and training) of her mobility difficulties arising from the neglect. These ratings improved as the training commenced, and the patient also showed improvements on cancellation tests. The improvements thus generalised to everyday life as well as to formal testing.

In the third case reported by Robertson et al., the treatment was again similar to the previous case, with the exception that this patient was not told to scan for his left arm. In other words, this study emphasised only the limb activation aspects of the treatment. Despite this constraint, the treatment produced therapeutic gains on cancellation tests (both visual and touch-based), and also improved ratings of mobility in everyday life.

Theoretical Implications of the Spatio-motor Cueing Treatment

The therapeutic effects of left arm activation on neglect in the last of the above three case studies were experimentally examined by Robertson and North (1992). Left hand finger movement was compared with an instruction to visually anchor perception on the left arm during letter cancellation. Only the finger movements significantly reduced neglect. Another comparison was between "out of sight" finger movements of the left hand in left and right hemispace, respectively. Only left hemispace "blind" finger movements significantly reduced neglect compared to the standard condition. Thirdly, blind left finger movements in left hemispace were compared with passive visual cueing (reading a changing number) and again it was found that only the finger movements reduced neglect. Finally, right finger movements in left hemispace were compared with left finger movements in left hemispace: only the latter reduced neglect. This suggests that, in the last of the three treatment cases at least, the potent effect of treatment was not the perceptual anchoring on the left arm, but rather the fact of mobilising a part of the hemiplegic side. Robertson and North interpreted these results by reference to the work of Rizzolatti and his colleagues (Rizzolatti & Berti, 1990).

Rizzolatti and co-workers suggest that multiple and dissociable spatial frames of reference exist in both humans and animals, and these may be selectively impaired. Rizzolatti has demonstrated in monkeys that space is coded in dissociable ways by different brain centres, and that damage to one centre may result in unilateral neglect for one spatial system but not another. For instance, frontal eye field neurons use visual information to control purposeful eye movements, while inferior area 6 neurons use somatosensory and peripersonal visual information to organise purposeful somatic movements. Lesions in these different areas produce corresponding different types of spatial deficit. A recent case study demonstrates related dissociations between neglect for peripersonal and locomotor space in man (Halligan & Marshall, 1990).

Rizzolatti proposes the existence of multiple representations of space by these different spatial systems, interacting together to produce a coherent spatial reference system against which purposeful motor movements are calibrated and organised. It is the parallel activity of these different perceptuo-motor neural maps which produces the representation of space and, conversely, it is their breakdown which creates distorted representations. Applying this theory to the case reported by Robertson and North (1992), the subject may have been suffering neglect with respect to *at least* two independent but nevertheless integrated spatial systems—a "personal" space related in some way to some somatosensory representation of his body, and a peripersonal or "reaching" space within which he manifested such deficits as neglecting the left in letter cancellation.

By inducing the subject to make voluntary movements with his left hand in left hemispace, it is possible that the left half of the somatosensory spatial sector was in some way activated or enhanced. Because of the integration of the somatosensory and peripersonal spatial sectors, this in turn produced enhanced activation of the impaired half of peripersonal space. Such is the interpretation which would follow from Rizzolatti's work. But why did not left hand movements in right hemispace similarly activate the left side of peripersonal space? After all, though left hemispace may not have been activated, the left side of the body was activated. One possibility is that reciprocal activation of more than one corresponding spatial sector of the closely linked neuronal maps in the brain must be activated to overcome the deficit in representing the left side of space.

In other words, cueing/recruitment of the hemispatial system was inadequate on its own. So also for the hemi-corporeal ("personal") system. Only when both were activated simultaneously did some improvement of spatial perception of the left arise, possibly by reciprocal activation across the related neuronal systems.

POSSIBLE FUTURE DIRECTIONS IN NEGLECT REHABILITATION

Dynamic Stimulation

Butters, Kirsch and Reeves (1990) argued in favour of a polymodal distributed spatial attention system similar to that proposed by Rizzolatti (described above). They argue that some aspects of this polymodal system, particularly some of the brainstem components, may be intact, and that if these are stimulated, then they in turn may increase functioning in related areas of the brain. The result is an overall increase in attention to the neglected side.

Butters and his colleagues reported that transient stimuli, particularly those moving in a jerky manner, are potent activators of neurons in the deep layers of the superior colliculus. They therefore proposed that dynamic stimulation on the neglected side should reduce neglect more than static stimuli. In a series of experiments, they demonstrated that this was indeed the case, using line bisection on a computer screen, with static and moving stimuli on the left side. Both stimuli reduced neglect over baseline, but the dynamic stimuli more so. However, the effects were transient and had no carry-over beyond the time of stimulation.

Butters et al. speculated that placing light-emitting diodes (LED) on the left frame of patients' spectacles might produce effects transferrable to everyday life. When they tried this during task performance, however, they found that there was no reduction in neglect. There was, however, a reduction in neglect when the same LEDs were placed to the immediate left of the sheets of paper containing the line bisection tasks, leading the authors to argue that dynamic stimuli must be mounted in the region where the patients perform the task and not just on the neglected side of space.

Eye-patching

Butters et al. (unpublished) evaluated a second type of manipulation of visual neglect, based on a suggestion by Posner and Rafal (1987), that patching the eye ipsilateral to the lesion in neglect patients should reduce neglect. This was predicted because retinal inflow to the right and left superior colliculi arises primarily in the contralateral eye. Hence, it is argued for cases of left neglect, patching the right eye should reduce retinal inflow (and hence activation) to the left superior colliculus. This would reduce the amount of inhibition that it exerts on the right superior colliculus, rendering the latter relatively "stronger" and hence more able to direct eye movements and attention to the left side.

Butters et al. went on to show the benefits of eye-patching in 11 of 13 patients with left neglect (in at least 1 of 5 tests in each case), though, as with the previous method, the effects lasted only as long as the manipulation (the eye-patch) was in place. In a subsequent experiment, Butters et al. combined eye-patching with dynamic stimulation and found that the combined effects were more powerful in reducing neglect than either method on its own.

Caloric (Vestibular) Stimulation

When around 20 cc of iced water is squirted into a neglect patient's left ear for approximately 1 min, dramatic improvements in visual and personal neglect are observable in many, but not all, cases and a similar result is obtained when a similar amount of warm water is inserted into patients' right ears (e.g. Cappa, Sterzi, Vallar, & Bisiach, 1987; Rubens, 1985; Vallar et al., 1990). Vallar et al. also found temporary remission of hemianaesthesia following vestibular stimulation.

The precise mechanisms for this effect are at present unknown, though arguments that it is attributable to induced ocular deviation are now hard to sustain given the evidence that hemianaesthesia may be reduced by the process (see Chapters 3 and 5 this volume, for further discussion). As with eye-patching, however, the effects are relatively transitory and tend to disappear 15–30 mins post-caloric stimulation, though there have been no controlled longitudinal follow-up studies.

Optokinetic Stimulation

Pizzamiglio et al. (1990) demonstrated that neglect could be reduced when line bisection was performed against a leftward moving background. Such a continuous movement produces a slow nystagmus in the direction of movement not dissimilar from that produced by caloric stimulation; indeed, Pizzamiglio and his colleagues argue that the two phenomena may share some common mechanisms. As with caloric stimulation, however, the beneficial effects only lasted as long as the stimulation was present.

Fresnel Prisms

Fresnel prisms produce a displacement of a retinal image to the right or left, depending on the orientation of the prism. Rossi, Kheyfets and Reding (1990) attached such prisms to the spectacles of 18 stroke patients who were said to have either homonymous hemianopia or unilateral neglect. The patients with field or neglect problems to the right were given prisms which displaced peripheral images on the right to a more central location in the visual field, with the reverse for patients with field or neglect problems on the left.

The patients wore these spectacles during the day for 4 weeks and were tested on a number of perceptual tasks at the end of this period while still wearing the prisms. Compared to a control group, the prism group performed better on a number of perceptual tasks, though their overall everyday life functioning was not significantly different. The effects on the patients' performance of removing the prisms were not reported.

OVERVIEW

The five methods described—dynamic stimulation, eye-patching, caloric stimulation, optokinetic stimulation and fresnel prisms—are among a number of manipulations which appear to reduce visual neglect in the short term, but which provide no carry-over after the manipulations are ended. Future research may establish ways of increasing the carry-over from such methods so as to increase general performance in everyday life. Clearer theoretical delineation of different types of unilateral neglect may lead to more sophisticated treatment procedures which are more closely tied to theory, and it is to be hoped that the chapters in Part II of this book will help provide the foundation of such an enterprise.

REFERENCES

Butter, C.M., Kirsch, N.L., & Reeves, G. (1990). The effect of lateralised stimuli on unilateral spatial neglect following right hemisphere lesions. *Restorative Neurology and Neuroscience 2*, 39–46.

Cappa, S.F., Sterzi, R., Vallar, G., & Bisiach, E. (1987). Remission of hemineglect and anosognosia during vestibular stimulation. *Neuropsychologia, 25*, 775–782.

Caramazza, A. & Hillis, A.E. (1990). Levels of representation, co-ordinate frames and unilateral neglect. *Cognitive Neuropsychology, 7*, 391–445.

Denes, G., Semenza, C., Stoppa, E., & Lis, A. (1982). Unilateral spatial neglect and recovery from hemiplegia: A follow-up study. *Brain, 105*, 543–552.

Fullerton, J., McSherry, D., & Stout, M. (1986). Albert's test: A neglected test of perceptual neglect. *Lancet*, 430–432.

Gordon, W., Hibbard, M.R., Egelko, S., Diller, L. Shaver, P., Lieberman, A., & Ragnarson, L. (1985). Perceptual remediation in patients with right brain damage: A comprehensive program. *Archives of Physical Medicine and Rehabilitation*, *66*, 353–359.

Gouvier, W., Cottam, G., Webster, J., Beissel, G., & Wofford, J. (1984). Behavioural interventions with stroke patients for improving wheelchair navigation. *International Journal of Clinical Neuropsychology*, *1*, 186–190.

Gouvier, W., Bua, B., Blanton, P., & Urey, J. (1987). Behavioural changes following visual scanning training: Observation of five cases. *International Journal of Clinical Neuropsychology*, *9*, 74–80.

Halligan, P.W. & Marshall, J.C. (1989). Laterality of motor response in visuo-spatial neglect: A case study. *Neuropsychologia*, *27*, 1301–1307.

Halligan, P.W. & Marshall, J.C. (1990). Left neglect for near but not far space in man. *Nature*, *350*, 498–500.

Halligan, P.W. & Marshall, J.C. (1991). Recovery and regression in visuo-spatial neglect: A case study of learning in line bisection. *Brain Injury*, *5*, 23–31.

Halligan, P.W., Manning, L., & Marshall, J.C. (1991). Hemispheric activation *vs* spatio-motor cueing in visual neglect: A case study. *Neuropsychologia*, *29*, 165–176.

Henley, S., Pettit, P., Todd-Pokropek, L., & Tupper, J. (1985). Who goes home? Predictive factors in stroke recovery. *Journal of Neurology, Neurosurgery and Psychiatry*, *48*, 1–6.

Joanette, Y. & Brouchon, M. (1984). Visual allesthesia in manual pointing: Some evidence for a sensori-motor cerebral organization. *Brain and Cognition*, *3*, 152–165.

Joanette, Y., Brouchon, M. Gauthier, L., & Samson, M. (1986). Pointing with left versus right hand in left visual field neglect. *Neuropsychologia*, *24*, 391–396.

Kinsella, G. & Ford, B. (1980). Acute recovery patterns in stroke patients. *Medical Journal of Australia*, *2*, 663–666.

Lawson, I.R. (1962). Visual-spatial neglect in lesions of the right cerebral hemisphere. *Neurology*, *12*, 23–33.

Lennon, S. (1991). Wheelchair transfer training in a stroke patient with neglect: A single case study design. *Physiotherapy Theory and Practice*, *7*, 51–55.

Lennon, S. (in press). Behavioural rehabilitation of unilateral neglect. In M.J. Riddoch & G.W. Humphreys (Eds), *Cognitive neuropsychology and cognitive rehabilitation*. Hove: Lawrence Erlbaum Associates Ltd.

Pizzamiglio, L., Frasca, R., Guariglia, C., Incoccia, C., & Antonucci, G. (1990). Effect of optokinetic stimulation in patients with visual neglect. *Cortex*, *26*, 535–540.

Posner, M.I. & Rafal, R.D. (1987). Cognitive theories of attention and the rehabilitation of attentional deficits. In M.J. Meier, A. Benton, & L. Diller (Eds), *Neuropsychological rehabilitation*. New York: Guilford Press.

Rizzolatti, G. & Berti, A. (1990). Neglect as neural representation deficit. *Revue Neurologique*, *146*, 626–634.

Rizzolatti, G. & Camarda, R. (1987). Neural circuits for spatial attention and unilateral neglect. In M. Jeannerod (Ed.), *Neurophysiological and neuropsychological aspects of neglect*. Amsterdam: North-Holland.

Robertson, I. (1991). Use of left versus right hand in responding to lateralised stimuli in unilateral neglect. *Neuropsychologia*, *29*, 1129–1135.

Robertson, I., Gray, J., Pentland, B., & Waite, L. (1990). Microcomputer-based rehabilitation of unilateral left visual neglect: A randomised controlled trial. *Archives of Physical Medicine and Rehabilitation*, *71*, 663–668.

Robertson, I.H. & Cashman, E. (1991). Auditory feedback for walking difficulties in a case of unilateral neglect. *Neuropsychological Rehabilitation*, *1*, 170–175.

Robertson, I.H. & North, N. (1992). Spatio-motor cueing in unilateral neglect: The role of hemispace, hand and motor activation. *Neuropsychologia*, *30*, 553–563.

Robertson, I.H., North, N., & Geggie, C. (1992). Spatio-motor cueing in unilateral neglect: Three single case studies of its therapeutic effects. *Journal of Neurology, Neurosurgery and Psychiatry*, *55*, 799–805.

Rossi, P.W., Kheyfets, S., & Reding, M.J. (1990). Fresnel prisms improve visual perception in stroke patients with homonymous hemianopia or unilateral visual neglect. *Neurology*, *40*, 1597–1599.

Rubens, A.B. (1985). Caloic stimulation and unilateral visual neglect. *Neurology*, *35*, 1019–1024.

Seron, X., Deloche, G., & Coyette, F. (1989). A retrospective analysis of a single case neglect therapy: A point of theory. In X. Seron & G. Deloche (Eds), *Cognitive approaches in neuropsychological rehabilitation*. Hillsdale, NJ: Lawrence Erlbaum Associates Inc.

Vallar, G., Sterzi, R., Bottini, G., Cappa, S., & Rusconi, M.L. (1990). Temporary remission of left hemianaesthesia after vestibular stimulation: A sensory neglect phenomenon. *Cortex*, *26*, 123–131.

Wade, D., Skilbeck, C., & Langton Hewer, R. (1983). Predicting Barthel ADL score at 6 months after acute stroke. *Archives of Physical Medicine and Rehabilitation*, *64*, 24–28.

Webster, J., Jones, S., Blanton, P., Gross, R., Beissel, G., & Wofford, J. (1984). Visual scanning training with stroke patients. *Behaviour Therapy*, *15*, 129–143.

Weinberg, J., Diller, L., Gerstman, L., & Schulman, P. (1972). Digit span in right and left hemiplegics. *Journal of Clinical Psychology*, *28*, 361.

Weinberg, J., Diller, L., Gordon, W., Gerstman, L. Lieberman, A., Lakin, P., Hodges, G., & Ezrachi, O. (1977). Visual scanning training effect on reading-related tasks in acquired right brain damage. *Archives of Physical Medicine and Rehabilitation*, *58*, 479–486.

Weinberg, M., Diller, L., Gordon, W., Gerstman, L., Lieberman, A., Lakin, P., Hodges, G., & Ezrachi, O. (1979). Training sensory awareness and spatial organisation in people with right brain damage. *Archives of Physical Medicine and Rehabilitation*, *60*, 491–496.

Young, G., Collins, D., & Hren, M. (1983). Effect of pairing scanning training with block design training in the remediation of perceptual problems in left hemiplegics. *Journal of Clinical Neuropsychology*, *5*, 201–212.

14 The Behavioural Management of Neglect

Leonard Diller
Rusk Institutre of Rehabilitation Medicine, MYU MC, USA

Ellen Riley
Jewish Home & Hospital for the Aged, Bronx, NY, USA

INTRODUCTION

Visual neglect denotes diminished awareness of space opposite to a damaged hemisphere. It has sometimes been referred to as hemineglect, spatial neglect, imperception, hemi-inattention, unilateral spatial agnosia, or visual spatial agnosia. Recent work has attempted to quantify observations with more precise measures to develop taxonomies of visual neglect (Gianutsos & Matheson, 1987), and to search for the causes and correlates of neglect. Thus visual neglect has been attributed to derivatives of impairment of defective visual processes (Battersby, Bender, Pollack, & Kahn, 1956; Gianutsos & Matheson, 1987) and attentional disturbances (Heilman, 1985). Historically, there have been attempts to relate visual neglect to motivational aspects of denial (Weinstein & Kahn, 1955). Application of cognitive science to clinical problems (McGlynn & Schachter, 1989) adds a new dimension to help understand visual neglect. In earlier work we found visual neglect was not a simple absence or deficiency in a skill, but consisted of several subsets of deficits involving motor impersistence, visual field cut, extinction, impulse control (Diller & Weinberg, 1977) and sluggish eye movements (Johnston, 1984). In addition, neglect is manifested in free-field search rather than being confined to delimited test conditions (Halligan, Marshall, & Wade, 1990).

From a rehabilitation perspective, neglect is not only a discrete clinical entity or part of a neuropsychological syndrome to be diagnosed and studied, it is a behaviour pattern with important prognostic consequences

293

(Lorenze & Cancro, 1962) and management concerns in rehabilitation. Given the problem which might be manifested in clinical or testing situations, what does one do to assist an individual who is disabled by this condition to return to normal living? The path we have followed and the leads we are pursuing will be the subject of this chapter.

This work has been concerned not only with techniques for altering neglect, but also with attempting to alter functional behaviours associated with neglect, developing methodology and principles to guide instruction in rehabilitation, and examining and addressing some of the clinical issues associated with neglect which impact rehabilitation. This chapter can be split into four sections: (1) studies conducted between 1966 and 1982; (2) studies conducted between 1983 and 1987; (3) current studies; and (4) future directions. Some of the earlier work has been summarised (Diller & Weinberg, 1977; Weinberg et al., 1977, 1979; Weinberg, Piasetsky, Diller, & Gordon, 1982). Most of the later work has been unpublished and will be presented here in more detail.

Our original approach to the management of visual neglect in a medical rehabilitation setting was to (1) define a central construct which expresses neglect; (2) develop an indicator of neglect which could be sensitive to change; (3) study the clinical correlates and (4) experimental conditions which influence neglect; (5) develop strategies for effecting change on the indicator; (6) identify functional markers as equivalents of the central indicator to test for the practical efficacy of the strategies; (7) develop further strategies for treating behaviours which had not been amenable to change. In the course of these studies, we found that both principles and procedures emerged to help promote an instructional frame for interventions. Since neglect is a complex phenomenon, each set of findings led to further questions touching eventually on the non-visual perceptual issues of arousal, depression and unawareness. Clinical management led to a wider range of considerations than originally anticipated. We therefore divide our presentation into phases to trace the path we followed to indicate some of this complexity.

DEFINING AND ALTERING VISUAL NEGLECT: A REVIEW OF EARLY STUDIES (1966–82)

A disturbance in visual scan is a central problem in neglect. In studying attention in individuals with right brain damage (RBD), we distinguished between disturbances via sensory modality (visual *vs* auditory, scan *vs* span). Scan refers to the aspect of attention involved in searching the environment (cancellation tasks). Span refers to the capacity for retaining information from the environment (digit span tasks). In presenting both types of tasks via auditory and visual modalities, in RBD the primary disturbance was visual scan. Visual cancellation became a useful indicator of the severity and nature of a visual scanning problem. The primary problem in RBD was errors of omission on a cancellation test, while the primary problem in left brain damage was slowness rather than errors (Diller & Weinberg, 1968).

To trace correlates of visual scanning disturbance, tests as well as observations in rehabilitation and natural settings were used. In addition to correlations with expected tests such as bisecting a line or Raven's Progressive Matrices, unexpected correlates emerged, including displacement to the right in the location of the backbone when touched along the shoulder (a sensory spatial task) and difficulty in reciting digits backwards (an auditory task). A wide network of problems in activities of daily living were found, including: accidents in learning to walk or transferring to and from a wheelchair (Diller & Weinberg, 1970); omission of food items on a hospital menu or missing food on the side of a tray; disturbance in grooming and dressing activities; and difficulties in reading. These difficulties were generally dismissed by patients (Diller & Weinberg, 1968) or attributed to external superficial factors ("Yes, I can read, but I left my glasses in my room"). Problems which are often unacknowledged lead to fear of social engagements due to misreaching for a cup of coffee, for example, or not being able to read a restaurant menu. In turn, avoidance of activity in public places or reduced recreational pursuits, such as going to theatres or concerts, become more prominent after in-patient treatment is finished. Extensive probing indicated that patients were often afraid that they were losing their sanity.

On cancellation tasks, varying the instructions can increase or decrease the manifestations of neglect. For example, the patient performs often differently if instructions are to start at the right or left, or to scan freely. Responses to instructions provided useful clues in developing clinically meaningful interventions. One could build training by starting with simple conditions and then increase the demand level. Thus factors such as instructions as to where to begin or altering size and density of stimuli could increase or decrease neglect (Diller et al., 1974).

Combining results from previous studies, three clinical training programmes in visual information processing (VIP) were developed. Each was built on the results of prior training programmes. It was possible to (a) improve scanning and the mechanics of reading and written arithmetic; (b) appreciate space on and off the body; and (c) enhance the search in figure ground problems (Weinberg et al., 1977; 1979; 1982). The procedures developed for each programme were derived from the more generic principles used with different kinds of materials and adapted to different rehabilitation environments (see Table 14.1).

We used a "scanning machine", which is a board with a target that can be moved around the periphery and requires the patient to point to the target

TABLE 14.1
Principles of Scanning Training

1. *Anchoring:* placing a strong cue at the point where scan begins. Early in treatment, anchoring might be needed for the end of the scan and the beginning of the next line
2. *Pacing:* providing a method for maintaining a steady search. Patients who are unaware of stimuli tend to scan too rapidly and miss targets. Reciting targets aloud slows impulsive behaviour
3. *Feedback:* confirming correct/incorrect responses
4. *Density:* increased distance between targets and enlarging targets reduces errors
5. *Arousing and maintaining awareness:* any technique which stimulates engagement in the problem is encouraged
6. *Repetition:* practice is important in converting new strategies into habits
7. *Platforms:* building a new set of skills, based on previous mastery

as it moves. The board was studded with lights, also serving as targets, to explore such phenomena as simultaneous stimulation and extinction (Weinberg et al., 1977). One virtue of the scanning machine was that it permitted engagement of patients who denied problems and rejected paper and pencil activities which are perceived as childish or a source of embarrassment when failed. Cancellation tasks were a primary tool to apply the principles because of their flexibility.

Combining previous interventions into a package and testing its effects, an experimental group was able to hasten improvement in skills and read more during leisure time on follow-up than a control group (Gordon et al., 1985). However, for the most part, the control group had caught up with the experimental group at 4 months follow-up. Despite improvements in both groups, cancellation measures were still far below normal and patients appeared to be depressed, socially isolated and passive.

EXPLORING NON-VISUAL CORRELATES OF NEGLECT: STUDIES 1983–87

Two questions were posed. The first was what the relationship is between visual neglect, depression, arousal and comprehension of affect. As indicated, depression and hypoarousal appeared to be prominent in the follow-up of patients (Gordon et al., 1985). Difficulties in affect comprehension might be an important marker in studying depression. In a study involving individuals with RBD who showed visual field defects ($n = 71$), there was a high incidence of difficulty in measures of VIP (91%), arousal (87%), depression (76%) and affect comprehension (80%). These problems were also common in people with RBD who had normal visual fields ($n = 79$) : VIP (61%), arousal (49%), depression (58%) and affect comprehension (60%) (Diller, Goodgold, & Kay, 1988). These disturbances, if untreated, remain at 1 year follow-up (Egelko et al., 1989). Disturbance in VIP without disturbance in affect or arousal is a rare event. Only 2% of patients with visual field defects and 4% of patients without visual field deficits had VIP problems alone.

The second question asked what the effect is of treating hypoarousal along with neglect. Arousal training was added to VIP training in a study which posed the question which training strategy was more effective, a depth programme which emphasised overlearning, or a breadth programme which emphasised generalisation? In the depth (overlearning) condition, a highly specific group of skills targeted to VIP was taught. Several exercises were repeated on a consistent, daily basis. The training materials were identical to those used in previous studies. They were accompanied by the orientation remediation module (ORM), a series of attention exercises developed for individuals with traumatic brain injury (Ben-Yishay, Piasetsky, & Rattok 1987), which were adapted for stroke patients to increase arousal. This highly structured context provided the opportunity to continue skill acquisition to the point of overlearning. Patients were challenged to maintain attention during repetitive exercises.

In the breadth (generalisation) condition, emphasis was placed on optimising consistent performance across a variety of tasks, rather than focusing on a specific task. Thus a given generic skill (lateral visual scanning) was practised in a variety of contexts. It was hypothesised that a broad range of exercises in treatment sessions would yield better carry-over to daily functioning. Less emphasis was placed on repeating VIP and ORM exercises, and more meaningful and personally relevant tasks were developed in consultation between the remediator and the patient (e.g. reviewing blueprints with an architect, menus with a chef). This model was designed to show patients how a generic skill deficit can interfere with functioning and heighten engagement in treatment by using personally relevant stimuli. Most importantly, with less uniform stimuli and task and environmental diversity, a wider degree of transfer and maintenance of skills over time was sought. The basic principles of treatment in the different models are the same (see Table 14.1), but the utilisation of tasks, the level of repetition, diversity, and the spatial environment in which the treatment occurs vary considerably.

Prior to the implementation of the depth and the breadth models, we had not attempted to treat the arousal/attention deficits associated with RBD and neglect. Based on the frequent co-existence of these deficits, and the encouraging findings in treating arousal/attention deficits in young traumatically brain-damaged adults (Ben-Yishay et al., 1987) and pilot studies in our programme, computerised exercises in simple reaction time, perceptual motor training and estimation of time intervals were incorporated into both models of treatment. Along with VIP training, the depth model emphasised daily repetition of these tasks, while the breadth model utilised them in conjunction with other tasks designed to increase alertness and participation in treatment. These tasks included engaging the patient in conversation on topics of personal interest, having the patient sort stimuli as quickly as possible, or engaging in semantic tasks, such as unscrambling sentences. The goal in both cases was to increase the patients' activation, directed attention, environmental responsivity and anticipatory alertness.

All consecutively admitted RBD stroke patients were screened for this study. To qualify for the programme, the patients had to meet the following criteria: at least 3 weeks post-onset unilateral stroke; neuroradiological evidence confirming the diagnosis of a unilateral RBD; right-handed for writing; primarily English speaking; corrected reading visual acuity of at least 20/85; between the ages of 45 and 85 years; no history of central nervous system (CNS) or psychiatric disturbance; and a passing score of 20 or above on a screening examination for dementia, the Mini-Mental State Exam (Folstein, Folstein, & McHugh, 1985). Only patients who met the criteria for deficits in the VIP or the arousal domain were accessed into this phase of the treatment studies. All patients who met the criteria for the study were assigned to either depth ($n = 21$), breadth ($n = 16$) or control group ($n = 41$). The latter received conventional occupational therapy, which typically is concerned with improving visual spatial functioning and encouraging patients with neglect to attend to the left. Within 2 weeks of admission, all patients were administered the full psychometric battery, listed in Table 14.2. The patients in the depth and breadth conditions received a minimum of 12 h of treatment and a maximum of 40 h of treatment. (Prior studies adopted a minimum of 20 h of treatment, but decreased rehabilitation in-patient stays to an average of 34 days at the time of this study, necessitated a change in this criterion.) All patients were re-tested prior to discharge (T_2) and 5 months post-discharge (T_3).

A series of covariance analyses was conducted with group (depth/ breadth/control) serving as the independent variable, T_2 performance as the dependent measure and T_1 performance as the covariate. These analyses revealed that the group effects which emerged from this study were primarily on the arousal measures. The depth and the breadth patients were significantly different from the controls on variable ORM reaction time, and the depth patients were significantly different from the controls on the fixed ORM reaction time. The depth and breadth patients were significantly different from the controls on clinical ratings of alertness, summed over 3 days of testing. (This effect should be interpreted cautiously as the testers were not blind to treatment condition.) There were also trends for the breadth patients to be less depressed and to perform better on the WAIS-R

TABLE 14.2
Psychometric Battery for Interventions

Visual information processing (VIP)
Double cancellation (cancel two targets)
Line bisection: left, right
Lateral asymmetric visual spatial attention (Piasetsky, 1981)
Raven's Coloured Progressive Matrices (RCPM)
Wide range achievement: reading
Simple written arithmetic
Facial recognition (Benton, Van Allen, Hammisher, & Levin, 1975)
Midline
Block design (WAIS-R)

Arousal-attention
Computerised reaction time (Ben-Yishay et al., 1987)
Computerised time estimates (Ben Yishay et al., 1987)
Portable reaction time
Motor inhibition (Downey, 1934)
Mini-Luria motor (6 motor items from the Luria Nebraska Motor Scale: Golden, 1981)
Rate of performance on double cancellation

Depression
Beck Depression Inventory (Beck et al., 1961)
Hamilton Rating Scale of Depression (Hamilton, 1967)
Multiple Affect Adjective Check List (MAACL) (Zuckerman & Lubin, 1965)

Cognitive flexibility
Mini mental state (Folstein et al., 1975)
Conceptual level analogy test (RCPM) (Willner & Strune, 1970)

Affect comprehension
Auditory affect comprehension (Unpublished)
Visual affect comprehension (Unpublished)

Miscellaneous verbal markers
Word fluency   (FAS: Spreen & Benton, 1969)
Digit span   (WAIS-R)
Comprehension   (WAIS-R)
Similarities   (WAIS-R)

Digit span than the depth patients. The fact that the depth and breadth patients performed significantly better than controls on the post-treatment arousal measures indicates that both treatment models impacted on the arousal deficits of these patients. Within-group t-tests comparing T_1–T_2 performance separately for the three groups were also conducted. The control patients improved significantly on 7 core visual measures, while the depth and breadth patients improved significantly on 8 and 10 visual measures, respectively. In contrast, the control patients did not improve on any core arousal measures from T_1 to T_2, whereas the depth and breadth patients improved on 6 and 5 arousal measures, respectively.

The covariance analyses of the 5-month post-discharge data indicated that the gains on the arousal measures were maintained over time. The breadth patients also performed better on a left-sided line bisection task, i.e. bisecting a line on the left side of a page, as opposed to the centre or right side of the page. This task is very sensitive to right hemisphere damage as measured on CT scan (Egelko et al., 1988) and is what we have termed a "far transfer" task, i.e. one that was not used directly in treatment. The T_1 deviation scores (measured in millimetres from the centre of the line) were as follows: breadth (16.9 mm) depth (15.9 mm), control (9.9 mm). At follow-up, the breadth group improved to 9.9 mm at T_2 and continued to improve to a score of 6.8 mm at T_3. The depth and control groups improved slightly at T_2 (13.3 and 8.6 mm, respectively) and those scores were maintained at T_3. This provided some encouraging evidence that the breadth model had a more sustained effect. There were also trends for the breadth patients to perform better than the controls on WRAT reading, a test with high face validity for real life functioning.

The T_1-T_3 within-group t-tests suggested that the pattern of results which emerged at T_2 was maintained over time. Specifically, the three groups looked similar with respect to their performance on VIP measures. The control patients did not improve significantly on the arousal measures, whereas the depth and breadth patients did improve in this domain. Moreover, the T_1-T_3 results suggest that the impact of the intervention programme in the arousal domain was better maintained over time in the breadth group. At discharge, the two experimental groups were comparable in the number of measures they improved on, relative to admission. Upon follow-up, however, the depth patients changed significantly on two measures, whereas the breadth patients changed on four. The fact that treatment-related gains in the arousal domain were better maintained in the breadth patients, provides evidence of the more generalised effect of the breadth model, relative to the depth model. An analysis of the activity patterns of patients upon follow-up at home revealed that the breadth patients spent time outside of the home more frequently than the depth or the control patients. Social isolation and reduction of leisure activities have been documented as persistent and prevalent problems among long-term stroke survivors (Feibel & Springer, 1982; Labi, Phillips, & Gresham, 1980). These problems are correlated with depression and are independent of severity of physical dysfunction. The finding of higher and more frequent levels of activity outside of the home in breadth patients fits with the gains noted in the arousal measures and may represent a generalised treatment effect with regard to alertness or energy level. The findings take on additional meaning in view of our previous study (Gordon et al., 1985), which involved only VIP training and did not yield an effect on activity patterns at 4 months follow-up.

A question which arises in the face of these results is why the treatment effects in this phase of our work was less pronounced on the VIP measures than in previous studies. The experimental patients did improve on VIP measures, but the control patients improved as well, and there was a great deal of variability on these measures both in terms of initial level of performance and degree of change. A variety of factors which may have contributed to this pattern of results speak to some pertinent issues about the treatment programme. First, the amount of time directed to the treatment of visual deficits in this phase of our studies was greatly reduced, relative to earlier phases, due to the combined treatment package for visual and arousal deficits, as well as to reduced in-patient stays. Patients in prior studies received between 30 and 35 h of VIP treatment. In this study, patients were selected on the basis of moderate-to-severe visual deficits, and sometimes received as few as 12 h of treatment, which targeted both VIP and arousal deficits.

To examine the impact of reduced stays on treatment-related gains, *t*-tests were used to compare the admission and discharge scores of those patients who received more than 20 treatment sessions to those who received less than 20 treatment sessions. The patients who received more than 20 treatment sessions, primarily as a result of longer hospital stays, were significantly more impaired at admission than the group which received less treatment. However, there were no significant differences between these two groups at discharge, suggesting that the more impaired group, which received more treatment, was brought up to the level of performance of the other group. These findings must be interpreted somewhat cautiously, as the more impaired group was younger, and the natural recovery of younger patients might account for these findings. Although the interpretation is ambiguous, it is rather compelling that these groups were significantly different on 12 core measures at admission, and that there were no significant differences at discharge.

Another set of factors may have led to a more pronounced effect on the arousal *vs* VIP results of this study. First, moderate and severe neglect patients were selected for treatment, based on their performance on a double letter cancellation task, eliminating the contamination of ceiling effects, but reducing the variability of performance at the base of the measure. In addition, the reaction time measures were derived from repeated observations for each patient, and reciprocal transformations were used to control for high outlying values, thereby providing a more stable measure of performance than is possible with any given VIP measure. Lastly, the programme of treatment research in our department had focused for the past 15 years on the visual deficits associated with neglect, and the restoration of orderly visual scanning. These remediation techniques have been widely disseminated and incorporated by other services within the institution, particularly occupational therapy. While this institutional effect is extremely beneficial clinically, the "control group" in our studies is not untreated but another group receiving similar but less focused treatment.

The group design model means that patients receive either a depth or a breadth treatment. From a clinical perspective, however, the depth model may be more effective for more severe patients and patients in the earlier stages of recovery, whereas the breadth model may be more effective for the milder patients and patients in the later stages of recovery. The depth model establishes the foundation of well-practised compensatory mechanisms, the patient's responsiveness to anchoring and cueing, through the use of uniform, repetitive and highly structured tasks. With a less severe patient, or a patient in the later stages of recovery, it may be more important to diversify the treatment tasks, the spatial environments in which treatment occurs, and the "transfer of responsibility" for cueing from the clinician to the patient. Ultimately, for treatment effects to be maintained over time, and different environmental and stimulus conditions, the neglect patient must self-cue.

Our early work in the treatment of neglect emphasised the development of a platform of skills. This stage of our work has emphasised the development of models or styles of treatment. Future work might focus on the development of a platform of treatment styles within a given module for a given patient. What is the optimum combination of the depth and the breadth approach, and how much of the treatment should be targeted to arousal deficits for any given patient, at any given stage of recovery? What works for whom and when?

In conclusion, current theories of neglect have focused on disturbances in the rapid, automatic shifting of visual attention—emphasising a disturbance in the disengagement of attention (Gianotti, D'Erme, Montebone, & Silveri, 1986), a disturbance in the shifting of attention (Posner, Walker, Friedrich, & Rafal, 1984), underarousal and hypokinesia (Heilman, 1985) and orientation to the impaired side of brain damage (Kinsbourne, 1977). The principles of anchoring and cueing, the hierarchy of treatment procedures, and the models of treatment are consonant with all of these theories. The fact that patients receiving arousal training were more active on follow-up in distinction to our prior study suggests other dimensions than straight VIP training yield an important impact on outcome. In implementing programmes, we observed that engagement and responsiveness to treatment were related to the awareness of the problem. While methods were designed to bypass unawareness, it was an important consideration. The observation was supported by a study described below.

UNAWARENESS: CURRENT STUDIES
(1988–PRESENT)

A cardinal feature of neglect—lack of awareness—has been noted by many (e.g. McGlynn & Schachter, 1989). From a remedial perspective, a number of leads might be useful. For example, when patients in the depth/breadth study were asked to state their problems and probed for changes in thinking, concentration and perception, three judges were able to rate the responses reliably (intraclass $r = 0.88$). The patients who were more aware of problems showed the most improvement on the VIP measures in all three conditions (breadth, depth and control). Awareness correlated with improvement scores while demographic, neurological and neuropsychological measures were not predictors of change. Awareness as a predictor of change and responsivity to treatment seemed worthy of further exploration.

The findings suggest three paths of study which are currently under investigation: the nature of verbal awareness of problems; the examination of non-verbal or "behavioural" awareness; and the analysis of response styles when being made aware of a problem.

Assessing Verbal Awareness

Students of the problem have distinguished between unawareness, as a function of brain damage, and denial, as a function of a motivated drive to avoid unpleasant experience. In rehabilitation, this distinction may be too simple. Awareness of deficit in rehabilitation of stroke patients encompasses a wide range of events including acknowledgement of stroke, paralysis, perceptual and cognitive difficulties, and anticipation of future consequences or implications of physical or cognitive deficits. Awareness can be examined along several dimensions. One dimension is the degree to which deficits are visible to the patient. Thus a paralysis is visible and offers a continuous reminder to the individual experiencing it. A perceptual deficit is not visible to the patient; its presence has to be inferred. Anderson and Tranel (1989) found that stroke patients endorsed the presence of visible impairments more frequently than they endorsed the presence of non-visible impairments. Barco et al. (1991) suggested another dimension. They noted distinctions between intellectual, emergent and anticipatory awareness in traumatically brain-damaged people which may be applicable to stroke patients. Anticipatory unawareness may be manifested in the observation, that it is common for stroke patients to postpone planning for the future as a consequence of impairments due to stroke (Powell, Diller, & Grynbaum, 1976).

To provide a systematic method for assessing the acknowledgement of the full range of problems associated with neglect and rehabilitation, we are developing an instrument called the Rusk Evaluation of Awareness of

Deficits in Stroke (READS). This instrument is in an interview format, and involves a layered approach to inquiry ranging from spontaneous statements concerning presence of problems to cued questions. In a preliminary study of patients with RBD, those with mild neglect (n = 18) rated themselves as equally impaired to those with severe neglect (n = 21). Awareness in mild patients is related to actual perceptual impairment. For severe patients, awareness is positively related to cognitive intactness (Simon et al., 1991).

Non-verbal Awareness

In a remedial situation, one may respond to cueing without verbal acknowledgement. This situation is similar to occurrences which have been cited in the procedural learning literature and may be related to implicit awareness (McGlynn & Schachter, 1989). We designed a four-tiered cancellation task to sample response to remediation. It consists of the following: (1) administration of a standard cancellation test; (2) administration of cancellation with remedial instructions and cueing, e.g. draw anchor on the left, say anchoring but no instructions. This approach samples the ability to profit from instruction and cues under structured and spontaneous conditions. It is similar in approach to Luria's (1961) zone of potential. This measure taps an individual's capacity for enhancing performance, but does not require explicit verbalisation.

Unawareness as Response Style

During remediation, a wide range of responses to confrontation with an unacknowledged problem can be observed. This may pose a clinical management problem in establishing and maintaining the rapport which is vital in a learning situation. Patients are often unaware of the VIP deficit, confused by their unawareness, and struggle to respond to cueing and reminders. Sometimes types of awareness may be disassociated. Thus, a patient can describe the deficit and yet act as if the deficit did not exist. For example, after spontaneously reporting a conversation with her physician about remediation and describing the importance of anchoring on the left side of space, a patient described only the right side of the room. When confronted with omission, responses vary from hostile resistance to making excuses for task failure (e.g. "I forgot my glasses", "I'm not interested") to initial resistance and reluctant acknowledgement to self-correction. In the course of perceptual remediation (Diller & Weinberg, 1993), we noted that it was possible to develop a typology of response styles in dealing with unawareness from active resistance to acceptance. The response styles were related to severity of impairments on cancellation tasks as well as other measures. This suggests that for the severe neglect patient, active resistance occurs because a reminder is seen as intrusive and discontinuous with current experience.

SOME FUTURE DIRECTIONS IN REMEDIATION OF NEGLECT

We have approached perceptual remediation as a problem in teaching and learning and found a number of related considerations which had to be addressed. In the spirit which has continually driven our inquiry, the following questions emerge from current studies. What are the interrelationships between different kinds of awareness measures? What is the relationship between awareness and the ability to transfer skills which have been taught? What further strategies can be developed to facilitate transfer of learned behaviours?

A problem which persists is that of inducing and maintaining generalisation. While there is a rich emerging literature in the field of developmental disabilities pointing to the need to build generalisation strategies from the onset of treatment, a number of converging leads from other arenas might be useful. Belmont (1989) noted that strategic learning in developing children takes place by having the child assume responsibility for a trained strategy from a response to cues, to self-generated cues, to application of the strategy even when the external elements of the task change slightly. Observation of responses to instruction yield useful insights into the way this unfolds. Since much of the effects of generalisations aim for performance in naturalistic situations, insights from studies in "enactive memory" may be relevant. Koriat, Ben-Zur and Druc (1990) noted that memory for acts to be completed in naturalistic situations tend to be context-dependent. It is unclear as to whether this is because attention is diverted by contextual events, or by the fact that people's responses are organised around their own cognitive structures leaving insufficient energy for their environments, or that motor encoding is more efficient for specific items than it is for relational information. At any rate, "enactive memory" bears resemblance to prospective memory, which has been found to be a complaint in populations of individuals with traumatic brain injury (Mateer, Sohlberg, & Crinean, 1987). This suggests that explication of "enactive" memory might be useful in providing ways of facilitating generalisation.

The study of differential impacts of instruction following procedural *vs* declarative training approaches also speaks to issues of generalisation. Our training included elements of both. It is apparent that individuals can talk about neglect but not carry it through in their actions. Others might show different patterns. It seems likely that such individuals might profit from different types of training.

Seemingly, at this stage in the development of treatment, the goal of neglect treatment should be to produce the habit of compensatory scanning, to provide the patient with "knowing how" to compensate for the deficit, to establish the sequence of learning–maintenance–generalisation, and to transfer the responsibility to the patient for self-cueing and self-structuring. The remediator will have to take into account that the visual information-processing component of neglect is often accompanied by disturbance in arousal, affect and awareness.

In this chapter, we have presented the results of studies which were conducted in group designs and we have tied our presentation closely to the data. However, these results are restricted in the sense that the data speak to delimited areas of transfer. Clinically, we have seen that patients who are treated for longer periods of time can translate their "knowing how" to behaviours outside of the treatment setting such as participating in cultural events and resuming employment. If this can be achieved, we have come a long way in overcoming the devastating effects of neglect on a person's ability to function in life.

ACKNOWLEDGEMENTS

This research was supported by grants G0083000009 and H133B80028 from the US Department of Education, NIDRR, to NYU Medical Center as a Research and Training Center in Head Trauma and Stroke, and Leonard Diller, Principal Investigator.

REFERENCES

Anderson, S.W. & Tranel, D. (1989). Awareness of disease states following cerebral infarction, dementia, and head trauma: Standardized assessment. *Clinical Neuropsychologist. 3*, 327–340.

Barco, P.B., Crosson, B., Bocosta, M.B., Werts, D., & Stout, R. (1991). Training awareness and compensation in head injury rehabilitation. In J.F. Kreutzer & P.H. Wehman (Eds), *Cognitive rehabilitation for persons with traumatic brain injury.* Baltimore, MD: Paul H. Brookes.

Battersby, W.S., Bender, M.D., Pollack, M., & Kahn, R.L. (1956). Unilateral partial agnosia (inattention) in patients with cerebral lesions. *Brain, 79*, 68–93.

Beck, A.T., Ward, J., Mendelson, M., Jock, J., & Erbaugh, J. (1961). An inventory for measuring depression. *Archives of General Psychology, 4*, 56–571.

Belmont, J.M. (1989). Cognitive strategies and strategic learning: The social instructional approach. *American Psychologist, 44*, 144–148.

Benton, A.L., Van Allen, M.W., Hammisher, K., & Levin, H.S. (1978). *Test of facial recognition* (Form SL). Iowa City: University of Iowa Hospitals, Department of Neurology.

Ben-Yishay, Y., Piasetsky, E., & Rattok, J. (1987). A systematic method for ameliorating disorders of attention. In M.J. Meier, A.L. Benton, & L. Diller (Eds), *Neuropsychological rehabilitation.* Edinburgh: Churchill-Livingstone.

Diller, L., Ben-Yishay, Y., Gerstman, L., Goodkin, R., Gordon, W.A., & Weinberg, J. (1974). *Studies in cognition and rehabilitation in hemiplegia*. Institute of Rehabilitation Medicine Monograph. New York: New York University Medical Center.

Diller, L., Goodgold, J., & Kay, T. (1988). *Final Report to National Institute of Disability and Rehabilitation Related Research*. Research and Training Center in Head Trauma and Stroke, Department of Rehabilitation Medicine, New York University Medical Center.

Diller, L. & Weinberg, J. (1968). Attention in brain damaged people. *Journal of Education*, *150*, 20–27.

Diller, L. & Weinberg, J. (1970). Evidence for accident prone behavior in hemiplegic patients. *Archives of Physical Medicine and Rehabilitation*, *51*, 358–363.

Diller, L. & Weinberg, J. (1977). Hemi-inattention in rehabilitation. The evolution of a rational remediation program. In E.A. Weinstein & R.P. Friedman (Eds), *Advances in neurology*, Vol. 18. New York: Raven Press.

Diller, L. & Weinberg, J. (1993). Response styles in perceptual retraining. In W.A. Gordon (Ed.), *Advances in stroke rehabilitation*. York, PA: Abington Publications.

Downey, E. (1934). *The Will–Temperament Scale and its Testing*. New York: World Book Co.

Egelko, S., Gordon, W.A., Hibbard, M.R., Diller, L., Lieberman, A., Holliday, R., Ragnarsson, K., Shaver, M.S., & Orazem, M.A. (1988). The relationship among CT scans, neurological exam, and neuropsychological test performance in right brain damaged patients. *Journal of Clinical and Experimental Neuropsychology*, *10*, 539–565.

Egelko, S., Simon, D., Riley, E., Gordon, W., Ruckdeschel-Hibbard, M., & Diller, L. (1989). First year after stroke: tracking cognitive and affective deficits. *Archives of Physical Medicine and Rehabilitation*, *70*, 297–302.

Feibel, J.H. & Springer, C.J. (1982). Depression and failure to resume social activities after stroke. *Archives of Physical Medicine and Rehabilitation*, *63*, 276–278.

Folstein, M.P., Folstein, S.E., & McHugh, P.R. (1975). Mini mental state. *Journal of Psychiatric Research*, *12*, 189–192.

Gianotti, G., D'Erme, P., Montebone, P., & Silveri, M.S. (1986). Mechanisms of unilateral spatial neglect in relation to laterality of lesions. *Brain*, *109*, 599–612.

Gianutsos, R. & Matheson, P. (1987). The rehabilitation of visual perceptual disorders attributable to brain injury. In M.J. Meier, A. Benton, & L. Diller (Eds), *Neuropsychological rehabilitation*. London: Churchill Livingstone.

Golden, C.J. (1981). A standard version of Luria neuropsychological tests. In S. Filskov & T.J. Boll (Eds), *Handbook of clinical neuropsychology*. New York: John Wiley.

Gordon, W.A., Hibbard, M.R., Egelko, S., Diller, L., Shaver, M.S., Lieberman, A.L., & Ragnarsson, K.T. (1985). Perceptual remediation in patients with right brain damage: A comprehension program. *Archives of Physical Medicine and Rehabilitation*, *66*, 353–360.

Halligan, P.W., Marshall, J.K.S., & Wade, D.T. (1990). Do visual field deficits exacerbate visual spatial neglect? *Journal of Neurology, Neurosurgery and Psychiatry*, *53*, 487–491.

Hamilton, M. (1967). Development of a rating scale for primary depressive illness. *British Journal of Social Clinical Psychology*, *6*, 278–296.

Heilman, K.M. (1985). Neglect and related disorders. In K.M. Heilman & E. Valenstein (Eds), *Clinical neuropsychology*, 2nd edn. New York: Oxford University Press.

Johnston, C. (1984). *Eye movements in right brain damaged persons*. Unpublished doctoral dissertation, Queen's College, City University of New York.

Kinsbourne, M. (1977). Hemi-neglect and hemispheric rivalry. In E.A. Weinstein, R. Freidlander (Eds.) *Hemi-inattention and hemispheric specialization*. New York; Raven Press.

Koriat, A., Ben-Zur, H., & Druc, A. (1990). *The contextualization of input and output events in memory*. Haifa: Institute of Information Processing and Decision Making, University of Haifa.

Labi, M.L., Phillips, T.F., & Gresham, G. (1980). Psychosocial disability in physically restored long term stroke survivors. *Archives of Physical Medicine and Rehabilitation*, *61*, 561–565.

Lorenze, E.J. & Cancro, R. (1962). Dysfunction in visual perception with hemiplegia: Its relation to activities of daily living. *Archives of Physical Medicine and Rehabilitation, 43,* 514–517.

Luria, A.R. (1961). An objective approach to the study of the abnormal child. *American Journal of Orthopsychiatry, 31,* 1–16.

Mateer, C.A., Sohlberg, M.M., & Crinean, J. (1987). Perceptions of memory function in individuals with closed-head injury. *Journal of Head Trauma Rehabilitation, 2,* 74–84.

McGlynn, S.M. & Schachter, D.L. (1989). Unawareness of deficits in neuropsychological syndromes. *Journal of Clinical and Experimental Neuropsychology, 11,* 143–205.

Piasetsky, E. (1981). A study of pathological assymetrics in visual spatial attention in unilaterally brain-damaged stroke patients. *Dissertation Abstracts International, 42,* 1213–1214.

Posner, M.I., Walker, J.A., Friedrich, F.J., & Rafal, R.O. (1984). Effects of parietal injury on covert orienting of attention. *Journal of Neuroscience, 4,* 1863–1874.

Powell, R., Diller, L., & Grynbaum, B. (1976). Rehabilitation performance and adjustment in stroke patients: A study of social class factor. *Genetic Psychology Monographs, 93,* 287–352.

Simon, D., Riley, E., Egelko, S., Newman, B., & Diller, L. (1991). *A new instrument for assessing awareness of deficit in stroke patients.* Poster presentation to 101st Annual Meeting of the American Psychological Association, San Francisco, CA, August.

Spreen, O. & Benton, A.L. (1969). *Neurosensory center comprehensive examination for aphasia.* Victoria, BC: University of Victoria, Department of Psychology.

Weinberg, J., Diller, L., Gordon, W.A., Gerstman, L., Lieberman, A., Lakin, P., Hodges, G., & Ezrachi, O. (1977). Visual scanning training effect on reading-related tasks in acquired right brain damage. *Archives of Physical Medicine and Rehabilitation, 58,* 479–486.

Weinberg, J., Diller, L., Gordon, W.A., Gerstman, L., Lieberman, A., Lakin, P., Hodges, G., & Ezrachi, O. (1979). Training sensory awareness and spatial organization in people with right brain damage. *Archives of Physical Medicine and Rehabilitation, 60,* 491–496.

Weinberg, J., Piasetsky, E., Diller, L., & Gordon, W.A. (1982). Treating perceptual organization deficits in non-neglecting RBD stroke patients. *Journal of Clinical Neuropsychology, 4,* 59–75.

Weinstein, E. & Kahn, R. (1955). *Denial of illness.* Springfield, IL: Charles C. Thomas.

Willner, A. & Strune, F. (1970). Analogy test for use with hospitalized psychiatric patients. *Archives of General Psychiatry, 23,* 428–437.

Zuckerman, M. & Lubin, B. (1965). *Manual of multiple affect adjective check list.* San Diego, CA: Educational Industrial Testing Service.

CODA

15 Contemporary Theories of Unilateral Neglect: A Critical Review

John C. Marshall
Neuropsychology Unit, Radcliffe Infirmary, Oxford, UK

Peter W. Halligan
Rivermead Rehabilitation Centre, Oxford, UK

Ian H. Robertson
Medical Research Council Applied Psychology Unit, Cambridge, UK

INTRODUCTION

From a clinical standpoint, there is some merit in taking a broad view of "neglect". It is useful to be alerted to the fact that some patients fail "to report, respond, or orient to novel or meaningful stimuli presented to the side opposite a brain lesion" (Heilman, Watson, & Valenstein, 1985) and that they hence appear to live in "only half the world" (Grusser & Landis, 1991). Similarly, one should know that such "negative" signs can occur in the absence of primary sensory or motor deficits, and that severe, persistent left neglect after right hemisphere damage is far more common than right neglect after left hemisphere damage. The "neglect syndrome" in this extended sense seems (typically) to reflect some underlying right hemisphere specialisation for spatial processing, just as "aphasia" reflects left hemisphere specialisation for language processing (in the vast majority of people).

Whether the "neglect syndrome" is a meaningful theoretical entity is, however, another question (Halsband, Gruhn, & Ettlinger, 1985). That the spectrum of disorders described by the clinical label "neglect" can all dissociate from each other suggests that they do not form a "natural kind" for purposes of explanation. Patients may show neglect in one situation but not another (Weinstein & Friedland, 1977), with respect to one class of material but not another (Cubelli et al., 1991; Young, De Haan, Newcombe,

& Hay, 1990) and within one "spatial frame" but not another (Karnath, Schenkel, & Fischer, 1991).

Dissociations can occur between different modalities (visual, auditory, or tactile: Barbieri & De Renzi, 1989) and between different spatial domains (personal, peripersonal and extra personal: Bisiach, Perani, Vallar, & Berti, 1986; Halligan & Marshall, 1991a). Likewise, motor neglect (the underuse of a non-paretic limb) can dissociate from perceptual neglect in any or all modalities (Laplane & Degos, 1983). In short, as Gainotti, D'Erme and Bartolomeo (1991) write: "... hemi-neglect is a multi-component syndrome".

The most popular current accounts of neglect stress attentional factors above all. But if this position is to have even limited validity, it is clear that "attention" must itself be fractioned. Barbieri and De Renzi (1989) summarise their discussion of the area as follows: "... the gamut of deficits covered by the concept of neglect do not constitute a unitary, coherent syndrome, which can be traced back to the disruption of a supramodal supervisor, controlling the deployment of attention to contralateral space". Similarly, Cubelli et al. (1991) conclude that "unilateral spatial neglect cannot be interpreted as a disruption of a single attentional mechanism, but rather it reflects impaired attentional mechanisms at several levels of cognitive processing". We concur, but wonder whether the attentional component of neglect may have been a little overstressed in recent theory. Accordingly, in the next section we outline the range of interpretations of visual neglect that are currently in play. The discussion will be restricted to "lateral" neglect, but it should be noted that neglect can also occur along radial and vertical orientations (Halligan & Marshall, 1989c; Mennemeier, Wertman, & Heilman, 1992). The spatial domain of perception and action is (at least) three-dimensional (Sakata & Kusunoki, 1992).

INTERPRETATIONS OF NEGLECT

Sensory Neglect

For investigators who do not like the "cognitive" in cognitive neuropsychology, there is always a temptation to "explain away" any specific disorder of higher mental functioning. This is usually achieved by postulating a combination of subtle sensory and/or motor disorder in the context of generalised intellectual impairment. With respect to unilateral visuo-spatial neglect, the stratagem would be to claim that the observed behaviour reflects the presence of an "uncompensated" visual field deficit (see De Renzi, 1982).

This particular manner of "explaining away" is usually thought to have little to recommend it, and is not supported by many (if any) current students of neglect. Many patients with neglect simply do not have a visual field deficit (uncompensated or otherwise). In patients who do have a visual field deficit, there appears to be no necessary interaction between that deficit and the severity of neglect (Halligan, Marshall, & Wade, 1990). Finally, it is unlikely that any kind of "sensory" account could cope with the observations of Bisiach and Luzzatti (1978) on left neglect of purely imaginal space.

One would be inclined to drop the issue at this point were it not for a number of oddities. First and foremost is the fact that, until quite recently, it has been customary to report the existence of patients with severe neglect but no visual field deficit, without further comment on how this state of affairs could be logically possible. If the patient "neglects" stimuli in the left field when the examiner is testing for neglect, why does the patient not also neglect a left-field stimulus when the examiner thinks he is testing for a field cut? Fortunately, there are now paradigms that help to distinguish between neglect and hemianopia (Walker, Findley, Young, & Welch, 1991); these procedures do, as one would expect, sometimes yield the conclusion that hemispatial visual inattention can masquerade as hemianopia (Kooistra & Heilman, 1989). Further support for this position can be found in studies of evoked potentials. Vallar, Sandroni, Rusconi and Barbieri (1991b) have reported normal somatosensory or visual evoked potentials on the left in patients with left neglect. The patients were without conscious perception (and hence verbal report) of the stimulation; their apparent hemianopia and hemianaesthesia may accordingly be a manifestation of neglect rather than primary sensory deficit.

It would, however, be surprising if some patients with neglect did not have a true associated hemianopia (after lesion of occipital cortex). Although in these patients the visual field deficit would not be the cause of their neglect, one might none the less expect some interaction between neglect and restricted vision. It is known, for example, that in normal subjects, the ability to discriminate the lengths of simultaneously presented horizontal lines falls off very dramatically if the size of the visual field is artificially restricted (Ikeda, Saida, & Sugiyama, 1977). Ikeda et al. suggest that "our excellent ability in length comparison may be possible only by using the peripheral retina", and that normal length comparisons are "only possible when we can observe the whole line at one time". If such results generalise to field restriction caused by occipital damage, there are obvious implications for "neglect" performance in the context of genuine hemianopia.

Some authors have interpreted neglect in terms of a spatial "cognitive" cut, analogous to a visual field cut. Bisiach, Bulgarelli, Sterzi and Vallar (1983) describe the typical rightwards bias on line bisection as a "representational scotoma" for a (variable) portion of the left side of a stimulus line; similarly, Nichelli, Rinaldi and Cubelli (1989) describe the phenomenon as "representational amputation". Such interpretations are incompatible with the fact that the bias is a constant *proportion* of stimulus length (Bruyer, 1984; Halligan & Marshall, 1991b; Marshall & Halligan, 1990). The recent finding (Chatterjee, Mennemeier, & Heilman, 1992b) that a power function describes the relationship between the number of stimuli in an array and the proportion of targets cancelled by a neglect patient is likewise problematic for any straightforward "amputational" theory.

A variant of the "sensory" interpretation of neglect places considerable stress upon the role of eye movements. While there is no doubt that eye movements are abnormal in many patients with neglect (Hornak, 1992; Karnath & Huber, 1992), it is less clear what explanatory role the disorder plays. In many testing paradigms, task analysis indicates that ocular movements *per se* can contribute little to the overt symptoms, while in others it is debatable whether the ocular disorder is cause or consequence. In monkeys, for example, neurons in parietal cortex that code for spatial position respond *before* saccadic eye movements are made to target positions (Duhamel, Colby, & Goldberg, 1992).

Sensori-perceptual Neglect

On the assumption that no firm demarcation line can be drawn between sensation and perception, failure to compute a full and distinct perceptual representation of left-sided space becomes one possible mechanism for some aspects of neglect. The dominant metaphor is of an internal "perceptual screen", with a "degraded" left side; the spatial extent and severity of the purported degradation varies from patient to patient. Denny-Brown and Banker (1954) could be regarded as supporting one early version of this hypothesis: Under the rubric of "amorphosynthesis", they interpret neglect as a lateralised disorder of spatial summation of sensory stimuli. If *elementary* sensation was intact but could not be integrated into a higher-order perceptual representation on the left, there would be no well-defined stimuli to be responded to in that spatial domain.

Interpretations of this nature are currently unpopular. The present consensus is that neglect is above all a disorder of spatial exploration which can be seen on tactile search tasks as well as on visual search tasks (Bisiach & Vallar, 1988). But such a rebuttal flies in the face of evidence for dissociations between visual and tactile neglect; it assumes the existence of a supra-modal explanation for all aspects of the "neglect syndrome". We accordingly stress that to advance a perceptual interpretation for some neglect phenomena is not incompatible with there being other explanations of other manifestations of neglect.

It thus remains possible that, on some tasks, "attention" is not captured by stimuli in left space precisely because those stimuli are perceptually too weak to attract attention. Bisiach and Vallar (1988) also claim that sensori-perceptual interpretations are "in an unfavourable position in facing the problem of hemispheric asymmetries concerning neglect". But again it is unclear to us why theorists who are happy to embrace differential hemispheric specialisation for attentional processes should not, in principle at least, be prepared to accept differential specialisation for some aspects of high-level perceptual representation. From Poppelreuter (1917) onwards, the phenomenon of visual extinction on double simultaneous stimulation has been regarded as a symptom of "visual inattention". Again, however, the unilateral capture of attention could be secondary to perceptual weakness.

It has been argued that the right hemisphere is dominant for the deployment of attention to all spatial locales (see Mesulam, 1985). The claim is that "attentional neurons" in the right cerebral hemisphere have bilateral receptive fields, whereas those in the left hemisphere are exclusively concerned with contralesional space. But exactly why the said neurons are "attentional" rather than "perceptual" is not entirely obvious. It thus remains an open issue whether performance on some standard tests of neglect (e.g. cancellation tasks and line bisection) can be interpreted in traditional psychophysical terms. We cannot yet rule out the possibility that perceptual discriminability (or even the assignment of basic figure–ground relationships) is impaired in left space (and gives rise to left-sided omissions on cancellation tasks). Similarly, it has been argued that "neglect" performance on bisection tasks is primarily a reflection of a greatly increased Weber fraction after right hemisphere damage (Marshall & Halligan, 1990). On this account, patients do not "neglect" (in the sense of "ignore") left portions of a line; rather, they judge that two segments thereof (demarcated by their transection mark) are subjectively equal when the discrepancy is far greater than one "just noticeable difference" for *normal* subjects.

Finally, it is worth noting that left-sided omissions on drawing or copying tasks could fall as easily under a perceptual as an attentional interpretation. The striking observation that patients fail to notice that they have omitted a left ear, eye or arm from a spontaneous drawing of a person is often described as "perceptual completion" (see Poppelreuter, 1917; Warrington, 1962). Although no convincing formal theory of the phenomenon exists, the basic process is surely perceptual or representational (Ramachandran & Gregory, 1991; Von der Heydt, Peterhans, & Baumgartner, 1984). Failure to complete overtly one side of drawings, paintings and even sculptures is seen in professional artists with neglect after unilateral brain damage, despite the fact that they have spent a considerable amount of time (and "attention") on the work (Halligan & Marshall, 1990). In some patients, "completion" is more accurately described as the misinterpretation of degraded left-sided information (Marshall & Halligan, 1992; Young, Hellawell, & Welch, 1992). One of the strangest results ever reported on "completion" is the following observation by Mesulam (1985). On (traditional) spontaneous clock-drawing, the patient (as is typical) missed out most of the numbers on the left side of the clock face. But performing the same task with his eyes shut, all 12 numbers were drawn (and in approximately the correct positions).

Perceptuo-representational Neglect

The most dramatic demonstration that visual neglect is not "purely" or "merely" visual was initially provided by Bisiach and Luzzatti (1978). Asked to describe a scene *from memory* (and a specified vantage point), some patients "neglect to report" landmarks on the left; but when the vantage point is reversed, the landmarks that were originally on the right are now neglected and the previously neglected items are correctly reported. Such observations are easy to replicate (although the effect is not found in all patients with "neglect"). We asked one of our patients to take an imaginary walk from the south coast of England to the Highlands of Scotland and report the towns she would pass through. She listed a series of east coast locales. When next asked to walk from Scotland to England, she listed a series of previously unmentioned west coast locales.

If this is "representational neglect", then the phenomenon undoubtedly exists (Perani, Nardocci, & Broggi, 1982). What type of explanation is demanded is less clear, although it is worth remarking that "seeing" and "imagining" appear to call upon many of the same central neural substrates (Farah, Soso, & Dasheiff, 1992; Kosslyn, 1987).

Further demonstrations of how left neglect can occur in contexts that do not directly involve the full extent of visuo-sensory co-ordinates are provided by "aperture" experiments (Morgan, Findlay, & Watt, 1982). In ingenious and elegant studies, Bisiach, Luzzatti and Perani (1979) and Ogden (1985) passed "nonsense" shapes horizontally behind a screen with a small slit; "vision" is thus restricted to the vertical meridian of the visual field. Under these conditions, where the full object has to be reconstructed from visual short-term memory, patients with left neglect still fail to make adequate discriminations of the left side of the stimuli.

One virtue of all such demonstrations is that they stress the "spatial" in visuo-spatial neglect. The meaning of the spatial term "left" in left neglect is multiply-ambiguous. "Left" can be interpreted as (at least) "left of the stimulus page midline", "left of the patient's midsagittal plane", "left of the patient's attentional focus", or "left of the principle axis of the depicted object (or objects)". The potential ambiguity is apparent on all tasks but was first noted by Apfeldorf (1962) on spontaneous drawing, and by Gainotti, Messerli and Tissot (1972) on copying tasks. The latter authors introduced a copying task in which the stimulus drawing represents a multi-object scene—from left to right, two trees, a fence, a house and another tree. Some (but not all) patients with neglect will miss out the left side of some of these objects while including the right side of an object that (on the page) is left of the "neglected" feature. Such "object-centred" neglect can also be seen in some (Driver & Halligan, 1991) but not all (Farah et al., 1990) paradigms that demand perceptual detection or discrimination with verbal report under free viewing conditions.

Emphasis upon neglect as a "representational" disorder draws attention to the fact that the visual world is normally "parsed" into object-filled spatial domains, as first pointed out by *Gestalt* psychologists (Ellis, 1938). The overall form of a visual configuration may accordingly determine whether, how and what components of a "scene" will be neglected (Halligan & Marshall, 1991c; Kartsounis & Warrington, 1989). Perceptual parsing, some aspects of which may be "pre-attentive" (Riddoch & Humphreys, 1987; Treisman, 1985), is discussed in the context of copying tasks in Marshall and Halligan (1993) and Halligan and Marshall (in press a).

A further twist to the story of "representational neglect" has recently been provided by Guariglia, Padovani, Pizzamiglio and Pantano (1992). Their patient, with a right *frontal* lesion, showed a deficit in left hemispace that was selective for visual *imagery*!

Attentional Neglect

The popularity of attentional accounts of neglect is not surprising; many of the basic clinical observations seem to demand an attentional explanation, and the phenomena can then be further investigated in sophisticated reaction-time experiments. The concept of "attention" does, however, cover a multitude of distinct processes. In some accounts of neglect, the emphasis is placed upon "arousal", and hypoarousal after damage (Heilman et al., 1985). There is evidence from *in vivo* neuroimaging techniques that the right hemisphere may play a leading role in generalised sustained attention (Pardo, Fox & Raichle, 1991). SPECT and PET studies have shown hypoperfusion of the damaged hemisphere in subcortical neglect (Bogousslavsky et al., 1988) and motor neglect (Fiorelli et al., 1991). That the right hemisphere is "dominant" for some tasks that require sustained attention is confirmed by the results of differential inactivation of the hemispheres by sodium amobarbital injection (Spiers et al., 1990). In other accounts, the basic concept concerns "selective" attention and disorders of "moving" an attentional "spotlight" (Posner, Walker, Friedrich, & Rafal, 1987; Posner & Driver, 1992).

In the acute phase, many patients with left neglect orient their eyes strongly to the right and appear incapable of "disengaging" (Gainotti et al., 1991; Posner et al., 1987) from that position. The whole head (or trunk) may be skewed rightward, and the ambulatory patient will often circle in a clockwise direction. In the chronic phase, the detection of targets in a lateral display shows a strong bias towards more accurate and faster response to the right-most element, with a progressive slowing for targets left thereof (De Renzi, Gentilini, Faglioni, & Barbieri, 1989). In some patients with left neglect, reaction times to the right relative position are actually faster than those of control patients without neglect (Ladavas, Petronio, & Umilta, 1990). As De Renzi et al. (1989) observe, the neglect patient seems to have a "magnetic attraction" to the extreme end of "right structural space".

The results described above are all found in "right space" with respect to fixation and the subject's mid-sagittal plane. They therefore provide strong support for a position advanced by Kinsbourne (1970; see also Chapter 3, this volume). Kinsbourne (1970) suggests that, in normal subjects, the two cerebral hemispheres have "opposing orientational tendencies". Hemineglect of space then occurs when a unilateral lesion provokes an imbalance in the direction of spontaneous attentional orientation. A system that is normally "in mutually inhibitory balance", mediated perhaps by the corpus callosum, becomes biased towards the ipsilesional spatial domain subserved by the intact hemisphere (Kinsbourne, 1974).

It is important to stress that Kinsbourne's account is "vectorial"; there is no dividing line (however defined) between "right" and "left"; attentional bias (and hence attentional "fall-off") is a continuous variable. The observed asymmetries between right neglect after left hemisphere lesion and left neglect after right hemisphere lesion are due to a pre-existent (normal) constraint; the right-orienting tendency of the left hemisphere is intrinsically stronger than the left-orienting tendency of the right hemisphere. There seems little doubt but that an attentional component will need to be invoked in the explanation of most (if not all) manifestations of neglect. The particular account proposed by Kinsbourne would appear to be the most appropriate framework to adopt within the class of "pure" attentional theories.

There remain, however, problems with any hypothesis that postulates only one attentional system per hemisphere. It is unclear how "domain-specific" or "modality-specific" neglects can be made to fit within such a framework. The amelioration of neglect by "cueing" to the neglected side is eminently compatible with vectorial attentional systems. But it would seem that they must be supplemented by the concept of general (non-lateralised) attentional difficulty (see Chapter 12, this volume). In some patients with left neglect, cueing to the left provokes "inattention" to the right side of a display (Marshall & Halligan, 1991; Robertson, 1989). For patients (or paradigms) where cueing makes little or no difference to performance, attentional and perceptual interpretations remain difficult to distinguish (Marshall & Halligan, 1991). The frequent finding that vestibular stimulation produces a temporary remission of unilateral neglect (Rode et al., 1992) is consistent with attentional accounts but hardly conclusive. An intriguing result by Hommel et al. (1990) suggests that neglect is ameliorated when listening to music (a predominantly right hemisphere function). The effect would appear to be input-specific as no comparable reduction in the severity of neglect was found when listening to speech. More studies of patients' spontaneous "search patterns" and their susceptibility to experimental manipulation (Chatterjee, Mennemeier, & Heilman, 1992a) are urgently required.

We also note that some results on the figural modulation of neglect (e.g. Halligan & Marshall, 1991c) seem to imply that the "focality" (narrow or wide) of attention plays a role distinct from the orientation of attention in determining final performance (see also Cohen & Rafal, 1991). In some patients, "wide focus" attention appears to be normal; it is only when attention must be "narrowed" to resolve fine detail that the rightward "skewing" of attention takes place (Halligan & Marshall, in press b).

Intentional Neglect

Watson, Miller and Heilman (1978) point out that many neglect tasks require the patient to make a manual response in left space. Could it be, then, that some patients are "unwilling" to perform such a movement? They appear "disinclined" to operate motorically in left space when the response would involve the right arm crossing the body midline. More generally, it seems difficult for them to make an intentional leftward movement. There is no doubt that exploratory-motor aspects of neglect can be dissociated from sensori-perceptual aspects (Liu, Bolton, Price, & Weintraub, 1992).

Some evidence for "directional hypokinesia" was reported by Heilman et al. (1985). Compared with control subjects, patients with left neglect showed a small but significant increase in reaction time to initiate a leftward movement of the (right) arm. Patients could, however, perform the task and their actual movement times (after initiation) were normal. Other evidence for directional hypokinesia in neglect is provided by Tegnér and Levander (1991a). Their patients performed a cancellation task in two conditions: with normal viewing of the stimulus array and viewing through a 90° angle mirror with direct view of the sheet on which the responses were made prevented. This latter condition "decouples the direction of visual attention and of arm movement" (Tegnér & Levander, 1991a). In this mirror condition, 4 out of 18 patients with left neglect cancelled only the lines in (true) right hemispace. This implies that they adequately perceived those lines in left hemispace (in the mirror) while responding motorically in right hemispace.

A similar decoupling was employed by Bisiach, Geminiani, Berti and Rusconi (1990) in a line bisection task. Their patients made their transection by moving a pointer that travelled either in the same or the opposite direction to the patient's hand. In some patients, neglect was ameliorated when a rightward movement of the hand drove the pointer leftward. But this improvement on bisection accuracy is not found in all patients when the directions of perceptual scanning (leftward) and motoric response (rightward) are made to conflict (Halligan & Marshall, 1989a). Likewise, in a study of spatial exploration, Mijovic (1991) found no evidence for directional hypokinesia. His patients searched for concealed targets on a stimulus display board in two conditions; either a covering panel with a window had to be moved over the board, or the stimulus board itself had to be moved beneath the now stationary covering panel. The direction of hand movement required to uncover targets in left space (leftward vs rightward) had no effect on response times to target detection.

Directional hypokinesia also fails to account for a very frequent finding on freehand line bisection; most patients who show left neglect on long horizontal lines bisect short lines to the left of true centre (Halligan & Marshall, 1988; Tegnér & Levander, 1991b). It is difficult to conceive of an intentional interpretation for why patients should be willing to make a mark in left space in one condition (short lines) but not another (long lines). The compelling evidence for left neglect in paradigms that require no manual response (discrimination or detection tasks with verbal report) cannot in principle receive any hypokinetic interpretation when eye movements are not involved (Bisiach et al., 1979).

None the less, some tasks do appear to show a crucial involvement of motor processes in neglect. Reuter-Lorenz and Posner (1990) report an amelioration of left neglect on line bisection when the examiner, rather than the patient, moves the pen along the stimulus line until the patient reports that the midpoint has been reached. The latter technique is potentially valuable, although it may introduce further confounds. A slowly moving pen allows for more direct comparisons of relative length than can be obtained with the traditional "quasi-ballistic" method of bisection. What would happen if the *patient* moved the pen along the line until it appeared truly bisected? Little (if anything) is known about "neglect" of *moving* targets. We also note that allaesthesic phenomena have been reported in conjunction with left neglect. Patients, who on detecting left visual field stimuli, may erroneously point to them in the contralateral (ipsilesional) hemispace (Joanette & Brouchon, 1984). Drawing and copying tasks sometimes provoke similar phenomena, as when left-sided stimuli are transposed to the right in the patient's response (Halligan, Marshall, & Wade, 1992).

A particularly striking example of "directional hypokinesia" was recently reported by Bottini, Sterzi and Vallar (1992). Their (acute) patient could name stimuli in left space when they were pointed out to her, but she could not reliably cancel them motorically with the right hand; the disorder was not secondary to optic ataxia and there was no overall inability to move the right hand into left space. The phenomenon is strangely reminiscent of "crossed avoiding reaction" in Marchiafava-Bignami disease (Lechevalier, Andersson, & Morin, 1977).

Currently, the terms "directional hypokinesia" and "intentional neglect" are used to cover a number of quite distinct phenomena. It will be vital in the very near future to distinguish between them (and thus add to the already overloaded vocabulary of cognitive neuropsychology!).

CONCLUSIONS

This brief review (and many of the other chapters in this volume) have attempted to show that an extremely large variety of phenomena have been regarded as manifestations of "neglect". The sheer range of (often dissociable) behaviours makes it unlikely that any unitary account of "the neglect syndrome" (or even the more restricted concept of "left unilateral visuo-spatial neglect") can be successfully formulated (Halligan & Marshall, 1992). The very fact that lesion to so many distinct anatomical locales can provoke "neglect" (in the wide sense of the term) should make one deeply suspicious that we are not dealing with a single well-defined system (either physiologically or functionally). A useful illustrative example is provided by Daffner, Ahern, Weintraub and Mesulam (1990). Their patient sustained two sequential right hemisphere strokes, the first frontal and the second parietal. The former stroke resulted in neglect only on tasks that "emphasize exploratory-motor components of directed attention"; the latter led to "the emergence of perceptual-sensory aspects of neglect".

Our inclination is, therefore, to "bite the bullet" and argue that the term "neglect" has the same status as, for example, the term "aphasia". There is no such *entity* as aphasia (although many patients with left hemisphere lesion have language disorders). No-one doubts that the language-faculty is a multicomponent system that can be impaired in many qualitatively distinct ways. The expression "aphasia" is no more than a (useful) clinical shorthand for any (or all) such impairments. By parity of reasoning, there is no such entity as unilateral visuo-spatial neglect (although many patients with right hemisphere lesions have perceptual, attentional, representational or intentional problems in dealing with "left" space). Why should we assume that spatial competence is any less complex than language competence, and hence any less liable to show qualitatively distinct forms of disorder in response to acquired brain damage? The title of a paper by Rizzolatti, Gentilucci and Matelli (1985), "Selective spatial attention: One centre, one circuit or many circuits?", points the moral we wish to draw. Rizzolatti et al. decide firmly in favour of "many circuits"; the only qualification we would make is to suggest that not all the manifestations that have gone under the label of "neglect" are necessarily "attentional" impairments, as that term is normally understood. The specific account of neglect proposed by Rizzolatti and his colleagues is probably not subject to our qualification here. In their theory, "selective attention is not conceived here as an independent function controlling the brain activity as a whole, but as a modular property intrinsically linked to the premotor activity" (Rizzolatti & Gallese, 1988). On this account, neglect arises at the interface between perceptual and motor systems (see also Milner, Brechmann, & Pagliarini, 1992, for some highly pertinent results on normal subjects).

Interactions between target positions and hand positions may play a vital role in determining how (and whether) neglect is made manifest (Duhamel & Brouchon, 1990; Goodale, Milner, Jakobson, & Carey, 1990; Halligan, Manning, & Marshall, 1991). Left neglect can ameliorate (Halligan & Marshall, 1989b; Joanette, Brouchon, Gauthier, & Samson, 1986; Robertson, 1991) in some patients when responses are made by the left (contralesional) hand (in those comparatively rare cases without left hemiplegia). The correct interpretation of these results remains open (and will probably differ from patient to patient). In some cases of callosal syndrome, left neglect is manifest when the right but not the left hand is employed (Kashiwagi et al., 1990; Sine, Soufi, & Shah, 1984). These findings are consistent with the proposal that the right hemisphere can attend to all spatial locales, while the left can only attend to contralateral space (Heilman & Van Den Abell, 1980), but they do not force that interpretation. It does, however, seem that, as Goldenberg (1986) writes, "a directional bias in favour of the right side is introduced when the left hemisphere processes sensory information to prepare a motor or verbal response" (see also Robertson & North, 1992). One cannot stress too strongly that most patients with left neglect are tested with the right hand and that primary control of that hand is vested in the (structurally) intact left hemisphere (Halligan & Marshall, 1989b). Even within a hemisphere, "the neural substrates of visual perception may be quite distinct from those underlying the visual control of action" (Goodale & Milner, 1992).

Although we believe that the concept of neglect *per se* is incoherent, in no sense are we proposing a counsel of despair: If language and language disorders can yield to theoretical understanding, there is no reason why spatial cognition and its disorders should not likewise become intelligible. Our worries on this latter score are concerned with the fact that few current "explanations" of "neglect" are anything more than a description of the phenomena phrased in terms that insinuate understanding without actually delivering. There is, in short, little deductive structure to any account of any "neglect phenomenon" with which we are familiar. To say that "neglect" is a "representational" disorder is to describe, not explain, the fact that some patients show the "Piazza del Duomo" effect; to say that "neglect" is an "intentional" disorder is to describe, not explain, the fact that some patients draw clock faces with all the numbers along the right hemi-circumference. We should give more consideration to the question of what levels of explanation are pertinent to the interpretation "neglect". It is probably unwise to jump to neurophysiological explanations without first constructing a full(ish) information-processing account of spatial cognition that is compatible with the varied patterns of spatial impairment.

At the highest level, we emphasise that among the many underlying disorders that provoke neglect in overt performance, neglect can be a disorder of "access to consciousness". There is growing interest in the elicitation of both autonomic (Vallar et al., 1991a) and indirect ("covert" or "tacit") behavioural responses (Audet, Bub, & Lecours, 1991; Bisiach & Rusconi, 1990; Marshall & Halligan, 1988; McGlinchey-Berroth et al., in press) to "neglected" stimuli. The data strongly suggest that, in some patients, the processing of undetected ("neglected") events can influence other responses without the patient's awareness of the grounds for that influence. A study by Berti and Rizzolatti (1992) provides convincing evidence for the facilitation of naming speed by categorical primes in the neglected field that the patients deny "seeing". The implications of this fact for any interpretation of neglect phenomena have yet to be explored in depth (but see Bisiach, 1992). The related concept of "extinction" remains problematic. At what stage or level of processing does extinction occur (Berti et al., 1992)? Exactly how much information (albeit degraded) may survive extinction to produce the sometimes spurious impression of "unconscious" perception (Farah, Monheit, & Wallace, 1991)?

The most telling criticism of (almost) all current theoretical accounts of any form of neglect remains, however, this: Investigators continue to report *quantitative* behavioural data with only *qualitative* interpretations thereof (but see Burnett-Stuart, Halligan, & Marshall, 1991). The law of diminishing returns will rapidly come to apply to such a situation. We recommend Mozer and Behrmann (1990) and Mozer (1991) as valuable preliminary attempts to break out of this uncharmed circle. Even if there should prove to be a well-defined notion of "neglect", many theoretical (and clinical) problems will remain to be solved. That "neglect" can influence other aspects of visuo-spatial perception is not incompatible with the possibility that other disorders of visual perception may modulate the expression of "neglect" (Oxbury, Campbell, & Oxbury, 1974).

REFERENCES

Apfeldorf, M. (1962). Perceptual and conceptual processes in a case of left-sided spatial inattention. *Perceptual and Motor Skills*, *14*, 419–423.

Audet, T., Bub, D., & Lecours, A.R. (1991). Visual neglect and left-sided context effects. *Brain and Cognition*, *16*, 11–28.

Barbieri, C. & De Renzi, E. (1989). Patterns of neglect dissociation. *Behavioural Neurology*, *2*, 13–24.

Berti, A., Allport, A., Driver, J., Dienes, Z., Oxbury, J., & Oxbury, S. (1992). Levels of processing for visual stimuli in an "extinguished" field. *Neuropsychologia*, *30*, 403–415.

Berti, A. & Rizzolatti, G. (1992). Visual processing without awareness: Evidence from unilateral neglect. *Journal of Cognitive Neuroscience*, *4*, 345–351.

Bisiach, E. (1992). Understanding consciousness: Clues from unilateral neglect and related disorders. In A.D. Milner & M.D. Rugg (Eds), *The neuropsychology of consciousness*. London: Academic Press.

Bisiach, E., Bulgarelli, C., Sterzi, R., & Vallar, G. (1983). Line bisection and cognitive plasticity of unilateral neglect of space. *Brain and Cognition*, *2*, 32–38.

Bisiach, E., Geminiani, G., Berti, A., & Rusconi, M.L. (1990). Perceptual and premotor factors in unilateral neglect. *Neurology*, *40*, 1278–1281.

Bisiach, E. & Luzzatti, C. (1978). Unilateral neglect of representational space. *Cortex*, *14*, 129–133.

Bisiach, E., Luzzatti, C., & Perani, D. (1979). Unilateral neglect, representational schema and consciousness. *Brain*, *102*, 609–618.

Bisiach, E., Perani, D., Vallar, G., & Berti, A. (1986). Unilateral neglect: Personal and extrapersonal. *Neuropsychologia*, *24*, 759–767.

Bisiach, E. & Rusconi, M.L. (1990). Breakdown of perceptual awareness in unilateral neglect. *Cortex*, *26*, 643–649.

Bisiach, E. & Vallar, G. (1988). Hemineglect in humans. In F. Boller & J. Grafman (Eds), *Handbook of neuropsychology*, Vol. 1. Amsterdam: Elsevier.

Bogousslavsky, J., Miklossy, J., Regli, F., Deruaz, J.P., Assal, G., & Delaloye, G. (1988). Subcortical neglect: Neuropsychological, SPECT and neuropathological correlations with anterior choroidal artery infarction. *Annals of Neurology*, *23*, 448–452.

Bottini, G., Sterzi, R., & Vallar, G. (1992). Directional hypokinesia in spatial hemineglect: A case study. *Journal of Neurology, Neurosurgery and Psychiatry*, *55*, 562–565.

Bruyer, R. (1984). Neglects in hemineglect: A comment on the study of Bisiach et al. (1983). *Brain and Cognition*, *3*, 231–234.

Burnett-Stuart, G., Halligan, P.W., & Marshall, J.C. (1991). A Newtonian model of perceptual distortion in visuo-spatial neglect. *NeuroReport*, *2*, 255–257.

Chatterjee, A., Mennemeier, M., & Heilman, K.M. (1992a). Search patterns and neglect: A case study. *Neuropsychologia*, *30*, 657–672.

Chatterjee, A., Mennemeier, M., & Heilman, K.M. (1992b). A stimulus–response relationship in unilateral neglect; The power function. *Neuropsychologia*, *30*, 1101–1108.

Cohen, A. & Rafal, R.D. (1991). Attention and feature integration: Illusory conjunctions in a patient with a parietal lobe lesion. *Psychological Science*, *2*, 106–110.

Cubelli, R., Nichelli, P., Bonito, V., De Tanti, A., & Inzaghi, M.G. (1991). Different patterns of dissociation in unilateral spatial neglect. *Brain and Cognition*, *15*, 139–159.

Daffner, K.R., Ahern, G.L., Weintraub, S., & Mesulam, M.M. (1990). Dissociated neglect behavior following sequential strokes in the right hemisphere. *Annals of Neurology, 28,* 97–101.

Denny-Brown, D. & Banker, B.Q. (1954). Amorphosynthesis from left parietal lesion. *Archives of Neurology and Psychiatry, 71,* 302–313.

De Renzi, E. (1982). *Disorders of space exploration and cognition.* New York: John Wiley.

De Renzi, E., Gentilini, M., Faglioni, P., & Barbieri, C. (1989). Attentional shift towards the rightmost stimuli in patients with left visual neglect. *Cortex, 25,* 231–237.

Driver, J. & Halligan, P.W. (1991). Can visual neglect operate in object-centred co-ordinates? An affirmative single-case study. *Cognitive Neuropsychology, 8,* 475–496.

Duhamel, J.-R. & Brouchon, M. (1990). Sensorimotor aspects of unilateral neglect: A single case analysis. *Cognitive Neuropsychology, 7,* 57–74.

Duhamel, J.-R. Colby, C.L., & Goldberg, M.E. (1992). The updating of the representation of visual spacve in parietal cortex by intended eye movements. *Science, 255,* 90–92.

Ellis, W.D. (Ed.) (1938). *A source book of Gestalt psychology.* London: Routledge and Kegan Paul.

Farah, M.J., Brunn, J.L., Wong, A.B., Wallace, M., & Carpenter, P.A. (1990). Frames of reference for allocation of spatial attention: Evidence from the neglect syndrome. *Neuropsychologia. 28,* 335–347.

Farah, M.J., Monheit, M.A., Wallace, M.A. (1991). Unconscious perception of "extinguished" visual stimuli: Reassessing the evidence. *Neuropsychologia, 29,* 949–958.

Farah, M.J., Soso, M.J., & Dasheiff, R.M. (1992). Visual angle of the mind's eye before and after unilateral occipital lobectomy. *Journal of Experimental Psychology: Human Perception and Performance, 18,* 241–248.

Fiorelli, M., Blin, J., Bakchine, S., Laplane, D., & Barton, J.C. (1991). PET studies of cortical diaschisis in patient with motor hemi-neglect. *Journal of the Neurological Sciences, 104,* 135–142.

Gainotti, G., D'Erme, P., & Bartolomeo, P. (1991). Early orientation of attention toward the half space ipsilateral to the lesion in patients with unilateral brain damage. *Journal of Neurology, Neurosurgery and Psychiatry, 54,* 1082–1089.

Gainotti, G., Messerli, P., & Tissot, R. (1972). Qualitative analysis of unilateral spatial neglect in relation to laterality of cerebral lesions. *Journal of Neurology, Neurosurgery and Psychiatry, 35,* 545–550.

Goldenberg, G. (1986). Neglect in a patient with partial callosal disconnection. *Neuropsychologia, 24,* 397–403.

Goodale, M.A. & Milner, A.D. (1992). Separate visual pathways for perception and action. *TINS, 15,* 20–25.

Goodale, M.A., Milner, A.D., Jakobson, L.S., & Carey, D.P. (1990). Kinematic analysis of limb movements in neuropsychological research: Subtle deficits and recovery of function. *Canadian Journal of Psychology, 44,* 180–195.

Grusser, O.-J. & Landis, T. (1991). *Visual agnosias and other disturbances of visual perception and cognition.* London: Macmillan.

Guariglia, C., Padovani, A., Pizzamiglio, L., & Pantano, P. (1992). Selective deficit of visual imagery in the left hemispace in a right frontal lesion. *Journal of Clinical and Experimental Neuropsychology, 14,* 373.

Halligan, P.W., Manning, L., & Marshall, J.C. (1991). Hemispheric activation versus spatio-motor cueing in visual neglect: A case study. *Neuropsychologia, 29,* 165–175.

Halligan, P.W. & Marshall, J.C. (1988). How long is a piece of string? A study of line bisection in a case of visual neglect. *Cortex, 24,* 321–328.

Halligan, P.W. & Marshall, J.C. (1989a) Perceptual cueing and perceptuo-motor compatibility in visuo-spatial neglect; A single case-study. *Cognitive Neuropsychology, 6,* 423–435.

Halligan, P.W. & Marshall, J.C. (1989b). Laterality of motor response in visuo-spatial neglect: A case study. *Neuropsychologia, 27*, 1301–1307.

Halligan, P.W. & Marshall, J.C. (1989c). Is neglect (only) lateral? A quadrant analysis of line cancellation. *Journal of Clinical and Experimental Neuropsychology, 11*, 793–798.

Halligan, P.W. & Marshall, J.C. (1990). *Art and visuospatial perception* (video film). Oxford: Oxford Medical Illustration.

Halligan, P.W. & Marshall, J.C. (1991a). Left neglect for near but not far space in man. *Nature, 350*, 498–500.

Halligan, P.W. & Marshall, J.C. (1991b). Spatial compression in visual neglect: A case study. *Cortex, 27*, 623–629.

Halligan, P.W. & Marshall, J.C. (1991c). Figural modulation of visuo-spatial neglect: A case study. *Neuropsychologia, 29*, 619–628.

Halligan, P.W. & Marshall, J.C. (1992). Left visuo-spatial neglect: A meaningless entity? *Cortex, 28*, 525–535..

Halligan, P.W. & Marshall, J.C. (in press a). When two is one: A case study of spatial parsing in visual neglect. *Perception*.

Halligan, P.W. & Marshall, J.C. (in press b). Homing in on neglect: A case study of visual search. *Cortex*.

Halligan, P.W., Marshall, J.C., & Wade, D.T. (1990). Do visual field deficits exacerbate visuo-spatial neglect? *Journal of Neurology, Neurosurgery and Psychiatry, 53*, 487–491.

Halligan, P.W., Marshall, J.C., & Wade, D.T. (1992). Left on the right: Allochiria in a case of left visuo-spatial neglect. *Journal of Neurology, Neurosurgery and Psychiatry, 55*, 717–719.

Halsband, V., Gruhn, S., & Ettlinger, G. (1985). Unilateral spatial neglect and defective performance in one half of space. *International Journal of Neuroscience, 28*, 173–195.

Heilman, K.M., Bowers, D., Coslett, H.B., Whelan, H., & Watson, R.T. (1985). Directional hypokinesia: Prolonged reaction times for leftward movements in patients with right hemisphere lesions and neglect. *Neurology, 35*, 855–859.

Heilman, K.M. & Van Den Abell, T. (1980). Right hemisphere dominance for attention: The mechanism underlying hemispheric asymmetries of inattention (neglect). *Neurology, 30*, 327–330.

Heilman, K.M., Watson, R.T., & Valenstein, E. (1985). Neglect and related disorders. In K.M. Heilman & E. Valenstein (Eds), *Clinical neuropsychology*. New york: Oxford University Press.

Hommel, M., Peres, B., Pollak, P., Memin, B., Besson, G., Gaio, J.-M., & Perret, J. (1990). Effects of passive tactile and auditory stimuli on left visual neglect. *Archives of Neurology, 47*, 573–576.

Hornak, J. (1992). Ocular exploration in the dark by patients with visual neglect. *Neuropsychologia, 30*, 547–552.

Ikeda, M., Saida, S., & Sugiyama, T. (1977). Visual field size necessary for length comparison. *Perception and Psychophysics, 22*, 165–170.

Joanette, Y. & Brouchon, M. (1984). Visual allesthesia in manual pointing: Some evidence for a sensorimotor cerebral organization. *Brain and Cognition, 3*, 152–165.

Joanette, Y., Brouchon, M., Gauthier, L., & Samson, M. (1986). Pointing with left versus right hand in left visual field neglect. *Neuropsychologia, 24*, 391–396.

Karnath, H.-O. & Huber, W. (1992). Abnormal eye movement behaviour during text reading in neglect syndrome: A case study. *Neuropsychologia, 30*, 593–598.

Karnath, H.-O., Schenkel, P., & Fischer, B. (1991). Trunk orientation as the determining factor of the "contralateral" deficit in the neglect syndrome and as the physical anchor of the internal representation of body orientation in space. *Brain, 114*, 1997–2014.

Kartsounis, L.D. & Warrington, E.K. (1989). Unilateral neglect overcome by cues implicit in stimulus arrays. *Journal of Neurology, Neurosurgery and Psychiatry, 52*, 1253–1259.

Kashiwagi, A., Kashiwagi, T., Nishikawa, T., Tanabe, H., & Okuda, J.-I. (1990). Hemispatial neglect in a patient with callosal infarction. *Brain, 113*, 1005–1023.

Kinsbourne, M. (1970). A model for the mechanism of unilateral neglect of space. *Transactions of the American Neurological Association, 95*, 143–145.

Kinsbourne, M. (1974). Lateral interactions in the brain. In M. Kinsbourne & W. Lynn Smith (Eds), *Hemispheric disconnection and cerebral function*. Springfield, IL: C.C. Thomas.

Kooistra, C.A. & Heilman, K.M. (1989). Hemispatial visual inattention masquerading as hemianopia. *Neurology, 39*, 1125–1127.

Kosslyn, S.M. (1987). Seeing and imagining in the cerebral hemispheres: A computational approach. *Psychological Review, 94*, 148–175.

Ladavas, E., Petronio, A., & Umilta, C. (1990). The deployment of visual attention in the intact field of hemineglect patients. *Cortex, 26*, 307–317.

Laplane, D. & Degos, J.D. (1983). Motor neglect. *Journal of Neurology, Neurosurgery and Psychiatry, 46*, 152–158.

Lechevalier, B., Andersson, J.C., & Morin, P. (1977). Hemispheric disconnection syndrome with a "crossed avoiding" reaction in a case of Marchiafava-Bignami disease. *Journal of Neurology, Neurosurgery and Psychiatry, 40*, 483–497.

Liu, G.T., Bolton, A.K., Price, B.H., & Weintraub, S. (1992). Dissociated perceptual-sensory and exploratory-motor neglect. *Journal of Neurology, Neurosurgery and Psychiatry, 55*, 701–706.

Marshall, J.C. & Halligan, P.W. (1988). Blindsight and insight in visuo-spatial neglect. *Nature, 336*, 766–767.

Marshall, J.C. & Halligan, P.W. (1990). Line bisection in a case of visual neglect; Psychophysical studies with implications for theory. *Cognitive Neuropsychology, 7*, 107–130.

Marshall, J.C. & Halligan, P.W. (1991). A study of plane bisection in four cases of visual neglect. *Cortex, 27*, 277–284.

Marshall, J.C. & Halligan, P.W. (1993). Visuo-spatial neglect: A new copying test to assess perceptual parsing. *Journal of Neurology, 240*, 37–40.

McGlinchey-Berroth, R., Milberg, W.P., Verfaellie, M., Alexander, M., & Kilduff, P.T. (in press). Semantic processing in the neglected visual field; Evidence from a lexical decision task. *Cognitive Neuropsychology*.

Mennemeier, M., Wertman, E., & Heilman, K.M. (1992). Neglect of near peripersonal space: Evidence for multidirectional attentional systems in humans. *Brain, 115*, 37–50.

Mesulam, M.M. (1985). Attention, confusional states and neglect. In M.M. Mesulam (Ed.), *Principles of behavioral neurology*. Philadelphia, PA: F.A. Davis.

Mijovic, D. (1991). Mechanisms of visual spatial neglect: Absence of directional hypokinesia in spatial exploration. *Brain, 114*, 1575–1593.

Milner, A.D., Brechmann, M., & Pagliarini, L. (1992). To halve and to halve not: An analysis of line bisection judgements in normal subjects. *Neuropsychologia, 30*, 515–526.

Morgan, M.J., Findlay, J.M., & Watt, R.J. (1982). Aperture viewing: A review and a synthesis. *Quarterly Journal of Experimental Psychology, 34A*, 211–233.

Mozer, M.C. (1991). *The perception of multiple objects: A connectionist approach*. Cambridge, MA: MIT Press.

Mozer, M.C. & Behrmann, M. (1990). On the interaction of selective attention and lexical knowledge: A connectionist account of neglect dyslexia. *Journal of Cognitive Neuroscience, 2*, 96–123.

Nichelli, P., Rinaldi, M., & Cubelli, R. (1989). Selective spatial attention and length representation in normal subjects and in patients with unilateral spatial neglect. *Brain and Cognition, 9*, 57–70.

Ogden, J.A. (1985). Contralesional neglect of constructed visual images in right and left brain-damaged patients. *Neuropsychologia, 23*, 273–277.

Oxbury, J.M., Campbell, D.C., & Oxbury, S.M. (1974). Unilateral spatial neglect and impairment of spatial analysis and visual perception. *Brain, 97*, 551–564.

Pardo, J., Fox, P., & Raichle, M. (1991). Localization of a human system for sustained attention by positron emission tomography. *Nature, 349*, 61–64.

Perani, D., Nardocci, N., & Broggi, G. (1982). Neglect after right unilateral thalamotomy. *Italian Journal of Neurological Sciences, 3*, 61–64.

Poppelreuter, W. (1917). *Die psychischen Schadigungen durch Kopfschuss im Kriege 1914/1916.* Leipzig: Voss.

Posner, M.I. & Driver, J. (1992). The neurobiology of selective attention. *Current Opinion in Neurobiology, 2*, 165–169.

Posner, M.I., Walker, J.A., Friedrich, F.J., & Rafal, R.D. (1987). How do the parietal lobes direct covert attention? *Neuropsychologia, 25*, 135–146.

Ramachandran, V.S. & Gregory, R.L. (1991). Perceptual filling in of artificially induced scotomas in human vision. *Nature, 350*, 699–702.

Reuter-Lorenz, P.A. & Posner, M.I. (1990). Components of neglect from right-hemisphere damage: An analysis of line bisection. *Neuropsychologia, 26*, 327–333.

Riddoch, M.J. & Humphreys, G.W. (1987). Perceptual and action systems in unilateral visual neglect. In M. Jeannerod (Ed.), *Neurophysiological and neuropsychological aspects of spatial neglect.* Amsterdam: North-Holland.

Rizzolatti, G. & Gallese, V. (1988). Mechanisms and theories of spatial neglect. In F. Boller & J. Grafman (Eds), *Handbook of neuropsychology,* Vol. 1. Amsterdam: Elsevier.

Rizzolatti, G., Gentilucci, M., & Matelli, M. (1985). Selective spatial attention: One center, one circuit or many circuits? In M.I. Posner & O.S.M. Marin (Eds), *Attention and performance. XI.* Hillsdale, NJ: Lawrence Erlbaum Associates Inc.

Robertson, I. (1989). Anomalies in the laterality of omissions in unilateral left visual neglect: Implications for an attentional theory of neglect. *Neuropsychologia, 27*, 157–165.

Robertson, I. (1991). Use of left versus right hand in responding to lateralized stimuli in unilateral neglect. *Neuropsychologia, 29*, 1129–1135.

Robertson, I. & North, N. (1992). Spatio-motor cueing in unilateral left neglect: The role of hemispace, hand and motor activation. *Neuropsychologia, 30*, 553–563.

Rode, G., Charles, N., Perenin, M.-T., Vighetto, A., Trillet, M., & Aimard, G. (1992). Partial remission of hemiplegia and somato-paraphrenia through vestibular stimulation in a case of unilateral neglect. *Cortex, 28*, 203–208.

Sakata, H. & Kusunoki, M. (1992). Organization of space perception: Neural representation of three-dimensional space in the posterior parietal cortex. *Current Opinion in Neurobiology, 2*, 170–174.

Sine, R.D., Soufi, A., & Shah, M. (1984). Callosal syndrome: Implications for understanding the neuropsychology of stroke. *Archives of Physical Medicine and Rehabilitation, 65*, 606–610.

Spiers, P.A., Schomer, D.L., Blume, H.W., Kleefield, J., O'Reilly, G., Weintraub, S., Osborne-Shaefer, P., & Mesulam, M.-M. (1990). Visual neglect during intracarotid amobarbital testing. *Neurology, 40*, 1600–1606.

Tegnér, R. & Levander, M. (1991a). Through a looking glass: A new technique to demonstrate directional hypokinesia in unilateral neglect. *Brain, 114*, 1943–1951.

Tegnér, R. & Levander, M. (1991b). The influence of stimulus properties on visual neglect. *Journal of Neurology, Neurosurgery and Psychiatry, 54*, 882–887.

Treisman, A.M. (1985). Preattentive processing in vision. *Computer Vision, Graphics, and Image Processing, 31*, 156–177.

Vallar, G., Bottini, G., Sterzi, R., Passerini, D., & Rusconi, M.L. (1991a). Hemianesthesia, sensory neglect and defective access to conscious experience. *Neurology, 41*, 650–652.

Vallar, G., Sandroni, P., Rusconi, M.L., & Barbieri, S. (1991b). Hemianopia, hemianesthesia, and spatial neglect: A study with evoked potentials. *Neurology, 41,* 1918–1922.

Von der Heydt, R., Peterhans, E., & Baumgartner, G. (1984). Illusory contours and cortical neuron responses. *Science, 224,* 1260–1262.

Walker, R., Findley, J.M., Young, A.W., & Welch, J. (1991). Disentangling neglect and hemianopia. *Neuropsychologia, 29,* 1019–1027.

Warrtington, E.K. (1962). The completion of visual forms across hemianopic field defects. *Journal of Neurology, Neurosurgery and Psychiatry, 25,* 208–217.

Watson, R.T., Miller, R.B., & Heilman, K.M. (1978). Nonsensory neglect. *Annals of Neurology, 3,* 505–508.

Weinstein, E.A. Friedland, R.P. (Eds). (1977). *Hemi-inattention and hemispheric specialization.* New York: Raven Press.

Young, A.W., De Haan, E.H.F., Newcombe, F., & Hay, D.C. (1990). Facial neglect. *Neuropsychologia, 28,* 391–415.

Author Index

Subject Index

Activities of daily living (ADL)
  functioning, 280
  problems with, 13, 295
Affect, comprehension of, 296–297, 299
Afferent dysgraphia, 247
Agnosia
  visual, 6, 8
  visuo-spatial, 78–79, 131–133
Alerting *see Vigilance*
Allaesthesia, visual, 16, 178–179
Amnesia, 42
"Amorphosynthesis", 108, 314–315
Anaesthesia, left-sided, and attention, 114
Anatomy and neglect, 27–52
  anatomical correlates, 29–36
    cortico-subcortical lesions, 29–33
    subcortical lesions, 34–36
  functional anatomy, 36–43
  neural correlates, 43–48
    extrapersonal *vs.* personal components, 48

pre-motor vs. perceptual
  components, 44–48
recovery mechanisms, 48–52
Animal studies
  activation imbalance, 68–69
  attentional gradients, 64–65
  neglect, 28–29, 36, 42–43
    and attention, 92–93, 172
    recovery, 49, 51
    and subsequent lesion, 93
    vertical, 97
  spatial neurons, 94–95
  two cortical visual systems, 134
  visual search and attention, 172
Anosognosia, 4, 33, 303–305
  assessing verbal awareness, 303–304
  and attention, 113–114
  non-verbal awareness, 304
  unawareness as response style, 304–305
  and vestibular stimulation, 100–101, 111

Neuropsychological Rehabilitation

Editor: Barbara A. Wilson
Deputy Editor: Ian H. Robertson

(Both: MRC Applied Psychology Unit, Cambridge, UK)

Neuropsychological Rehabilitation provides an international forum for the publication of well-designed and properly evaluated intervention strategies, surveys, and observational procedures which are clinically relevant and may also back up theoretical arguments or models.

The Research Digest is a regular feature in *Neuropsychological Rehabilitation*. The digest editors regularly scan a wide range of journals and other publications for material of particular interest to those working in rehabilitation. This section will be an invaluable resource providing both bibliographic references and informal comment and discussion.

RECENT PAPERS

Anosognosia and Extrapersonal Neglect as Predictors of Functional Recovery Following Right Hemisphere Stroke **B. Gialanella & F. Mattioli**

Reflections on the Treatment of Brain-Injured Patients Suffering from Problem-Solving Disorders **D. Yves von Cramon & G. Matthes-von Cramon**

How Does Post-Traumatic Amnesia differ from the Amnesic Syndrome and from Chronic Memory Impairment? **B.A. Wilson, A. Baddeley, A. Shiel & G. Patton**

When is a Cue not a Cue? On the Intractability of Visuospatial Neglect **P.W. Halligan, C.A. Donegan & J.C. Marshall**

Patients with Semantic Memory Loss: Can They Relearn Lost Concepts? **M. Swales & R. Johnson**

Differential Effects of Covert and Overt Training of the Syntactical Component of Verbal Number Processing and Generalizations to Other Tasks: A Single-Case Study **G. Deloche et al**

Forthcoming Special Issues

Coma and the Persistent Vegetative State **Guest Editors: T.M. McMillan, S. Wilson**

Issues in Neuropsychological Rehabilitation of Children with Brain Dysfunction **Guest Editor: G. Prigatano**

SUBSCRIPTION INFORMATION
Volume 3 (4 issues), 1993, ISSN 0960-2011
Individuals: E.E.C. £25.00 / U.S.A. $47.50 / Rest of World £27.50
Institutions E.E.C. £50.00 / U.S.A. $95.00 / Rest of World £55.00

Orders and enquiries to: *The Journals Department, LEA Ltd, 27 Church Road, Hove, East Sussex BN3 2FA, UK. Fax 0273 205612*

NEGLECT AND THE PERIPHERAL DYSLEXIAS

A Special Issue of Cognitive Neuropsychology

M. JANE RIDDOCH (University of Birmingham), Ed.

A wide variety of quantitatively different forms of reading disorder have been identified and extensively described. These may be broadly classified into the peripheral and central dyslexias, according to whether the patients have impaired prelexical or impaired lexical/post-lexical processes. The Special Issue concerns peripheral reading disorders. These may be produced by various functional deficits, which may manifest themselves in clinical syndromes of neglect dyslexia and letter-by-letter reading. Detailed study of these syndromes should allow better understanding of how visual lexical access may normally be obtained.

0-86377-162-9 1991 344pp. $57.95 £35.00 hbk

LAWRENCE ERLBAUM ASSOCIATES
27 Church Road, Hove, East Sussex, BN3 2FA, UK.